WORLD WIDE WEB

BEYOND THE BASICS

Edited by
Marc Abrams

Department of Computer Science
Virginia Tech

An Alan R. Apt Book

PRENTICE HALL, Upper Saddle River, New Jersey 07458

Library of Congress Cataloging-in-Publication Data

Abrams, Marc
   World Wide Web: beyond the basics / Marc Abrams
      p. cm.
   Includes bibliographical references and index.
   ISBN: 0-13-954785-1
1. World Wide Web (Information retrieval system) I. Title
TK5105.888.A254 1998
004.67'8—dc21   98-6363
                            CIP

Publisher: **ALAN APT**
Editor: **LAURA STEELE**
Production editor: **EDWARD DEFELIPPIS**
Editor-in-chief: **MARCIA HORTON**
Managing editor: **BAYANI MENDOZA DE LEON**
Assistant Vice President of Production and Manufacturing: **DAVID W. RICCARDI**
Art director: **HEATHER SCOTT**
Cover designer: **BRUCE KENSELAAR**
Cover art: **JOSEPH REISS**
Composition: **MACQUISTAN CONSULTING**
Manufacturing buyer: **PAT BROWN**
Editorial Assistant: **KATE KAIBNI**

©1998 by Prentice-Hall, Inc.
Simon & Schuster / A Viacom Company
Upper Saddle River, New Jersey 07458

The author and publisher of this book have used their best efforts in preparing this book. These efforts include the development, research, and testing of the theories and programs to determine their effectiveness. The author and publisher make no warranty of any kind, expressed or implied, with regard to these programs or the documentation contained in this book. The author and publisher shall not be liable in any event for incidental or consequential damages in connection with, or arising out of, the furnishing, performance, or use of these programs.

Printed in the United States of America

10 9 8 7 6 5 4 3 2

ISBN: 0-13-954785-1

Prentice-Hall International (UK) Limited, *London*
Prentice-Hall of Australia Pty. Limited, *Sydney*
Prentice-Hall Canada Inc., *Toronto*
Prentice-Hall Hispanoamericana, S.A., *Mexico*
Prentice-Hall of India Private Limited, *New Delhi*
Prentice-Hall of Japan, Inc., *Tokyo*
Simon & Schuster Asia Pte. Ltd., *Singapore*
Editora Prentice-Hall do Brasil, Ltda., *Rio de Janeiro*

Preface

by the Editorial Board:
Ashish Shah, George Chin, Felicia Doswell, Calin Groza, Pris Sears

*T*he evolution of the World Wide Web has reached a point where it is easy for a Web user or developer to get lost in day-to-day Web developments, and miss longer-term trends. New technologies and standards are being proposed almost daily, leaving people with a nebulous view of the Web. This book was designed to structure various facets of existing Web technology into a coherent whole.

World Wide Web: Beyond the Basics caters to a dual audience: casual users, who want a fundamental knowledge about existing and evolving Web technology; and professionals, who want in-depth infomation on specific topics. The book addresses six major areas of the Web:

- History and evolution of the Web

- Existing and evolving Web standards

- Effective representation of information on the Web

- Use of object technology for the Web

- Social and legal issues surrounding the Web

- The future of the Web.

The book is a product of a graduate-level Computer Science course, World Wide Web: Beyond the Basics (http://ei.cs.vt.edu/~wwwbtb/), taught by Prof. Marc Abrams at Virginia Tech in Fall 1996. Having the class write an online book about the course is a novel approach to teaching. There were pedagogical and practical purposes for this. A single person could not know enough about the Web to teach a comprehensive course on it in only one semester. In addition, the

Computer Science Department at Virginia Tech has been looking for ways to incorporate large-scale teamwork in the curriculum. So the class offered a break with traditional teaching methods, employing a constructivist approach in which students together accumulate knowledge about a subject, with the teacher serving as a guide. Students learned by discovering information, writing about it, and critiquing each other's work.

After researching an assigned or chosen topic and presenting the chapter's material to the class, each student wrote one chapter for the book. Each student also served additional roles in the preparation of the book as a whole. They were required to review two other articles and serve as a member of one of the functional committees, such as the editorial board or the style board.

The idea of writing the electronic book came from Prof. Ben Shneiderman at the University of Maryland at College Park. Shneiderman described in a lecture at Virginia Tech a course he taught in Fall 1993 (CMSC 828S, Virtual Reality and Telepresence), in which his students wrote two online works: *The Encyclopedia of Virtual Environments* and *The Journal of Virtual Environments* (http://www.cs.umd.edu/projects/hcil/vrtp.html).

There are many different voices and viewpoints in this book, and we hope that others interested in the Web will find it valuable, too.

C O N T E N T S

Foreword

*T*he book you are reading started as electronic articles about the Web. The topics were chosen to present a comprehensive picture of one of the most rapidly developing systems created by any civilization.

The original versions of the articles were written by graduate students who took a class from me at Virginia Tech in the Fall of 1996. Following the posting of the articles on the Web, I received numerous comments from around the world on the book, and requests for a hardcopy edition. At the same time, the World Wide Web has been growing up. The most rapid changes have occurred in the social issue of freedom of speech in the Internet, and in the technical areas of HTML, Java, Objects, and Web access through non-PC based devices. Thus in preparing a printed version, I worked with one of the authors, Ashish Shah, to reorganize, revise, update, and in some cases extensively rewrite the material to develop a coherent picture of the Web.

The preface describes more about the origin of the book. If you visit the Web site at Virginia Tech mentioned in the preface, you'll see the original, outdated manuscript. However, to accompany this book a new Web site containing an electronic copy was created at Prentice-Hall (http://www.prenhall.com/abrams/). Some electronic chapters contain additional hypertext links in the text, code examples that can be executed, and links in all reference lists will be updated periodically.

In addition to the authors of the original manuscript, many other individuals made the printed book possible. At Prentice Hall, thanks go to Alan Apt for overseeing the process of transforming the book from an electronic to a printed form, to Toni Holm for communicating with the 25 authors, and to Laura Steele and Ed DeFelippis for production of the book and Web site. Special thanks go to Ashish Shah, who put in many months of work helping to revise selected chapters and assisted with the mechanics of updating the book; to Joseph W. Reiss for

1

creating the artwork; to Felicia Doswell for updating the Web site in the months to come; and to Virginia Tech for granting me a sabbatical leave from teaching over one thousand Computer Science students so that I could complete this project.

— Marc Abrams

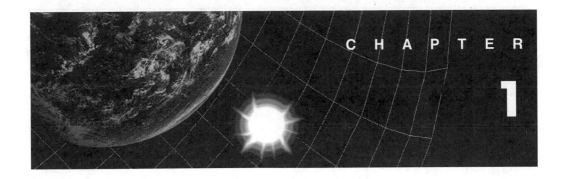

History of the Web

by Shahrooz Feizabadi

This chapter presents the history of the Web and of a number of ideas and underlying technologies from which the Web emerged. The history is presented in a sequential format, while events and technologies of particular significance have been discussed in individual sections. As the Web, in the most basic sense, is a networked hypertext information-delivery mechanism, particular attention is given to the above-mentioned fundamental technologies of hypertext and networking. More recently, with the advent of technologies such as Java, the Web has gone through another transformation, which among other things has provided the ability to deliver applications and distributed objects across the Internet. A section on the evolution of Java has therefore been included to provide historical context for this relatively new technology.

Chapter Content

1. History of Hypertext

- Memex

- Hypertext

- Xanadu

- Other Landmarks

2. History of the Net

1.1 History of Hypertext

Memex

The history of hypertext begins in July of 1945. President Roosevelt's science advisor during World War II, Dr. Vannevar Bush, proposed Memex in an article titled "As We May Think" [1], published in *The Atlantic Monthly*. In the article, Bush outlined ideas for a machine that would have the capacity to store textual and graphical information in such a way that any piece of information could be arbitrarily linked to any other piece. In his own words:

> *"He [the user] can add marginal notes and comments, taking advantage of one possible type of dry photography, and it could even be arranged so that he can do this by a stylus scheme, such as is now employed in the telautograph seen in railroad waiting rooms, just as though he had the physical page before him. All this is conventional, except for the projection forward of present-day mechanisms and gadgetry. It affords an immediate step, however, to associative indexing, the basic idea of which is a provision whereby any item may be caused at will to select immediately and automatically another. This is the essential feature of the memex. The process of tying two items together is the important thing."*

Moreover, Memex would also give the user the capability to create an information trail of traveled links which could later be retrieved. The following excerpts further outline Dr. Bush's vision:

> *"The real heart of the matter of selection, however, goes deeper than a lag in the adoption of mechanisms by libraries, or a lack of development of devices for their use. Our ineptitude in getting at the record is*

largely caused by the artificiality of systems of indexing. When data of any sort are placed in storage, they are filed alphabetically or numerically, and information is found (when it is) by tracing it down from subclass to subclass. It can be in only one place, unless duplicates are used; one has to have rules as to which path will locate it, and the rules are cumbersome. Having found one item, moreover, one has to emerge from the system and re-enter on a new path.

"The human mind does not work that way. It operates by association. With one item in its grasp, it snaps instantly to the next that is suggested by the association of thoughts, in accordance with some intricate web of trails carried by the cells of the brain. It has other characteristics, of course; trails that are not frequently followed are prone to fade, items are not fully permanent, memory is transitory. Yet the speed of action, the intricacy of trails, the detail of mental pictures, is awe-inspiring beyond all else in nature.

"Man cannot hope fully to duplicate this mental process artificially, but he certainly ought to be able to learn from it. In minor ways he may even improve, for his records have relative permanency. The first idea, however, to be drawn from the analogy concerns selection. Selection by association, rather than by indexing, may yet be mechanized. One cannot hope thus to equal the speed and flexibility with which the mind follows an associative trail, but it should be possible to beat the mind decisively in regard to the permanence and clarity of the items resurrected from storage.

"Consider a future device for individual use, which is a sort of mechanized private file and library. It needs a name, and to coin one at random, "memex" will do. A memex is a device in which an individual stores all his books, records, and communications, and which is mechanized so that it may be consulted with exceeding speed and flexibility. It is an enlarged intimate supplement to his memory.

"It consists of a desk, and while it can presumably be operated from a distance, it is primarily the piece of furniture at which he works. On the top are slanting translucent screens, on which material can be projected for convenient reading. There is a keyboard, and sets of buttons and levers. Otherwise it looks like an ordinary desk.

"In one end is the stored material. The matter of bulk is well taken care of by improved microfilm. Only a small part of the interior of the memex is devoted to storage, the rest to mechanism. Yet if the user inserted 5000 pages of material a day it would take him hundreds of years to fill the repository, so he can be profligate and enter material freely."

Hypertext

In 1965, Ted Nelson coined the terms *"hypertext"* and *"hypermedia"* in a paper to the ACM 20th national conference [7, 2]. In an article published by *Literary Machines*, Nelson explained:

> *"By 'hypertext' I mean nonsequential writing—text that branches and allows choice to the reader, best read at an interactive screen."*

The first hypertext-based system was developed in 1967 by a team of researchers led by Dr. Andries van Dam[1] at Brown University. The research was funded by IBM and the first hypertext implementation, *Hypertext Editing System*, ran on an IBM/360 mainframe. IBM later sold the system to the Houston Manned Spacecraft Center, which reportedly used it for the Apollo space program documentation. A year later, in 1968, van Dam developed FRESS, a *File Retrieval and Editing System*, which was an improvement of his original *Hypertext Editing System* and was used commercially by Philips [2, 11].

Doug Engelbart[2] of the Stanford Research Institute, inventor of the mouse, was also inspired by the hypertext idea. In 1968 he introduced his NLS, *the oN Line System*, which held in a *"shared journal"* over 100,000 papers, reports, memos and cross references [2, 12, 13, 14, 15, 11].

In 1972, researchers at Carnegie-Mellon University began development of *ZOG* (which doesn't stand for anything!). ZOG was a large database designed for a multiuser environment. The ZOG database consisted of *frames*. Each frame included a title, a description, a line with standard ZOG commands, and a set of selectable menu items which led to other frames [2]. The ZOG database was text-only and originally ran on an IBM mainframe. A PERQ workstation implementation of ZOG was used on the nuclear-powered aircraft carrier *USS Carl Vinson*. Two of the original developers of ZOG, Donald McCracken and Robert Akscyn, later developed KMS, *Knowledge Management System,* which was an improved version of ZOG. KMS ran on Sun and HP Apollo workstations with much enhanced performance. Though KMS included a crude GUI, its interface still remained a predominately text-based system. It was intended to be a collaborative tool, in that users could modify the contents of a frame and the changes would be immediately visible to others through dynamically updated links [2, 11, 14].

In 1978, Andrew Lippman of the MIT Architecture Machine Group, led a team of researchers that developed what is argued to be the first *true* hypermedia system, the *Aspen Movie Map*. This application was a virtual ride simulation through the city of Aspen, Colorado. Four cameras, pointing in different directions, were mounted on a truck which was driven through the streets of Aspen. The cameras took pictures at regular intervals, and all the pictures were

---

[1] http://www.cs.brown.edu/people/avd/

[2] http://www.std.sri.com/public/bootstrap/home.html

compiled onto videodiscs. The images were linked in a way that would allow the user to start at a given point and move forward, back, left, or right. Once a route through the city was chosen, the system could display the images in rapid succession, creating a movielike motion. The system also included images of the interior of several landmark Aspen buildings, so the user could take a virtual tour of these buildings. Another interesting feature of the system was a navigation map which was displayed in addition to the movie window. The user could jump directly to a point on the city map instead of finding a route through the city streets to that destination. The Aspen Movie Map was a landmark in hypermedia development in that, through a sophisticated application, it demonstrated what could be achieved with the technology available at the time [2, 11, 14].

Xanadu

In researching the history of Web computing, this author has not encountered any subject as passionately discussed as Xanadu. Its followers believe in it with almost religious zeal and its skeptics bash it with equal conviction. Theodor Holm Nelson, a writer, filmmaker, and software designer, conceived the idea of Xanadu in 1981. In his own words, "explaining it quickly" [3]:

1. Xanadu is a system for the network sale of documents with automatic royalty on every byte.

2. The transclusion feature allows quotation of fragments of any size with royalty to the original publisher.

3. This is an implementation of a connected literature.

4. It is a system for a point-and-click universe.

5. This is a completely interactive docuverse.

Andrew Pam, in his "Where World Wide Web Went Wrong" article,[3] explains transclusion as:

> *"'Transclusion' is a term introduced by Ted Nelson to define virtual inclusion, the process of including something by reference rather than by copying. This is fundamental to the Xanadu designs; originally transclusions were implemented using hyperlinks, but it was later discovered that in fact hyperlinks could be implemented using transclusions! Transclusions permit storage efficiency for multiple reasonably similar documents, such as those generated by versions and alternates as discussed above."*

---

[3] http://www.xanadu.com.au/xanadu/6w-paper.html

In the Xanadu scheme,[4] a universal document database (docuverse) would allow the addressing of any substring of any document from any other document. "This requires an even stronger addressing scheme than the Universal Resource Locators used in the World-Wide Web." [2] Additionally, Xanadu would permanently keep every version of every document, thereby eliminating the possibility of a broken link and the ever-so-familiar HTTP return code *404-Document Not Found* error. Xanadu would only maintain the current version of the document in its entirety. The previous versions could then be dynamically reconstructed from the current version through a very sophisticated versioning system which would keep track of modifications made to each generation of the document. Nelson named his project after the Xanadu in Samuel Taylor Coleridge's poem, *Kubla Khan*, Xanadu, a "magic place of literary memory" where nothing is ever forgotten [3, 18].

Xanadu was never implemented. In his article in *Wired* magazine, "The Curse of Xanadu,"[5] Gary Wolf writes:

> *"Xanadu, a global hypertext publishing system, is the longest-running vaporware story in the history of the computer industry. It has been in development for more than 30 years. This long gestation period may not put it in the same category as the Great Wall of China, which was under construction for most of the 16th century and still failed to foil invaders, but, given the relative youth of commercial computing, Xanadu has set a record of futility that will be difficult for other companies to surpass."*

Despite these harsh words, Wolf later writes:

> *"Nelson's writing and presentations inspired some of the most visionary computer programmers, managers, and executives—including Autodesk Inc. founder John Walker—to pour millions of dollars and years of effort into the project. Xanadu was meant to be a universal library, a worldwide hypertext publishing tool, a system to resolve copyright disputes, and a meritocratic forum for discussion and debate. By putting all information within reach of all people, Xanadu was meant to eliminate scientific ignorance and cure political misunderstandings."*

Wolfsbane,[6] published by the Xanadu project, is Nelson's retort to Gary Wolf's "Curse of Xanadu" in *Wired* magazine.

After years of frustration, Ted Nelson accepted an invitation from Japan in 1994 and founded the Sapporo HyperLab where he continued his Xanadu

---

[4] http://xanadu.net/the.project

[5] http://www.hotwired.com/wired/3.06/features/xanadu.html

[6] http://xanadu.net/wolfsbane

research. He is currently a Professor of Environmental Information at the Sho-
nan Fujisawa Campus of Keio University.

Other Landmarks

Other landmarks in the history of hypertext include Janet Walker's 1985 *Sym-
bolics Document Examiner*, which was the first hypertext-based system to gain
widespread acceptance and usage. The system provided the manual for Symbol-
ics computers in hypertext format, a useful alternative to the 8000-page printed
version. This application was significant in that it was generic enough to be used
for general purposes. This was a change from other hypertext applications of the
time, which were written for more specific needs. The application also gave users
the option to *bookmark* nodes within the document database [2].

Also in 1985, Xerox released *NoteCards*, a LISP-based hypertext system.
NoteCards' unique features included scrolling windows for each notecard, preformatted specialized notecards, and a separate browser/navigator window.
Another hypertext application released in 1985 was Brown University's *Interme-
dia* for the Macintosh A/UX system [2].

In 1986 Office Workstations Ltd. (OWL) introduced *OWL-Guide*, which was
a hypertext system developed for the Macintosh. Developed in 1982, the original
version of Guide was a PERQ workstation hypertext system based on the work of
Peter Brown of the University of Kent at Canterbury. OWL-Guide was later
ported to the IBM-PC platform and became the first multiplatform hypertext
system. The application gained widespread acceptance due to the popularity of
the Macintosh platform [2].

In 1987, Bill Atkinson of Apple Computer developed *HyperCard*. Apple bundled the application free with all Macintosh machines. HyperCard soon became
the most widely used hypertext system and many HyperCard-based applications
were developed. Many believe HyperCard to be the application that contributed
the most to the popularization of the hypertext model. ACM held the first Conference on Hypertext later that year [2].

Then in 1989 the Web came along....

1.2 History of the Net

Having discussed the origin of hypertext, we next discuss the other technology
underlying the Web: the Internet. This section provides an outline of events that
comprise the history of the Internet. Each event is presented individually, and its
significance is assumed to be self-evident. A detailed historical treatment of each
event is beyond the scope of this section and has no direct relevance to the history of the Web. The section may lack continuity, since the items contained here

are too diverse and disjointed to be put in narrative format in any cohesive fashion. This section, for the most part, is an abbreviated version of [17].

1858

- The "Atlantic cable" was installed across the ocean with the idea of connecting the communication systems of the U.S. and Europe. While this was a great idea, the 1858 implementation of it was only operational for a few days.

1866

- The implementation was attempted again, this time with great success. The original Atlantic cable laid in 1866 remained operational for almost 100 years.

1957

- In 1957, the Soviet Union launched Sputnik. As a response to the Soviet research efforts, president Dwight D. Eisenhower instructed the Department of Defense to establish the Advanced Research Projects Agency, or ARPA. The agency started with great success and launched the first American satellite within 18 months of the agency's conception. Several years later, ARPA was also given the task of developing a reliable communications network, specifically for use by computers. The primary motivation for this was to have a network of decentralized military computers connected in such way that in the case of destruction of one or several nodes in a potential war, the network would still survive with communication lines between remaining nodes.

1962

- In 1962, Dr. J.C.R. Licklider was given the task of leading ARPA's research efforts in improving the use of computer technology in the military. It was due to Dr. Licklider's influence that ARPA's primary research efforts moved from the private sector to universities around the country. His work paved the way for the creation of ARPANET.

- Paul Baran of RAND Corporation published the paper "On Distributed Communications Networks," which introduced Packet-Switching (PS) networks. PS networks have no single outage point.

1965

- ARPA sponsored a study that proposed a "cooperative network of time-sharing computers." The TX-2 at MIT Lincoln Lab and Q-32 at System Development Corporation (Santa Monica, CA) are directly linked (without packet switches).

1967

- At the ACM Symposium on Operating Principles, a plan was presented for a packet-switching network. Also, the first design paper on ARPANET was published by Lawrence G. Roberts.

1968

- PS-network was presented to the Advanced Research Projects Agency (ARPA).

- It is argued that the first packet-switching network was operational and in place at the National Physical Laboratories in the U.K. Parallel efforts in France also resulted in an early packet-switching network at Société Internationale de Télécommunications Aéronautiques in 1968–1970.

1969

- First ARPANET node was established at UCLA's Network Measurements Center.

- Subsequent nodes were established at Stanford Research Institute (SRI), University of Utah in Salt Lake City, and UCSB (UC Santa Barbara).

- Information Message Processor (IMP) was developed by Bolt Beranek on a Honeywell DDP 516. The system delivered messages within the 4-node network above.

- First RFC (Request For Comments), "Host Software," was submitted by Steve Crocker.

1970

- Norman Abrahamson developed ALOHAnet at University of Hawaii. ALO-HAnet provided the background for the work which later became Ethernet.

- ARPANET hosts started using Network Control Protocol (NCP). This protocol was used until 1982 at which time it was replaced with TCP/IP.

1971

- ARPANET had grown to 15 nodes connecting 26 hosts: UCLA, SRI, UCSB, University of Utah, BBN, MIT, RAND, SDC, Harvard, Lincoln Lab, Stanford, UIUC, CWRU, CMU, and NASA (Ames).

1972

- RFC 318, TELNET specification, was published.

- Ray Tomlinson wrote an e-mail program to operate across networks.

- Inter-Networking Working Group (INWG), headed by Vinton Cerf, was established and given the task of investigating common protocols.

- Public demonstration of the ARPANET by Bob Kahn of BBN. The demonstration consisted of a "packet switch" and a Terminal Interface Processor (TIP) in the basement of the Washington Hilton Hotel. The public could use the TIP to run distributed applications across the U.S. According to Vinton Cerf, the demonstration was a "roaring success."

1973

- ARPANET went international:
  - University College of London—U.K.
  - Royal Radar Establishment—Norway.

- First published outline for the idea of Ethernet: Bob Metcalfe's Harvard PhD thesis.

- RFC 454, File Transfer Protocol (FTP), was published.

1974

- The design of TCP was given in "A Protocol for Packet Network Internetworking" by Vinton Cerf and Bob Kahn.

1976

- UUCP (Unix to Unix Copy Program) was developed at AT&T Bell Labs and distributed with UNIX the following year.

1977

- RFC 733, Mail specification, was published.
- THEORYNET, a UUCP based e-mail system with over 100 users, was established at the University of Wisconsin.
- First demonstration of ARPANET/Packet Radio.

1979

- Computer scientists from the University of Wisconsin, NSF, DARPA, and other universities met to establish Computer Science network.
- Tom Truscott and Steve Bellovin implemented USENET.
  - Only between UNC and Duke.
  - All groups originally under net.
- Internet Configuration Board was created by ARPA.
- PRNET (Packet Radio Network) was established.

1981

- BITNET (Because It's Time NETwork) established.
- CSNET (Computer Science NETwork) established.
  - Based on funding from NSF.
  - Stated goal of providing network access to universities without ARPANET access.

1982

- TCP (Transmission Control Protocol) and IP (Internet Protocol) was selected as the protocol suite for ARPANET.
- TCP/IP selected by Dept. of Defense as standard.
- RFC 827, External Gateway Protocol, published.

1983

- Name server developed at University of Wisconsin.
- Gateway between CSNET and ARPANET was established.
- ARPANET was split into ARPANET and MILNET.
- UNIX machines with built-in TCP/IP gained in popularity.
- Internet Activities Board (IAB) replaced ICCB.
- Tom Jennings developed FidoNet.

1984

- Domain Name Server (DNS) introduced.
- Over 1000 hosts were now present.
- Japan Unix Network operational.

1986

- NSFNET created.
  - Originally composed of five supercomputer centers connected with 56 Kbps lines.
  - Other universities joined in.
- Network News Transfer Protocol (NNTP) created.
- Mail Exchanger (MX) records developed by Craig Partridge allowed non-IP network hosts to have domain addresses.

1987

- NSF and Merit Network, Inc. agreed to manage the NSFNET backbone.
- Over 10,000 Internet hosts were now present.

1988

- On November 1, Internet worm affected 10% of Internet hosts.
- Dept. of Defense adopted OSI.
- NSFNET backbone was upgraded to T1 (1.544 Mbps).
- Canada, Denmark, Finland, France, Iceland, Norway, and Sweden were added to NSFNET.

1989

- Over 100,000 hosts were now present.
- CSNET merged into BITNET to form Corporation for Research and Education Networking (CREN).
- Internet Engineering Task Force (IETF) was created.
- Internet Research Task Force (IRTF) was created.
- NSFNET added Australia, Germany, Israel, Italy, Japan, Mexico, Netherlands, New Zealand, Puerto Rico, and the U.K.

1990

- NSFNET replaced ARPANET.
- Peter Deutsch, Alan Emtage, and Bill Heelan at McGill released Archie.
- NSFNET added Argentina, Austria, Belgium, Brazil, Chile, Greece, India, Ireland, South Korea, Spain, and Switzerland.

1991

- Wide Area Information Servers (WAIS) was invented by Brewster Kahle.
- Gopher was released by Paul Lindner and Mark P. McCahill from the University of Minnesota.
- Tim Berners-Lee at CERN released World Wide Web.
- NSFNET backbone was upgraded to T3 (44.736 Mbps).
- NSFNET traffic passed 1 trillion bytes/month and 10 billion packets/ month.

- NSFNET added Croatia, Czech Republic, Hong Kong, Hungary, Poland, Portugal, Singapore, South Africa, Taiwan, and Tunisia.

1992

- Internet Society (ISOC) was formed.

- Over 1,000,000 hosts were now present.

- Veronica, a gopherspace search tool, was released by the University of Nevada.

- NSFNET added Cameroon, Cyprus, Ecuador, Estonia, Kuwait, Latvia, Luxembourg, Malaysia, Slovakia, Slovenia, Thailand, and Venezuela.

1993

- InterNIC was created by the NSF.

- U.S. National Information Infrastructure Act was passed to further Internet development.

- Web proliferated at a 341,634% annual growth rate of service traffic. Gopher's growth rate was 997%.

- NSFNET added Bulgaria, Costa Rica, Egypt, Fiji, Ghana, Guam, Indonesia, Kazakhstan, Kenya, Liechtenstein, Peru, Romania, the Russian Federation, Turkey, Ukraine, UAE, and the Virgin Islands.

1994

- NSFNET traffic passed 10 trillion bytes/month.

- Percent packets and bytes in order:
  - FTP
  - WWW
  - TELNET.

- NSFNET added Algeria, Armenia, Bermuda, Burkina Faso, China, Colombia, French Polynesia, Jamaica, Lebanon, Lithuania, Macau, Morocco, New Caledonia, Nicaragua, Niger, Panama, Philippines, Senegal, Sri Lanka, Swaziland, Uruguay, and Uzbekistan.

1995

- NSFNET reverted back to a research network. Main U.S. backbone traffic rerouted through interconnected network providers.

- Web surpassed FTP-data in March as the service with greatest traffic on NSFNet based on packet count, and in April based on byte count.

- Traditional online dial-up systems (Compuserve, American Online, Prodigy) began to provide Internet access.

- Registration of domain names was no longer free. Beginning 14 September, a $50 annual fee was imposed, which up until then was subsidized by NSF. NSF continued to pay for .edu registration, and on an interim basis for .gov.

- Technologies of the Year: WWW, Search engines.

- Emerging Technologies: Mobile code (JAVA, JAVAscript), Virtual environments (VRML), Collaborative tools.

1.3 History of the Web

CERN WWW Research

It all began when Tim Berners-Lee,[7] a graduate of Oxford University, got frustrated with the fact that his daily schedule planner, his list of phone numbers, and his documents were stored in different databases on different machines, thus making it difficult to access them simultaneously. He set out to fix this problem. The year was 1980, and the place was CERN.

Tim Berners-Lee started working at CERN (Conseil Européen pour la Recherche Nucléaire, or European Laboratory for Particle Physics) as a consultant in 1980. At that time, several platform-dependent and proprietary information storage and retrieval methods were being used at CERN. Additionally, several systems such as "CERNET" and "FOCUS" were developed in-house. In general, as with other institutions, data was stored and manipulated in isolated machines with practically no interaction or connectivity. Tim Berners-Lee's data was scattered over several such systems. He wished to develop a system that would allow him, for example, to quickly and transparently retrieve a mailing address from a remote database for a letter he might be composing on his local

---

[7] http://www.w3.org/pub/WWW/People/Berners-Lee

word processor. "I wanted a program that could store random associations between arbitrary pieces of information," he recounts. His first program to address this issue was "Enquire-Within-Upon-Everything," "Enquire" for short. The name for the program was based on an 1856 book *Enquire Within Upon Everything*, a how-to book for the Victorian era. In a recent interview, Berners-Lee said that at the time of creation of "Enquire," he had only been marginally exposed to the ideas of Ted Nelson and the concept of hypertext. At the time, he was simply concerned with solving a technical problem he was facing at CERN [15].

Berners-Lee left CERN shortly after the completion of the "Enquire" system, which went mostly unused after his departure. He worked as a consultant in the area of networking and made contributions to the RPC (Remote Procedure Call) system. In the meantime, the Internet and TCP/IP were introduced at CERN in 1984. By 1989 CERN had become the largest Internet site in Europe. In 1989 Tim Berners-Lee returned to CERN. The "computing culture" at CERN revolved around the then-new ideas of distributed computing and object-oriented programming. Berners-Lee's background in network and socket programming was completely consistent with the new ways of computing at CERN. Additionally, with the advent of revolutionary object-oriented technologies introduced by NeXT, rapid systems development and prototyping in a UNIX environment had become more feasible. The conditions were just right [15, 3].

In March of 1989, Tim Berners-Lee submitted "Information Management: A Proposal"[8] to his superiors at CERN. In a later paper ("World-Wide Web: An Information Infrastructure for High-Energy Physics"), he mentioned that the motivation for this system arose "from the geographical dispersion of large collaborations, and the fast turnover of fellows, students, and visiting scientists," who had to get "up to speed on projects and leave a lasting contribution before leaving." In his original "Information Management: A Proposal," Berners-Lee described the deficiencies of hierarchical information-delivery systems such as UUCP and outlined the advantages of a hypertext-based system. The proposal called for "a simple scheme to incorporate several different servers of machine-stored information already available at CERN." A distributed hypertext system was the mechanism to provide "a single user-interface to many large classes of stored information such as reports, notes, data-bases, computer documentation and on-line systems help" [9]. As outlined by Relihan,[9] the proposal's main objectives were:

- To provide a simple protocol for requesting human-readable information stored in remote systems accessible using networks.

- To provide a protocol by which information could automatically be exchanged in a format common to the information supplier and the information consumer.

---

[8] http://www.w3.org/pub/WWW/History/1989/proposal.html

[9] http://itdsrv1.ul.ie/Research/WWW/utwww.ps

- To provide some method of reading text (and possibly graphics) using a large proportion of the display technology in use at CERN at that time.

- To provide and maintain collections of documents, into which users could place documents of their own.

- To allow documents or collections of documents managed by individuals to be linked by hyperlinks to other documents or collections of documents.

- To provide a search option, to allow information to be automatically searched for by keywords, in addition to being navigated to by the following of hyperlinks.

- To use public-domain software wherever possible and to interface to existing proprietary systems.

- To provide the necessary software free of charge.

Berners-Lee envisioned a two-phase approach in his "Proposal for a Hyper-Text Project."[10] In the first phase, CERN would "make use of existing software and hardware as well as implementing simple browsers for the user's workstations, based on an analysis of the requirements for information access needs by experiments." In the second phase, they would "extend the application area by also allowing the users to add new material." The proposal requested four software engineers and a programmer, and the development time for each phase was projected to be three months. Initially, the proposal did not have complete support, but in 1990 Berners-Lee recirculated the proposal and received the needed resources to begin work. In October of 1990, his project proposal was reformulated with help from Robert Cailliau[11] and the name World Wide Web was selected [3, 18].

As an aside, it is interesting to note that the birth of the Web was a "side effect" of research in the area of particle physics. CERN provided the type of environment in which scientists and researchers were given the opportunity to cultivate any new and creative ideas. Ben Segal[12] recalls in an interview [3]:

> "As it happened many times in the history of science, the most impressive results of the super-large scale scientific efforts were far from the main directions of these efforts. I hope you agree that Web was a side effect of the CERN's scientific agenda. After World War II, the nuclear centers of developed countries around the world became the places with highest rate of the concentration of talented people per square of Labs. Some of the most talented persons among the national scientists usually were invited to the international CERN's Laboratories. The

---

[10] http://www.w3.org/pub/WWW/Proposal

[11] http://www.w3.org/pub/WWW/People.html#Cailliau

[12] http://wwwcn1.cern.ch/~ben/

specific kind of the CERN's intellectual "entire culture" was constantly growing from one generation of the scientists and engineers to another during about four decades."

Berners Lee and others at CERN were impressed with some of the new paradigms of computing as implemented by NeXT Software, Inc., founded by the one of the architects of the desktop computer revolution, Steve Jobs. The initial Web program was developed in November of 1990 using NeXT's object-oriented technology. The program was a browser which also allowed WYSIWYG editing of Web documents. The first Web server was also developed and implemented on NEXT-STEP. The software was ported to other platforms in 1991 and released to the public. Berners-Lee and his team at CERN paved the way for the future development of the Web by introducing their server and browser, the protocol used for communication between the clients and the server, Hypertext Transfer Protocol (HTTP), the language used in composing Web documents, HyperText Markup Language (HTML), and the Universal Resource Locator (URL) [3].

So it began.

Mosaic and Netscape

Once the Web concepts and the protocols were placed in the public domain, programmers and software developers around the world began introducing their own modifications and improvements. Marc Andreessen was one such programmer. Andreessen, a graduate student at the University of Illinois' NCSA (National Center for Supercomputing Applications), led a team of graduate students (including Eric Bina) which in February of 1993 released the first alpha version of his "Mosaic for X" point-and-click graphical browser for the Web implemented for UNIX. In August of 1993, Andreessen and his fellow programmers released free versions of their *Mosaic* for Macintosh and Windows operating systems. This was a significant event in the evolution of the Web in that, for the first time, a Web client, with a relatively consistent and easy to use point-and-click GUI (Graphical User Interface), was implemented on the three most popular operating systems available at the time. By September of 1993, Web traffic constituted 1% of all traffic on the NSF backbone [3].

Andreessen left NCSA in December of 1993 to move to California and accepted a position with a small software company. At that time, he had no intention of continuing work on Mosaic. Within four months, however, Andreessen and Eric Bina (from the original Mosaic team at NCSA), along with the founder of SGI, Jim Clark, started "Mosaic Communications Corp.," which is now known as Netscape.[13] Andreessen recalls:

---

[13] http://www.netscape.com

"At the NCSA, the deputy director suggested that we should start a company, but we didn't know how. We had no clue. How do you start something like that? How do you raise the money? Well, I came out here and met Jim, and all of a sudden the answers starting falling into place." [3]

By May of 1994, practically all the members of the original Mosaic development team at NCSA had joined Netscape. The Marc Andreessen Interview Page [10] provides an interesting view on the history of Mosaic and Netscape.

The creation of the Web by Tim Berners-Lee, followed by release of the Mosaic browser (and the eventual establishment of Netscape Inc.) can arguably be viewed as the two most significant contributing factors to the success and popularity of the Web today. The list that follows contains links to other locations with additional information on the history of the Web.

- The World Wide Web Consortium (W3C), was formed in December of 1994. Tim Berners-Lee currently holds the position of the director of the organization. W3C's main objective is "to promote standards for the evolution of the Web and interoperability between Web products by producing specifications and reference software." W3C provides a linear and sequential history of the Web in the document "A Little History of the World Wide Web" [15].

- The International Web Conferences[14] are held regularly to bring together developers of Web technologies and provide another forum for discussion of innovative ideas.

- The "World Wide Web Research" page [16] includes several papers which contain the original design philosophy for the Web.

1.4 History of Java

At first glance, it may appear that Java was developed specifically for the Web. However, interestingly enough, Java was developed independently of the Web, and went through several stages of metamorphosis before reaching its current status of de facto programming language for the Web. Below is a brief history of Java from its infancy to its current state.

---

[14] http://www.w3.org/pub/Conferences/Overview-WWW.html

Oak

According the Java FAQ [4], Bill Joy, currently a vice president at Sun Microsystems, is widely believed to have conceived the idea of a programming language that later became Java. In late 1970's, Joy wanted to design a language that combined the best features of MESA and C. In an attempt to rewrite the UNIX operating system in 1980's, Joy decided that C++ was inadequate for the job. A better tool was needed to write short and effective programs. It was this desire to invent a better programming tool that swayed Joy, in 1991, in the direction of Sun's "Stealth Project"—as named by Scott McNealy, currently Sun's CEO [4].

In January of 1991, Bill Joy, James Gosling, Mike Sheradin, Patrick Naughton (formerly the project leader of Sun's OpenWindows user environment), and several other individuals met in Aspen, Colorado for the first time to discuss the ideas for the Stealth Project. The goal of the Stealth Project was to do research in the area of application of computers in the consumer electronics market. The vision of the project was to develop "smart" consumer electronic devices that could all be centrally controlled and programmed from a handheld-remote-control-like device. According to Gosling, "the goal was ... to build a system that would let us do a large, distributed, heterogeneous network of consumer electronic devices all talking to each other." With this goal in mind, the Stealth group began work [8].

Members of the Stealth Project, which later became known as the Green Project, divided the tasks among themselves. Mike Sheradin focused on business development, Patrick Naughton began work on the graphics system, and James Gosling identified the proper programming language for the project. Gosling, who had joined Sun in 1984, had previously developed the commercially unsuccessful NeWS windowing system as well as GOSMACS—a C language implementation of GNU EMACS. He began with C++, but soon afterward was convinced that C++ was inadequate for this particular project. His extensions and modifications to C++ (also known as C++ ++ − −) were the first steps toward the development of an independent language that would fit the project objectives. He named the language "Oak" while staring at an oak tree outside his office window! The name "Oak" was later dismissed when a patent search determined that the name was copyrighted and used for another programming language. According to Gosling, "the Java development team discovered that Oak was the name of a programming language that predated Sun's language, so another name had to be chosen" [8, 4].

"It's surprisingly difficult to find a good name for a programming language, as the team discovered after many hours of brainstorming. Finally, inspiration struck one day during a trip to the local coffee shop," Gosling recalls. Others have speculated that the name Java came from several individuals involved in the project: **J**ames gosling, **A**rthur **V**an hoff, **A**ndy bechtolsheim [MCCAR].

There were several criteria that Oak had to meet in order to satisfy the project objective. Given the wide array of manufacturers in the consumer electronics market, Oak would have to be completely platform independent and function seamlessly regardless of the type of CPU in the device. For this reason, Oak was designed to be an interpreted language, since it would be practically impossible for a complied version to run on all available platforms. To facilitate the job of the interpreter, Oak was to be compiled to an intermediate "byte-code" format which would then be passed around across the network and executed/ interpreted dynamically [8, 4, 6].

Additionally, reliability was of great concern. A consumer electronics device that would have to be "rebooted" periodically was not acceptable. Another important design objective for Oak would then have to be high reliability, achieved by minimizing programmer-introduced errors. This was the motivation for several important modifications to C++. The concepts of multiple-inheritance and operator overloading were identified as sources of potential errors and were eliminated in Oak. Furthermore, in contrast to C++, Oak included implicit garbage collection, thereby providing efficient memory utilization and higher reliability. Finally, Oak attempted to eliminate all unsafe constructs used in C and C++ by only providing data structures within objects [8, 6].

Another essential design criterion was security. By design, Oak-based devices were to function in a network and often exchange code and information. Inherently, security is of great concern in a networked environment, especially in an environment as network-dependent as the conceived Oak-based systems. For this reason, pointers were excluded from the design of Oak. This would theoretically eliminate the possibility of malicious programs accessing arbitrary addresses in memory [8, 6].

If Oak was going to be widely accepted and used within the consumer electronics industry, it would have to be simple and compact, so that the language could be mastered relatively easily and development would not be excessively complex. Some would argue that Oak/Java is C++ done right, but the jury is still out on that.

In April of 1991, Ed Frank, a SPARCstation 10 architect, joined the Green Project. He led the project's hardware-development effort. In two months they developed the first hardware prototype, known as star-seven (*7). The name *7 was somewhat demonstrative of the project's objective. *7 was the key combination to press on any telephone to answer any other ringing telephone on their network. In the meantime, Gosling was beginning work on the Oak interpreter. By August of 1991, the team had a working prototype of the user interface and graphical system, which was demonstrated to Sun's co-founders Scott McNealy and Bill Joy [8].

Development of Oak, the Green OS, the user interface, and the hardware continued through the summer of 1992. In September of that year, the *7 prototype was complete and demonstrated to McNealy and Joy. The prototype was a PDA-like (personal digital assistant) device that Gosling described as a "handheld remote control." Patrick Naughton proclaimed that "in 18 months, we did the equivalent of what 75-people organizations at Sun took three years to do—an

operating system, a language, a toolkit, an interface, a new hardware platform"
[8].

While impressive, this type of technology lacked market appeal, as later
demonstrated by Apple's Newton PDA. The Green Project's business planner,
Mike Sheradin, and hardware designer, Ed Frank, had envisioned a technology
similar to that of Dolby Labs, which would become the standard for consumer
electronics products [8].

FirstPerson

In November of 1992, the Green Project was incorporated under the name First-
Person. Given Java's lack of success in the consumer electronics industry, the
company's direction was somewhat uncertain. Under Sun's influence, the company began reevaluating its mission.

In early 1993, Time-Warner issued an RFP (request for proposal) for a set-
top box operating system and interactive, video-on-demand technology. First-
Person identified this area as a new target market and began working in that
direction. However, despite FirstPerson's great efforts, SGI was granted the contract by Time-Warner. By mid 1993 Sun began negotiating with 3DO to provide a
Java-based OS for their set-top box. The negotiations were, however, unsuccessful and a deal was never made. FirstPerson was left on its own without any viable business prospects. Another attempt by the company to market its
interactive TV technology failed when in February of 1994 a public launching of
their products was canceled [8].

A higher-level review of FirstPerson determined the interactive TV market
to be immature in 1994. FirstPerson then shifted its focus yet again. Business
plans were submitted to Sun's executives for developing Oak-based on-line and
CD-ROM applications. Sun's response was not favorable, and FirstPerson was
dissolved. Most of FirstPerson's employees moved to Sun Interactive to work on
digital video data servers. However, a few individuals from FirstPerson still pursued the objective of finding a home for Java in a networked desktop market [8].

Java and the Web

In June of 1994, Bill Joy started the "Liveoak" project with the stated objective of
building a "big small operating" system. In July of 1994, the project "clicked" into
place. Naughton got the idea of putting "Liveoak" to work on the Internet while
he was playing with writing a Web browser over a long weekend. Just the kind of
thing you'd want to do with your weekend! This was the turning point for Java
[8].

The Web, by nature, had requirements such as reliability, security, and platform independence that were fully compatible with Java's design parameters. A
perfect match had been found. By September of 1994, Naughton and Jonathan

Payne (a Sun engineer) start writing "WebRunner," a Java-based Web browser which was later renamed "HotJava." By October 1994, HotJava was stable and was demonstrated to Sun executives. This time, Java's potential, in the context of the Web, was recognized and the project was supported. Although designed with a different objective in mind, Java found a perfect match in the Web. Introduction of Java marked a new era in the history of the Web. Information providers were now given the capability to deliver not only raw data, but also the applications that would operate on the data.

Sun formally announced Java and HotJava at SunWorld '95. Soon afterward, Netscape Inc. announced that it would incorporate Java support in their browser. This was a great triumph for Java, since it was now supported by the most popular browser in the world. Later, Microsoft also announced that they would support Java in their Internet Explorer Web browser, further solidifying Java's role in the Web.

And the rest is, well, in Chapter 7.

1.5 References

[1]   Bush, Vannevar. "As We May Think."
        <http://www.isg.sfu.ca/~duchier/misc/vbush> (31 Nov 1996).

[2]   De Bra, P. "History of hypertext and hypermedia."
        <http://www.win.tue.nl/win/cs/is/debra/cursus/history.html> (31 Nov 1996).

[3]   Gromov, Gregory R. "History of Internet and WWW: View from Internet Valley" <http://www.internetvalley.com/intval.html> (31 Nov 1996).

[4]   Harold, Elliotte R. "comp.lang.java FAQ."
        <http://sunsite.unc.edu/javafaq/javafaq.html> (31 Nov 1996).

[5]   Lee, Chang-Jae. "What's in a name & history."
        <http://web.sec.samsung.co.kr/~cjlee/www-kr/Mirror/jhjeon/TP/java/sld008.html> (31 Nov 1996).

[6]   McCarthy, Vance. "Gosling On Java."
        <http://www.datamation.com/PlugIn/java/03ajava2.html> (31 Nov 1996).

[7]   Nielsen, Jakob. "History of Hypertext."
        <http://www.sun.com/950523/columns/alertbox/history.html>
        (31 Nov 1996).

[8]   O'Connell, Michael. "Java: The inside story."
        <http://www.sun.com:80/sunworldonline/swol-07-1995/swol-07-java.html>
        (31 Nov 1996).

[9]   Relihan, L., *et al*. "Untangling the World-Wide Web."
       <http://itdsrv1.ul.ie/Research/WWW/utwww.html#Origins> (31 Nov 1996).

[10]   Stark, Thom. "The Marc Andreessen Interview Page."
       <http://www.dnai.com/~thomst/marca.html> (21 Oct. 1997).

[11]   Swedish University of Agricultural Sciences. "A Hypermedia Timeline"
       <http://ulmo.stud.slu.se:8001/kurser/it-kurs-vt96/ew3_intro.html> (31 Nov
       1996).

[12]   The World Wide Web Consortium. "W3C—The World Wide Web Consor-
       tium." <http://www.w3.org/pub/WWW> (31 Nov 1996).

[13]   The World Wide Web Consortium. "Talks."
       <http://www.w3.org/pub/WWW/Talks> (31 Nov 1996).

[14]   The World Wide Web Consortium. "Short History of Hypertext."
       <http://www.w3.org/pub/History> (31 Nov 1996).

[15]   The World Wide Web Consortium. "A Little History of the World Wide Web."
       <http://www.w3.org/pub/WWW/History.html> (31 Nov 1996).

[16]   University of Limerick. "World Wide Web Research."
       <http://itdsrv1.ul.ie/Research/WWW/www-research.html> (31 Nov 1996).

[17]   Zakon, Robert. "Hobbes' Internet Timeline."
       <http://info.isoc.org/guest/zakon/Internet/History/HIT.html> (17 Feb 1998).

[18]   Zeltser, Lenny. "The World Wide Web: Origins And Beyond."
       <http://homepage.seas.upenn.edu/~lzeltser/WWW/#About_WWW>
       (31 Nov 1996).

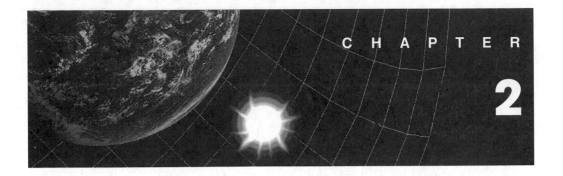

C H A P T E R

2

Demographics and Demographic Tools

by Mei See Yeoh
(updated by Ashish Shah)

What is all this hype about the Web? What's the "magic" about it that makes people spend hours and hours on it? Who are the people using the Web, and what are they using it for? These questions plague those who have yet to jump on the bandwagon. They are of great interest to the commercial media. Much as it may surprise those of us who are using the Web, less than ten percent of the United States population and less than one-tenth of a percent of the world population use it, according to the GENic and Georgia Tech user survey during June of 1996.

Plenty of Web demographic studies and surveys can be found on the Web. Results of these demographic studies, the effectiveness of using current methods for gathering consumer demographics, and proposed techniques are addressed in this chapter.

Chapter Content

1. Introduction
2. Collecting Web Demographics

- Current Methods
- Proposed Methods

2.1 Introduction

What is the Web? According to the Internet Literary Consultants, there are two possible meanings [13]. Defined loosely, it is all the resources that can be accessed using *Gopher, FTP, HTTP, telnet, USENET, WAIS,* and some other tools. The second definition, which will be used in this chapter, is that the Web is the "universe of hypertext servers" *(HTTP servers),* which are servers that allow text, graphics, sound files, etc. to be mixed together.

Although the Web was first introduced by CERN in 1991, it only really gained popularity and attention with the release of NCSA's Mosaic Web browser in 1993. The original version of today's Netscape, Mosaic made the Web and Internet more accessible to the general public through its user-friendly interface and its wide availability across popular platforms. Businesses and the media started to take notice of the Internet and its possibilities. The commercial community began to directly connect to the Internet in 1994.

Just three years after its debut, there were at least thirty million Web users, and today this number is growing rapidly. One good measure of how fast the Web has grown is to look at the number of Web sites: it has grown from 130 [9] in June of 1993 to 1,269,800 [16] in August of 1997.

This chapter focuses on demographics of the Web. Numbers tell a story, and this chapter will provide some insight to these numbers. The first part of this chapter focuses on what Web demographics really mean, who is collecting this information, and why. The methods of collecting demographics on the Web are discussed, followed by a survey of Web user evolution and characteristics. Demographics of Web usage for the purpose of education and commerce are discussed in the next two sections. A conclusion then summarizes this chapter.

2.2 Collecting Web Demographics

According to the Webster dictionary, "demography" is the "statistical study of human population, especially with reference to size and density, distribution, and vital statistics" [3]. For the Web, demography is the study of the characteristics of the users, their tastes, preferences, and behavior on the Web.

Why collect demographics? Aren't you curious about who is accessing your Web pages? To the Web service provider and other information content providers, demographics are clues to helping them improve their Web page content and services. All Web service providers would like to know what information users would like to have and how they want this information presented and delivered. By knowing the tastes, preferences and demographics of users, Web service providers can offer quality content and an effective presentation of the information. They can provide businesses and commercial institutions demographics to help determine effective ways of marketing their products. Most of the information on the Web is currently free, provided to users by users. Because of this, users have the tendency to expect information on the Web to be free. Businesses who wish to sell their information on the Web have the challenge of breaking through this barrier; knowledge of user behavior and characteristics will help in this. Businesses would like to know what products sell best, and how to produce effective, attractive advertisements on the Web. Web service providers, too, would like to analyze the traffic flow to ensure a good balance between load and service to the users.

Web demographics are essentially unique; people's behavior in private is usually different from public behavior. The Web is a world where users may be nameless, faceless, and even voiceless, where the users have control of their identifying information. The flow of electronic data in the Web is inherently difficult to track because it is ephemeral and intangible. Thus, those who conduct demographics have to be creative in their ways of capturing that information. The fact that the Web is evolving fast without a central control also makes collecting demographics more difficult. The current and proposed methods of collecting Web demographics are presented here.

Current Methods

The current methods of collecting information on the Web are through HTTP logging, surveys and guest-books, user/password authentication and cookies.

HTTP Logging

The first method of collecting information, HTTP logging, extracts information regarding user/machine requests. "HTTP" (Hypertext Transfer Protocol) is the communication protocol used in the Web. HTTP logs are maintained by the Web server software which is responsible for serving Web pages. These logs contain information about document requests, such as information about the HTTP GET, POST, and HEAD messages received, the client and server machine, the date and time of the request, the URL of the request, browser information, and possibly user ID. (For further information regarding the HTTP protocol, refer to Chapter 23.) Therefore, user requests on the Web can be recorded to a certain extent. Note that this type of information can be collected by the information provider without the user's knowledge. This method is often employed by network administrators and Web service providers to collect information regarding network load (number of bytes requested and transferred), Web page requests, and response time, to provide better service to the users. Advertisers may use these methods to determine the effectiveness of an advertisement.

Logging may occur at four levels: client, server, proxy, and network. At the client level, the client machine collects users' Web-page-request information that is sent out to different servers. The possible advantage of client logging is that actions of each user may be identified. At the server level, Web requests from clients may be logged. A proxy is a machine usually at the client network that filters information that flows in and out of the network. HTTP requests from different machines may be logged at this level. The advantage of proxy caching is that HTTP requests from different machines may be logged at the same time. Network-level logging is HTTP logging by an independent machine (neither the client, server, or proxy machine). Abrams and Williams propose logging at the network level to collect information on Web usage, using *tcpdump* [1]. The advantage of network logging is that it is secure; only the owner of the network monitoring device can access the data, and it does not impact the performance of clients, proxies, servers or networks. One problem that may occur with logging is caching; caching documents at the client, server or network levels may distort information collected from HTTP logs. Caching usually occurs at the client level to reduce network traffic and retrieval time.

Problems that result from caching are:

- Web users may access Web pages many times without the client requesting information directly from the server.

- More than one user may request the same pages, but this won't be reflected at the server log. These problems may be solved by specifying a short time-to-live period for each document retrieved. However, this will nullify the purpose of a cache proxy to reduce network traffic and improve user response time. Mirroring also distorts log information collected at the server level.

Other limitations of using HTTP logs are:

- Logging is limited to only collecting information at each site, usually at the client or server site. It cannot collect information about user behavior at other sites, and unless Web administrators pool their resources together, limited inference can be made about user actions.

- Logs at the server level can only tell user's behavior for one session, i.e., when a user accesses pages from one Web site at one sitting. Logs usually cannot identify users over different sessions unless the userID is specified in the HTTP requests. This, too, makes the data very limited in terms of its use.

These limitations create difficulty in making generalizations of user behavior. However, there are benefits from logging information, such as:

- User anonymity is usually preserved. Only the machines that users use, and not userIDs, are logged. Information can be collected automatically using scripts.

- Since participation is automatic, users don't select themselves.

User Surveys

The second form of collecting demographics, complimentary to the first, is through user surveys. Personal information such as gender, age, preferences, beliefs, lifestyles, and opinions can be collected through this method. Businesses often hire or sponsor organizations to conduct these surveys. Some organizations also conduct surveys to record the evolution of the Web and to provide this information online for the general public. These surveys are conducted on the Internet, through forms on Web browsers and e-mail. Surveys are also conducted over telephones, and through postal mail and personal interviews. Most of the online surveys are, typically, extremely long (at least several pages) and require many types of reply formats, including paragraph-long replies! These surveys run from the typical demographic surveys, to surveys on net addiction, and surveys for sea surfers. However, there are limitations to surveys. Respondents select themselves for the surveys; hence these surveys may not accurately represent the general Web population as a whole. Furthermore, respondents may provide inaccurate or false information; survey results may be affected by the type of questions used and the order and phrasing of the questions. Forms-based surveys limit their respondents to those who use forms-supporting browsers. However, despite their limitations, surveys today remain the main source of demographic information because of privacy concerns.

Web users value their anonymity highly and are very concerned with having control of demographic information. Surveys provide the simplest solution to user concerns at the moment. It is also a way to gain information regarding Web users and their usage patterns that cannot be collected from HTTP logs. Surveys need not be limited to a specific site or network of users as they are in logging. Guestbooks are similar to surveys except that they are placed on a specific set of Web pages in which the guestbook author is interested.

Cookies and User/Password Authentication

Netscape introduced a way to collect some limited information, yet protect user anonymity to a certain extent, through Netscape cookies. Now also available through the Microsoft Internet Explorer, cookies provide a way for servers to save a limited amount of information to the user's files. This information may include the domain server identity, unique value of the cookie, and a field for a server-defined code to identify the client machine. When the user accesses the Web site again, the server can retrieve the information it had originally saved. One limitation of the use of cookies is that it is browser-dependent and enables only limited information about the Web user.

Another method of collecting information that is widely used is through user/password authentication. Many users are turned off by this feature because it lacks security: anyone with knowledge of a user's ID and password may pretend to be that user.

Demographics from Collaborative Filtering

An interesting source of demographic data is from collaborative filtering environments in the Web. An example of such a site is Firefly [7]. This site provides ways for users to view sites that are recommended by other members and recommend different sites to each other. Members can also provide information about themselves through Web pages. Although this service is free, users provide some general information to the site and access the site through an alias/password authentication. Such collaborative systems are a gold mine of information as they not only provide user profiles but also show users' interests, tastes, and preferences in Web sites.

Proposed Methods

A few ideas have been proposed for alternative or complementary ways to survey users. The World Wide Web Consortium (W3C) has proposed methods for gathering consumer demographics [22]. One proposal is that the user agent, i.e., a client browser, sends a randomly generated sessionID at the beginning of each HTTP session. That sessionID is then monotonically increased at each request in that session. This will allow the server to track the information that is being requested by the client. Another suggestion is using a business card record, where the HTML browser maintains a user profile on behalf of the user. This profile includes the user's full name, e-mail address, home URL, affiliation, postal address, and business phone number. When a form is processed, the initial values of the matching user information will be filled with the given user profile. Security is an important issue in this, so users must have control of access to their own profile.

Another tool that is suggested is anonymous authentication. This works in a similar manner to Netscape cookies, without being browser-dependent. A 128-bit random number is chosen for a user for each site server and saved in the user's own file. This unique number is accessed when the user agent requests information from a server.

There are other methods that are being employed by companies to collect demographic information. Companies like I/PRO, NetCount and WebTrac market tools to monitor and analyze Web sites. Some of the problems currently faced by all these demographic tools are firewalls, cache proxies, and site mirroring. However they provide a useful technique for understanding consumer online behavior.

2.3 Web User Demographics

An inherent difficulty in collecting user demographics for the general Web population is the Web's lack of a central control. There is no one common tool that is used by all Web servers and/or clients to gather demographic information. HTTP logging, as explained in the previous section, provides limited demographics information. Those who collect demographics may not be willing to share their information with others. Currently, surveys are the most effective method of collecting information about the general user. Results of a few of the important surveys are presented here. Note that due to the limitations of surveying, these figures may not accurately reflect the general Web population; however, some insight is better than no insight.

Organizations and businesses first began to conduct general surveys a year after the introduction of NCSA's Mosaic. One of the largest, oldest and widely regarded surveyors, the Graphics, Visualization and Usability Center's World Wide Web User Surveys, began its work in January 1994 [10]. This center was one of the first organizations to demonstrate the Web as a powerful surveying medium. Surveys were done using forms; after the first survey, adaptive questioning was used. Since its inception, it has taken a total of seven surveys. The eighth survey is currently being conducted. From these surveys, it can be observed that the characteristics of the Web populations have changed significantly in a very short time.

Web User Evolution

The first survey featured the characteristics of the early Web adopters; the users were mostly male (94%), relatively young (56% between 21 and 30), and living in North America (69%). They were mostly professionals (45%) or graduate students (22%) and had over ten years of programming experience (77%). These users had high income, with an average of $69,000 per year. These were the early technology adopters who were eager to learn new tools and held careers in the computer industry. The fact that 88% of the surveyed users used UNIX as their platform is another good indication that these were users who were involved in a computer-related industry or in an education environment. These early users were heavy Web users, too; 97% of them used the browser at least a few times a week.

The continuing surveys indicate that the Web population has gradually become closer to the norm; the female Web population ratio has gradually increased to 31.3%, the average annual income has decreased to $58,000 per household, and the users in other occupations, such as management, have gained a greater share. These trends indicate that the Web is gradually becoming more accessible to everyone. Table 2–1 shows the gradual adoption of the Web by groups who were not "technology developers/pioneers."

Table 2–1 Change in Web User Demographics over Time

Surveys	1st Survey (Jan. 94)	3rd Survey (April 95)	5th Survey (April 96)	7th Survey (April 97)
Age	56% between 21 and 30	30% between 21 and 30	Average = 33.0	Average = 35.2
Gender	94% male	82% male	68.5% male	68.7% male
Average Income	N/A	$69,000	$59,000	$58,000
Main Profession	N/A	Computer-related 31.4%	Education-related 29.6%	Computer-related 30.24%
% in the U.S.	69% in North America	80.6% in U.S.	73.4% in U.S.	80.05% in U.S.

A prime factor in the popularity of the Web today could be its ease of use and installation; today's improved Web browsers such as Netscape and Microsoft Internet Explorer do not require any technical knowledge for installation or for usage. Even children at the elementary level can point and click to "go places" on the Web. The main barrier to Web usage today is getting access to the Internet. Most users today access the Internet through home (60.38%) or work (32.43%). Those who do not have a computer at home or at work are left out from the information superhighway. Today, even that barrier is whittling away, as coffee-shops, software vendors and other shops in large cities are starting to provide fee-based access to the Internet. Other less expensive alternative ways to access the Web, such as set-top boxes, smart phones, palm-tops and PDAs, are now being offered by companies in the communications industry.

For the moment at least, a telephone survey by Yankelovich Partners Inc.[1]finds that the biggest obstacles to going online for those without a PC are the cost of a computer and the perceived complexity of surfing the Internet. For those who do have PCs, only 10 percent use commercial on-line services, and another three quarters are seeking ISPs with a set rate for unlimited usage [20].

Web Users Today

How many Web users are there today? Who are they and what are they doing on the Web? This section describes first the general characteristics of the Web users and then their Web activities.

User characteristics

Currently the latest GVU survey, conducted in April 1997, indicates that:

- a majority of the users are still highly educated; 54.24% of the users have at least a college degree. The average age is still relatively young (35.2 years old).

- the proportion of female users is increasing (31.30%).

- many of the users surveyed were in the education-related fields (24.48%) or computer related fields (30.24%).

Of those surveyed, a large percentage of the users (25.34%) indicate that they have been on the Internet for less than a year. Out of this, a large number of them are females (38.29% of females are reported to be new users) and those in the over-50 age group (33.72% are new users). The increasing number of female Web users is probably due to the increase in female college students, and the emphasis of educators on education tools on the Web, education being primarily a female-dominated profession. Another group of new users are those in the age group of 19–25 who have been online for 1 to 3 years (43.99%). Students who are introduced to these facilities in college probably contribute to this large percentage.

Users were also surveyed on their opinions on Web-related issues. An important topic that users felt strongly about was censorship (33.58%), closely followed by privacy (26.17%). Anonymity was valued very highly among the respondents, and the complete authority to control demographic information came a close second. Most users, however, would agree to part with personal information if "a statement regarding how the information would be used" or a statement regarding "what information was being collected" was provided. Note, however, that more than a quarter of users have provided false information! The third most important issue facing the Internet is navigation (13.14%) [12].

---

[1] http://www.yankelovich.com

Web-related activities and demographics

Results from the 7th GVU survey [12] have some interesting statistics:

- **Location of Access:** 60.38% from home, 32.43% from work, 5.74% from other places, and 1.44% from more than one place.

- **Connection Speed:** 33.70% with 28.8K modems, 19.16% with 33.6K modems, 11.02% with 14.4K modems, and 11.03% with 1M connections.

- **Responsibility of Payment:** 65.04% self, 32.78% work, and 13.34% from school, 5.16% parents, and 3.31% other.

- **Frequency of access:** 85.16% at least once a day, 14.33% at least once a week.

The numbers above are closely related to each other; it can be seen that some of the 60.38% who access the Internet from home and 5.74% who access it from other places contribute to the 65.04% who pay for the access themselves. Note also that the responsibility-of-payment percentages add up to greater than a hundred, which implies that users are either accessing the Web at more than one place or sharing the cost of access. The fact that only 48.4% of users actually subscribe to online services is closely related to the number of users who access the Internet from home and those who pay for their own access. Online services provide a package of software tools to more easily access information, and give access to magazines, newsletters and forums online. It is interesting to note that 51% of users who subscribe to online services prefer local service providers to the larger online services. America Online, however, still has a very large share of the online service market, with 34.3% of the online service subscribers.

What do users do on the Web? A frequent activity is using the Web for reference. Of those surveyed, 86.03% have used the Web for reference and gathering information. Another popular activity is searching (63.01%). Only 54.05% of the users have actually used the Web for work-related activities. Other interesting user characteristics are:

- **Frequency of Use:** 43.47% of respondents access the Web 1 to 4 times a day, 41.69% use it more frequently and 14.84% use it less frequently.

- **Other Purposes of Use:** 61.29% simply browsing, 45.48% entertainment, 47.02% communication, 52.21% education, 18.65% shopping.

- Web users are giving up TV viewing time to browse and surf online instead.

With a majority of the respondents coming from either the U.S. (80.05%), Canada and Mexico (7.09%), or Europe (6.84%), one might think that the demographics may be biased toward users in these regions. However, studies on non-U.S. users' profiles by geographic region show otherwise. It was found that overall, the demographics of Web users were very similar throughout every continent.

Classifying Web Users

Some attempts have been made to classify Web users to determine what they do on the Web. According to Thomas E. Miller in his article *Segmenting the Internet* [15], users of the Web are best classified into different age groups. How users perceive the function of the Web is based on when they are introduced to it and the stage of life they are in. Based on the FindSVP's American Internet user survey [6], it was found that younger users are more likely to socialize through e-mail, online chat, and newsgroups. They are more likely to browse and experiment, instead of just searching for specific information. They are also more likely to browse the music and entertainment Web sites, while their older counterparts are more likely to access online news and many other categories of online information. "This is partly due to the fact that younger users have more discretionary time, and more like to put priority on socializing."

Another interesting segment of users are those in the over-50 age group. From the GVU surveys, there is a distinct difference in their behavior on the Web. They are more likely to access the Web from home (78.1%) and pay for their own access (83.1%). These users are more likely to use the online services (57%) than the average user (48.4%). They are also more likely to access economic/financial and government information on the Web than any of the other age groups.

Other methods of classifying Web users are through education level, gender, income, frequency of use, and purpose for using the Web.

2.4 Educational Institutions and Resources on the Web

The foundations of the Internet were laid with a large effort from universities. It cannot be denied that tertiary educational institutions played an important role in laying the groundwork for the Internet and Web. Universities and colleges were the first organizations to link up to the Internet; they used it for research and educational purposes. Educational institutions provide a rich source of information to students through the Internet and the Web. The primary and secondary educational institutions are beginning to catch up with their tertiary counterparts in getting connected to the Web; this means that pre-tertiary educators and students are using the Web for educational pursuits. This section gives a cursory idea of the connectivity of K12 institutions on the Web.

Based on the Web66 International WWW Schools Registry [23], a project funded by $3M^2$ to facilitate introduction of Web technology to schools, there are about 4000 schools worldwide that have their own Web servers.

More than 87% of these are in the United States. Another ten percent of the schools are in Canada. This is followed by Australia and Japan, with 307 and 213 schools (less than 1 percent) online, respectively. United Kingdom came in a far fifth with 77 schools, and Germany sixth with 75 schools. In the United States, all the schools with Web servers are concentrated in 901 districts. California has the largest number of schools that have Web servers: 465 schools in 78 districts, with Illinois coming second with 201 schools in 40 districts. This is followed by Washington (171 schools), Virginia (159), New York (154), Florida (132), and Texas (123) and Minnesota (123). For a complete and updated list of all K–12 schools on the Web, refer to Web66's International WWW Schools Registry [23].

There are also a number of Web sites to help promote education on the Web. The Web66 Project by the University of Minnesota provides a variety of interesting resources to help schools set up their Internet servers and to use Web resources for primary and secondary school education. Other resources include K–12 Technology [14], Galaxy's K–12 Education Resources [8], and TRFN General K–12 Education Sites [21]. For more information on education on the Web refer to Chapter 21. For Web-based collaboration for educational purposes, refer to Chapter 20.

2.5 Commerce on the Web

In this world of increasing free-market enterprise, whenever there is a new form of communication, there exist advertisers who will want to use it to market their products and services. Businesses also use the Web as an important form of communication with clients. With the advent of better, more accessible software, and more companies who are willing to offer Web and Internet services, many companies are jumping onto the information superhighway.

Businesses Online

Table 2–2 summarizes a study conducted by O'Reilly and Associates[3] conducted in June 1996 [19]. This study was done by conducting interviews with MIS directors and Web masters of companies sampled from the Dun & Bradstreet database of over 7 million enterprises.

[2] http://www.mmm.com

[3] http://www.ora.com

Table 2–2 Businesses Online

Business Size	% on Web (June '96)	% on Web (est. Dec. '96)
Large	51	66
Medium	25	42
Small	9	17

Are Consumers Buying?

How successful are businesses on the Web? According to the 5th GVU Survey, 38.53% of the users have never used the Web for online shopping and 37.43% have used it only a few times [10]. It was also found that those in the over-50 age group were most likely to have tried shopping at least once, and were the most frequent shoppers overall. Younger adults have less money and thus spend less on online-shopping, although they contribute to a large amount of CD and music sales on-line. However, in a Coopers & Lybrand[4] survey conducted in the first quarter of 1996, consumers expect to use the Internet for purchases once security measures are in place [5]. Internet commerce will not take off until consumers are satisfied that this new medium has effective security safeguards. In the meantime, the survey found that the print medium has gained a lot of business from the Internet. In fact, books on the Internet are generating more sales than actual online commerce. The survey found that consumers are spending from $300 to $600 million annually on books and magazines on the Internet, compared to the $200 to $300 million in electronic commerce conducted on the Internet last year.

The most popular item to purchase over the Web is software under $50 (36.2%). Other than hardware and software, the two most popular items to seek information about, and to purchase over, the Web are travel arrangements and books or magazines. Over 40% of users report spending over $100 in purchases over the Web in the past six months.

Impact of Advertising on the Web

Users may not actually buy products/services through the Internet because of security reasons, but what is the impact of advertisements in the Internet on the users? The Coopers & Lybrand survey shows that 37% of the consumers are turned off by advertiser-supported content on the Internet, while the remainder of the users are most interested in interactive ads. Ads with detailed information

---

[4] http://www.colybrand.com

on the products, coined "advermation" by Coopers & Lybrand, gained the most favor (41%), while "customization" ads, tailored to meet the consumer's interest, had 25% of the vote of users who weren't turned off by ads. Another 25% of the users liked "advermarts," ads that facilitate ordering (25%), while only 9% of the users were interested in primarily interactive ads.

In the meantime, businesses, armed with the knowledge that current Web users on the whole are more affluent than the average consumer, are spending heavily on advertisements. According to a report from Frost & Sullivan [4], Internet advertising accounts for 3.4 percent or $85 million of all ad dollars spent in 1996. The market is expected to grow to 22.2 percent or $5.48 billion by 2002.

Another type of commerce that is generated through the Web is access to information. Some Web servers have begun to charge for access to their database of information. There are no statistics about how widely used these services are, but since most of the information in cyberspace is currently free, most users will be very hesitant to pay for information if they think that they can get it free from other sources on the Web.

2.6 Concluding Remarks

In their report *Online & Internet Statistics Reality Check,1996*, NuNet Inc. [17] believes there are only 15 million people on-line (encompassing the Internet, Web and commercial services), accounting for only 6% of the U.S. population and 11% of households [18]. In comparison, Jupiter Communications and Find/SVP in their study *The American Home Financial Services Survey* suggest an incredible 18.7 million children in the U.S. may have Internet access and about 23 million adults are using the Internet from home, representing U.S. 15.1 million households [18]. Why such widely different figures?

The quote from Anamorph's Irresponsible Internet Statistics says it all [2]: "The problem is this: **there is no absolute way to measure any statistic regarding the growth of the Internet.** As John Quarterman of MIDS says:

> "The Internet is distributed by nature. This is its strongest feature, since no single entity is in control, and its pieces run themselves, cooperating to form the network of networks that is the Internet. However, because no single entity is control, nobody knows everything about the Internet. Measuring it is especially hard because some parts choose to limit access to themselves to various degrees. So, instead of measurement, we have various forms of surveying and estimation.

"So all the statistics presented here are based on estimates and conjecture. And even if they were absolutely true, growth rates change ... There is only one conclusion that can possibly be drawn from such vague data:
"The Internet is getting big, and it's happening fast."

2.7 References

[1] Abrams, Marc and Stephen Williams. "Complementing Surveying and Demographics with Automated Network Monitoring," *World Wide Web Journal*, Vol. 1, No. 3, June 1996.
<http://www.w3j.com/3/s3.abrams.html> (21 Nov 1997).

[2] Anamorph. "Irresponsible Internet Statistics Generator," 1996. <http://www.anamorph.com/docs/stats/stats.html> (22 Oct 1996).

[3] Bennet Yee. "Hypertext Webster Interface."
<http://c.gp.cs.cmu.edu:5103/prog/webster> (22 Oct 1996).

[4] Brown, Patricia. "Internet Ads May Finally Pay Off," October 25, 1996.
<http://techweb.cmp.com/ia/iad_web_/newsnow/oct21-25/oct25/oct25-4.htm> (2 Nov 1996).

[5] Coopers & Lybrand. "Coopers & Lybrand Consulting Study Reveals Winners & Losers in the Evolution of the Internet & the World Wide Web," CLC Telecom and Media Group, June 3, 1996.
<http://www.colybrand.com/industry/infocom/mediapr.html>
(22 Oct 1996).

[6] FIND/SVP. "Internet Realities: New Findings from the American Internet User Survey," Workshop on Internet Survey Methodology and Web Demographics, January 28, 1996.
<http://www.ai.mit.edu/projects/iiip/conferences/survey96/findsvp/sld001.html> (22 Oct 1996).

[7] Firefly. "Firefly MainPage." <http://www.firefly.com> (22 Oct 1996).

[8] Galaxy, "K12 Education Resources" <http://galaxy.tradewave.com/galaxy/Social-Sciences/Education/K12-Education.html> (10 Aug 1997).

[9] Gray, Matthew. "Web Growth Summary," 1996.
<http://www.mit.edu:8001/people/mkgray/net/web-growth-summary.html">
(22 Oct 1996).

[10] Graphics, Visualization, and Usability (GVU) Center, Georgia Tech "GVU's WWW User Surveys." <http://www.cc.gatech.edu/gvu/user_surveys> (22 Oct 1996)

[11] GVU Fifth WWW User Survey, April 1996.
<http://www.cc.gatech.edu/gvu/user_surveys/survey-04-1996/>
(22 Oct 1996).

[12] GVU Seventh WWW User Survey, April 1997.
      <http://www.cc.gatech.edu/gvu/user_surveys/survey-1997-04/>
      (10 Aug 1997).

[13] Internet Literacy Consultants. "ILC Glossary of Internet Terms."
      <http://www.matisse.net/files/glossary.html> (22 Oct 1996).

[14] K–12 Technology <http://www.cvu.cssd.k12.vt.us/k12tech/k12tech.htm>
      (10 Aug 1997).

[15] Miller, Thomas. "Segmenting the Internet," *American Demographics*, July
      1996.   <http://www.demographics.com/Publications/AD/96_AD/9607_AD/
      9607AF04.htm> (22 Oct 1996).

[16] Netcraft Ltd. "The Netcraft Web Server Survey."
      <http://www.netcraft.co.uk/Survey/> (22 Oct 1996).

[17] NuNet, Inc. "Online and Internet Statistics Reality Check."
      <http://www.nni.com> (24 Oct 1997).

[18] NUA Ltd. "NUA Internet Surveys" <http://www.nua.ie/surveys/> (10 Aug
      1997).

[19] O'Reilly Research. "Conducting Business on the Internet," 1996.
      <:http://www.ora.com/research/business/index.html> (22 Oct 1996).

[20] Seminerio, Maria. "Survey finds users want their Internet TV," *PCWeek
      Online*, October 28, 1996.
      <http://www.pcweek.com/news/1028/30estudy.html> (2 Nov 1996).

[21] TRFN, "General K-12 Education Sites."
      <http://trfn.pgh.pa.us/Education/K12/general.html> (10 Aug 1997).

[22] World Wide Web Consortium. "Proposals for Gathering Consumer Demo-
      graphics," Nov 6, 1995. <http://www.w3.org/Privacy/Proposals.html> (22
      Oct 1996).

[23] Web 66. "International WWW Schools Registry."
      <http://web66.coled.umn.edu/schools.html> (22 Oct 1996).

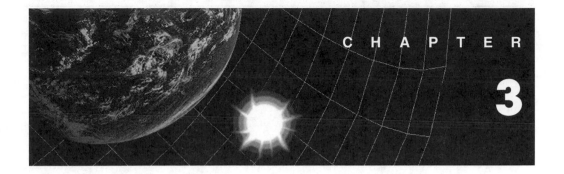

CHAPTER

3

Web Access for the Masses

by Theodoros P. David and Marc Abrams

*D*espite the explosive growth of the Web and the Internet in general, the percentage of the world's population that gets connected to the world's biggest network is still minuscule. There are two main obstacles blocking Web access by the "masses," meaning the general public. First, the Internet historically has only been accessed through a computer. Second, a large number of today's netizens use telephone lines via slow modems to access the Internet. But the introduction of the Web has created a universal demand to access Web pages which are rich in multimedia content but slow to download.

The purpose of this chapter is to investigate ways to overcome these two obstacles. New emerging technologies in both the end-user Internet device and the communication medium promise to make Internet for the masses a reality.

Chapter Content

1. Introduction
2. Internet Appliances

- Network Computer Overview
- NC Reference Profile
- Mobile Network Computer Reference Specification
- Who Will Use the NC
- Other Internet Appliances

3. Broadband Public Networks

- Cable TV Networks

- Telephone Networks

- Satellite Networks

4. Conclusion

5. References

3.1 Introduction

Despite the explosive growth of the Web and the Internet in general, the percentage of the world's population that gets connected to the world's biggest network is not as impressive. While the world's population is almost six billion, an estimated group of only 30 million people have accessed the Internet.

Due to the high cost of personal computers (PCs), coupled with the high degree of technical sophistication required to operate them, over 65% of the U.S. population alone still does not own a PC. They are, therefore, unable to gain access to the information super-highway. So, an inexpensive, easy-to-use Internet/Web access service should be provided to the general public. The most promising devices proposed so far are Network Computers (NCs), Network PCs, TV set-top boxes, and cellular phones with displays.

The other constraint is the medium for Internet connection. Many of today's Web users manage with telephone lines via slow modems, while a fortunate few are connected by T1 (1.5 Mbps) or T3 (45 Mbps) connections. With the introduction of the Web, network speed became a necessity. Gone are the days when a 2,400 kbps telephone modem was more than enough for accessing what used to be an almost entirely text-based Internet. Today a person using a 28,800 kbps telephone modem struggles to download a picture of a company's home page on the Web. The Web is rich with multimedia content such as graphics, color imagery, video and voice. And users are hungry to get as much as they can. The U.S. Telecommunications Bill of 1996 has given the computer and communications industries the flexibility to invent new ways for fast access to the Internet. They are now free to provide their services in any telecommunication domain. And the industries have responded with ISDN, ADSL, VDSL, cable modems, and satellite connections to provide mass Web access.

3.2 Internet Appliances

The Internet makes it possible to share information and services among millions of people around the world. The nature of the Internet opens up the possibility of redefining the desktop computer paradigm into one that utilizes more affordable, easier to use, and easier to maintain devices to access the Internet.

The terms *Internet appliance*, *network appliance*, *access appliance*, and *information appliance* have been coined to describe alternatives to the desktop computer that are used on a network to access server computers. The term "appliance" is used because the devices are intended to become high-volume, low-cost devices, like televisions or refrigerators. The term also suggests that the devices are interchangeable components: if one breaks, it can be replaced by another identical device. In contrast, PCs are not interchangeable because they store files that customize an individual PC.

A variety of appliances have come to market or are about to:

- Network Computers, or NCs (specification written by Apple, Inc., IBM, Oracle Corp., Netscape Communications Corp., and Sun Microsystems, Inc.) [2]

- Mobile NCs (specification spearheaded by Apple, IBM, Oracle, Netscape, Sun, and 10 other companies) [3]

- Network PCs, or NetPCs (specification by Microsoft and Intel with support from several PC manufacturers)

- Television set-top devices (competing systems offered by WebTV, Philips, Sega, and others)

- Televisions with built-in electronics for Internet access

- Telephones and cellular telephones with displays (such as AT&T's Pocket-Net, which delivers conventional analog cellular voice and Cellular Digital Packet Data)

- Personal Data Assistants (PDAs) and Personal Information Managers

- Two-way pagers.

The new roles assumed by Internet appliances vary. They may serve as a true network interface, or a point-of-entry device, between the Internet, customer or business premises network, and consumer or business electronics equipment. Or they may serve as a network controller, much like a computer, among the numerous digital devices in the home using an advanced navigation capability [4].

Internet appliances all share a screen that at a minimum displays a few lines of text, a network interface of some form, and a keyboard or keypad. Appliances may also include a pointing device, text input capability, audio output, and

VGA or NTSC video output. Internet appliances are intended for use by the general public for general purposes. Thus they usually rely on common multimedia formats, such as JPEG, GIF, WAV (Waveform Audio Format, July 1993), AU (SUN Audio File Format, 1992), and MPEG. They use standard Internet protocols, including Transmission Control Protocol (TCP), User Datagram Protocol (UDP), File Transfer Protocol (FTP), Network File System (NFS), Simple Mail Transfer Protocol (SMTP), and telnet.

One function of Internet appliances is to display Web pages. Network computers and network PCs directly support existing Web standards (HTML and HTTP). Television set-top devices use some modified HTML tags (such as WebTV [22]) to facilitate Web page display on televisions through NTSC signals, which offers lower resolution than a VGA computer monitor. Cellular telephones with displays, such as AT&T's PocketNet, may use a proposed standard called the Handheld Device Markup Language (HDML) [12].

Another function of Internet appliances is to run client software applications. Certain Internet appliances run so-called "thin" clients, meaning that the client software requires a minimum amount of memory and processor power to run the user interface and possibly a small amount of local computation on the appliance. The thin client connects over the network to a server program running on a server computer. The server program performs more complex computation, and the server computer stores files or databases required by the client. Two approaches exist to thin clients:

- The thin client can act simply as a terminal to a program running on the server. No code needs to be downloaded to the appliance, and the appliance needs minimal memory and processing power. One example is the Windows Terminal. Another example is Cruise Technologies, Inc.'s Cruise-Connect firmware that connects a handheld appliance via a radio link to a Windows NT application server running a multiuser version of NT, such as Citrix Systems, Inc.'s WinFrame.

- The thin client can be a Java program downloaded to the appliance. In this case, the appliance must be a full-fledged computer, with sufficient memory to store and execute the Java program. The desktop NC and mobile NC specifications use this approach [6].

Another requirement for Internet appliances is a hardware design that permits low cost. The goal for network computers has been to produce an appliance for under $500, making it slightly more expensive than a moderate quality television. However, network computers available in 1997 range are typically closer to $1000, equipped with at least 4 Mb of RAM and usually without any disk drive. Network PCs are expected to start below $1000.

Three conditions are necessary to reach a price below $500:

- A sufficiently high production volume of the appliance will drive the price down.

- The cost of the most expensive component, the monitor, must drop.

- The cost of the electronics must drop due to the use of fewer integrated circuits.

The third of these conditions is occurring first: National Semiconductor plans to offer a single chip which combines most of the electronics needed for an appliance: a 10/100 Mbit/sec Ethernet adaptor, I/O, power management, and a Pentium and Pentium-II class processor. Meanwhile dropping the monitor cost may be the most challenging condition to achieve. The remainder of this section discusses the NC in detail, and then briefly describes other Internet appliances.

Network Computer Overview

The NC is the most extensively developed Internet appliance. Apple, IBM, Oracle, Sun and Netscape announced on May 20, 1996, a set of guidelines called the Network Computer Reference Profile that define low-cost, easy-to-use network computing devices [2]. The specification lets software developers write one application that runs on NCs from different vendors, and lets NCs manufactured by one vendor work with servers manufactured by another vendor.

The NC is a set of appliances based on open standards for networked computing and communications. The NC provides inexpensive Internet and Web access and applications for a wide range of consumers, and those in businesses, educational institutions, and developing countries. The NC redefines what a computer should be: small, inexpensive, easy to use, and lacking the complexity and cost associated with today's personal computers (PCs).

To understand the NC, first consider the PC. A PC stores an operating system, application programs, and user files on a hard disk. On the positive side, a PC is a stand-alone device—it does not have to be attached to a network to work. On the negative side, a lot of time, effort, and cost go into maintaining a PC: making backups of user files on the hard drive, installing upgrades to the operating system and software applications, and diagnosing problems which arise because of the way a PC is customized by its user (i.e., by setting preferences, loading new software that modifies system library files, and removing software and files).

In contrast, a basic NC lacks a hard drive, floppy drive, and CD-ROM. The NC cannot be used in a stand-alone mode. Whenever a user turns an NC on, the NC must load an operating system from a server over the network. When a user invokes a software application, the application is loaded over the network. Every user file is stored on the server, and hence reads and writes to user files travel over the network.

The only software that the NC retains after you turn off the power is stored in a small amount of persistent memory (e.g., read-only memory [ROM]). At a minimum the persistent memory must contain code implementing a simple protocol to load the operating system over the network from a server.

If the NC has a hard drive, it is usually only used to cache files that were recently loaded over the network. Caching can reduce the time that a user spends waiting for files to download, the load on the network, and the load on the server that would otherwise supply the file.

The fundamental advantage of an NC over a PC is that it centralizes many maintenance operations. A system administrator never has to visit a user's office, or even remotely administer a user's machine over a network, because only servers store software and files. All software installations and upgrades need be done only at the server. Thus users can instantly get the most recent version of all software. All file backups are done only at the server. A system administrator has fewer problems to diagnose, because all users share one copy of the operating system, one copy of each software application, and one copy of all system library files. NC users are not permitted to modify or delete these files. A technology like data encryption (Chapter 12) can be installed once on servers to permit its use throughout an organization, rather than having to be installed on each individual PC.

Various estimates of the cost savings of using an NC over a PC have been made [15]. They usually include the purchase cost of the NC or PC; the cost of software; the system administrator's time; and the user's time in trying to install, upgrade, and fix software. Sun estimates the annual cost of a PC to be $11,900, compared to an estimated $2,500 annual cost of a Sun NC (a Java-Station). An IBM commissioned study estimates the PC cost to be $5,713 compared to $3,144 for the IBM NC (an IBM Network Station).

But NCs have disadvantages. One is reliability: the server, the network, and the NC all must be up and running to even turn on an NC. Another is cost. More bandwidth is required in a network that connects NCs than one connecting PCs. High-powered servers are required, and these can cost up to 100 to 1000 times the price of a single NC.

At present there is a debate on the utility of NCs versus PCs. Companies that make their money from PCs often argue that the purchase cost of a cheap PC is only marginally higher than that of an NC. Further, they argue, new administration initiatives under development at Microsoft, such as "Zero Administration for Windows" initiative, can achieve the cost savings of NC administration. Another argument is that users want more sophisticated software running their desktop machine to make computers easier to use, and hence users will need high-end PCs rather than NCs with slower processors and less RAM. Finally, Microsoft and Intel have proposed NetPCs and Windows Terminals to bring the NC benefits to organizations that presently use PCs running Microsoft

Windows operating systems. NetPCs uses an IBM PC architecture in a "sealed" case that limits hardware modifications by the user, and protects system files through access-control lists to prohibit software modification by a user.

Meanwhile NC manufacturers argue that NCs are a logical replacement for "dumb" or text-only terminals. They also argue that for people in many industries, from bank tellers to hospital nurses, they can do everything on an NC that they now do on a PC, but with fewer problems.

NC Reference Profile

The NC specification [2] gives a minimal set of features that an NC must implement. Vendors are free to incorporate additional features. An NC consists of a processor that can execute a Java virtual machine (see the section on "Platform Components" on page 154), at least four megabytes of memory, input/output devices (a VGA display [640 by 480 pixels], a pointing device, text input and audio output capabilities), a network interface, and a way to establish network service. Optionally, an NC can support an ISO 7816 SmartCard (e.g., that contains a user's identity and preferences).

Processor

The NC specification is architecture neutral, and thus does not require a particular processor. For the initial prototype of the NC, the CPU used was the ARM 7500 processor, a multimedia, 32-bit RISC chip with performance equivalent to that of a 66 MHz Intel 486. The ARM 7500 is a highly integrated silicon package that incorporates many functions that have been handled separately from the CPU chip: video and I/O subsystems, keyboard input, audio capability, memory bus, network graphics, etc.

In future NCs, a logical processor choice will be one that directly implements the Java virtual machine. For example, Sun is developing several chip-level Java engines: picoJava (low-cost implementation for low-cost consumer devices, such as phones), microJava (higher performance, adding application-specific I/O, memory, communications and control functions to picoJava), and UltraJava (high-performance implementation, for network computers, incorporating 2D and 3D imaging and graphics support, video compression and decompression, audio, networking, encryption) [19]. See the section on "Java Application Environments" on page 156 for more details.

Network Interface

NCs are intended to be connected to networks running the Internet's IP protocol. The original NC specification supports standard network interfaces: modems, Ethernet, 25 megabit/sec ATM (for corporate installations), high-speed E1 and T1 telephone lines, and ISDN (Integrated Services Digital Networks).

The NC will need to adapt to new communication technologies that are introduced to satisfy the bandwidth requirements of the future. Some of these technologies have already appeared, and they are discussed in Section 3.3.

Input/Output Devices

The NC supports keyboards, mice, joysticks, microphones, headphones, speakers and infrared remote interfaces. The infrared connectivity is potentially useful to home users, eliminating the need for cables stretching across the living room from the NC to the TV.

Protocols, Software, and Multimedia Formats

The NC supports the TCP, FTP, telnet, NFS, Universal Datagram Protocol (UDP), Simple Network Management Protocol (SNMP), SMTP, Post Office Protocol Version 3 (POP3), Internet Message Access Protocol Version 4 (IMAP4), and HTTP protocols. In addition, when the NC is powered on, it can obtain an IP address dynamically using the Dynamic Host Configuration Protocol (DHCP) and a boot volume containing the operating system by using the Bootp protocol.

NC software must include a Java Application Environment, the Java Virtual Machine and runtime environment, Java class libraries, and a Web browser. Supported multimedia formats are the JPEG image and GIF graphic formats and the WAV and AU audio formats.

Mobile Network Computer Reference Specification

About a year after the NC Reference Profile (page 49) was developed to specify desktop devices, an extension was created for mobile devices (PDAs, phones with screens, low-end or reduced size laptops): the Mobile Network Computer Reference Specification [3]. Products based on the specification are expected in 1998.

Unlike a desktop machine, a mobile device has a nonpersistent network connection of relatively low bandwidth and a small screen. For example, users of a reduced-size laptop with a cellular phone modem may spend most of their time "offline," or disconnected from the network. The user would connect over the modem temporarily, and during the connection period would experience a network connection running at least an order of magnitude slower than a local area network connection (e.g., Ethernet). Another consideration is that the network connection may be unreliable. If the laptop is in a car, the network connection may be disrupted as the user approaches the boundary of a cell.

The specification distinguishes three categories of mobile NCs:

- *Professional assistant*: Has full capability of a desktop NC, but is a mobile device (e.g., a laptop) with the constraints of non-persistent, slow, and unreliable network connection.

- *Information access device*: Has less memory and processing capability than a professional assistant, runs a limited number of applications (e.g., terminal emulation, calendar program, Web browser, and e-mail client), and usually requires a network connection to function.

- *Basic device*: Includes phones, PDAs, and pagers, offers the least common denominator from among the three classes, offers limited Web browsing, and is intended just to "keep in touch with the office" [3].

Architecturally, there are three chief differences between mobile and desktop NCs. First, mobile devices must be able to boot stand-alone. Therefore there must be persistent storage to retain what is termed base code, namely the operating system kernel and key applications (e.g., a Web browser or a terminal emulator). These can be refreshed with newer copies when a network connection is available. Persistent storage, if large enough, can also be used to cache recently used applications.

Second, mobile devices must offer two distinct modes: online and offline. There may be a procedure to transition between the online and offline mode (e.g., an e-mail client may send queued email before the device disconnects from the network). Furthermore, persistent storage may be used to cache data to permit the device to work in the offline mode (e.g., browsing of previously downloaded Web pages). There must also be a mechanism to synchronize a cached copy of data on the mobile device and the original copy on a server. This might be implemented using the concepts of data consistency and replication used with databases. The specification describes a file-based consistency mechanism [3].

Third, a proxy program will run on a server, and the mobile devices will communicate with the proxy. The proxy appears to other servers as a full-featured client (e.g., a desktop client). However, the proxy will transform or distill the data stream sent to the mobile device to fits its capabilities, such as screen resolution. The proxy may also address other issues: security and optimization of the data stream sent to conserve bandwidth.

Mobile NCs fitting the professional assistant category should offer at least the following:

- For input and output, a monochrome screen of 320×240 pixels, each represented by 2 bits; a pointing device; an "Instant On" capability when the device is powered down; power management software and hardware interfaces; text input capability (e.g., keyboard, pen input, or even speech recognition); audio output of AU or WAV files with optional recording; and JPEG, GIF, HTML, and optionally MPEG4 for content delivery. Database access is offered via the Java Database Connectivity (JDBC). A SmartCard may also be supported.

- For protocols, TCP, IP, UDP, Point-to-Point Protocol (PPP), IMAP4, SMTP, Domain Naming System (DNS), and Lightweight Directory Access Protocol (LDAP), DHCP, and Bootp. Optional protocols include NFS, FTP, telnet, Network News Transfer Protocol (NNTP), and Mobile IP (see Chapter 16).

- For security, several optional facilities are Secure Socket Layer (SSL, see Section 12.3); IP Security (IPSEC), being developed in the Internet Engineering Task Force for key management when IP is used with encryption; and Password Authentication Protocol (PAP) or Challenge Handshake Authentication Protocol (CHAP) for authentication over dial-up network connections.

In the future, mobile NCs will support emerging standards for teleconferencing and collaborative applications.

Who Will Use the NC

The variety of version of NCs facilitates a broader range of users than the PC.

Corporations
Most users, including those in corporations, have PCs to perform simple tasks like database and Web access, word processing, spreadsheets, and e-mail.

Market research suggests that the NC can potentially replace up to 50 to 70 percent of the PCs now in place in corporations. Even though the corporate NC may be equipped with a larger monitor and more memory than a typical home model, it will have a lower acquisition cost than a PC. More importantly, corporations can drastically reduce by up to 70% their administration, support and training costs [6].

The corporate NC can be integrated into corporate Webs (Intranets) on existing LANs, peacefully coexisting on the same networks with the conventional PCs required by power-users.

Consumers
For the average consumer, telecommuter or home student, a device that is as easy to buy and set up as a telephone and provides simple access to many different services is an extremely attractive option. Whether a computer-literate user wants better multimedia capabilities or a second machine for accessing the Web, or a person who has never used a computer wants a less daunting way to explore the Web and communicate electronically, the NC is an inexpensive and easy-to-use solution. Typically plugged into a TV in the den or a hotel room, or into a monitor or small TV on a desk or kitchen table, the NC holds tremendous promise for making computing available to everyone.

Education
In schools, acquisition costs present the most difficult problem to realizing the dream of placing modern computers in every classroom. Many schools are

attempting to recycle old PCs for student use, but face problems of inconsistency, software compatibility, ongoing support, and administrative overhead.

Imagine the educational system if every student had a low-cost NC supported by a big server network. Students and teachers would have access to online research and textbooks, up-to-date news information, the Web, and e-mail. The development of more cost-effective wireless transmission methods for feeding the NC to a whole classroom creates all of these extraordinary and exciting possibilities.

One trial of the NC is in the James Flood Science and Technology Magnet School in Menlo Park, California. Oracle planned to provide an NC for each student desktop and to rewire the school to support NCs [14].

Developing Countries

Many developing countries with increasing needs for low-cost communications and computing infrastructures will benefit from the NC. With a lower cost of ownership than a PC, the NC offers to bring these countries to full participation in the worldwide Internet community in a relatively short time, perhaps five years or less, as opposed to the ten or more it would take with PCs.

Other Internet Appliances

In addition to the NC, other Internet appliances include TV-top boxes that provide Web access, such as WebTV; hybrid TV/PCs; and cellular phones with a display that can access Web pages. Each is briefly described below.

TV-top Boxes

Television set-top devices without a keyboard in 1997 range in price from $199 for Sega's Saturn to $349 for Microsoft's WebTV, licensed to Philips and Sony [20]. In addition, the user pays a monthly online service fee ranging from about $20 to $25 per month. The devices offer e-mail access via the POP3/SMTP protocols, storage of email on a server, sometimes access to other online services (e.g., America Online), newsgroup access, and a Web browser that provides varying degrees of HTML 3.2 compatibility.

Due to limited memory in set-top boxes, the Web browsers have limited features. Capabilities to display Java applets, frames, and dynamic HTML are often missing. PC browsers, such as Netscape Navigator and Microsoft Internet Explorer, require 6–12 Mb of memory, which is prohibitive for a diskless set-top box.

The main problem with using a television for Internet access is that text is hard to read on a television monitor. Televisions interlace the scan lines to effectively refresh the entire display 30 times a second. In contrast, computer monitors are not interlaced, and refresh the display 60 or more times a second. The slower refresh rate of a television makes text flicker. Also, televisions use color triads, while PCs use color strips [4]. To compensate for lower text display quality, some set-top boxes provide a magnifying glass tool in their Web browsers to view small fonts on a Web page despite the limited resolution of a standard television.

Hybrid TV/PCs

Televisions with built-in electronics for Internet access are due to market in 1998. They offer the advantage of lower cost than a set-top box (e.g., one power supply shared by the television and the Internet access electronics), a potentially better picture due to direct connection to the television, and a single remote control for both television and Internet access. When digital televisions arrive on the market, the disadvantage of poor television resolution for displaying text compared to computer monitors should be dispelled, making Internet televisions a popular alternative to PCs.

In designing a hybrid TV and PC, companies are left with uncertainty about what combination of features and price will appeal to consumers [4]. At one extreme in price, Gateway introduced its $3500 to $5000 Destination hybrid, which uses a Pentium motherboard, a 31-inch VGA monitor, and a wireless keyboard. The quality of text is high due to the use of a VGA monitor, but this results in a high price. At the opposite extreme in price, television manufacturers want to add only $300 to $600 in the price of a television to add Internet access.

Another design constraint is that the hybrid TV/PC should appeal to people who have limited computer experience, and work as simply as a television does. Therefore the presence of an underlying operating system on a motherboard inside the TV/PC, such as Windows, should be invisible to the consumer. This has proved to be difficult to hide in early prototypes [4].

User interface issues arise in the TV/PC. Early offerings are expected to operate in two separate modes: TV versus Internet access. More mature offerings are expected to blend the two. A television picture might be offered in one window, with a Web browser in another window on the screen.

Telephones with Displays

Cellular telephones with displays cost about $500 to $600 in 1997. The AT&T PocketNet service, first tested in 1996 and launched in 1997, gives users access to send and receive e-mail, view Web pages, and send faxes.

The PocketNet phone contains a 3 line by 22 character screen that displays text only. The phone uses a Cellular Digital Packet Data (Section 16.4) modem for network data access at rates up to 19.2 Kbps [17].The service was initially offered for a $45 activation fee in addition to the normal cellular voice charge, a $40 monthly charge allowing 500 Kb of data transmission, and a charge of 8 cents per kilobyte transmitted over 500 Kb.

Web pages that use HDML [12] are viewed with UP.Link, a text browser for handheld devices produced by Unwired Planet, Inc. Web sites must offer HDML, in addition to HTML, to be accessible by PocketNet. Uses envisioned for

PocketNet phones include accessing airline flight schedules, obtaining stock quotes, and accessing directories (telephone numbers, etc.)

HDML assumes that the display screen is at least 12 characters wide, scrolls vertically, displays ASCII characters, has a way to enter numeric and alphabetic characters, has a way to choose an alternative (e.g., arrow keys), and has one or two programmable keys, and has two keys labeled ACCEPT and PREV. HDML organizes information that is displayed into a deck consisting of a set of cards. There are four types of cards:

Entry cards: Contains a message and allows user to enter text

Choice cards: Contains a message and allows user to select one item from list of alternatives

Display cards: Contains a message only

No-display cards: Executes an action without showing anything to the user.

Besides displaying screens, as HTML does, HDML can also notify (or push) information to the handheld device. HDML is loaded to the phone from a proxy server, the UP.Link Gateway, using the Handheld Device Transfer Protocol (HDTP). Unlike HTTP, which runs over the connection-oriented TCP protocol, HDTP runs over a connectionless or datagram protocol. HDTP offers privacy, integrity, and authentication mechanisms, as HTTPS does (see Chapter 12). The UP.Link proxy server communicates with normal Web servers via HTTP.

3.3 Broadband Public Networks

The Web boom has exposed the low bandwidth of the Internet. No matter where they live or what they do, Internet users have the same complaints. The Graphic, Visualization, & Usability Center's 6th WWW User Survey [8] (run from October through November 1996) reports that "speed continues to be the number one problem of Web users (76.55%), and has been since the Fourth Survey when the question was first introduced." For example, the survey asked "how often people surf without images being loaded for each page automatically," and found that "as one might expect due to the slow transoceanic connection between US and Europe, more Europeans turn image loading off."

Sometimes slow downloads and displays simply aren't under your control, but result from poor connectivity at the server end. It is everybody's wish that the Information Highway will someday consist of high-bandwidth fiber-optic cables that run to every user's machine. But that day is not in the near future. Nevertheless, much of the data highway already exists in the vast web of fiber-optic strands, coaxial cables, radio waves, satellites, and lowly copper wires now spanning the globe.

More often, however, the bottleneck is at the *user* end of the connection. This *last-mile user connection* is the connection from the Telephone Company's End-Office to the user's home. Unfortunately, the latest analog modems offer bandwidth only up to 56 Kbps.

Studies have shown that users are "consuming" much more information than they are "producing." The telecommunications industry is taking advantage of this fact and is developing new asymmetric technologies that give huge *downstream* bandwidth to the user, but allow only a fraction of it for *upstream* bandwidth from the user [9]. In fact, to the user's advantage, there is a race among cable, telephone and satellite companies, each giving a different answer to the user's desire for more bandwidth.

Cable TV Networks

One day you might be tuning into the Internet Channel on your PC. Of all the high-speed Internet access solutions, cable TV systems are probably the most talked about. That's partly because they leverage existing broadband cable TV networks and partly because they promise to deliver high-speed access at an affordable price.

But there are considerable technical hurdles: While satellites are only one-way devices, cable modems can work in both directions if cable operators make their one-way networks interactive. Once that's accomplished, the technology could offer the best price/performance combination of any Internet access method to date, delivering close to 30-Mbps speeds at less than $50 per month—about three times the cost/performance factor of ISDN access [7].

Cable Modems

Today, making the cable-to-PC connection requires a cable modem to modulate and demodulate the cable signal into a stream of data. The similarity with analog modems ends there, however. Cable modems also incorporate a tuner (to separate the data signal from the rest of the broadcast stream); parts from network adapters, bridges, and routers (to connect to multiple computers); network-management software agents (so the cable company can control and monitor its operations); and encryption devices (so your data isn't intercepted or sent someplace else by mistake).

Each cable modem has an Ethernet port that connects to the computer (or network) on one side and to the cable connection on the other. You install an Ethernet adapter in the PC, then connect it to the cable's Ethernet port via a standard RJ-45 connector. You then configure the PC with standard TCP/IP software. As far as your PC is concerned, it's hooked directly to the Internet via Ethernet. There are no phone numbers to dial and no limitations on serial-port throughput (as is the case with ISDN modems). What you do get is lots of speed:

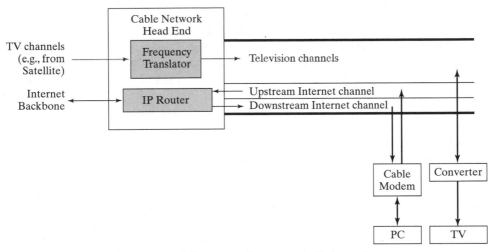

Figure 3–1 Two-way cable network access to Internet

Downlinks vary from 500 Kbps to 30 Mbps, while uplinks can, potentially, range from 96 Kbps to 10 Mbps [9].

Internet over Cable TV Networks

In each community, cable operators install a head end that receives both satellite and broadcast TV signals. Coaxial cable carries these signals to each subscriber's home. Depending on the number of homes and the distance between them, the operator may need to install amplifiers and filters to maintain signal strength.

Typical cable systems serve between 500 to 2,500 homes on one line [5]. Because the cable is broadband, it carries multiple signals, or channels. Most of these channels are devoted to TV programs. A TV channel occupies 6 MHz of the spectrum, and sometimes cable operators multiplex several channels into one. If the cable system were used strictly for data, it could deliver gigabytes of that data per second over hundreds of individual networks.

But TV signals consume most of the potential bandwidth. And most cable systems send these signals in one direction only: from the head end to your home. Internet access, obviously, is two-way: a Web browser sends URLs to Web servers, an e-mail client sends mail messages, and so on.

Two-Way Street: To become interactive, cable operators must allocate spectrum on the cable for upstream signals so you can send data from the PC back to the Internet. This is shown in Fig. 3–1. Typically, the upstream signal is transmitted via a low-frequency band that has not been used to carry a TV channel. (These low frequencies are noisy: Ham and CB radios, household appliances, lights, and other devices generate interference, which must be filtered somewhere between the head end and the cable recipient.) [16]

Another problem is that all homes (or offices) connected to the same cable drop share the bandwidth available in this one transmission channel. Downstream transmissions generated by all users on the cable drop share a single channel. Just like Ethernet, too many nodes competing for bandwidth slow network performance. If your neighbors do lots of downloads, your throughput will suffer, unless the cable operator provides additional capacity or extra routers and channels.

Cable operators will also have to modify their cable amplifiers to separate the upstream and downstream signals. In some regions, they'll end up replacing most amplifiers, putting fiber closer to each home. Finally, cable operators will have to set up a community-wide Internet point of presence (POP) to serve all the networks associated with a particular head end. This will require the cable companies to plan very carefully and to gain an enormous understanding of TCP/IP networking. They'll have to set up routers and servers at the head end and at strategic places around the cable system to manage Internet traffic.

The Institute of Electrical and Electronics Engineers (IEEE) has assigned a working group committee, 802.14 "Standard for Cable-TV Based Broadband Communication," to define a common media-access control scheme for sending data over cable [11]. The committee is presently selecting the best elements from among 17 different proposals.

Telephone Networks

Cable companies are not alone in having an existing wired network that runs into many homes. Telephone companies also have existing wiring into most homes. The shielded coaxial cable used by cable companies can carry a higher potential bandwidth than the unshielded twisted-pair wiring for phone service that runs through today's buildings. A technological challenge has been to maximize the bandwidth that existing twisted pair wiring can handle. Telephone companies are using two different technologies. The older technology, which has not seen widespread use in the United States, is Integrated Services Digital Network (ISDN). But ISDN offers only moderate increases in bandwidth compared to analog modems, and ISDN's bandwidth is insufficient to carry full-motion video (minimum 1.5 Mbps for MPEG movies). A newer technology that is sufficient for video and is more competitive with the higher bandwidth offered by cable modems is Asymmetric Digital Subscriber Line (ADSL). We next discuss ISDN, followed by ADSL.

Integrated Services Digital Network (ISDN)
Instead of a modem moving bits between analog telephone lines and digital applications, ISDN is a digital solution from end to end. Rather than connecting to the Internet at 28.8 Kbps, you can reach speeds of 56 to 128 Kbps, depending

on where you live, where your Internet service provider (ISP) is located, and what equipment lies in between.

This extra bandwidth is useful for everything from downloading files to browsing graphics- and multimedia-rich Web pages. If you need to download *and* upload data, then ISDN offers the best connection speed; alternatives such as satellite or cable links are currently one-way technologies that either require a separate dial-in line for uploads (satellite) or don't traditionally handle them at all (cable).

If you frequently connect to the Internet but do not like waiting for data modems to negotiate the call, then you'll like ISDN's almost instantaneous connection: Being completely digital, it takes only seconds to place a call. In fact, of all the high-speed Internet access methods, ISDN is furthest along in its deployment, availability, and products.

ISDN Basics: For home users and small offices, an ISDN service called 2B+D in phone company parlance, or Basic Rate Interface (BRI), is offered [7]. The 2B+D service offers three channels: two higher-speed "B," or bearer, channels and one lower-speed "D," or data, channels. ISDN works over existing twisted pair wiring used in homes and businesses. However, when a twisted pair is used for ISDN it cannot be used for common analog telephones. Either a second twisted pair is required, or a voice phone designed for ISDN must be used.

A phone company uses the D channel to handle control and signaling information, such as identifying the calling party's phone number and the amount of bandwidth the line occupies.

The two remaining B channels can carry voice, data, or both. Each B-channel can operate at either 56 Kbps or 64 Kbps, depending on the equipment at your local phone company switch or central office. The two B-channels can also be *bonded* to act as a single 128-Kbps channel. ("Bonding" is an acronym for Bandwidth ON Demand INteroperability Group.) Some ISDN equipment even supports dynamic bonding, which you use when you require the extra bandwidth—for downloading a large file, for example. With dynamic bonding, you pay for the connectivity only when you need it. Once you've downloaded the file, your ISDN router disconnects automatically, saving you the telephone connect charges.

For corporate intranets that require connections between offices in different cities or ISPs linking their backbone networks, an alternative ISDN service is offered: Primary Rate Interface (PRI). PRI handles either 23 or 30 bearer channels. It's often called 23B+D (used in the U.S.) or 30B+D (used in Europe and Japan) and can run at 1.544 and 2.048 Mbps, respectively (over the B channels). High-capacity PRI is most useful, though, for connecting large networks or for ISPs linking their backbone networks. For small-office and home users, BRI is clearly the way to go.

Asymmetric Digital Subscriber Line (ADSL)

ADSL is a newer alternative to ISDN offering the promise of high-speed transmissions over the copper wiring that already connects to each home. Besides higher bandwidth, ADSL has another advantage to consumers: a single twisted pair can carry both voice calls using existing analog lines and high-speed digital data.

To do this, ADSL carries three separate frequency channels over the same line. The first set of frequencies carries plain old telephone system (POTS) conversations. Another series of frequencies transmits a 16- to 640-Kbps data signal (different products use different speeds) that carries information upstream from your home to the Internet. Like ISDN, this is a digital signal; but unlike ISDN, each channel goes in only one direction. The third signal is a high-speed downstream connection, which can run anywhere from T1 speeds, 1.5 Mbps, on up to 9 Mbps [1].

The assumption here, of course, is that most of us will be downloading more from the Internet than we'll be transmitting to it. This is a huge gamble, one that cable and satellite vendors are also betting on. The difference is that satellite and cable technologies are much further along. One point in cable's favor is that there are many more cable modem vendors than ADSL modem vendors.

To use ADSL you'll need an external ADSL modem. There will also be an ADSL modem in the phone company's central office. While ADSL modems are still being developed, one prototype, from Aware, has three connectors on the back of the unit: One goes to the wall jack and then out to the phone company; one is for a standard RJ-11 phone jack for analog phone service; and one is an Ethernet twisted-pair RJ-45 connector that hooks the ADSL modem to your computer equipment.

This means that once you install an ADSL modem, you won't need special interface electronics to run your analog phones. That's a big plus, one that could speed ADSL's adoption as a single solution for home PC users and small businesses that don't want to install and pay for an extra data line. Also, most home PCs are located near phone wall jacks, which will make ADSL easier to install than, say, cable modems.

Another, similar technology, referred to as Very-high-data-rate Digital Subscriber Line (VDSL), promises even greater speeds. VDSL can operate at ultrafast rates, from 13 to 55 Mbps, but over about half the loop distances as ADSL [18]. And VDSL and ADSL equipment aren't compatible, though they share many of the compression and modulation technologies to achieve such high throughput.

Satellite Networks

While vendors such as NII Norsat International have announced plans to offer Internet access via satellite, the only product shipping today is Hughes Network Systems' DirectPC. Configuring and maintaining satellite dishes takes patience and a tolerance for cutting-edge technology. And when all is said and installed, ISDN is probably still a better bet for individual users with access to ISDN service. That's because satellites don't deliver the throughput rates they promise, setup is complex, and satellites cannot be used to upload data from users. To transmit data to the Internet, you still need a separate dial-in account to an ISP.

Why do you need the analog line and modem? The satellite dish is a non-powered receiver: It can't transmit information back to the Internet. So every time you type at the keyboard, your modem needs to dial your ISP and send that information back to the Internet. The information you requested is then relayed via the satellite back to your computer. The result is a highly asymmetrical network: 400 Kbps downstream and modem speed (e.g., 33.6 Kbps) upstream [10]. These speeds are well short of what cable modems and ADSL offer.

The connection between the dish and the PC is straightforward. The coaxial cable connects directly to an ISA adapter card, which is set up like a network adapter card (with a few caveats, which we'll discuss in a moment).

Interestingly enough, eliminating dial-in connections in favor of satellite links accentuates other Internet bottlenecks. Many sites have poor connectivity: Either they link to the Internet via slow-speed lines or are choked with so many users that effective throughput is on a par with ISDN lines. In fact, depending on traffic, the time of day, and the number of users accessing a site, your satellite link may not buy as much bandwidth as you'd expect.

Among the three asymmetric public network technologies the most prominent seems to be cable networks. The huge downstream bandwidth they provide will satisfy most home users. The fact that some cable modems are already in the market, while most of them are in the final trial stages at different cable networks around the world, gives them a definite advantage. ADSL trials, on the other hand, are still in the early stages. Nevertheless, the dedicated bandwidth will attract many users concerned about privacy and need fixed bandwidth. As for satellite networks, they need to provide more and reliable bandwidth. These will be ideal for isolated areas where there are no telephone or cable networks installed.

The ambiguity about which technologies will dominate has been reflected in recent high-cost business deals. First, Teledesic Corp. was founded to deploy a $9 billion network of 840 low-Earth orbital satellites for worldwide coverage, with primary investors Bill Gates of Microsoft and Craig McCaw, founder of AT&T's McCaw Cellular. On the other hand, Gates' Microsoft later invested $1 billion in cable company Comcast, the nation's fourth-largest cable television operator [13].

3.4 Conclusion

What started off as a personal computer-based ideology has now evolved into a Web of services and content that is being accessed by customers via desktop browsers. In effect, the PC workstation has moved from a primary role as a content processor and application-specific workstation to a secondary role as a content access mechanism. The Web servers and Internet/intranet (INET) networks are now dominant. They provide access to vast amounts of content and services. The limited set of applications that can run on a single PC is overwhelmed by the content of INET-based networks and a tremendous richness of functionality.

This might have been expected since, in a sense, Internet appliances mirror our world and our lives. Internet appliances are designed and optimized for sharing knowledge. No person is a community unto herself/himself, and Internet appliances do not expect or require every participant in the network community to be an isolated survivalist. People in everyday life do not maintain their own electric, water, and gas supply. As a world—and computing—community we have learned to share specialties and information because that is what makes most economic sense. Sharing allows us to save time and energy and obtain the benefits of economies of scale.

The Internet appliance, however, will not "exterminate" the PC, but it will complement it. Power users such as engineers and scientists will not be satisfied with the performance of most Internet appliances. Issues like privacy and security will scare other users away from the Internet appliances and toward the most centralized architecture of the PC. For the vast majority of the general public some form of the Network Computer will be more than enough.

Performance on INETs and Internet appliances is very much dependent upon available bandwidth. Organizations will have to manage their intranetworks just like they have to manage their current WANs and LANs. Increased bandwidth may not even be necessary initially if usage levels remain at current levels. Clearly, as the market for Internet appliances gains momentum, bandwidth infrastructure will have to grow to accommodate the potential explosion of users.

That's where the broadband telecommunication technologies being developed by the telephone and cable companies over their existing networks will come to the rescue. Telephones were useless before the telephone companies began stringing wires. Cable TV was only a backwater business before the cable companies went national. Automobiles weren't very practical before governments began paving roads. Indeed, ADSL and cable modems give to the *hungry-for-bandwidth* "masses" *all-you-can-eat* access to the Web and Internet.

3.5 References

[1]   ADSL Forum. "ADSL Tutorial."
         <http://198.93.24.23/adsl_tutorial.html> (26 Oct. 1996).

[2]   Apple, IBM, Netscape, Oracle and Sun. "Network Computer Reference Pro-
      file." May 1996. <http://www.nc.ihost.com/nc_ref_profile.html> (25 Aug.
      1997).

[3]   Apple, IBM, Netscape, Sun. "Mobile Network Computer Reference Specifi-
      cation, Version 23." June 1997.
      <http://www.sun.com/smi/Press/sunflash/mncrs-spec.html> (25 Aug. 1997).

[4]   Day, Rebecca. "The Great PC/TV Debate." *OEM Magazine*. May 1996.
      <http://techweb.cmp.com/oem/docs/cover.html> (25 Oct 1996).

[5]   Debevc, Matjaz. "Internet Access Through Cable TV."
      <http://teja.uni-mb.si/personal/matjaz/CableEng.html> (25 Oct. 1996).

[6]   Finkelstein, Richard. Performance Computing, Inc. "Network Computers—
      The Birth of a New Industry."
      <http://www.oracle.com/products/nc/html/finkelstein.html> (25 Oct. 1996).

[7]   Gillett, S.E. "Connecting Homes to the Internet: An Engineering Cost
      Model of Cable vs. ISDN."
      <http://www.tns.lcs.mit.edu/publications/mitlcstr654.html> (20 Sep. 1996).

[8]   Graphic, Visualization, & Usability Center. "6th WWW User Survey."
      <http://www.cc.gatech.edu/gvu/user_surveys/survey-10-1996/>   (16   Dec.
      1996).

[9]   Halfhill, Tom R. "Break the Bandwidth Barrier." *Byte*. Sep. 1996.
      <http://www.byte.com/art/9609/sec6/art1.htm> (25 Oct. 1996).

[10] Hughes Network Systems. "DirectPC Web Page."
      <http://www.direcpc.com/about/index.html> (14 Oct. 1996).

[11] IEEE. IEEE Standards Status Report.
      <http://standards.ieee.org/cgi-bin/status?802> (26 Aug. 1997).

[12] King, Peter and Tim Hyland. Handheld Device Markup Language 2.0.
      <http://www.w3.org/TR/NOTE-Submission-HDML-spec.html>, 11 Apr. 1997
      (25 Aug 1997).

[13] Microsoft Corporation. Press Release. 9 June 1997.
      <http://www.microsoft.com/corpinfo/press/1997/Jun97/ComcasPR.htm>
      (26 August 1997).

[14] Oracle Corporation. "Oracle CEO Ellison to Receive Award for Contribution
      to Education." Press Release. Feb. 3, 1997.
      <http://www.oracle.com/corporate/press/html/PR020397.200754.html>
      (26 Aug. 1997).

[15] Pang, Albert and Elissa Palmer. "The Network within Your Reach." *ZD Internet Magazine*, Jan. 1997. pp. 50–56.

[16] Robertson, Douglas M., Robert Atkinso, and Lela Cocoros. "Motorola Multimedia CableComm Technology." Motorola Inc. <http://www.mot.com/MIMS/Multimedia/comp/PR/PR_CCTech.html> (8 Oct. 1996).

[17] Rupley, Sebastian. "AT&T's Internet Phone Becomes Official." *PCMagazine Online*. 16 July 1996. <http://www8.zdnet.com/pcmag/news/trends/t960716a.htm>   (26   Aug. 1997).

[18] Sallee, Debbie, Motorola Inc. "Motorola's CopperGold ADSL Transceiver." <http://www.mot.com/SPS/MCTG/MDAD/adsl_whitepaper.html> (25   Oct. 1996).

[19] Sun Microelectronics. "Java Processors Intro." <http://www.sun.com/sparc/java/> (25 Aug. 1997).

[20] Taschek, James. "Television: Tune in to the Web." *ZD Internet Magazine*. May 1997.

[21] Unwired Planet, Inc. Handheld Device Transfer Protocol Specification, version 1.1—Draft. 15 July 1997. <http://www.uplanet.com/pub/hdtp11.pdf>, Unwired Planet, Inc. (25 Aug. 1997).

[22] WebTV Networks, Inc. *HTML Reference*. 9 Aug 1997. <http://webtv.net/ primetime/preview/technology/newHTMLRef/HTML_Reference.fm.html> (29 Aug. 1997).

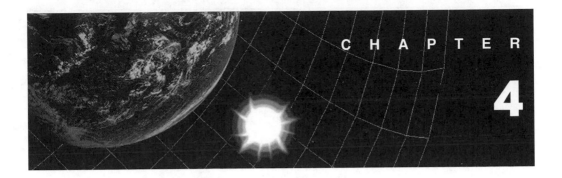

HTML Origins, Owners, Good Practices

by Pris Sears

*T*here are many worthy documents available on learning and authoring HyperText Markup Language (HTML). This is not one of them, although it offers guidelines on what constitutes good HTML practice. This chapter attempts to detail the history and original intent of HTML, how commercial interests have fragmented the device independence that is so critical to HTML, where HTML tags come from, how an HTML author can ensure that documents are readable by all users, and how an individual can get involved in evolving the HTML specifications.

HTML, when used properly, can allow anyone in the world to share information with anyone else in the world who has a connection to the Internet and a Web browser. The future of portable HTML is in the hands of each individual author's dedication to using markup that is not dependent on a particular operating system or Web browser.

Chapter Content

1. Introduction
2. Origins

- Origins of HTML
- What Is HyperText Markup Language?
- Timeline for the Evolution of HTML

3. Owners—The Factions that Vie for Control of HTML

- CERN and NCSA
- W3C—The World Wide Web Consortium
- IETF
- Browser Manufacturers
- HTML Authors

4. Good Practices

- HTML Good Practices—How to Ensure Everyone Can Get Your Information
- How Nonstandard HTML Can Be Harmful
- Standard HTML Tags from HTML 1.0 and 2.0

5. How to Get Involved in Adding to HTML Specifications

- Proposing New Features

6. Conclusion

7. References

4.1 Introduction

This is a quick overview of HTML. The topics covered here will be examined in detail later in this chapter.

When the Web was first created, a fundamental decision made was to represent documents using a markup language that separated document content from appearance. HTML is device independent, which means that HTML documents should be viewable by any Internet-connected computer with any HTML-aware Web browser. HTML is not a programming language; it is a markup language, based on the older Standard Generalized Markup Language (SGML). SGML was chosen as a base because it is device independent, well documented, and the specifications are freely available in the public domain.

The first HTML specification and browser was produced and given away for free to the general public in summer 1991 by Tim Berners-Lee while he was at CERN. Additions to HTML were debated, tested, and finalized as HTML 1.0 in March 1993. In November 1993, NCSA produced and distributed Mosaic, a free multiplatform Web browser. Mosaic complied with the HTML 1.0 specification. Later, a revised HTML 2.0 specification was introduced. The popularity of the Web placed demands on Web page appearance that could not be satisfied by the simple HTML 2.0 specification. Users wanted control over stylistic elements, such as fonts and text placement. In addition, common document elements, such as tables, could not be represented in HTML 2.0. An ambitious HTML 3.0 draft that addressed these points was debated by the World Wide Web Consortium.

While HTML 2.0 and 3.0 were developed, the Web was commercialized. In April 1994, Netscape Corporation was created by James H. Clark, founder of Silicon Graphics, Inc., and Marc Andreessen, creator of the NCSA Mosaic research prototype for the Internet. Netscape introduced the Navigator Web browser. In 1995, Microsoft changed directions and began supporting the Internet, which led to introduction of its Internet Explorer Web browser. Other commercial Web browsers were brought to market.

Netscape and Microsoft responded to the competition in attracting customers by independently defining their own enhancements to HTML 2.0. The rate of competition did not match the slow debate on HTML 3.0 in the World Wide Web Consortium (W3C), and so Netscape and Microsoft introduced their own enhancements independently of W3C and without going through the established channels of proposal, comment, and approval that would normally accompany changes in HTML. This introduced a Tower of Babel into the Web, because Web pages began to appear that used features only available in one company's Web browser. The enhancements, while satisfying the needs of some authors, were detrimental to users with old Web browsers and text-only computer displays. Also, disabled users that depend on HTML-to-speech or HTML-to-Braille depend on a standard for HTML that has been designed with consideration for representing Web pages by speech. More fundamentally, the Netscape and Microsoft enhancements (such as allowing fonts to be specified), violated HTML 1.0's premise of separating document content from appearance. So for a while people wondered if there would ever be another standard version of HTML. Eventually, the Netscape and Microsoft enhancements were reconciled into HTML 3.2. However, the single standard HTML 3.2 was not long-lived. Two new HTML developments followed HTML 3.2: cascading style sheets and "dynamic" HTML. In cascading style sheets, W3C attempted to restore to HTML the property that an HTML file describes content. A style sheet lists attributes that control appearance, from font sizes to positioning. There can be multiple style sheets (e.g., for a document, for a Web site, for the Web browser, for an individual user), giving rise to the notion of cascading style sheets. The result was the cascading style sheet 1 (CSS-1) specification. Meanwhile in 1997 Netscape and Microsoft introduced new versions of their Web browsers implementing "dynamic" HTML. The term "dynamic" refers to several new features: the ability to specify positioning and layering, the use of style sheets, and the ability of a scripting language to treat elements of an HTML document between tags as an "object" that can be manipulated by a scripting language. However, Netscape and Microsoft introduced incompatible enhancements to HTML 3.2, thereby returning the Tower of Babel to the Web.

Given the continual flux in the state of HTML, individual HTML authors have to know what tags belong to what versions of HTML and make careful decisions on the use of non-standard tags will affect users. This may become even more critical in the future, as less developed countries join the Internet community. The most plentiful computers may be older, low powered machines that lack the screen resolution, memory, and CPU speed to quickly render high quality graphics. Use of non-standard HTML makes Web pages inaccessible to persons using text-only Web browsers as well as disabled users.

In the next section, we will look at the origins of HTML.

4.2 Origins

Origins of HTML

The original concept of hypertext was invented by Theodor Holm Nelson, the famous prophet of the "Xanadu" network [6]. (See Section 1.3 for more on Xanadu.)

For the source of the concept, Nelson quotes an essay by Vannevar Bush written in 1945 and read to him by his father as a boy: "The human mind ... operates by association. With one item in its grasp, it snaps instantly to the next that is suggested by the association of thoughts, in accordance with some intricate web of trails carried by the cells of the brain." Expanding this idea from a single human brain to a global mind, Nelson opened the way for the World Wide Web.

Tim Berners-Lee wrote the first Web client and server in the NeXTSTEP environment at CERN, the European Particle Physics Laboratory which is on the Swiss-French border near Geneva [1]. (The acronym CERN is, in French, "Conseil Européen pour la Recherche Nucleáire.") In 1989, Berners-Lee and Robert Cailliau proposed a global networked hypertext project for High-Energy Physics collaborations to be known as the World Wide Web. This work was started in October 1990, and the program "WorldWideWeb" was made available within CERN in December, and on the Internet at large in the summer of 1991. Berners-Lee subsequently defined the URL, HTTP and HTML specifications.

In November 1993, using the work made public by Berners-Lee, the National Center for Supercomputing Applications at the University of Illinois released NCSA Mosaic, a software tool that enabled people to easily browse the thousands of different types of documents proliferating on the Internet.

Tim Berners-Lee gave HTML, and the Web in general, to the world. NCSA took his work and produced Mosaic, which was given away as well. Then in April 1994, Marc Andreessen, creator of NCSA Mosaic, left NCSA to found the Netscape Corporation. Netscape set the stage for Microsoft and other commercial firms to add to the fragmentation of the Web by introducing proprietary HTML

tags in contradiction to the charter of the W3C. The W3C, its function and charter, will be examined more closely later in this chapter.

What Is HyperText Markup Language?

HTML is a text markup language. The term "markup" refers to the process
of adding extra tags to the text of a document that specify how to format the document [12]. HTML is not a programming language, although it can be viewed as
a "glue" that holds together many programming languages, such as JAVA, PERL,
and C++. (CGI and Java are discussed in detail in Chapters 7 and 8, respectively.)

HTML is an application of ISO Standard 8879[1] (1986) Information Processing Text and Office Systems; Standard Generalized Markup Language (SGML).
The SGML specification (ISO Standard 8879:1986) defines the "text/html" Internet Media Type (RFC 1590) and MIME Content Type (RFC 1521).

SGML is a type of markup used on IBM mainframes to generate formatted
documents. SGML, like HTML, is a sign-style language: a markup tag sets a
type style, which continues to hold until another tag is encountered.

There are certain constraints that are meant to be followed when using
HTML. The following list of requirements is quoted from the W3C's position
statement regarding HTML [13].

Requirements

A simple scalable document format that can be used for information exchange on
virtually any platform:

- Graphical User Interfaces, such as Windows, Macs, and X11/Unix

- Text-only systems, for instance VT-100 terminals

- Text-to-Speech devices

- Rendering to Braille

The document format should be, as far as is practical, backwards-
compatible with existing HTML documents. It should support both paged and
scrolling layout models. It should work well with separate style sheets, but not
require support for this in browsers. It should support the common needs of
information providers for delivering services over the World Wide Web. It should
make it practical to create HTML documents by directly editing the markup;
with WYSIWYG (What You See Is What You Get—that is, the input looks just
like the output) editors for HTML; with filters from common word processing formats; and from other SGML document types.

---

[1] http://www.iso.ch/cate/d16387.html

It should work well with separate style sheets but not require support for this in browsers. It should support the common needs of information providers for delivering services over the World Wide Web. It should be practical to create HTML documents either by directly editing the markup, with WYSIWYG editors for HTML, and with filters to translate common word processing formats.

The next section takes a look at the history of HTML and its specifications.

Timeline for the Evolution of HTML

1989

- Tim Berners-Lee and Robert Cailliau propose a networked Hypertext project for High-Energy Physics collaborations while at CERN.

1990

- The system is available on the NeXTSTEP operating system. Further proposals are made for a Hypertext project for CERN. The name World-Wide Web is decided on.

1993

- HTML 1.0 Document Type Definition (DTD) is finalized in March 1993. NCSA releases X-Mosaic and Mac and PC versions of Mosaic.

1994

- Web traffic overtakes Gopher traffic. Netscape "buys up" all manpower from NCSA and releases Netscape 1.0. Tim Berners-Lee leaves CERN for MIT. The W3C is founded.

1995

- European development is transferred from CERN to INRIA. WWW and the Internet become one entity in the minds of non-specialists. HTML is standardized by the WWW consortium as Internet Engineering Task Force (IETF) RFC 1866, commonly referred to as HTML Version 2. Netscape 2.0 is released. March, 1995, HTML 3.0 draft specification is released and later in the year expires.

1996

- W3C Announces Release of HTML 3.2 (also known as Wilbur): Improving Interoperability of HTML, a W3C Proposed Recommendation. HTML 3.2 is not an official specification, but a snapshot of current practice. Netscape releases version 3.0. Microsoft jumps into the browser business with Internet Explorer.

1997

- W3C releases CSS-1 specification. Netscape and Microsoft introduce "dynamic" HTML.

Next, we will examine who is in control of the evolution and implementation of HTML.

4.3 Owners—The Factions that Vie for Control of HTML

There is no single group that controls HTML. HTML originated from CERN and NCSA, scientific and educational facilities, but has been largely preempted by commercial companies. The two main groups currently involved in HTML standards are the W3C and the IETF.

The established process to modify HTML standards is to write Internet Drafts, which are published, tested, and commented on, and when finalized become Document Type Definitions. DTDs are used as standards for Web browsers and HTML authors. This process is circumvented by browsers authors, who add to HTML and support the additions in their particular browsers. These kinds of additions may eventually be codified as current practice or may be abandoned, depending on how well the Web community likes them and uses them. The final control of HTML lies with individual authors who choose to use only tags from an HTML specification or instead choose to use non-standard, exclusionary markup.

CERN and NCSA

Although HTML came from CERN and NCSA, these two entities have been superseded, mostly by commercial concerns. They are no longer involved in HTML's evolution.

W3C—The World Wide Web Consortium

The W3C has been the single body with the most influence on HTML develop-
ment. W3C is hosted by the Laboratory for Computer Science at MIT, by INRIA
(Institut National de Recherche en Informatique et en Automatique—The
French National Institute for Research in Computer Science and Control), and
Keio University with support from DARPA (Defense Advanced Research Projects
Agency) and the European Commission. Members include Netscape, Microsoft,
Spyglass, Sun, Apple, and many others.

Any organization or company can sign the membership agreement and pay
the membership fees. Individuals cannot join the W3C, but may participate by
subscribing to the *World Wide Web Journal*, the official journal of the W3C, published quarterly by O'Reilly and Associates.

The W3C is a non-profit organization; however the fee for becoming a Full
Member for companies with gross revenues over $50 million is $150,000. Other
companies join as Affiliate Members for $15,000. One-third of the total fee is due
at the time an organization joins, and one-third is due in each of two subsequent
years. Members get new information and specifications before they are released
to the general public.

The Consortium claims its purposes are to support the advancement of
information technology in the field of networking, graphics and user interfaces
by evolving the World Wide Web toward a true information infrastructure, and to
encourage cooperation in the industry through the promotion and development
of standard interfaces in the information environment known as the "World Wide
Web." MIT and INRIA's role is to provide the vendor-neutral architectural, engineering and administrative leadership required to make this work. The Consortium began operation October 1, 1994. But membership in the W3C does not
means the members have to, or will, abide by its constraints and charter.

IETF

The Internet Engineering Task Force is the protocol engineering and development arm of the Internet. The IETF is a large open international community of
network designers, operators, vendors, and researchers concerned with the evolution of the Internet architecture and the smooth operation of the Internet. It is
open to any interested individual.

The IRTF (Internet Research Task Force) is tasked to consider the long-
term research problems in the Internet. The Internet Society (ISOC), formed in
January 1992, provides the official parent organization for the IETF. The ISOC
Board of Trustees appoints the members of the IAB (Internet Architecture
Board). The IETF and IRTF Chairs are also IAB members. The IAB provides the
final technical review of Internet standards.

Browser Manufacturers

Although there are many Web browser makers, Netscape and Microsoft are the main players here. Other browsers are available, such as Mosaic and Lynx, but they are not addressed here because they are not well known for adding tags to HTML.

Netscape

Andreessen developed the idea for the NCSA Mosaic browser for the Internet in the fall of 1992 while he was an undergraduate student at the University of Illinois and a staff member at the university's National Center for Supercomputing Applications in Champaign, Illinois. He created the navigational tool for the Internet with a team of students and staff at NCSA in early 1993, basing their work on Tim Berners-Lee's efforts, which were given to the world for free. In addition to Andreessen, Netscape Communications' core technical team includes five of the six other original NCSA Mosaic developers from NCSA: Eric Bina, Rob McCool, Jon Mittelhauser, Aleks Totic, and Chris Houck. The team also includes Lou Montulli, author of Lynx, the best known text-based browser for the Internet, other University of Illinois alumni, and several software engineers formerly with Silicon Graphics, Lucid, and General Magic Corporation.

Microsoft

Although late on the HTML scene, Microsoft has plunged into the Web, offering its own browser, Internet Explorer, and, of course, its own proprietary tags. Recently Microsoft has proposed to W3C as a draft standard each modification it makes to HTML, in an effort to support the standardization process.

HTML Authors

The final control of HTML rests squarely on the shoulders of individual authors of HTML documents. If authors can be seduced by blinking, barking, and spinning proprietary tags, and do not care who is excluded by such practices, the Web will become more and more fragmented. If authors decide that the most important facet of HTML is its device independence, its ability to make information sharable to everyone in the world, regardless of software and hardware, then they will adhere to standardized HTML and generate blander Web sites. A browser company cannot force anyone to use frames or blinking text; all they can do is make up the tags and see if the authoring community uses them. It is critical that authors understand the proprietary nature of such tags and make informed decisions on their use.

Next we will examine what good HTML practices are and then look at the nuts and bolts of HTML, exactly which tags are "safe" (defined in a finalized specification) and which tags are potentially harmful non-specification additions.

4.4 Good Practices

HTML Good Practices—How to Ensure Everyone Can Get Your Information

A Web page designer can adopt one of two philosophies in creating pages. On the one hand a designer can stress the overall appearance and impact of a page. This often argues for choosing tags appearing in the most recent incarnation of HTML. On the other hand, the designer may need to insure that the page content can be shared by everyone worldwide regardless of their computer and software. This argues for using the "lowest common denominator" among browsers and computers (e.g., HTML 2.0).

Listed below are tips for page designers in the second category of desiring universal accessibility.

- Familiarize yourself with the HTML specs, so that you have a good understanding of what HTML is most widely supported.

- Validate your pages—that is, use a validator to check your markup. Some software, such as BBEdit, has built-in HTML validators. There are also many online validators that require no more software than a Web browser. Try A Kinder, Gentler Validator or the WebTechs validator (also known as the "HALSoft validator").

- Don't assume that because you created your pages using one browser they will look the same on all browsers—they won't! Test your pages with other browsers and platforms if possible. A good lowest-common-denominator test is to check your pages with Lynx, a text-only browser. Users without access to Lynx can use Lynx-me, a free online service that will take a URL and display the page as Lynx would render it.

- Make reasonably-sized documents, that is, less than 50 Kb.

- Carefully weigh content. Is it really critical? Could it be represented in a simpler way? Is it helpful or distracting?

- Identify your audience. Is your information critical for users worldwide, or is it only going to appeal to a tiny group?

- Provide alternate pages—if you are going to take the time to do fancy stuff, take a little more time to make a text version. Use your Web server to dynamically detect and redirect browsers to an appropriate page, or provide a simple entry page with links to plain and fancy versions. (The fancy page is where to put those "download blah now" blurbs.)

- Put a link to an alternative, text-only page at the top of your document.

- If you must use frames, use <noframe> outside of the <frameset> tags so that users without a frame-capable browser can view a version of your page. Put the <noframe> at the top of the page for critical links and text.

- Don't count on the following to convey your information properly. Many browsers do not see these the way you expect they will (or at all)—this is not a comprehensive list.

  - centering
  - font information (size, colors, etc.)
  - graphics (inline or background)
  - tables—use the <pre> tag to format tables with a fixed-width font and spacing, possibly on alternate pages
  - blinking text
  -
  - plug-ins
  - frames

- Use pictures sparingly. Many folks cannot or do not want to look at them; many folks are paying by the minute for Web access, and wasting time and bandwidth sometimes seems criminal.

- Use the ALT attribute in tags that include graphics, especially when using graphics as links.

- Some browsers ignore ALT attributes; include text in the body for descriptions and links. Put pictures on their own pages, and make a link to the page with a note as to its content and the size of graphics.

- Use transparent and interlaced GIFs to improve download time.

Next we'll look at how nonstandard HTML fragments the Web, defeats its original intent of device independence, and keeps users from getting information.

How Nonstandard HTML Can Be Harmful

"Anyone who slaps a 'this page is best viewed with Browser X' label on a Web page appears to be yearning for the bad old days, before the Web,

when you had very little chance of reading a document written on another computer, another word processor, or another network." [2]

Use of proprietary HTML coding that is hardware or software specific can deprive seekers of information. The ultimate test of who might be hurt is to determine who the audience is. If the documents under consideration are personal vanity pages, it might be appropriate to use non-standard HTML. If the documents are intended for an Intranet in which the software and hardware can be dictated and supplied, then anything goes. If the information is critical to the world it would be best to use the simplest, most widely supported HTML.

Who Is Being Left Out?

Relying heavily on graphics and nonstandard markup, and not providing text/plain HTML alternatives, leaves out many users:

- Anyone using a plain DOS or UNIX connection that is text only. (There are lots of them about and there are bound to be more, as old DOS machines are cheap and easily available and can meet the demand for access to the information on the Web.)

- Users who access the Net via public libraries, universities and other text-only vehicles.

- A user who is sight impaired may be using a text to speech or text-to-Braille mechanism to use the Web. In this case, it is mandatory to use standard HTML, or the conversion software will not work properly.

- Power-users with very fast connections still travel with graphics off. People trying to get to information or make purchasing decisions may be in a hurry.

- Users with mobile devices, such as PDAs and small machines such as laptops, are severely limited by the markup that is effective on a small display screen. This is another Web access mode that is only going to grow.

Daniel W. Connolly, editor of HTML 2.0, has this to say about nonstandard markup, and the role of the W3C:

"So please, everybody, stop asking 'what would it break?' and start asking 'what is the design rationale behind the current spec, and is there new evidence that suggests the spec should be changed?'

"Once you've got an argument that the spec should change, then we'll all start to look real hard at compatibility and deployment issues." [5]

In the next section, we will take a look at exactly what HTML tags are "safe," that is, understandable by any browser that visits.

Standard HTML Tags from HTML 1.0 and 2.0

The following list of tags are from HTML 1.0 and 2.0 They considered safe, that is, usable by any browser [3].

Required Tags

<HTML></HTML> encloses the entire document and defines it as HTML

<HEAD></HEAD> comes after the opening <HTML> tag and contains the <TITLE>

<TITLE></TITLE> contains the name of the document and must be enclosed by <HEAD> tags

<BODY></BODY> contains all of the rest of the document—it is opened after the closing </HEAD> tag and is closed at the end of the document. The only tag to go after the closing </BODY> tag is the closing </HTML> tag.

HTML 1.0

Following are the original tags in HTML 1.0 (HTML 1.0 DTD, March 1993):

A—anchor

ADDRESS—formatting tag, often shown in italics

B—formatting tag, bold

BASE—optional head element, sets base URL for related documents

BLOCKQUOTE—formatting tag, to indicate portions of text included from other documents

BODY—required, see above

BR—line break

CITE—formatting tag, to indicate text is a citation from another source

CODE—formatting tag, to indicate text is program source code

DD—list tag, definition

DIR—list tag, directory

DL—list tag, definition list

DT—list tag, definition term

EM—formatting tag, to indicate text is to be emphasized

H1—structural heading, top (largest) level

H2—structural heading

H3—structural heading

H4—structural heading

H5—structural heading

H6—structural heading, bottom (smallest) level

HEAD—required, see above

HR—horizontal rule

HTML—required, see above

I—formatting tag, italics

IMG—image anchor

ISINDEX—optional head element, indicates document is a searchable
index

KBD—formatting tag, indicates expected user in source code

LI—list tag, list item

LINK—indicates relationship between documents, varies from
browser to browser

MENU—list tag, compacted

META—optional head element, information for client software such
as last revision date

NEXTID—optional head element used by automated markup systems
to keep track of anchors

OL—list tag, ordered list

P—paragraph break

PRE— formatting tag, indicates text should be preformatted (monospaced, preserve whitespace)

SAMP—formatting tag, used to mark text output from a computer program

STRONG—formatting tag, strongly emphasize text

TITLE—required, see above

TT—formatting tag, typewriter text, show text in fixed font

UL—list tag, unnumbered list

VAR—formatting tag, indicates a variable in program source code

HTML 2.0

HTML 2.0 introduced forms support, which added the following tags [4]:

FORM—encloses a form block

INPUT—a form input field (text entry field, radio button, check box, etc.)

OPTION—the list items in a SELECT element

SELECT—for pull-down lists in forms

TEXTAREA—for large text input fields in forms

4.5 How to Get Involved in Adding to HTML Specifications

Proposing New Features

Those who would propose new features or modify old ones should research available information first.

Ideas are taken more seriously if they follow Internet draft guidelines.[2]

Research Links:

Internet Engineering Task Force:[3] IETF is the protocol engineering and development arm of the Internet, open to all interested.

---

[2] http://info.internet.isi.edu:70/in-drafts/1id-guidelines.txt

[3] http://www.ics.uci.edu/pub/ietf/html/

Internet Monthly Reports:[4]   The purpose of these reports is to communicate to the Internet Research Group.

Internet Architecture Board:[5]   The IETF is a standards body and the IAB is drawn from the IETF in order to help it achieve its goals of better standardization.

HTML World Wide Web Consortium:[6]   The W3C is an industry consortium which seeks to promote standards for the evolution of the Web and interoperability between Web products by producing specifications and reference software. Although W3C is funded by industrial members, it is vendor-neutral, and its products are freely available to all.

W3C hosts several e-mail lists:[7]

- www-announce (WWW announcements of general interest);[8]

- www-talk (Technical discussions of WWW issues);[9]

- www-html (Discussions of proposed future enhancements to HTML);[10]

- Web4lib (Delivery of Library services via WWW).[11]

W3 Consortium information on HTML:[12]   HyperMail archive of the HTML-WG mail server[13]

- 100 Web-related sites are searchable at verity.com[14]

- comp.infosystems.www.authoring.html[15]

- comp.infosystems.www.authoring.misc[16]

---

[4] http://www.isi.edu/in-notes/imr/

[5] http://www.iab.org/iab/

[6] http://www.w3.org/Markup

[7] http://www.w3.org/Mail/Lists.html

[8] http://lists.w3.org/Archives/Public/www-announce/

[9] http://lists.w3.org/Archives/Public/www-talk/

[10] http://lists.w3.org/Archives/Public/www-html/

[11] http://sunsite.berkeley.edu/Web4Lib/

[12] http://www.w3.org/MarkUp/Activity

[13] http://www.acl.lanl.gov/HTML_WG/archives.html

[14] http://www.verity.com/vlibsearch.html

[15] news:comp.infosystems.www.authoring.html

[16] news:comp.infosystems.www.authoring.misc

People:

- HTML Working Group Chair
    - Dan Connolly[17]
- Editor of the HTML 2.n Specification:
    - Dan Connolly[17]
- Editor of the 3.n Specification
    - Dave Raggett[18]
- Editors of the 4.n Specification
- Dave Raggett[18]
    - Arnaud Le Hors[19]
    - Ian Jacobs[20]

Finally, we will move on to the conclusion.

4.6 Conclusion

HTML is the language that powers the World Wide Web. Its greatest strength is its ability to allow sharing of textual and graphical information freely, regardless of the hardware and software used by the author or the user.

With the out-of-control growth of the Web has come a plethora of HTML tags added by commercial Web browser manufacturers. These tags are specific to a particular browser and may be presented by other browsers in an unexpected way, or not at all.

HTML is limited in its ability to present document formatting; it is especially weak in presenting mathematical formulas. This is being addressed by cascading style sheets, which give authors much more control of presentation, as well as math support.

The future of the Web, and HTML, ultimately rests with HTML authors. Authors must understand which tags have been introduced by commercial concerns and carefully choose what kind of HTML to use, based on their document content and expected audience. Information that is useful to the world and has a long "shelf-life" should be marked up with HTML that is as widely usable as possible. Nonspecification HTML is more appropriate for information that is meant for a small audience, or an intranet, where the author knows what kind of software and hardware the users will have.

[17] mailto:connolly@w3.org

[18] mailto:dsr@w3.org

[19] mailto:lehors@w3.org

[20] mailto:ij@w3.org

4.7 References

[1]   Berners-Lee, Tim. "Online Biography."
       <http://www.w3.org/pub/WWW/People/Berners-Lee-Bio.html/Longer.html>
       (20 Nov. 1996).

[2]   ——. *Technology Review,* July 1996.

[3]   Connolly, Daniel W. "HTML DTD Reference." 30 Nov. 1994.
       <http://www.w3.org/pub/WWW/MarkUp/html-spec/L1Pindex.html>
       (22 Nov. 1996).

[4]   ——. "Public Text of the HTML 2.0 Specification." 21 Sept. 1995.
       <http://www.w3.org/pub/WWW/MarkUp/html-spec/html-pubtext.html>   (22
       Nov. 1996).

[5]   ——. <connolly@w3.org> "Re: What are the problems with IDML?" 26 Aug.
       1996. <www-html@w3.org> (26 Aug. 1996).

[6]   Gilder, George. "The Coming Software Shift." Forbes ASAP, 28 Aug. 1995.
       <http://homepage.seas.upenn.edu/~gaj1/shiftgg.html> (20 Nov. 1996).

[7]   Netscape. "Extensions to HTML 2.0."
       <http://home.netscape.com/assist/net_sites/html_extensions.html>
       (22 Nov. 1996).

[8]   ——. "Extensions to HTML 3.0."
       <http://home.netscape.com/assist/net_sites/html_extensions_3.html>
       (22 Nov. 1996).

[9]   ——. "Frames—Syntax."
       <http://home.netscape.com/assist/net_sites/frame_syntax.html>   (22   Nov.
       1996).

[10]   ——. "New HTML 3.0 Proposals."
       <http://home.netscape.com/assist/net_sites/new_html3_prop.html>
       (22 Nov. 1996).

[11]   ——. "Tables as Implemented in Netscape 1.1—Netscape 1.1 Tables and the
       Proposed HTML3.0 Spec."
       <http://home.netscape.com/assist/net_sites/tables.html> (22 Nov. 1996).

[12]   Powell, James. "HTML Plus!" Wadsworth Publishing Co., 1997.
       <http://scholar.lib.vt.edu/jpowell/htmlplus/> (20 Nov. 1996).

[13]   Raggett, Dave. "W3C Activity: Hypertext Markup Language (HTML)."
       <http://www.w3.org/pub/WWW/MarkUp/Activity> (20 Nov. 1996).

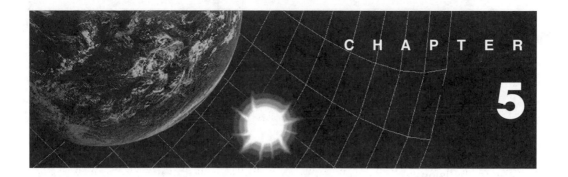

C H A P T E R

5

Graphical Design

by Joseph W. Reiss

*L*ayout and design professionals have been honing their craft since publishing began hundreds of years ago. However, the early years of each new publishing revolution always seem to be spent rediscovering this knowledge. This happened in the 1980s with desktop publishing, when every page contained 20 different fonts and several pieces of clip art. It is happening again in the 1990s on the Web. There is a strong tendency to include design elements simply because one can, and not because one should.

This chapter provides some hints on how to produce designs that are both attractive and effective, without being browser exclusive. Some are drawn from print media. Others come from the areas of hypermedia and multimedia. And a few others are specific to the Web. We will also look at some pitfalls of bad design and discuss better ways to present the same information.

Chapter Content

- If You Can't Beat Them, Create a New Standard

4. Multimedia

- The Bleeding Edge

- Proceed with Caution

5. Conclusions
6. References

5.1 Introduction

The Web has been hailed by many as perhaps the greatest revolution ever in the publishing industry. For the first time in history, the "common man" has been given the ability to distribute information to potentially thousands or even millions of people. In the past, such widespread circulation could only be achieved by a select few who were judged worthy by editors and publishers. Now, anyone can be their own editor and their own publisher. All they need is an account with an Internet service provider and a few lessons in HTML.

Yet let us look back a few years to the last great publishing revolution. In the mid-80s, Desktop Publishing, or DTP, was creating a similar stir in publishing and computer circles. Here again was a technology that was giving lay persons the ability to do things that were previously reserved only for those with fancy printing presses and large design staffs. Now everyone could be their own designer and printer. All they needed was a computer, a printer, and a DTP package.

Sound familiar?

Of course, the problem with the DTP revolution became obvious very quickly. Yes, people had the tools to create all sorts of wonderful documents. Unfortunately, what they didn't have were the skills to use these tools effectively. The results were documents with 15 different fonts on a page, clipart images put in not because they were needed but just because there weren't any on the page yet, etc. The average user had little or no knowledge of the art of design, a subject to which many people devote their entire careers.

Today, we're seeing the same pattern played out on the Web. While there are millions of pages available, many of them are poorly designed. Their lack of structure often makes them difficult to navigate. Large in-line images are common, dramatically increasing page download times, but often producing a very weak visual effect. Animations run endlessly around the screen, distracting the reader from the actual content of the document, if there is any.

The Web is passing through a phase almost identical to what DTP went through. Many people perceive it as a new toy. For this reason, they often do things on their Web pages not because they need to but simply because they can.

While this can be a fun and sometimes an enlightening exercise, it does not make for good design.

In this chapter, we'll look at Web design from three different perspectives. First, we'll examine how past work with hypertext navigation leads to suggestions for imparting an easily navigable structure upon a Web document. Second, we'll pull some tips from printed media for making pages more visually appealing while enhancing their usefulness. Finally, we'll take a look at multimedia, the latest craze to hit the Web, and examine its place in effective design.

5.2 Hypermedia

From its earliest incarnations, the Web has been conceived first and foremost as a global hypertext system. One of the goals of the Web's original creators was to provide a uniform interface to the Internet's existing services such as news and FTP. At the same time, they wanted to provide a simple medium for cross-platform information exchange between members of their own particular scientific community [2]. The simplicity of the hypertext model made it a natural way to accomplish both. News articles could be mapped into hypertext by parsing the reference headers to locate related articles. Meanwhile, many existing graphical tools for accessing FTP sites also used a point-and-click method to select files, and this readily mapped to a hypertext format.

Conceptually, hypertext is a very elegant concept. When the user wants additional information about a particular topic, she needs only to click on (or in some other way select) the text referring to that topic. More information about that item is then displayed. However, a simple concept often has complex problems that aren't immediately obvious. Such is the case with hypertext.

Lost in Hyperspace

When users interact with any interface, they tend to form a mental model of the process being controlled. A good interface will help the user build a fairly accurate model of the system. Certain aspects may be abstracted somewhat because they are not meaningful to the user, but the basic concepts of the model should be fairly faithful to reality. If they are not, then the users may try to manipulate the interface in ways that make sense given their mental model but make no sense in the real system. Even worse, the actions they take may have radically different effects than what they intended because of the model mismatch. At best, this will cause the user significant frustration. At worst, it could cause data loss or even more catastrophic results.

The same thing happens when a user begins navigating in an information space. Whether that space is a book, a card catalog, or a hypertext system is irrelevant; the user tends to develop a structure for the information in their mind. Ideally, this helps relate pieces of information to each other and helps guide searches to an appropriate location in the information space. However, while a book is a highly linear space with a fairly straightforward model, a hypertext document is often highly nonlinear. Information flow can branch outward from many locations within the text. By following a link, the user may be taken to a completely different part of the document, and it may not be entirely clear how the new-found information relates to the document as a whole. It may not even be clear how to get back to the location in the document that contained the link to this page.

When a user gets so deep into a hypertext system that she can no longer figure out where the current information fits into the grand scheme of things or how the current information was found in the first place, that user is said to be "Lost in Hyperspace" [5]. Typically, this situation arises because the mental model that the user formed of the information system is chaotic—a jumbled mess of pages and links that have no real structure beyond the linkages themselves. If this is a faulty model, that's bad enough. Too often, however, this is the *only* model that applies to a great many hypertext systems.

This problem is only exacerbated on the Web. In a stand-alone hypertext system, the author has control over the entire document. If she has a coherent view of the document structure, then there's a good chance of conferring this model to the user. On the Web, however, a hypertext link can lead to anywhere, including to a completely different site on a completely different server with a completely different structural model that is out of the original author's control.

Beginning to see the problem?

Guiding the User

The situation is not hopeless, of course. Many things can be done to design Web pages so that they aid the user in forming an accurate and organized model of the information available on the site. The Yale C/AIM Style Manual [8] discusses many of these techniques.

Perhaps the first important point to stress is the need for consistency. In most interface designs, this is a desirable thing. In Web design, it is one of the most important concepts to learn. Moreover, consistency can and should be applied at many different levels of the design, from consistency between pages to consistency in layout and in imagery.

To begin with, interpage consistency within a site is a must. If all the pages in a site have a common visual thread running through them, then a reader will quickly know when a link has been followed to an external site because the look will change.

Creating this kind of consistency can be quite simple. One effective technique is to use a single banner at the top of all pages, as is done in the electronic version of this book. Such a banner provides a strong visual identity to the site. The banner does not even have to be exactly the same on all pages; simple variations in color and/or imagery can help indicate different high-level topics within the site. Just be sure that all the variations remain similar enough that there's no doubt they're from the same site.

Another type of interpage consistency involves buttons, or images used as links. If a button on one page performs a similar function to a button used on a different page (e.g., go to next page), it will help the reader if both buttons use the same image. This way, when the user learns the meaning of that particular image, she will be able to apply that knowledge whenever that image reappears.

Consistency within a page is important, too. For example, when a page is divided into multiple sections and each section is introduced by a header, the format of that header should be consistent throughout the page (and perhaps throughout the site). If an image is included as part of that header, which is often a good way to visually separate sections, all the images should be the same size and should occupy the same position horizontally on the page. This avoids the "clown's pants" phenomenon where images and text are scattered haphazardly around the page, leading to a general sense of disorder and confusion. Again, the Yale C/AIM Style Manual [8] provides an excellent example of this.[1]

The Web designer also needs to keep in mind that on the Web, other people can link to any page within your site. Therefore, you cannot count on the reader's having been to your top-level page or any other pages within your site. You have to assume that the reader could enter the system anywhere. Here, you can help the user by providing a consistent set of navigational links on every page. These are usually placed at the top or bottom of the page, or sometimes in both places. At the very least, a link should be provided to return the user to some top-level page in your document space. If your document is arranged in a roughly hierarchical form, a link to the current page's parent is also useful. And if there is a linear flow to the information on your site, as there is with the sections of this book, then links to the previous and next pages can be quite handy. By giving users these links on every page, you help them navigate through the site as well as form their mental model based on the structure these links create.

Yahoo [16] is an excellent example of a consistent visual look and navigational links, though the links are slightly different than those described above. At the top of each and every page is an image map that contains links to several of the most important pages in the site. This banner serves the dual purpose of establishing a visual identify for the site and aiding in site navigation. More importantly, however, the header on each page lists every step in the categorizational hierarchy above the current page. In this way, a user who enters the site at one of the inner nodes can quickly and easily see how the page relates to other available information and can also get to this other information via a single click.

There are other techniques beyond simple consistency to help users form a good mental model. One simple step is to make the text within links as meaningful as possible. Too often, one sees a link saying only "Click here" for information.

---

[1] http://info.med.yale.edu/caim/manual/pages/balanced_pages.html

The user will be whisked off somewhere, but who knows where? It takes very little effort to make link text meaningful. It also helps the readers when they quickly scan through a document looking for highlighted links; meaningful names make it easy to quickly discern what each link is about. Well-chosen link text conveys the relationship between the document with the link and the document being linked to. It also helps some Web indexes categorize the content of the linked page. Moreover, some browsers for those with disabilities may present a list of links to the user so that they can chose which ones to follow. In this situation, "Click here" does not provide adequate information.

Another way to help the user build relationships in an information space is to keep file sizes small. Generally, hypertext links are created so that users can find out more about a particular topic being mentioned in the current document. If particular concepts can be isolated on their own short pages, then the users can quickly fill in the gaps in their knowledge without having to spend a great deal of time searching for the relevant information. Moreover, the user will be able to see directly how the new information relates to the original document. If the second page contains lots of extraneous information, or information on several different subjects, this relationship will be obscured.

One soon realizes that choosing the right amount of information for a page is always a balancing act. Enough information must be provided to successfully explain the concept. Too much information will overwhelm the user. There is no one guideline to determine what size is right. It's dependent on the information itself and on the prior knowledge of the target audience. Sometimes, you'll just have to try something and then see if people like it or not. After a while, you may begin to just get a feel for the right size. Experience is always a great teacher.

5.3 Printed Media

Despite the advances in modern publishing technology, including electronic publishing on the Web, many of the basic tenets for graphical design continue to come from the realm of printed media. After all, it is the oldest form of modern publishing. As such, it has provided the greatest avenue for study and experimentation.

Still, many Web designers have a tendency to ignore most of these guidelines. Even those guidelines that have gained some level of acceptance have often done so only after they were "rediscovered" in this new medium. At first, this repetition of effort seems somewhat silly and wasteful. Yet there are a few good reasons why things happen this way.

When Philosophies Collide

The original vision of the Web was as a platform-independent method of information exchange. The designers wanted to create a system that could be navigated by software running on the most basic text-based computers as well as high-end graphical workstations and personal computers [2]. Moreover, they also wanted the Web to be accessible by people with physical impairments that might make reading traditional computer displays difficult or impossible. Therefore, the Web was designed so that its information could be presented using synthesized speech or braille displays or other similar techniques.

These criteria imposed many restrictions on the Web's design. Such restrictions are particularly visible in early versions of HTML. In particular, directives to control the visual layout and appearance of elements in a Web document are conspicuously absent. Virtually all HTML tags differentiate portions of text not by their visual attributes but by their function. For example, in HTML 2.0 [3], all but a few tags only indicate the function of the text (header, quote, etc.), not how it is to be displayed. There is no way to indicate that a particular block of text should be displayed in a larger-than-normal font size. There is no way to indicate that an in-line image should be centered horizontally. There is no way to indicate that text should be arranged in multiple columns.

Naturally, it wasn't long before Web page designers found themselves wanting to do these very things. However, the content-based design paradigm that was an inherent part of early HTML standards did everything it could to prevent them from doing so. After all, how can you let a page designer specify a change in font when a user viewing the document on a text-only computer terminal or listening to a synthesized voice read the page would be unable to see or hear the difference?

Even between graphical browsers, designers couldn't rely on consistent appearance of elements. Some browsers displayed headers as larger text. Some centered headers on screen. Some changed the font style. The only thing that designers could safely assume was that headers would appear visually distinct from the surrounding body text.

Of course, as the Web's popularity grew and an increasing number of classically trained graphical designers began to become interested in the new technology, this situation rapidly became unacceptable. They wanted this kind of control.

And one way or another, they were going to get it.

Working within the System

Even though HTML is defined based on content rather than presentation, certain visual interpretations of the HTML tags have become almost de facto standards themselves. Motivated by Web authors' desire for at least some level of consistent behavior, and aided by the early dominance of a single Web browser (namely NCSA Mosaic [9]), the developers of early Web browsers consistently chose to apply many of the original design choices made in Mosaic. When Netscape [10] became the driving force in the market, others began to imitate its design choices. Web authors have, therefore, been able to exploit some of these consistent constructs to control appearance in ways that the Web's original designers never envisioned.

One popular "trick" is to use a <PRE> block to provide more precise control over the positions of text and graphics on the screen. Within a <PRE>...</PRE> block, a monospaced font is used so that all letters are the same width. Moreover, any sequence of spaces, tabs, and newlines is drawn on screen exactly as it appears in the document rather than being collapsed into a single space as is normally done. Therefore, the Web author is able to arrange text in multiple columns, simulating a tabular layout even in browsers that don't support the newer <TABLE> extensions. This technique was more popular before <TABLE> support was widespread, but it's still seen occasionally today.

Perhaps the most prominent example of reliance on standard renderings is the HTML header construct. Virtually all current graphical browsers display these in a larger point size than normal body text. So many Web designers have used headers to increase point size even when the text in question wasn't actually a header. With the arrival of Netscape as the dominant browser, headers became used for even odder things. Why? Because in Netscape, an <H6> header is actually drawn smaller than normal text. Many other browsers, in an attempt to be compatible with Netscape, have imitated this behavior. The result is that many authors use <H6> headers to include "fine print," such as copyright notices, in their designs.

One common mistake is often made by designers when using HTML headers and other constructs such as bold text to grab reader attention. There is a common fallacy which says that making everything on the page an <H1> header or making a large passage of text bold makes the entire page stand out. This is usually not the case. These enhancements rely on visual contrast to make their point. If everything is big and bold, then nothing stands out. Therefore, such tags should be used only when they really make sense.

Related to this is one of Tufte's fundamental precepts of graphical design [14]. Basically what this says is that the most important information should be the most visually salient. Too often, the important information is overwhelmed by pure decoration or details of lesser importance. Tufte's books show many examples that present a large amount of information but do not appear to be cluttered. This effect is often achieved by using bright, fully saturated colors for the key information, while less important information is drawn with more subdued colors, causing it to fade into the background and not compete as strongly for the reader's attention. Primary information also tends to be larger than secondary information, again drawing the eye.

This idea translates directly into Web design. Frequently, Web sites feature brightly colored background images. These tend to distract the reader and compete with the text for attention. For an albeit exaggerated example of this, see [13]. Backgrounds running behind text should not be busy; they should be very subdued. Also, many sites incorporate large and colorful image maps into their designs. This can be useful if the information in the image itself is of importance, like the maps at MapQuest [6]. However, when the imagery in the picture is simply decorative or is so elaborate that it becomes difficult for a user to determine what is a clickable region and what is not, image maps can do more harm than good. They also increase download time significantly.

Image maps also have the drawback that they cannot be used properly by people with text-based browsers. Even people who by default turn off the downloading of images, due to the delays involved when surfing over slow modem connections, will be unable to use image maps until they specifically download the image. Many people feel that the visual impact of an image map outweighs these shortcomings. Still, these issues should be kept in mind when deciding if an image map is really needed. Often a similar effect can be achieved using regular images inside links, then arranging the images within a <TABLE> or a <PRE> block. When an image map *is* used, a set of equivalent plain text links should also be provided, if at all possible, for those who cannot use the image map directly.

At the same time, the visual appeal of a colorful image can be very effective when used to break up large bodies of text. Using images as headers and subheaders gives the eye a visual resting point, a place to pause while perusing a large grey mass of text. When using images this way, of course, it is even more important than ever to include an ALT string within the image so that people with nongraphical browsers will still have the very important header text available. Actually, every graphic should have an ALT string. Even a graphic that is pure decoration should have an empty ALT string to indicate that it serves no real purpose.

Of course, there are other ways to break up large bodies of text besides including in-line images. One thing that is frequently done by magazines and newspapers is to include a quote in the middle of a long article. Such a quote is generally set off from the text by horizontal rules and is frequently set in a larger type size. This is another good way to give the eye a rest. All sorts of things that break up the monotony of large expanses of text can help make a Web page easier to read.

Many of the Web magazines and newspapers use these techniques on a regular basis. A look through C|Net's News.com reveals many interesting techniques for breaking up large sections of text, such as using in-line images to create displayed quotes [4].

If You Can't Beat Them, Create a New Standard

In early 1994, frustrated with, among other things, the slow evolution of Web standards, Marc Andreessen left his position as one of the chief developers of

NCSA Mosaic to create his own company and his own browser: Netscape Navigator. Almost immediately, Netscape began to redefine HTML, adding many new extensions thought to be useful to Web designers. Many people took issue with Netscape's strategy, pointing out that proprietary extensions went against the model of a universal standard for information exchange. Nevertheless, the market had spoken. Netscape, with all of its nonstandard extensions, quickly became the most popular Web browsing software available. More extensions followed in rapid succession.

At the same time, the World Wide Web Consortium (W3C) continued to try and define standards for the Web that would allow information to be accessible to as broad a user base as possible. In May of 1996, the W3C announced HTML 3.2, a new official version of the Web's defining language [12]. This new standard incorporated many of the most popular HTML extensions, thereby giving developers and designers a more up-to-date baseline against which to judge their browsers and their pages. Many of these extensions (such as <FONT>, <CENTER>, and several new <IMG> attributes) are undeniably presentation driven.

Perhaps the most important and useful extension included in HTML 3.2 was the <TABLE> tag. Authors can now use these tables instead of preformatted blocks to lay out columns of information. Layout artists have long recognized the importance of organizing a layout around a grid. Horizontal and vertical "eye lines" help guide the reader around a page. These eye lines are seldom actual lines, however. They are formed from the edges of images and columns of text. Thus, aligning the edges of such design elements often increases the effectiveness of the design. HTML tables allow designers to create eye lines. Again, Web magazines and newspapers use this technique frequently [15]. And once again the Yale style manual [8] provides some thoughtful suggestions on the use of grids in Web design.[2]

Of course, a perfect grid arrangement where everything is exactly lined up can become boring easily. Therefore, designers will often "break" an eye line by placing an element across the line. This can be accomplished in HTML by creating an table cell with a COLSPAN or ROWSPAN value of two or more. Then, an image centered within this cell will straddle the eye line formed by the edges of the other cells in its column or row. Care must be taken, however, because an element which deviates only slightly from an eye line tends to be very distracting. When breaking an eye line, it's best if the element doing the breaking extends about an inch over each side of the line. Therefore, an image used in this manner should be large enough that the intent to break the line is clear. Otherwise, it will simply look like a sloppy line. When done properly, however, this technique of creating an eye line and then breaking it can be very effective.

Another common use of tables is to simulate the multicolumn layouts common in magazines and newspapers. Wide columns with narrow leading (between-line space) can be very difficult to read. The eye tends to skip lines or

---

[2] http://info.med.yale.edu/caim/manual/pages/design_grids.html

read lines multiple times. By using tables to create narrower columns, a designer can make large bodies of text much easier to read.

The <FONT> extension can also be used to help remedy this situation. Try including a space within a <FONT SIZE=+2>...</FONT> block on each line (or regularly enough that you can be assured that one will appear on each line when the text wraps). The larger space will act as a "hydraulic jack" and will pry the lines apart, thereby increasing their leading and making them easier to read [7].

Other HTML extensions are less commonly implemented and are somewhat more controversial. Even the more common tags such as tables are not implemented in many browsers. If you are not careful with your use of these extensions, you run the risk of making your page unreadable to people not using a Netscape-compatible browser. While some companies consider this to be a fair assumption when designing their corporate Web pages, it can reflect badly on them if they are targeting a broad audience. The conscientious designer will view her Web pages with two or three different browsers to ensure that her design displays nicely in the absence of any proprietary HTML extensions.

In another attempt to overcome the limitations of HTML, Adobe defined the PDF document format [1]. This is effectively a merger of HTML-style hypertext links with a language similar to Adobe's popular Postscript. As such, it provides much greater flexibility in design. Almost any layout is possible. However, the PDF format has yet to receive popular acceptance. Until more mainstream tools are written to take advantage of PDF, it seems HTML and its various extensions will continue to be the *lingua franca* of the Web.

5.4 Multimedia

As computers have become increasingly powerful, software designers have sought out new ways to take advantage of this power. The most pervasive of these has been multimedia. Playback and manipulation of digital sound and video are both very resource intensive and have only become practical in the last few years.

For these reasons, multimedia is still very much an experimental technology. When it is combined with the Web, another technology that is only slightly more stable, the results can be quite unpredictable.

The Bleeding Edge

Because multimedia is so new, standards are only now beginning to emerge. Moreover, the standards that do exist have a tendency to change frequently or to be completely usurped by new standards. Most multimedia software extensions are very proprietary in nature. As such, they are only available for platforms to which the software has been ported. While virtually all of the most popular

additions are available for both Macs and PCs, the Unix community is at a definite disadvantage due to the large variety of hardware on which Unix runs; only
a small subset of Unix machines ever see these multimedia ports.

Even the mainstream operating systems have problems with multimedia.
There are large numbers of older computers still in use today in both industry
and the private sector. Many of these machines simply cannot provide the processor power and storage space needed to support real-time audio and video.

Multimedia is also problematic because it is usually implemented via
browser extensions, which are called such things as "drop-ins," "plug-ins," etc. So
even if a user is browsing the Web using a powerful and supported machine, they
often have to download and install the extensions before the multimedia content
can be viewed. Many users find this to be a difficult process, though the leading
software developers have made certain inroads in simplifying the procedure.

Still, even if a user has managed to meet all these criteria, the act of
accessing the multimedia data is still quite daunting. Digitized sound and video
files are notoriously huge. Thirty seconds of video can easily take up several
megabytes of disk space. Audio is somewhat better, but the files are still quite
large. Given that the majority of Web surfers today access the net over low-speed
modem connections, download times are quite lengthy for files of this size. Many
users are simply unwilling to put up with the wait.

Proceed with Caution

Not all forms of multimedia share these problems in equal measure. For example, most animated GIFs are relatively small. Browsers that support them generally do so internally without the need for cumbersome extensions. And browsers
that don't support them can still display a single frame of the animation.

Even so, Web designers should exercise caution when using any form of
multimedia on their pages. In-line animations of any kind can be very distracting for the user. A constantly running GIF animation will tend to draw the
reader's eyes, pulling them away from the text and other meaningful content on
the page. Considering that most of these images are used more for decoration
than to convey meaningful information, it usually isn't a good idea for them to be
drawing that much attention to themselves, as was discussed by Tufte [14].
These animations really aren't much better than the hated Netscape <BLINK>
tag.

When dealing with large multimedia files included as links rather than
being in-line, some small and simple courtesies can make for a much happier
user community. In particular, one should always indicate the size of the multimedia data near the link to the actual file. This lets the user gauge the probable
download time and decide if it's really worth it. Other dimensions such as running time or, in the case of video, width and height of the image are also good
items to include. They give the user an idea of what it is they will be getting
before they take the time to download it.

The designer should strive to provide the user with the most information possible about a large download. In this way, the user can better judge if they want to take the time needed to retrieve it. One effective way of informing the user is to include a smaller version of the actual document in-line as part for the link. For audio, this may mean writing out any dialogue in the file or describing what sounds it contains. For video, this may be a frame or two from the film itself or a small animated GIF. Even for large still images, a smaller "thumbnail" image is often included so that the user doesn't have to spend time downloading a picture that is of no interest.

5.5 Conclusions

The Web is in many ways a radical new medium with a host of peculiar idiosyncrasies for designers to learn about and overcome. At the same time, it borrows from things that have come before, as all new things do. It does not stand alone, but rather it combines aspects of hypermedia, printed media, multimedia, and more within a new framework. That framework itself is still evolving, and it probably will continue to change for years to come. Such is the nature of new ideas.

All of these peculiarities make the Web a challenging place for today's graphic designers. It is often frustrating trying to hit such a rapidly moving target. It is just as often elating when a design finally comes together and everything clicks. Of course, the same extremes exist in all fields of design. And the Web is not the only medium that changes rapidly. Pick up an old book or magazine sometime and compare it with today's designs. Style, like the Web, is constantly evolving. You never master design because of this constant change. You can only master the techniques that allow you to change with it. It is a situation familiar to anyone working in a technological field.

To this end, there is perhaps one cardinal rule that underlies all the many different forms of media—a rule that has held true for hundreds of years. A good designer working in any arena must develop a skill for observation. You must learn to look critically at designs that other people create. When a particular design grabs your attention, you must examine it and figure out what it is that sets it apart from the rest. You must learn to adapt the things you see to fit your own design needs, to pick and choose from a tool box of design tricks that will grow constantly as you train yourself to notice these details. Look at magazines and newspapers. Look at Web sites and their HTML code. Look at cereal boxes and gum wrappers. Graphical designs surround you every day of your life. You must simply learn to see them.

5.6 References

[1]   Adobe Systems Inc. "Adobe Acrobat Overview."
       <http://www.adobe.com/prodindex/acrobat/> (9 Sept. 1997).

[2]   Berners-Lee, Tim. "The Original Proposal of the WWW," Mar. 1989.
       <http://www.w3.org/pub/WWW/History/1989/proposal.html> (22 Oct. 1996).

[3]   Connolly, Daniel W., *et al.* "HTML 2.0 Proposed Standard Materials," Nov.
       1995. <http://www.w3.org/pub/WWW/MarkUp/html-spec/> (22 Oct. 1996).

[4]   CNET Inc. "Rumor Mill." *News.com.*, Nov 1996.
       <http://www.news.com/Rumormill/Archives/rum11_08_96.html>
       (28 May 1997).

[5]   Edwards, D., and L. Hardman. "Lost in Hyperspace: Cognitive Mapping
       and Navigation in a Hypertext Environment." in *Hypertext: Theory into
       Practice*. Ed. Ray McAleese. Norwood, NJ: Ablex Pub. Co., 1989. pp. 105–
       125.

[6]   Geosystems Global Corp. "MapQuest." <http://www.mapquest.com/>
       (18 Nov. 1996).

[7]   Gillespie, Joe. "Web Page Design for Designers."
       <http://ds.dial.pipex.com/pixelp/wpdesign/wpdintro.htm> (18 Nov. 1996).

[8]   Lynch, Patrick J. and Sarah Horton. "Yale C/AIM Style Manual."
       <http://info.med.yale.edu/caim/manual/contents.html> (27 May 1997).

[9]   National Center for Supercomputing Applications, University of Illinois.
       "NCSA Mosaic Home Page."
       <http://www.ncsa.uiuc.edu/SDG/Software/Mosaic/> (27 May 1997).

[10]   Netscape Communications Corp. "Welcome to Netscape."
       <http://www.netscape.com/> (27 May 1997).

[11]   NeXT Software, Inc. "Welcome to NeXT Software Inc."
       <http://www.next.com/> (18 Nov. 1996).

[12]   Raggett, Dave, Daniel W. Connolly, *et al.* "Introducing HTML 3.2.," 1997
       <http://www.w3.org/pub/WWW/MarkUp/Wilbur/> (9 Sept. 1997).

[13]   Shirky, Clay. "B1FF#S K3WL H0M3 PAG3!!!"
       <http://www.panix.com/~clays/biff/> (28 May 1997).

[14]   Tufte, Edward R. *The Visual Display of Quantitative Information, 1983.*
       Cheshire, CT: Graphics Press, 1992.

[15] USA Today. "USA Today." <http://www.usatoday.com/> (18 Nov. 1996).

[16] Yahoo! Inc. "Yahoo." <http://www.yahoo.com/> (30 Sept. 1996).

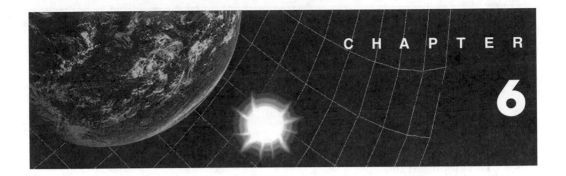

Web Applications

by Constantinos Phanouriou
(edited by Ashish Shah)

Latest surveys estimate that over 40 million individuals are currently using the Internet. Most organizations have either implemented or are planning to implement Internet-based applications or, as most commonly known, *Web applications*. This is an amazing rate of adoption, especially when one considers the short history of the Web. Enterprises are rushing to port their existing client/server applications to the Web environment, because of the universal accessibility of the Web. Web applications are also easy to deploy and maintain. They provide more control and flexibility over who can execute them, when, and where as compared to traditional applications.

This chapter explains the basics of Web applications and examines the advantages and disadvantages of accessing applications over the Web. We also introduce some existing tools that ease the development of Web applications and take a brief look at what the future has in store for this exciting technology.

Chapter Content

1. Introduction
2. Why Web Applications?

- Client/Server Computing
- Advantages
- Web Challenges

3. Application Development Paradigms

- HTML and CGI

- Java

- ActiveX

4. Development tools

- Javamatic

- WebObjects

- Castanet

5. A Look into the Future

- Distributed Objects

- Oracle's Network Computing Architecture

6. Conclusion
References

6.1 Introduction

"Imagine a computing environment where your word-processor software does not reside on your PC's hard disk. Instead, the executable code sits on a remote server. That server might be owned by your corporation or government agency, and might only be a short walk from your desk. Or the server could be owned by the developer of the word-processor software and might be physically located hundreds, even thousands of miles away. Imagine that the word-processor works equally well on your Intel-based PC or your Macintosh, is always the newest version, and costs the same regardless of the operating system. In a sense the network is the operating system, and your enterprise network is the part of the World-Wide that's behind your firewall." Vision propounded by Scott McNealy, CEO of Sun Microsystems

Web applications are client/server applications designed to be used by any authorized user, with a Web browser and an Internet connection. The application code usually resides on a remote Web server and the user interface is presented at the client's Web browser. Web applications are by nature, platform independent, and the client can be running software on any device connected to the Internet, such as a WebTV, high-end workstations, or even two-way pagers. These applications leverage off of the accessibility of the Web. In the Web environment, hundreds of thousands of distributed servers combine to behave like a single application server. This is made possible by introducing four new technologies on top of the existing Internet infrastructure [14]: graphical Web browsers [6], the HTTP RPC [9], HTML-tagged documents [19], and the URL global naming convention [20].

Initial efforts at creating Web applications were limited to simple applications such as clocks, scrolling banners, educational support tools, and games. With the introduction of new technologies, large commercial applications have started appearing on the Web. More and more companies are trying to make their enterprise's applications accessible over the Web.

In this chapter we examine how Web applications can change the fundamental client/server computing paradigm and provide a rich model for user interaction with applications. We also discuss the challenges faced in developing Web applications. After that, we present the current development paradigms for Web-accessible applications and describe some tools that ease application development and deployment. In the final section, we discuss the future of Web applications and describe a novel architecture proposed by Oracle Corp., for building large-scale, distributed, client/server applications.

6.2 Why Web Applications?

The best way to justify a new idea is to provide motivation for it; let's consider the following scenario: A researcher is trying a complex simulation on a high-end workstation in his company's laboratory. After a few hours of playing with input variables, the researcher decides to let the simulation run, and goes for a cup of coffee at the local cyber-cafe. While enjoying his coffee, the researcher discovers that one of the input variables was wrong. Usually, he would run back to the laboratory and fix it, but this time he remembers that the simulation is running as a Web application. Using one of computers at the cafe he is able to change the input variable and continue the simulation. Confident about his simulation, he decides to go home and rest. Later, using his home computer, he is able to monitor the progress of his simulation.

Web applications allow a user to interact with them over the Web. The user need not worry about installing, upgrading, or maintaining the application; most of the application overhead is absorbed by the server.

Client/Server Computing

Applications first appeared as mainframe-based monolithic applications. Users had to have access to the machine where the application resided and had to compete with others in sharing the machines resources (e.g., CPU time, memory). Client/server applications sliced these centralized monolithic applications into two halves [15]. The client typically provides the graphical interface, while the server provides access to shared resources, such as enterprise computing resources, databases and so on. Several technologies such as SQL databases, Transaction Processing Monitors (TP Monitors), and visual builder tools let you deploy your client/server applications more quickly. Unfortunately, such applications consist of two monoliths instead of one: one running on the client and another running on the server. Traditional client/server applications essentially remain difficult to build, manage, and extend. Web applications are based on the same model as client/server, but here the client and the server are not directly related. The client is a regular Web browser and can communicate with any server on the Internet.

The Web is attractive as an application platform for client/server applications because it eliminates the time and cost associated with application deployment. In the Web environment, deployment is instantaneous because the application resides on the Web server rather than the client. From the server, the application can be accessed from anywhere in the world, since the Web browser is the universal client.

Advantages

There are many advantages to using Web browsers as the application interface and the entire Web as an application server. The most important being wide accessibility. Traditional applications are typically limited to one user and one machine; Web applications leverage off of the accessibility of the Web and allow virtually everybody and everything to interact. Thus, collaborative work is now possible since many users can share a single program and its associated data. The hypertext model of the Web makes it simple for Web interfaces to contain embedded documentation and links to related material. This makes Web applications self-documenting.

Many users do not have the time to download an application and install it, to evaluate it or get the new version every time it is released. They prefer to stick with the older version even if the newer version offers more features. Web applications upgrade themselves transparently to the users. The developer can install a newer version, apply patches, or upgrade the application at the server and all the client users will immediately benefit from the changes without any effort on their part.

When developers design a new application or add a new feature to an existing application, they want to know how many users actually use it. With traditional applications, they can look at the sales figures and see how many people actually purchase the software. However, the sales figures do not tell them how many times each person uses the software. Web applications allow developers to know exactly how many times each application was used and for how long. Thus, Web applications enable open, low-cost deployment. Consumers also benefit from this, since they do not have to pay the full price if they just want to use an application only once.

As mentioned earlier, the executable code is on a remote server and the user interface is on the local client. Traditional applications were restricted to a single machine and if that machine was overloaded, the users had to wait for their application to execute. With Web applications the load can be distributed across multiple server transparently to the user, thus increasing throughput time.

Web applications solve the *fat client* problem. Fat clients, found in client/server computing, are characterized by ample resident memory, persistent storage, and high end multimedia and content creation capability. On the other hand, thin clients are characterized by minimum of resources, little persistent storage, and simple content creation. Fat clients are also relatively more expensive than thin clients. Web browsers are thin clients. Most of the resources used by the application reside on the server, the browser is only responsible for displaying the user interface.

Web Challenges

The Web, while providing significant benefits as a platform for large-scale, distributed applications, introduces new technical challenges. It lacks scalability, mission-critical services such as persistence and transactions, and security. As the Web evolves from a library of HTML documents to an electronic business platform for conducting secure transactions on the Internet, it needs to provide the rich services of the client/server world and provide robust, scalable, and reusable extensibility. The following are some of the main challenges faced by Web technology:

- Web applications can face unpredictable and potentially enormous peak loads. This demands a high performance architecture that is extremely scalable.

- The Web is a stateless environment, in which the client and server are loosely coupled. Applications must keep state information from one page to another if they are to avoid requiring users to re-enter information such as user name and password from page to page.

- The Web presents new security issues for companies wishing to make internal databases accessible to external users. User authorization and authentication are more challenging in the Web environment because of the large number of potential users.

- The Web is changing rapidly and standards are still evolving.

- Robust Web applications must provide reliable, secure, and stable processing under heavy demands.

Web applications must deal with all these challenges in order to be competitive with traditional applications. Most of the challenges mentioned above are due to rapid expansion of the Web. Although the technology is advancing at an equal rate, integrating it to the real world has been a slow process. Most people are not connected to the Internet, and those who are use low-end PC's and slow telephone lines. In time, Internet connections will become faster and more reliable, Web standards will be robust and proven, and security issues will be resolved.

6.3 Application Development Paradigms

The Web has become the largest source of information. Anyone with an Internet connection and a Web browser can access any information he or she wants. Most Web browsers provide access to different types of media such as text, image, audio, video, and 3D models (VRML). With the integration of all these media, the functionality of Web pages has been greatly enhanced.

To recap, Web applications are platform-independent, client/server applications. The application code usually resides on a remote Web server and the user interface is presented in the client's Web browser. In this section, we will look at the various paradigms currently used for development of Web applications.

HTML and CGI

The Web started out as a collection of hypertext documents, containing images and text, and interlinked in a variety of ways. The first large-scale, distributed application of network computing was surfing the Web. In late 1993, the Mosaic Web browser came out as the first client/server application environment on top of the Internet. It supported HTML pages. However, HTML pages are static and user interaction is very limited, even when enhanced with all the different media.

Although this environment is great for presenting information, it is not suited for running applications where user interaction is need. The addition of HTML forms and the Common Gateway Interface (CGI) [7] server protocol in 1995 provided support for slightly more interactive applications but was limited to form-filling. This simple interaction model is sufficient for products such as online questionnaires, database queries, or simple data collection, but does not scale up for large dynamic applications. CGI applications constitute the major chunk of Web applications that have been deployed. Chapter 7 covers the CGI protocol and CGI application development in detail.

The Web is a stateless environment, in which the client and server are loosely coupled. Applications must keep state information from one page to another if they are to avoid requiring users to re-enter information such as user name and password from page to page. HTTP Cookies [8] are a general mechanism which server side connections (such as CGI scripts) can use to both store and retrieve information on the client side of the connection. The addition of a simple, persistent, client-side state significantly extended the capabilities of Web-based client/server applications and enabled a host of new types of applications to be written for Web-based environments. Shopping applications can store information about the currently selected items and free the client from retyping a userID on every Web page. Sites can store per-user preferences on the client and have the client supply those preferences every time that site is connected.

Java

In "The Java Language: A White Paper," [17] Sun describes Java as follows:

"Java: A simple, object-oriented, distributed, interpreted, robust, secure, architecture neutral, portable, high-performance, multi-threaded, and dynamic language."

Java [18], starting out as an Internet programming language, has quickly transformed itself into a novel computing platform that provides benefits for developers as well as users. Java is very well suited for programming applications for a heterogeneous, distributed computing environment such as the Internet, because of its architecture neutrality. Also, Java programs can be dynamically downloaded from the Net and run without any setup or installation. The Java revolution started off with Java applets. Applets are small Java programs that can be embedded in a Web page; the program code is dynamically downloaded while loading the HTML page and is executed by the Java interpreter built into the Web browser.

Java applets provide a much better user interface than is possible with HTML forms. Java's Abstract Windowing Toolkit (AWT) allows programmers to design full-fledged graphical user interfaces (GUIs) that provide better control to the user in terms of interaction among the interface elements, and it enables the development of better, more intuitive user interfaces. Naturally, Java provides a good choice for creating interactive Web applications with nice user interfaces. Yet that's not the only reason Java is becoming more and more popular for programming Web applications. Java has many features that ease the development of distributed client/server applications, such as a predefined classes for network communications, a client/server method invocation paradigm, a mechanism for accessing SQL databases, and many more. Thus, Java is fast becoming the platform of choice for developing dynamic Web applications that can convert the Web browser into a truly interactive application environment.

Chapter 8 provides an introduction to the Java platform and its capabilities. Chapter 9 discusses Java in terms of the capabilities it provides for programming distributed client/server applications and for developing software components that can plug-and-play over the Web in a transparent manner.

ActiveX

ActiveX [4] controls are reusable software components developed by software vendors. These controls can be used to quickly add specialized functionality to Web sites, desktop applications, and development tools. For example, a stock ticker control can be used to add a live stock ticker to a Web page, or an animation control can be used to add animation features. ActiveX controls are not platform-independent by nature, as they rely on the presence of Microsoft's Common Object Model (COM) as the underlying software framework. Thus, Web pages that embed ActiveX controls can only be viewed with browsers running on the MS Windows platform.

6.4 Development Tools

The Web is a compelling platform for database-driven, interactive applications. It is platform independent, provides instant global access, and significantly lowers deployment and training costs. In search of these benefits, many organizations are building Web applications or moving existing client/server applications to the Web.

Until recently, there were few organizations building commercial Web applications because of the lack of development tools. Applications had to be custom coded in PERL or C++. As tools that lower the cost of application development and maintenance mature, organizations are increasingly turning to the Web as a platform for commercial applications.

The Internet and the private Intranets are slowly emerging as the new platform for software. Unlike the generation of applications and content developed for stand-alone personal computers, Web applications take advantage of the Internet's connectivity. This means much more than HTML pages on the Web. With the Internet as the platform, applications can be deployed dramatically faster and more easily. And, those applications can be tailored for each individual customer, utilizing the two-way communications of the Internet. Companies can develop specifically for the Internet, much as they develop for specific stand-alone hardware/software environments today.

We will now look at some of the tools available for developing Web applications. Note that these are not the only tools available; there are a host of other development environments available for Web applications.

Javamatic

Javamatic is a tool for adding a Web-based interface to a command-line driven system [16]. Javamatic automatically generates a graphical user interface from a high-level description of the application which is User Interface (UI) independent, combined with a set of UI mapping rules. It then invokes commands in the legacy system transparently to the user. The application is wrapped with an interface server; thus multiple clients can use the application through the Web.

Javamatic was originally written to reduce the time spent to design, develop, and maintain interface code in Chitra, a statistical system used to visualize, statistically analyze, and model traces of data. Chitra is composed of several small commands which are command-line driven. Every time a new command was added to the system, the interface had to be manually updated. This caused the interface to be inconsistent and difficult to maintain. Also, Chitra only runs on a UNIX system and requires a high-end workstation to operate efficiently. Javamatic reduces the time needed to update the interface and makes the system widely accessible to any user with a Java-capable Web browser.

WebObjects

WebObjects [1] is a tool designed to help corporations develop dynamic, server-based applications for the Web. These dynamic applications can be deployed on a private Intranet or to the global Internet. WebObjects was originally developed by NeXT Computer, Inc., which is now a part of Apple Computers, Inc.

WebObjects is designed to preserve investments in existing computing resources. Using WebObjects, Web applications can be easily integrated with legacy technology and data spanning the entire computing environment, from the desktop to the mainframe. WebObjects is also an open technology, supporting all major Web standards, browsers, HTTP servers, and scripting languages, with the ability to embrace new technologies as they evolve.

Castanet

Castanet is a collection of tools and technologies for easier and more efficient deployment of rich content and applications within an Intranet or across the Internet. Castanet was developed by Marimba [3], a company founded in February 1996 by four key members of Sun Microsystems' original Java development team.

A Castanet channel, which is an application with its data, is automatically distributed and installed like a Java applet but appears to users more like an application. Each channel can create persistent data, such as documents and preferences, and can communicate data, such as usage patterns, back to its server. All these make it possible to deliver personalized applications and content to each individual client. Castanet mirrors the channel software on the client machine; thus applications operate as quickly and reliably as conventional applications. "Since any change made to an application can be immediately delivered to every desktop, developers can continually modify and enhance their applications—without worrying how to install new versions on users' computers. We designed Castanet to be able to simultaneously deploy application and content updates to millions of users worldwide—surpassing the capabilities of traditional systems and application management tools," stated Kim Polese, Marimba's president.

Marimba's Castanet suite includes a Tuner, a Transmitter, a Proxy, and a Repeater. The Castanet Transmitter (server) is responsible for distributing and maintaining channels to Castanet Tuners (clients). Each channel can be personalized through a Plug-In API. The Castanet Transmitter and Castanet Tuner work together to keep software and content always up-to-date. The Proxy and the Repeater are used to improve the performance and transmission capacity of the system, respectively. Marimba has also developed Bongo, a visual tool that makes it easy to design and implement GUIs for Java applications and create channels for distribution and maintenance by Castanet.

6.5 A Look into the Future

The Web is rapidly becoming the platform of choice for deploying enterprise computing applications, both on the public Internet and on the vast numbers of private intranets. Within this relatively new domain, many technologies are competing for providing the infrastructure for building large-scale, distributed, client/server applications. Some of these technologies exist as standards, some come from research in academic fields, and some come from individual vendors. These include HTTP/HTML, Java/JavaScript, CORBA/IIOP, DCOM/ActiveX, and others. Each of these technologies provides new capabilities to the developer and the user and offers unique possibilities for enhancing development productivity. What is needed, however, is an infrastructure that leverages the best of each environment with relatively little compromise, and preserves the enterprise's investment in existing client/server technology.

In this section, we will briefly look at a technology that can form the basis of such an infrastructure, and also consider a single approach based on this technology.

Distributed Objects

Object technology has gained wide-spread popularity as the correct approach to developing complex enterprise applications. Object-oriented applications are easy to develop, maintain, and extend. Object technology speeds application development and cuts down development costs. In classical object-oriented applications, objects are confined to a single program running on a single machine. In contrast, distributed objects are intelligent software components that are location- and implementation-independent, and can interoperate with each other as effectively as objects bound to a single machine.

Distributed objects can serve as the building blocks for the next generation of client/server systems. Distributed object technology is extremely well suited for creating flexible client/server systems because the data and business logic are encapsulated within objects, allowing them to be located anywhere within a distributed system. Distributed objects have the potential to allow software to plug-and-play, interoperate across networks, run on different platforms, coexist with legacy applications through object wrappers, roam on networks, and manage themselves and the resources they control [14]. Chapter 9 discusses distributed object technology in detail and describes how it can be used to build enterprise client/server systems that are Web-accessible. The next subsection describes a vendor's solution to using distributed objects for creating an infrastructure for such systems.

Oracle's Network Computing Architecture

The Network Computing Architecture (NCA) [13], created by Oracle Corp. [12], is an extensible, network-based architecture that provides a way to integrate client/server computing with the Internet using distributed object architectures. Oracle created the NCA with the assumption that no single technology is sufficient for providing all the tools needed to build large-scale Web-accessible applications. The needs can be met by a combination of the best new and existing technologies.

The Network Computing Architecture is implemented on top of the industry standard CORBA/IIOP environment. CORBA stands for Common Object Request Broker Architecture. It is a set of specifications defined by a consortium of over 600 companies called the Object Management Group (OMG). CORBA defines the architecture for a software bus that acts as a client/server middleware on which object components written by different vendors can interoperate across networks and operating systems. The main component of the CORBA environment is the ORB (Object Request Broker) which basically forms the object bus. The ORB enables transparent communication between local and remote objects. There are many commercially available ORBs on the market today from companies such as IONA, Sun, HP, IBM, Expersoft and Visigenic. While the ORB provides for communication between distributed object-oriented client/server applications, IIOP provides for communication between different ORBs. IIOP stands for Internet Inter-ORB Protocol. IIOP is based on TCP/IP and serves as the backbone for Object Request Brokers to communicate with each other.

According to the NCA whitepaper [11], the critical elements behind the Network Computing Architecture are:

- **Pluggable components (objects) called cartridges.** Cartridges are containers for objects that are independent of implementation language, operating platform, object models and APIs. Cartridges can be developed at all three tiers of development: client, server, and database. Cartridges can obtain standard services such as invocation, security, registration, and so on, by accessing Universal Cartridge Services. Additional cartridge services such as transactions, messaging and queuing, and database access can be obtained through Scalable Cartridge Services and Specialized Cartridge Services.

- **Inter-component communication** through a software bus called Inter-Cartridge Exchange (ICX). Cartridges access other cartridges, clients, application servers, and cartridge services through ICX. ICX uses both IIOP and HTTP protocols for communication, making the required translations between environments. ICX provides integration with Java (through Java IDL and JDBC), ActiveX/COM clients, and with legacy systems.

- **Extensible clients, applications servers and database servers.** The NCA supports a wide range of clients such as Netscape's ONE (Open Network Environment) client, ActiveX clients, HTML and Java clients, and even the Network Computer. It can also incorporate any new client through appropriate interfaces. This allows developers to used their choice of Java/JavaScript, C/C++, Visual Basic, and SQL-based languages to create cartridges.

- **Integrated development and management of cartridges**.

The Network Computing Architecture insulates both developers and businesses from the risks associated with rapidly evolving technology by providing a unifying, standards-based architecture for client/server, the Web, and distributed objects. Support for key open and de facto standards guarantees that developers can use clients of their choice, a language that suits the application, and an appropriate programming model for rapid deployment.

We are not saying that this is the only architecture available or possible, but it surely is representative of future distributed computing architectures.

6.6 Conclusion

Web-based Internet applications are possible today and are quickly evolving to become an important part of today's software market. A competitive and open software and hardware marketplace is driving companies to make improvements in the technology to enhance the range of what it can do and how easily Web applications can be managed and deployed.

As the Internet continues to mature, Web sites are acquiring better application development tools, middleware products for connecting to legacy systems, and system management tools. These new tools will allow support for research-based and innovative systems without sacrificing control. Improved security and administration tools will ensure that users are authorized to access the information they seek. Information management tools will also provide integrated search technology to search across distributed servers.

6.7 References

[1]   Apple Computer, Inc. "WebObjects." <http://software.apple.com/webobjects/> (9 Sept. 1997).

[2]   Gosling, J., B. Joy, and G. Steele. *The Java Language Specification*. Reading, MA: Addison-Wesley, Aug. 1996.

[3]   Marimba Inc. "Marimba Home Page." <http://www.marimba.com/> (9 Sept. 1997).

[4]   Microsoft Corporation. "ActiveX." 1997. <http://www.microsoft.com/activex/> (9 Sept. 1997).

[5]   Network Computer Inc. "NC." <http://www.nc.com/> (9 Sept. 1997).

[6]   National Center for Supercomputing Applications. "NCSA Mosaic." <http://www.ncsa.uiuc.edu/SDG/Software/Mosaic/> (9 Sept. 1997).

[7]   National Center for Supercomputing Applications. "The Common Gateway Interface (CGI)." <http://hoohoo.ncsa.uiuc.edu/cgi/> (9 Sept. 1997).

[8]   Netscape Communications Corporation. "HTTP Cookies." <http://home.netscape.com/newsref/std/cookie_spec.html> (9 Sept. 1997).

[9]   Network Working Group. "Hypertext Transfer Protocol." <http://ds.internic.net/rfc/rfc1945.txt> (9 Sept. 1997).

[10] Object Management Group. "OMG Home Page." <http://www.omg.org/> (9 Sept. 1997).

[11] Oracle Corporation. "Network Computing Architecture: An Oracle White Paper." June 1997. <http://tiburon.us.oracle.com/odp/public/spotlite/nca/info/ncatwp.pdf> (9 Sept. 1997).

[12] Oracle Corporation. "Oracle Home Page." <http://www.oracle.com/> (9 Sept. 1997).

[13] Oracle Corporation. "Network Computing Architecture." <http://www.oracle.com/nca/> (9 Sept. 1997).

[14] Orfali, R., D. Harkey, and J. Edwards. *The Essential Distributed Objects Survival Guide*. New York: Wiley, 1996.

[15] ——. *The Essential Client/Server Survival Guide*. New York: Wiley, 1996.

[16] Phanouriou, C., and M. Abrams. "Transforming Command-Line Driven Systems to Web Applications." in *Proc. Sixth Intl. World Wide Web Conf.*, 1997. <http://proceedings.www6conf.org/HyperNews/get/PAPER41.html> (9 Sept. 1997).

[17] Sun Microsystems. "The Java Language: An Overview." <http://www.javasoft.com/doc/Overviews/java/java-overview-1.html> (9 Sept. 1997).

[18] Sun Microsystems. "Java Home Page." <http://www.javasoft.com/> (9 Sept. 1997).

[19] World Wide Web Consortium. "HyperText Markup Language." <http://www.w3.org/pub/WWW/MarkUp/> (9 Sept. 1997).

[20] World Wide Web Consortium. "Web Naming and Addressing Overview." <http://www.w3.org/pub/WWW/Addressing/> (9 Sept. 1997).

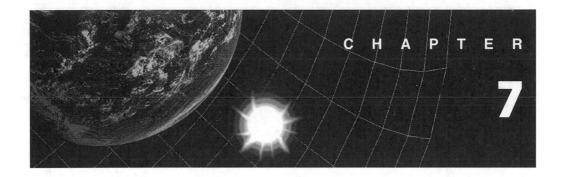

Common Gateway Interface

by J. Patrick Van Metre
(edited by Ashish Shah)

The Common Gateway Interface (CGI) is an interface specification that lets HTTP servers run other programs on the server machine in a platform-independent manner. It provides a way for passing parameters to those programs and getting output from them. The CGI is a major driving force behind many of the interactive features on Web pages. Programs executed in this manner using CGI are commonly referred to as CGI scripts or CGI applications. Many Web sites use CGI scripts for dynamic Web page creation, for parsing forms, for sending e-mail, for building on-the-fly page counters, and for providing a Web-based interface to other applications, such as databases.

Issues that one must consider when using CGI to expand a Web site, include the following: the language used to create the CGI applications; whether or not the applications should be compiled or interpreted; the required performance of the CGI applications and how it will affect the server; and the portability of the applications, should a new server or operating system be chosen for the site. We will discuss these issues, explain the process of creating CGI applications, and present some examples in this chapter. We will also take a brief look at the new FastCGI protocol.

Chapter Content

1. Introduction
2. Creating CGI Applications

- Output from a CGI Applications
- Handling Input
- Side Effects
- Making CGI Applications Accessible

3. Issues

- Security
- Language
- Performance

4. Examples

- Date and Time
- Finger Gateway
- Access Counter

5. References

7.1 Introduction

The Common Gateway Interface (CGI) is a simple interface that lets Web servers run other programs and incorporate their output, whether it be text, image, or audio, into the output sent back to the Web browser client. This interface makes it possible to run programs on a Web server in a platform-independent manner, and is a major driving force behind interactivity on the Web. The programs executed in this manner using the CGI interface are commonly referred to as CGI scripts or CGI applications. Many Web sites use CGI scripts for dynamic Web page creation, for parsing forms, for sending e-mail, for building on-the-fly page counters, and for providing a Web-based interface to other applications, such as databases.

HTML forms allow users to enter data for processing. This data can also be used to create dynamic HTML documents on the fly. The information entered by the user is collected by the browser and sent to the Web server specified in the HTML form. When the server receives the request to process the user data, it starts a CGI program, also specified in the HTML form, that can process the collected information.

A Web server has a set of legal URLs that it makes available to Web clients. Every legal URL that a server provides corresponds to a file on that server. Normally, those files are images, HTML files, or other static documents. When a server is asked to supply such a static document, it simply returns the document's contents. However, when a Web client asks for a URL that points to a CGI application, or when a user submits an HTML form, the following things happen:

1. **The Web client (e.g., browser) sends a request to the HTTP server.** This request gives the name and location of the CGI application and provides parameters to the application.

2. **The HTTP server starts the application.** The server passes the parameters sent by the client to the program. It also provides some extra environment and transaction information to the CGI application.

3. **When the CGI application terminates, all output produced by the application is returned to the client.** Some additional information is added by the Web server to the HTTP header produced by the CGI before the output is returned.

The client treats the output from the CGI application the same as it would if the data had come from a static file. So, if a CGI script produces HTML, it will appear as a normal HTML page in the browser. A CGI application isn't limited to creating HTML pages. It can produce any type of data, including images and sound files. These three steps are discussed in more detail in the next section.

CGI applications can be written to perform other actions on the server in addition to producing HTML pages. A CGI application can act as a gateway to other applications on the Web server, hence the name. For example, there are many telephone directory services available on the Web; these services maintain large databases that contain publicly listed names, addresses, and telephone numbers. Users can access the information in these databases over the Web through a CGI forms-based front-end. When a user asks for information on a person, the client browser sends a query to a CGI application on the HTTP server. This application acts as a gateway to the database and generates a Web page containing the information requested in the query.

Sometimes, however, the output from a CGI application is secondary to the application's side effects (see the section on "Side Effects" on page 119).

7.2 Creating CGI Applications

There are many things that one must consider when designing CGI applications. This section covers the basic requirements for creating such applications, including the input and output needed to make a CGI script work, and how side effects can be used to an advantage. Section 7.3 discusses some more general issues which are important to creating effective CGI applications.

A CGI program can be written in any programming language; however, the most popular languages are Perl and C. Since a CGI program is an executable, it is basically the equivalent of letting anyone run a program on your machine, which may be a security risk depending on how the program functions. CGI programs are generally required to be put in a special directory which is under the direct control of the Webmaster, prohibiting the casual user from creating CGI programs. Other ways to allow access to CGI scripts are mentioned in the section on "Making CGI Applications Accessible" on page 120.

A CGI program is an external program being invoked by the Web server, and the interface across which the Web server and the CGI program communicate is the Common Gateway Interface. Thus a CGI program is like any other executable program, except that it has to confirm to the CGI specification for input and output. We describe this input-and-output interface in the next two sections.

Output from a CGI Application

The output from a CGI application contains two sections: the header and the body. The header is always the first output that a CGI-app generates. A blank line immediately follows the header information, and the body follows this blank line. Usually, the header includes information about the data contained in the body. Generally, writing output from the application is just a matter of writing to the standard output stream defined by the programming language (e.g., stdout in C).

Header Output

Usually, a CGI application doesn't need to produce much header information. When a Web server returns a static or dynamic object to a client, it includes information about the object in the header. This information could be the date of object creation, time of last modification, the type of encoding used for the object, etc. [10]. Such information is provided to the client by the server whether or not the page is created by a CGI application. If it is, then this information is merged with the header information that the application produces. There are three main pieces of information that a CGI application can include in its header.

Content type: This describes the type of data contained in the body that the CGI application generates. This must always be included in the header. If this information isn't included, then the Web client that receives the output from the application will not know what it is, and how to handle it.

The content type of a document should be a valid MIME type/subtype combination, and it should correspond with the type of data within that document. For example, if a CGI application produces an HTML document, it should have the MIME type/subtype combination of **text/html**. Table 7–1 contains examples of document types and their associated MIME type/subtype combinations.

Table 7–1 Some MIME Types

Document Type	MIME type/subtype
HTML	text/html
ASCII text	text/plain
GIF image	image/gif
QuickTime movie	video/quicktime

The content type should appear in the header output on a single line as follows:

```
Content-type: type/subtype
```

where `type/subtype` is the MIME type/subtype combination for the data contained in the output body.

Location: This gives an alternate location for the client to access. How this location is used is up to the client. This location should appear in the CGI header output on a single line as follows:

```
Location: URL
```

where `URL` is the alternate location.

Status: This returns a status code to the Web client, as described in "Status codes in HTTP" [11]. This should appear in the CGI header output on a single line as follows:

```
Status: XXX Message
```

where `XXX` is a three-digit status code and `Message` is a message string.

Body

The body of the application output follows the blank line which separates it from the header. The body contains all of the data which is to be displayed by the Web client. If the content type specified by the header is **text/html**, then the body should contain the HTML code that the CGI application generates. If a CGI-app generates a GIF image, then the body of the output should contain the bytes that make up a valid GIF image.

Handling Input

When a client requests the URL corresponding to a CGI application, the server will execute it in real-time. The client can provide input to the application in a variety of ways. There are three important ways to send input from a client to a CGI application:

1. Through a query string
2. Through the command line
3. Through standard input

Query String

A Web client can send a **query** to a CGI application by appending a "?" followed by a query string to the URL for the CGI application. This query string is composed of name-value pairs in the form of *name=value*, where *name* is the name of a variable and *value* is the value assigned to it. Each name-value pair in the query string is separated by an "&". The query string is sent to the CGI application through the environment variable QUERY_STRING. It is the responsibility of the CGI application to decode the query string and extract the name-value pairs.

The most common way to send a query string to a CGI application is by setting up an HTML form that uses the HTTP GET method [12]. Each input field in the form that can take on a value is given a unique name. When the form is filled out by a user, the user's Web client sends back the names of the items and the entered values in the form of a query string. The CGI application to which the client sends this information can then dissect the query string to find the information provided by the client.

Since the query is appended to the URL for the CGI application, it is "URL encoded" and must be decoded. There are some characters that have special meaning in a URL, such as the colon (":") and forward slash ("/"). Some characters are not allowed to appear in URLs at all, such as spaces. For this reason, URLs are encoded in a special way. All spaces are replaced by a plus sign ("+"), and all special characters are replaced by *%xx*, where *xx* is the hexadecimal representation of the ASCII value for the character. All URL encoded strings must be decoded before they can be used properly.

Command-Line Parameters

Passing parameters to a program on the command line is an easy way to provide information to an application. This method, however, is rarely used for CGI applications. It is useful, though, when an author of a CGI application wants to pass a single parameter to the application without having to parse a query string. This method was originally designed for use with the ISINDEX tag [1], but it may be used in other ways.

Let's say that there is a server called "www.nowhere.com", and on that server in a directory called "cgi-bin" exists a CGI application called "foo.cgi". This application may be accessed through the following URL:

```
http://www.nowhere.com/cgi-bin/foo.cgi
```

If we send a query to this CGI application with no equals sign ("=") in the query string, then the query string is passed to the CGI application through the command line. If an equals sign is present in the query string after the question mark ("?") (see the section on "Query String" on page 118), then the entire query string is provided through the QUERY_STRING environment variable. So, if the following URL were accessed:

```
http://www.nowhere.com/cgi-bin/foo.cgi?chicken
```

then the string "chicken" would be the first parameter passed to foo.cgi when the server started its execution. If the following URL were accessed:

```
http://www.nowhere.com/cgi-bin/foo.cgi?yummy=chicken
```

then the string "yummy=chicken" would be placed in the QUERY_STRING environment variable; foo.cgi should ignore anything in the list of command-line parameters passed to it upon execution.

Standard Input

Information is only given to a CGI application through standard input when the CGI is accessed with either the **POST** or **PUT** methods [12]. The body of the POST or PUT request, sent by the client to the server, is used as the standard input to the CGI application. The information in the body transferred by the POST method is also URL encoded.

For example, if a user fills out an HTML form, the Web client can send the user's form data to a CGI application using the POST method. The CGI application which receives this data will have the form information provided to it through standard input. In fact, the format of the information will be the same as if it were provided in the QUERY_STRING environment variable via the GET method.

Side Effects

In programming context, "a **side effect** of a function... occurs when a function changes either one of its parameters or a global variable" [8]. In some cases, such a modification may not be a desirable occurrence, but there are many situations where global information may need to be modified, especially on a Web server. In fact, such "side effects" may be desirable and may be the main purpose of a CGI application.

Whenever a Web server uses the Common Gateway Interface to allow people to access the contents of a database, the server makes that database information global. In one sense, a CGI application is essentially a function; it takes input and produces output. If a CGI application that is acting as a gateway to a database modifies the data within that database, then this is technically a side effect to the CGI application; it is acting as a function that has modified global variables. Whenever another user accesses the modified information, they will see the changes made by the other CGI application. This is the intended function of the application, but it is technically a side effect.

Most Web servers are capable of serving more than one request at a time; that is, a server can operate with some concurrency. This can cause problems when designing CGI applications that modify a global information space. For more information on concurrency issues, consult an Operating Systems text [2].

Making CGI Applications Accessible

When a CGI application is ready to be made available to users, it must be stored in a special directory that can be accessed by the Web server running on the host machine. This way, when a user tries to access the URL that points to that CGI application, the server will have the ability to execute it. The server must, however, know that the file to which the user's URL points is a CGI application and not a static document, such as a text or HTML file. There are usually two ways of accomplishing this:

- **Store the CGI application in a place that is used solely for CGI programs**

    Usually, Web servers have certain directories into which only CGI applications are placed. Depending upon how the server is configured, it may be necessary to have administrative access to place CGI applications into these directories.

    If your Web site uses a version on the NCSA HTTPd server, there will be a /cgi-bin directory accessible from the server's document root directory. This is the special directory mentioned above where all CGI applications reside.

- **Add a certain extension to the CGI application file name**

    If the file name for a CGI application ends with an extension that lets the server know that the file is a CGI application, then the server will execute it instead of trying to return it as a static document. This file name extension mapping has to be defined by the Webmaster in the server's configuration files.

7.3 Issues

In this section we will discuss some important issues related to developing CGI applications, such as server security, choice of programming language, and application response time. We will also introduce the new FastCGI protocol, which can be used to boost application performance.

Security

Malicious Attacks

A server program that can access the host computer's data resources can provide potential security leaks. If a server provides read-only access to a set of documents, there is a possibility that documents may be read by people for whom they are not intended. If a server provides write access, then the computer is subject to many more security threats. But it is when a server provides the ability to run programs on the host computer that the worst consequences can arise, unless the server is adequately protected.

Read access: The main purpose of a Web server is to provide the world with the ability to read certain documents. The server must be set up properly, so that it prevents anyone from reading files that were not meant to be accessible, such as system configuration files or password files. If we assume that this is the case, then there are really only two ways to limit access to the public documents: through server controls, and through CGI application-based authorization.

Most Web servers are designed to allow Webmasters to restrict access to the documents that the system provides. For example, a server may grant read access only to client requests coming from within a certain Internet domain. Or, a server may only grant read access only to users who authenticate themselves (see also Chapter 12). CGI authorization relies on some means of authentication, and is discussed in the section on "Authentication and CGI Applications" on page 123.

Write access: Some Web servers allow clients to write directly to the document space that the server makes available. This allows a great deal of flexibility, yet provides the potential for some sticky security problems. Write access is provided by servers in the form of the PUT and DELETE methods of HTTP/1.1, and the multipart/form-data encoding type, which allows file uploads from a Web form [4].

It is up to the server to ensure that no one is allowed to maliciously alter the document space using the PUT and DELETE methods. But it is also up to the server administrator to ensure that any files uploaded to the host machine are appropriate and that they don't contain any viruses. The use of forms for file uploading requires the use of a CGI application to process the completed form that is POSTed to the server. This CGI application can take the responsibility of placing any uploaded documents in a safe place until they can be reviewed, or can automatically perform virus checking on the documents. In this way, CGI applications can provide some safeguards against attacks while still providing flexibility to users.

Execute access: The greatest potential for security problems occurs when a server allows users to execute programs on the host computer. Consider this: a person can't get a virus from reading an e-mail message (reading a message only involves viewing text characters), but if a person executes a program attached to an e-mail message, and that program has a virus, then the person's system will probably become infected by the virus. The virus can only spread when part of it is being executed by the computer.

When a CGI application is used as a gateway to another application, it will often make system calls—that is, it will execute other programs on the host system. Frequently, the application will pass parameters in these system calls, and the information provided in these parameters may come from a query string sent by a Web client. If a user designs a clever query string, and the CGI application can not sense what the user is doing, it is possible for a user to gain the ability to issue commands on the host system as if logged onto the system. Sometimes, servers will execute CGI applications with administrative access privileges, which may give the intrusive user full control over the system!

A common illustration of this potential security hole is a "finger" gateway. The "finger" utility is a way of finding out a little bit of information about users of a system—information that the users provide about themselves to the public. For example, if one were to issue the command "finger vanmetre@csgrad.cs.vt.edu" on a Unix or similar system, one could find out some more about the author of this section. Common "finger gateways" are CGI applications that accept a user name as a query string from a Web client, perform a system call to the finger utility, and return the results to the client. So, if a client were to access a CGI application called finger.cgi with the URL

```
http://www.nowhere.com/cgi-bin/finger.cgi?vanmetre
```

the CGI-app would issue the system command

```
finger vanmetre
```

and return the results to the Web client. Now suppose a user submit the URL

```
http://www.nowhere.com/cgi-bin/finger.cgi?vanmetre;rm+-rf+%2F
```

After the CGI decodes this, it will issue the system command

```
finger vanmetre;rm -rf /
```

If the CGI-app was executed with full system privileges, this will not only return the finger information for user vanmetre, but it will also erase the contents of the hard drives on the system! Even if the CGI-app was not executed with full privileges, a user could create a query string that could mail off a password file, open a remote telnet connection, or do something else that would aid a break-in to the system. More information on secure CGI scripting can be obtained from Lincoln Stein's *WWW Security FAQ* [9].

Authentication and CGI Applications

There are two important steps to maintaining a certain level of security within a Web site: authentication and authorization. Authentication is how a server identifies users and makes sure that they really are who they say they are (see Chapter 12). Authorization is the process of determining to which documents an authenticated user has access.

Often, in the context of the Web, authentication is provided by a simple name/password combination. When a user enters a protected site, the server asks the user's Web client for authentication. The Web client then asks the user for a name/password combination, which is then sent back to the server. If the combination is a valid one, the user is authenticated, and can then be authorized to access the documents from the server. Each time the authenticated user makes a request for a protected document, the name/password combination is resubmitted by the client to the server.

Servers can also provide authorization protection for specific documents or for sets of documents within the server document space. For example, all of the contents of a directory on a server can be assigned a list of authorized users, who must properly be authenticated before they can access the directory; all users who fail authentication will be denied access.

To provide a bit more flexibility with document control, authorization can be left up to a CGI application. When an authenticated user accesses a CGI application, an environment variable is set which provides the name of the user to the application; the application can decide whether or not to provide access to the user. In addition, a CGI application that generates complex Web pages can present different pages to different users, as long as they are authenticated. A Web site can keep a list of preferences or configuration details for each user and apply these preferences to the page-generation methods of the site.

Language

There are many points to consider when choosing a language to use for developing CGI applications. Here is a list of the important ones:

Interpreted vs. Compiled: There are many interpreted languages, such as PERL, that have become popular among CGI application developers, and some compiled languages, including C, are popular, too. There are advantages and disadvantages to both; these must be considered before developing CGI applications.

Programs written in compiled languages generally run faster than equivalent programs written in interpreted languages. However, interpreted languages can be more flexible and can make prototyping much easier. If any changes need to be made to a CGI application, they can be made to an interpreted version much more quickly than to a compiled version, because the compiled version must be recompiled before the changes can take effect. Once a CGI application is in place, though, a user may not see much of a difference between an interpreted application and its compiled equivalent.

Portability/Modifiability: When developers choose a language to use for a CGI application, they must always think of the long term. They must consider how the site will operate in several years to make sure that the CGI application will not only meet the needs of the site today, but also in the future. The Web is changing extremely rapidly, so it is often difficult to keep the future in perspective.

The needs of a Web site are always changing. As server technology advances, it is likely that a site will undergo some hardware and/or software modifications, while the contents of the site must stay the same. To make such transitions as smooth as possible, one must consider the portability and modifiability of CGI applications. If a language is chosen for a site that uses proprietary hardware or software, then the applications developed with that language may not be usable should that hardware or software change. One should choose a stable, flexible language, such as C, that will persist while needs and resources may fluctuate and evolve.

Development Time: Quite often, a Web site needs to be constructed very quickly. If CGI applications are needed at that site, then it may be necessary to choose a language that allows rapid development, yet may be weaker in other areas. CGI creation often takes the greatest proportion of development time, so any steps to minimize that development time may weigh heavily when a language is to be chosen. For a site that will not exist for very long, like a site that provides up-to-date Olympics results, development time is much more important than preparing for the future of the site. Interpreted languages such as PERL are often used for rapid development.

Systems Interfacing: When a CGI application provides an interface to a second application, the dominant concern for language choice is often dictated by that second application. If a developer is creating a CGI-based Web interface to a proprietary database, then the CGI applications will have to access the database's programming interface, which may be very limiting. Many CGI applications are forced to make system calls (run programs from the command line) to interface with other applications; in this case, the secondary application may not have as much influence on language choice.

Performance

For Web sites that serve mainly static document requests, the performance bottleneck is often the server's network connection. It doesn't take much time or computational power to read a file from a hard disk, but it does take some time to send that file over a slow network connection. As servers gain faster and faster network connections, the source of congestion may not be the network.

This is especially true on Web servers that provide many dynamically produced documents. In this case, to serve one client request, it takes much more time and effort than it does to simply read a file and return it. When running a CGI application, the system needs to start a new process, execute the code (which could be complex), collect the results, and then return them. If the application is a gateway to a second application, say, a database, then there may be much time spent by the second application to provide any data needed by the CGI application. While such applications increase the flexibility of a server, they can significantly decrease the server's performance.

In order to reduce the performance penalties of CGI, a new protocol named **FastCGI** [6] has been developed by *Open Market* [5]. FastCGI is basically an extension of CGI. Like CGI, FastCGI applications are run in separate, isolated processes. The main performance advantage of FastCGI comes from the fact that FastCGI processes are persistent; they are reused to handle multiple requests. Thus, unlike CGI, a new process does not have to be created for each request. Another performance benefit is related to communication between the Web server and the application: instead of using operating-system environment variables and pipes, the FastCGI protocol multiplexes the environment information, standard input, output and error over a single full-duplex connection. As an added benefit, this allows FastCGI programs to run on remote machines that do not host a Web server, using TCP connections between the Web server and the FastCGI application [7].

7.4 Examples

Presented next are examples of CGI applications. The Web version of this chapter (http:// www.prenhall/abrams/) contains links to execute the examples.

Hello World

Description / Motivation
This CGI application is designed to say "hello" to its viewer. It takes no input, and the only output it provides is the HTML to display a simple message. This example demonstrates sever important aspects of CGI applications:

Producing Header Information: The MIME type of the output produced by the CGI application is one of the most important items a CGI-app must provide. "Hello World" demonstrates this, as well as how to separate the header information from the body with a blank line of text.

Producing Basic HTML Body Output: The output that "Hello World" produces is always the same, and is nothing more than a simple Web page. A user can see how the output from "Hello World" is returned to a Web client and how it is interpreted in the same way that a static Web page is interpreted.

Source Code

```
/*      helloworld.c --
 *      "Hello World"
 *      Written by J. Patrick Van Metre for
 *      World Wide Web: Beyond the Basics
 *      CS 6204 at Virginia Polytechnic Institute and State University
 *
 *      This CGI application says hello to the world
 */

#include <stdio.h>

void main()
{

/* Output header information (followed by blank line): */
/*      MIME type of contents of body                  */

  printf("Content-type: text/html\n\n");

/* Output body */

  printf("<HTML>\n\n");

  printf("<HEAD>\n");
  printf("<TITLE>Example 12.1</TITLE>\n");
  printf("</HEAD>\n\n");

  printf("<BODY>\n");
  printf("<H1>Hello world</H1>\n");
  printf("</BODY>\n\n");

  printf("</HTML>\n");

}
```

Date and Time

Description / Motivation

This CGI application displays the date and time (relative to the Web server on which the CGI application executes). The capabilities demonstrated by this CGI application are:

Displaying Dynamic Data: Every time this CGI application is executed, it will produce different output. This CGI-app exemplifies the dynamic nature of all CGI applications in a very simplistic manner.

Interfacing with Other Functions: The heart of creating a Web interface to other applications lies in the functions used to address them. CGI-apps are a way of placing a user-friendly front-end on other applications, and the success of this approach depends on the interface between the two parts.

Source Code

```
/*      date.c --
 *      "Date and Time"
 *      Written by J. Patrick Van Metre for
 *      World Wide Web: Beyond the Basics
 *      CS 6204 at Virginia Polytechnic Institute and State University
 *
 *      This CGI application displays the current date and time
 */

#include <stdio.h>
#include <stdlib.h>

#define STRING_LENGTH 256

void main()
{
  time_t Local;
  char TimeString[STRING_LENGTH];

/* Output header information (followed by blank line): */
/*      MIME type of contents of body                  */

  printf("Content-type: text/html\n\n");

/* Compute local time and store text version in TimeString */

  time(&Local);
  strftime(TimeString, STRING_LENGTH,
          "It is now %I:%M:%S %p on %A, %e %B, %Y",
          localtime(&Local));
```

```
/* Output body */

  printf("<HTML>\n\n");

  printf("<HEAD>\n");
  printf("<TITLE>Example 7.2</TITLE>\n");
  printf("</HEAD>\n\n");

  printf("<BODY>\n");
  printf("%s\n", TimeString);
  printf("</BODY>\n\n");

  printf("</HTML>\n");

}
```

Finger Gateway

Description / Motivation

This CGI application is a gateway to the "finger" utility. The finger system, when queried about a certain user, returns information about that user (such as their real name, or their office telephone number). So, this finger gateway provides a Web interface to this system. This example demonstrates:

Passing input through the command line: The user forms a query to the finger gateway, providing the name (and possibly the home system) of the person about which information is desired. So, to query the finger gateway about the author, one would access the following URL:

> http://csgrad.cs.vt.edu/vanmetre-cgi/finger.cgi?vanmetre

At the end of the URL, "finger.cgi?vanmetre" means to send the name "vanmetre" to the finger gateway. If one wished to find out information about the account on example.system.com belonging to Joe_Blow, one could access the following URL:

> http://csgrad.cs.vt.edu/vanmetre-cgi/
> finger.cgi?Joe_Blow@example.system.com

(The "at" sign @ should really be encoded as %40)

Checking parameters for security: As shown before on page 121, a finger gateway can leave open a large security hole. This example demonstrates two ways to close this hole.

The example on page 121 shows that if a user accesses the URL

> http://www.nowhere.com/cgi-bin/finger.cgi?vanmetre;rm+-rf+%2F

it will cause the server to issue the system command

```
finger vanmetre;rm -rf /
```

This is a problem if the finger gateway doesn't recognize the semicolon and issues the command through a system call or through a shell. In C, when a system call is executed, the calling program starts another process—a shell—and lets that shell execute a command. It is the shell that allows the semicolon in the above command to split the command into two separate instructions that are executed sequentially. There are two main ways to bypass this problem.

1. **Remove the semicolon and all subsequent text**
   This will ensure that there is only one parameter to be passed to the finger program, and that only one command, the finger command, can be executed. It is also wise to do remove any ampersands and any subsequent text. This finger gateway example starts at the beginning of the query passed to it and searches through each character until it reaches the end or it finds a semicolon or an ampersand. If it finds either, it replaces the offending character with a null character (ASCII 0) which terminates the string. This effectively removes any potentially offensive command that may have followed the semicolon or ampersand.

2. **Don't execute any commands through a shell**
   Since it is the shell that interprets a semicolon as a character which separates two commands, it follows that bypassing the shell would be a satisfactory way of eliminating the problem. To do this, one can use the execvp function call. This ends the calling program and starts the program provided in the execvp call. The new program keeps the same process ID as the calling program. The finger gateway described in this example does just this. After retrieving the user's query and producing the header output, the gateway launches the finger utility through an execvp call.

A system call creates a new process, uses execvp to turn that new process into a shell, and tells the shell to execute a particular command; the calling process waits for the shell to finish before continuing execution. The finger gateway example given here does two things differently: it doesn't launch a new process, and it doesn't start a shell. This not only saves processing overhead, but it also reduces the potential for security problems by bypassing the shell.

Source Code

```
/*      finger.c --
 *      "Finger Gateway"
 *      Written by J. Patrick Van Metre for
 *      World Wide Web: Beyond the Basics
 *      CS 6204 at Virginia Polytechnic Institute and State University
 *
 *      This CGI application is a gateway to the finger utility
 */

#include <stdio.h>
#include <stdlib.h>
#include <string.h>

#define STRING_LENGTH 256
#define FINGER_CMD "finger"

void main(int argc, char *argv[])
{
  char Name[STRING_LENGTH];
  int i, len;
  char *execargv[3];

/* If no parameter is given, or if too many are given, */
/*   exit gracefully (only one name is expected)       */

  if (argc != 2)  {
    printf("Content-type: text/html\n\n");
    printf("<HEAD><TITLE>Finger gateway -- ERROR");
    printf("</TITLE></HEAD>\n\n");
    printf("<H1>ERROR:</H1>\n");
    printf("You must provide a name.\n");
    exit(1);
    }

/* If the name passed in contains a semicolon or an    */
/*   ampersand, replace the offending character with   */
/*   a null character to cut off the rest of the string */

  strcpy(Name, argv[1]);
  len = strlen(Name);
  for (i = 0; i < len; i++)
    if ((Name[i] == ';') || (Name[i] == '&'))
      Name[i] = 0;

/* Output header information (followed by blank line): */
/*     MIME type of contents of body                  */

  printf("Content-type: text/plain\n\n");
```

```
/* Make sure that the output buffer is empty before we */
/*   call "finger"; otherwise, we may not output the   */
/*   header properly.                                  */

  fflush(stdout);

/* Set up the parameters to be passed to "finger" as */
/*   if they were typed at the command line          */

  execargv[0] = (char *) malloc(STRING_LENGTH);
  strcpy(execargv[0], FINGER_CMD);
  execargv[1] = (char *) malloc(STRING_LENGTH);
  strcpy(execargv[1], Name);
  execargv[2] = NULL;

/* Start the finger utility */

  execvp(FINGER_CMD, execargv);

}
```

Access Counter

Description / Motivation

This example presents a rough yet functional access counter. The CGI application in this example doesn't return any HTML code or images. Instead, it returns pointers to GIF images. A Web document that wishes to contain this counter includes in its source n images, each of which has its source specified by this CGI. Each of these n images is a digit in the count of accesses to the parent document. The SRC attribute of the IMG tag which displays these images is a call to counter.cgi; in this call, a query is made which specifies the digit to be displayed. This query is in the form of digit=i, where i is the 10^i place. For example:

```
<IMG SRC="http://csgrad.cs.vt.edu/vanmetre-cgi/counter.cgi?digit=1">
```

will display the digit in the tens place.

Whenever a page asks counter.cgi for a digit, the URL of the referring page is passed to counter.cgi in the HTTP_REFERRER environment variable. Each time the ones digit for a URL is accessed, counter.cgi increments the access count for the referring URL and stores this value in a database on the host server. This is an example of a desirable side effect. A global variable, the database file, is being modified, and these modifications will affect all others who access this global object at a later time. This example demonstrates the following features of CGI applications:

Passing input through a query: The digit to be displayed is passed into the CGI application through a query. The query is passed from the requesting client to the server using the GET method [12], and the query is given to the CGI through the `QUERY_STRING` environment variable.

Intended side effects: Updating the database when a page is requested is an intended side effect.

Document referral. As stated before, this CGI application doesn't return any data; it returns in the header output the location of the data to be displayed. This location points to a GIF image, which is a static document stored on a Web server.

Source Code

HTML Source

```
<H1>Hello!</H1>

<TABLE BORDER=0>
  <TR>
    <TD>I have been accessed</TD>
    <TD>
      <TABLE CELLSPACING=0 CELLPADDING=0 BORDER=3>
        <TR>
<TD><IMG SRC="http://csgrad.cs.vt.edu/vanmetre-cgi/
counter.cgi?digit=2"><IMG SRC="http://csgrad.cs.vt.edu/
vanmetre-cgi/counter.cgi?digit=1"><IMG SRC="http://
csgrad.cs.vt.edu/vanmetre-cgi/counter.cgi?digit=0"></TD>
        </TR>
      </TABLE>
    <TD>times!
  </TR>
</TABLE>
```

CGI Source

```
/*      counter.c --
 *      "Access Counter"
 *      Written by J. Patrick Van Metre for
 *      World Wide Web: Beyond the Basics
 *      CS 6204 at Virginia Polytechnic Institute and State University
 *
 *      This CGI application returns the location of a GIF image which
 *          can be displayed to represent a single digit in the count of
 *          accesses to a Web page.
 */

#include <stdio.h>
#include <stdlib.h>
#include <string.h>
```

```c
#include <sys/file.h>

#define STRING_LENGTH 1024
#define SEPARATOR '&'
#define DATABASE "/home/vanmetre/cgi-db/counter/counter.db"
#define PICTURE_LOC "http://csgrad.cs.vt.edu/~vanmetre/numbers/"
#define LOCK_FILE "/home/vanmetre/cgi-db/counter/LOCK"

/* GetParam -- Accepts a query string in Query and searches it
 *             for a term named Name.
 *             Returns the value assigned to Name in Dest.
 */

void GetParam(char *Dest, const char *Name, const char *Query)
{
  int Pos=0, copy, QueryLen;

  QueryLen = strlen(Query);

/* Iterate through query looking for Name; if found, copy to Dest */
  while (Pos < QueryLen)  {
    if (!strncmp(Query+Pos, Name, strlen(Name)))  {
      Pos += strlen(Name)+1;
      copy = 0;
      while ((Query[Pos] != SEPARATOR) && (Pos < QueryLen))
        Dest[copy++] = Query[Pos++];
      Dest[copy] = 0;
      return;
      }  /* if */
    else  {                          /* If not found, move along to the next */
      Pos += strlen(Name)+1;         /*  name-value pair in query */
      while ((Query[Pos] != SEPARATOR) && (Pos < QueryLen))
        Pos++;
      Pos++;
      }  /* else */
    }  /* while */

  }  /* GetParam */


void main()
{
  char Query[STRING_LENGTH];
  char ReqDigit[STRING_LENGTH];
  char Location[STRING_LENGTH];
  char Temp[STRING_LENGTH];
  char TempLocation[STRING_LENGTH];
  char NewDBName[STRING_LENGTH];
  char Command[STRING_LENGTH];
  int NumAccess, Value, Work, CurrDigit, Digit;
  int TempNumAccess;
```

```
  int Found = 0;
  FILE *OldDB, *NewDB;
  int lock_fd;

/* Remember the query string and the URL of the page being counted */

  strcpy(Query, getenv("QUERY_STRING"));
  strcpy(Location, getenv("HTTP_REFERRER"));

/* Retrieve the value for "digit=" from the query string */

  GetParam(ReqDigit, "digit", Query);
  Digit = atoi(ReqDigit);

/* Get a lock on the counter database file */

  lock_fd = open(LOCK_FILE, O_RDONLY | O_CREAT, 256+128+32+16);
  if (lock_fd < 0)   {
    printf("<H1>Error opening lock file</H1>\n");
    exit(1);   }
  flock(lock_fd, LOCK_EX);

/* Open the database file for reading */

  OldDB = fopen(DATABASE, "r");
  if (OldDB == NULL)   {
    printf("Content-type: text/html\n\n");
    printf("Couldn't open db for reading\n");
    exit(1);
    }

/* We only update a location's counter when the ones digit is ac-
cessed */

  if (Digit == 0)   {

/* And when we update, we write a new database file, then rename
it */

    sprintf(NewDBName, "%s.new", DATABASE);

    NewDB = fopen(NewDBName, "w");
    if (NewDB == NULL)   {
      printf("Content-type: text/html\n\n");
      printf("Couldn't open db for writing\n");
      exit(1);
      }

    }

/* Read through the database file looking for the accessed URL */
```

```
   while (!feof(OldDB))  {
      fgets(Temp, STRING_LENGTH, OldDB);            /* Read one line */
      if (!feof(OldDB))  {
         sscanf(Temp, "%d %s", &TempNumAccess, TempLocation);
         if (!strcmp(TempLocation, Location))  {
/* If the accessed URL is already in the database increment the
number of accesses */
            NumAccess = TempNumAccess;
            Found = 1;
            NumAccess++;
            if (Digit == 0)
               fprintf(NewDB, "%d %s\n", NumAccess, Location);
            }
          else  {
           if (Digit == 0)
              fputs(Temp, NewDB);
          }
       }
     }

   fclose(OldDB);

   if (Digit == 0)  {

      fclose(NewDB);

      sprintf(Command, "cp -f %s %s", NewDBName, DATABASE);
      system(Command);

      }

/* If the URL isn't in the database, then just stick it on the end */

   if (!Found)  {
      OldDB = fopen(DATABASE, "a");
      if (OldDB == NULL)  {
         printf("Content-type: text/html\n\n");
         exit(1);
         }

      NumAccess = 1;
      fprintf(OldDB, "%d %s\n", 1, Location);
      fclose(OldDB);
      }
/* Unlock the database file */

   flock(lock_fd, LOCK_UN);
   close(lock_fd);
```

```
  Value = 0;
  CurrDigit = 0;
  Work = NumAccess;

/* Isolate the digit we want */

  while (Work != 0)  {
    if (CurrDigit == Digit)
      Value = Work % 10;
    CurrDigit++;
    Work /= 10;
    }

/* Refer the accessed URL to the location of the digit image */
/*    by putting it in the header output                      */

  printf("Location: %s%d.gif\n\n", PICTURE_LOC, Value);

}
```

7.5 References

[1] Berners-Lee, T., and D. Connolly. "Hypertext Markup Language—2.0—Document Structure." 1995.
     <http://hopf.math.nwu.edu/html2.0/html-spec_5.html#SEC28>   (20   Nov.
     1996).

[2] Deitel, Harvey M. *Operating Systems*. 2nd Ed. Reading, MA: Addison-Wesley Publishing Company, Inc., 1990. Chapter 5.

[3] National Center for Supercomputing Applications. "The Common Gateway Interface." <http://hoohoo.ncsa.uiuc.edu/cgi/> (14 Aug. 1997).

[4] Netscape Communications Corp. "Extensions to HTML 3.0."
     <http://home.netscape.com/assist/net_sites/html_extensions_3.html>
     (20 Nov. 1996).

[5] Open Market, Inc. "Open Market Home Page."
     <http://website-1.openmarket.com/> (14 Aug.1997).

[6] ——. "FastCGI Home Page." <http://www.fastcgi.com> (14 Aug. 1997).

[7] ——, "FastCGI: A High-Performance Web Server InterFace." April 1996.
     <http://www.fastcgi.com/kit/doc/fastcgi-whitepaper/fastcgi.htm>   (14   Aug.
     1997).

[8]   Sebesta, Robert W. *Concepts of Programming Languages*. 3rd Ed. Reading, MA: Addison-Wesley Publishing Company, Inc., 1997. p. 258.

[9]   Stein, L.D., "WWW Security FAQ: CGI Scripts." <http://www.genome.wi.mit.edu/WWW/faqs/wwwsf4.html> (14 Aug. 1997).

[10]   World Wide Web Consortium. "HTTP: A protocol for networked information: Object Header lines in HTTP." <http://www.w3.org/pub/WWW/Protocols/HTTP/Object_Headers.html> (20 Nov. 1996).

[11]   ——. "HTTP: A protocol for networked information: Status codes in HTTP." <http://www.w3.org/pub/WWW/Protocols/HTTP/HTRESP.html>   (20   Nov. 1996).

[12]   ——. "HTTP: A protocol for networked information: Predefined Methods." <http://www.w3.org/pub/WWW/Protocols/HTTP/Methods.html>   (20   Nov. 1996).

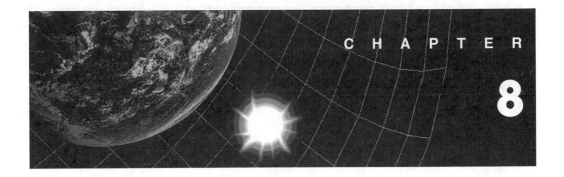

C H A P T E R

8

Java

by Guowei Huang and Ashish Shah

Java, which started out as an Internet programming language, has quickly transformed itself into a full-fledged computing platform that has unparalleled versatility in the history of computing. At times one may think: is there any computing task which can not be done using Java? Java has grown so much in so little a time that it is quite a formidable task to write a chapter that talks about everything that is Java, and still make sense of it.

Java is progressing towards becoming a platform of choice for application development in key areas such as Internet and intranet development, distributed computing, enterprise computing, and so on. With the Java platform being deployed in more and more widely used operating systems, Java is well on its way to becoming the most important computing platform that promises "Write Once, Run Anywhere" capability.

In this chapter we attempt to provide an overall view of Java, just enough to arouse the reader's interest in the various capabilities of this technology. We begin with a short overview of how Java came into being and into the limelight, followed by a brief discussion of the Java Programming Language. Then we go on to talk about the Java Computing Platform and its components and benefits. Finally we describe the family of products and APIs available from JavaSoft that are actually used in developing Java applications and applets.

Chapter Content

139

- Java Language Features
- Applets and Applications
- Java API Categories
- Overcoming Performance Limitations

3. The Java Platform

- Platform Components
- Java Application Environments
- Benefits of the Java Platform

4. JavaOS

- The Java Platform with and without JavaOS
- Performance Issues
- Advantages of JavaOS

5. Java Development Tools

- Java Development Kit
- Java Runtime Environment
- Java Foundation Classes
- Other Java Development Tools

6. Summary
7. References

8.1 Background

The **Sun Microsystems, Inc.'s** *Java* programming language development started in 1991 when James Gosling was designing a new language as a part of a large project to develop advanced software for consumer electronics. During his efforts at developing a more platform-neutral process, Gosling extended the C++ compiler and added many extras to C++ in the hope of making it work. However, this led him to realize that C++ is not suitable for the job. As a result, a small, reliable and architecture-independent language—Java, originally known as Oak—was born.

In 1993, as the Java team continued to work on the design of the new language, the Web appeared on the Internet and took it by storm. The team realized that an architecture-neutral language like Java would be ideal for programming on the Internet. By the early fall of 1994, Patrick Naughton and fellow Sun engineer Jonathan Payne finished writing *WebRunner*, a Mosaic-like Web browser written in the *Java* language. This early version of the *HotJava browser* demonstrated the potential of the Java language and impressed decision-makers in Sun. In 1995, Sun launched the HotJava browser as the first Web browser to support Java applets. Java applets are relatively small, compiled Java programs that can be downloaded from the Internet and run locally by the browser software. HotJava visibly exhibited the power of the Java language to programmers and to the rest of the world. In early 1996, Sun released the JDK 1.0—the first version of the Java Development Kit. Programmers could use this development kit to write applets that would run in all Java-enabled browsers, as well as to write applications that could be run locally outside the browser environment. With a lot of expectation from the computer world, Sun released the JDK 1.1 in early 1997. JDK 1.1 greatly enriches the features of JDK 1.0, and brings improvements in functionality, performance, and quality to the Java Platform. The shipment of JDK 1.1. is a milestone indicating that Java is fast becoming a sturdy, mature platform for robust application development.

Two factors contributed to the great success of Java: marketing strategy and timing. The availability of the JDK and the Java source code for free and the open specification development process have been the driving force in generating broad product interest and acceptance. This benefited both the software developers and the average consumers and helped open up a huge new marketplace for Java. Java arrived right at the time when the Internet fueled the demand for platform-independent applications. The idea of isolating hardware platform issues from the high-level language and compilation issues is not new. Historically, the UCSD p-code system was the best that used a binary-code interpreter to achieve platform-independent portability. But it did not make much advance because the performance penalty was too severe twenty years ago.

Today, Java is no longer just a programming language. It is a platform in its own right. By building this platform on top of other platforms or hardware, applications written in Java language can run wherever the Java platform is present. The emergence of the Java computing platform gives people a chance to rethink the basic design of computer applications and has made true distributed computing a reality.

In the next section we will look at the features of the Java programming language and how it relates in performance to other development environments. We also take a brief look at how the performance of Java can be improved, using new tools such as Just-in-time compilers.

8.2 The Java Programming Language

The Java programming language, when introduced in late 1995, took the Web by storm. JavaSoft released a newer version of Java (JDK 1.1) in early 1997, with a string of new features and Application Programming Interfaces (APIs). Although Java started out as an Internet programming language, it has many nice features that make it an ideal language for software development in other key areas. This is especially true for programming in the world of heavily networked, heterogeneous-platform computing. If we cut through all the hype surrounding Java, we can see that Java is basically a programming language and Java APIs basically define a class hierarchy just like any other object-oriented programming language.

In this section we describe the features of Java as compared to C and C++, introduce the Java predefined classes, and talk about some limitations of the Java language and how these are addressed.

Java Language Features

Java originated as part of a research project at Sun to develop advanced software for a wide variety of network devices and embedded systems. The goal was to develop a simple, robust, portable, distributed, and real-time operating platform. Design and architecture decisions for Java were drawn from a variety of object-oriented languages such as SmallTalk, Eiffel, Objective C, and Cedar/Mesa. The result was a language platform that has proven ideal for developing secure, network-based end-user applications which can be deployed in environments ranging from the Web and the desktop to network-embedded systems.

In its white paper *The Java Language: An Overview* [4], Sun describes Java as a simple, object-oriented, network-savvy, interpreted, robust, secure, architecture neutral, portable, high-performance, multithreaded, dynamic language. Let's see what these terms actually mean:

- *Java is simple.* "Simple" means that Java contains fewer syntactic and semantic rules than C++ and "looks like" C++. Thus existing C++ programmers can easily start programming in Java without extensive training. Sun designed Java as closely to C++ as possible in order to make the system more comprehensible, but removed from C++ many of those features that have become programmers' burdens in producing reliable applications. These primarily include operator overloading, multiple inheritance, extensive automatic coercions, and go to statements.

  The most important simplification is that Java does not use pointers and implements automatic garbage collection to eliminate headaches caused by dangling pointers, invalid pointer references, and memory leaks. It automatically handles referencing and dereferencing, and memory management is not an issue while programming.

In order to keep the language small, one design goal has been to enable the construction of software that can run stand-alone on small machines. The size of the basic interpreter and class support is about 40 Kb; the basic standard libraries and thread support require an additional 175 Kb.

- **Java is object-oriented.** This means that the programmer can focus on the data in his application and the interface to it, rather than thinking in terms of procedures. In an object-oriented system, a *class* is comprised of data and methods that operate on that data. Together, the data and methods define the state and behavior of an *object*, which is an instance of a class. A class can inherit data and behavior from another class, and thus a class hierarchy is formed.

  As compared to C++, Java is more strict in terms of its object-oriented nature. In Java, everything except the primitive types (numeric, character, boolean) is an object. Even strings are represented by objects. The entire application must be viewed as a collection of objects of various classes. A short introduction to object technology is also provided in Section 9.1. An added benefit with Java is that it comes with an extensive pre-defined class hierarchy, which saves the programmer from writing code for a lot of support functions. The classes in the Java class hierarchy are organized in different *packages*. We will talk about the various Java packages in the next subsection.

  The object-oriented paradigm fits well with Java's distributed client/server model. In recent years, many software developers have been focusing on applying object-oriented technology to distributed computing. By adopting object-oriented concepts, developers can dynamically build up complex distributed systems with prefabricated components that are ready for network installation. These componentized computing systems promise more reliable services, lower maintenance cost, and easier software upgrades.

- **Java is network-savvy.** Java is designed to support applications on networks. It supports various levels of network connectivity through pre-defined classes for handling TCP/IP protocols like HTTP and FTP with ease. For instance, the URL class provides a very simple interface to networking—you can open and access an object referred to by a URL on a remote site as easily as you would open and access a local object. It also provides classes that support datagram and streaming sockets.

- **Java is robust.** Java is designed for writing highly reliable or robust software. First of all, it is a strongly typed language. It employs early checking to catch potential problems and requires explicit method declarations, unlike C/C++. Moreover, it removes pointers to eliminate the possibility of overwriting memory and corrupting data and uses automatic garbage collection to prevent memory leaks. Instead of pointer arithmetic, Java has true arrays with bounds-checking.

The exception handling is also an important feature that makes Java robust—programmers can use try/catch/finally statements to simplify the task of error handling and recovery by grouping all of their error-handling code together.

- *Java is secure*. Security is an integral feature of the Java platform, since it was designed for deployment in networked environments. Toward that end, Java implements several security mechanisms to ensure that malicious code that tries to invade your file system cannot gain access to system resources. These include three major components: the class loader, the bytecode verifier, and the security manager. They define how Java classes are loaded over the network, and ensure that untrusted classes will not execute dangerous instructions or gain access to protected system resources. Classes loaded over the network will not be put in the same namespace as classes loaded from the local system. The Java bytecode verification process checks all untrusted Java code for violation of namespace restrictions, invalid Java Virtual Machine code, stack overflow or underflow, incorrect use of registers, and illegal conversion of data types. The removal of pointers also makes Java secure, since applications cannot forge pointers or do memory arithmetic, which could give it access to the underlying machine.

- *Java is architecture-neutral and portable.* Java programs are compiled to an architecture neutral bytecode format, rather than to a platform-specific binary format. The Java byte-codes are instructions for the Java Virtual Machine (JVM) that runs on top of a specific computing platform. This allows a Java application to run on any system that implements the Java Virtual Machine.

Besides distributed computing, architecture-neutrality also has benefit for single-system software distribution. To achieve the same level of compatibility for its database, Oracle has to compile its source code to 80 different Unix platforms, plus other personal computers, minicomputers, and mainframes. In the present computer market, software developers have to produce versions of their application that are compatible with different platforms. Noticing that, besides the Unix platforms, there are various other personal computers, minicomputers, and mainframes, one can imagine how difficult it will be to produce software that runs on all platforms.

Java's portability actually comes from its architecture-neutrality. But Java goes even further by explicitly specifying the size of each of the primitive data types and their arithmetic behavior to eliminate implementation dependencies. Another example of the portability of Java is that the Java compiler is written in Java. Sun's new "100% Pure Java" program helps developers ensure that their Java code is completely portable [6].

- *Java is interpreted*. The Java compiler generates bytecodes for the Java Virtual Machine. The JVM actually consists of the Java interpreter and the run-time environment. The interpreter is used to actually execute the compiled byte-codes.

- *Java is high-performance.* Java, being an interpreted language, is never going to be as fast as a compiled language like C. It is probably reasonable to say that compiled C code runs ten times faster than interpreted Java bytecodes. This speed is usually enough for event-driven, GUI-based applications, or for networking applications. Much of the speed-critical portion of the Java run-time environment has been implemented with efficient native methods (mostly in C). Compared to some high-level, fully-interpreted scripting languages, the performance of Java is quite superior. We will talk more about the performance of Java in a later subsection.

- *Java is multithreaded*. It is not hard to imagine why multithreading has become a must for a language like Java. In a GUI-based network application such as a Web browser, there are usually multiple things going on at the same time—you can scroll down a page while the browser is loading contents you want to see. Java provides support for multiple threads of execution that can handle different tasks with a Thread class in the java.lang API package. Java multithreading comes with a set of synchronization primitives based on the monitor and condition variable paradigm introduced by C.A.R. Hoare [3]. This makes programming in Java with threads much easier than programming in the conventional single-threaded C and C++ style.

- *Java is dynamic*. One thing among many others that makes Java so popular is its server/client model—Java applications or applets reside on the network in centralized servers. A Java program can load in classes as they are needed, even from a remote site, and execute them. This is what happens when a Web browser downloads a Java applet. This allows clients to dynamically gain intelligence they did not have before, so they can adapt much more easily to an evolving environment. This also makes software upgrades much easier and effective and cuts down maintenance cost.

Java's classes have a run-time representation: instances of the class named *Class* represent the run-time class definition. You can find out what class an object belongs to based on the run-time type information. With Java 1.1 it is even possible to query an object regarding its run-time data and methods. In C or C++, you have a pointer to an object but you can never tell what type of object it is.

By now we should have a good idea of what the Java language is all about. These interesting features are where Java is different from other languages and where Java gets started; taken individually they can all be found in different development systems, but none integrates them as Java does. More information on the features of the Java language and the language environment can be found in the white paper *The Java Language Environment* by James Gosling and Henry McGilton [5]. The book *Java in a Nutshell* by David Flanagan is an excellent reference on the Java language and its predefined class hierarchy [2].

Applets and Applications

The Java language and run-time environment enables developers to create two different kinds of programs:

- **Applets.** Applets require a Web browser to run. The <applet> tag is embedded in a Web page and names the program to be run. When a page containing the <applet> tag is accessed by a Java-enabled browser, the browser automatically downloads the applet code from the code base specified in the tag, and runs it on the local machine. The browser software for a Java-enabled browser has a built-in Java interpreter which uses the Java class libraries that come with the browser.

  The start of the Java revolution was fueled in most part by people developing jazzy applets and putting them up on their Web pages. The Internet community was really impressed with interactive capability added by applets to Web pages. Applets must be designed small or modular, to avoid large download times. Since an applet is downloaded from an untrusted source, it runs under certain restrictions within the local machine and is prevented from doing certain system tasks such as creating or editing files on the local file system. This restriction can be relaxed when applets can be marked with digital signatures, which ensure that the applet has been downloaded from a trusted source.

- **Applications.** Java applications are similar to application programs developed in other languages. They do not require a browser to run, and they do not have any built-in downloading mechanism. An application is run from the command line using the Java interpreter. Like an applet, an

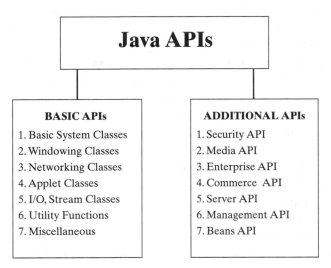

Figure 8–1   Java API Categories

application also requires the Java platform, with its Java virtual machine and class libraries, to run. The platform itself can be available as an independent program or can be embedded inside the operating system.

Both applets and application have access to most of the language capabilities. An applet does not have access to system services and system resources, while an application has full access to all of these. An application has to be used when access to the local file system is required.

Java API Categories

The Java language comes with a set of predefined classes that aid the user in accomplishing complex tasks with minimum coding. This set of classes is called the Java Application Programming Interface (Java API). APIs are grouped into Java packages by function. A package in Java provides a separate unique namespace. The Java APIs are divided into the Java Base APIs and the Java Standard Extension APIs. For the purposes of this chapter we will divide the API categories as shown by Fig. 8–1.

Basic Java APIs

The default Java environment currently consists of several different Java packages implementing a diverse set of fundamental classes. They include the following:

1. Basic System Classes (java.lang, java.lang.reflect)

The java.lang package contains basic Java classes: classes representing all the primitive data types (Boolean, Character, Byte, Short, Integer, Long, Float, Double), the superclass of all classes (Object), string classes (String, StringBuffer), and classes dealing with the extended capabilities of the language such as System, Security Manager, Thread, and Throwable (the root class of the Java exception and error hierarchy). The System class is a very important class that provides the connection to the language environment and the underlying system environment. Other important classes in this package include: Class (the class representing the run-time class information of an object), Run-time, and Process (provides a platform-independent interface to platform-dependent processes). The classes in the java.lang.reflect package enable a Java program to query a run-time Java class or object about its structure. The package contains classes that represent the fields, methods, and constructors of a class.

2. **Windowing Classes (java.awt, java.awt.event, java.awt.datatransfer, java.awt.image)**

The **java.awt** package is the Abstract Windowing Toolkit (AWT) which allows you to deal with GUI objects without regard to the system. The big advantage is that your program will automatically run on all supported Java platforms. The current java.awt is a least-common-denominator GUI toolkit. The classes of this package may be roughly divided into three categories:

- Graphics: These classes define colors, fonts, images, polygons, and so forth.

- Components: These classes are GUI components such as buttons, menus, lists, and dialog boxes.

- Layout Managers: These classes control the lay out of components within their container objects.

The **java.awt.peer** package consists entirely of interface definitions. The AWT allows you to deal with GUI objects regardless of system, because each one of the java.awt Component or MenuComponent classes has a corresponding java.awt.peer interface. This interface defines the methods that must be supported by the GUI components on a specific platform. The **java.awt.event** package contains classes that support the AWT event model; **java.awt.datatransfer** contains classes that support application-independent data transfer such as cut-and-paste and drag-and-drop. The **java.awt.image** package contains classes that deal with images and their manipulation.

3. **Networking Classes (java.net)**

The **java.net** package contains classes to support network programming. These classes provide powerful tools dealing with sockets, Internet addresses, network datagrams, uniform resource locators (URLs), and content handlers for data from a URL. For example, the URL class allows you to download an object referred to by the URL with a single call, and the Socket class allows you to connect to a specified port on a specified Internet host and read and write data.

4. **Applet Classes (java.applet)**

   The **java.applet** package contains the Applet class and three related interfaces. The Applet class implements an applet and is the superclass of all applets. You can create your own applet by creating a subclass of this class and overriding some or all of its methods.

5. **Input/Output and Stream Classes (java.io)**

   The **java.io** package contains classes to support reading and writing streams, files, and pipes. Most classes implemented in this package are subclasses of InputStream or OutputStream. InputStream and OutputStream are classes that implement methods for reading and writing data from a byte stream.

6. **Utility Classes (java.util, java.util.zip)**

   The **java.util** package contains general-purpose utility classes for data structures, such as dictionaries, hashtables, dates, stacks, bits, and strings. Since Java depends directly on several of the classes in this package, it is an integral part of the Java language. The **java.util.zip** package implements classes for computing checksums on streams of data and for compressing and archiving (and the reverse) streams of data, using the ZLB compression library and the ZIP and GZIP file formats.

7. **Miscellaneous Packages (java.math, java.text)**

   The **java.math** contains only two classes, which support arithmetic on arbitrary-sized integers and arbitrary-precision floating-point numbers. Classes in the **java.text** package are used for internationalization.

Additional API Categories

1. **Java Security API**

   The Java Security API is a framework for developers to easily and securely include security functionality in their Java applets and applications. This functionality includes cryptography with digital signatures, encryption, and authentication. This API is still under development, and part of it has been included in the Java 1.1 release. Chapter 11 discusses the Java security model and the security API in great detail. For more information on cryptography see Chapter 12.

2. Java Media API

The Java Media API defines the classes that support a wide range of media, and interactive multi-media related activities. It is composed of several distinct components, each associated either with a specific type of media such as 3D, audio, and video, or a media-related activity such as collaboration, telephony, and animation. The components of this API are still under development and will be released with future releases of Java. The various components of the Media API are as follows:

- **Java Media Framework**

  The Java Media Framework (JMF) provides for common control, synchronization, and composition of all time-based media as well as for media filters and processors. It is designed to handle streaming data, live or stored, compressed or raw, as well as from sampled audio and video streams. It also accommodates the ever-changing suite of media transports, containers, and encoding formats.

- **Java Collaboration API**

  Java Collaboration allows for interactive full-duplex multi-party communications over a variety of networks and transport protocols. It enables synchronization and session management, and allows sharing of both "collaboration-aware" and "collaboration-unaware" applets and applications.

- **Java Telephony API**

  This API provides the classes to integrate telephones with computers. It provides the basic functionality for control of phone calls: 1st party call control (simple desktop phone), 3rd party call control (phone call distribution center), teleconferencing, call transfer and caller ID.

- **Java Animation API**

  This API provides for motion and transformations of 2D objects. It makes use of the Media Framework for synchronization and composition.

- **Java 3D API**

  This API provides high-performance, interactive, 3D graphics support. It supports VRML, and provides a model for behavior and control of 3D objects.

More up-to-date information about the Java Media APIs can be found at the JavaSoft *Java Media and Communications Home Page* [9].

3. **Java Enterprise API**

   The Enterprise APIs support connectivity of Java-powered applets and applications to enterprise information resources such as databases, and legacy applications. Using these APIs, developers can build client/server applications in Java that run on any OS or hardware platform in the enterprise. There are currently four methods of connectivity:

   - **Java Database Connectivity (JDBC)**

     JDBC provides a standard interface for accessing local and remote SQL databases such as ORACLE. It provides uniform access to a wide range of relational databases. This API has been included in the Java 1.1 release. In conjunction with JDBC, JavaSoft has also released the JDBC-ODBC bridge implementation that allows access to any of the existing Microsoft ODBC-based databases.

   - **Remote Method Invocation (RMI)**

     RMI lets programmers create Java objects whose methods can be invoked from another virtual machine. RMI is the object-oriented counterpart of remote procedure calls (RPC) in the procedural-programming world. Section 9.2 provides more information on RMI. RMI is now part of the core Java APIs and is available with Java 1.1.

   - **Interface Definition Language (IDL)**

     IDL is a language-neutral way to specify an interface between an object and its client when they are on different platforms. Java IDL provides seamless connectivity and interoperability with applications written using the industry-standard CORBA (Common Object Request Broker Architecture) system for heterogeneous computing. It provides a Java-to-IDL mapping specification, and an IDL-to-Java compiler.

- **Java Naming and Directory Interface (JNDI)**

  This is a new API that provides a uniform interface to heterogeneous directory services in the enterprise.

Again, more up-to-date information about the Java Enterprise APIs can be found at the *Java API Overview and Schedule* Web site [8].

4. **Java Commerce API**

The Java Commerce API brings secure purchasing and financial management to the Web. The initial component of the Commerce API is JavaWallet, which defines and implements a client-side framework for credit card, debit card, and electronic cash transactions. See Chapter 13.

5. **Java Server API**

The Java Server API aids in the development of Internet and intranet servers in Java. The server API framework consists of server-side class libraries for server administration, access control, and dynamic server resource handling. This API also enables the creation of Java servlets. Servlets are server-side counterparts of applets. Servlets may reside locally on the server or may be downloaded from the network under security restrictions. More information about the Java Server API can be found on the *Java Server* Web pages [10].

6. **Java Management API (JMAPI)**

This API provides a rich set of extensible Java objects and methods for building applets that can manage an enterprise network over the Internet. More information on the Management API can be found on the *Java Management* Web pages [11].

7. **JavaBeans API**

The JavaBeans APIs define a portable, platform-neutral set of APIs for building software components that can be plugged into existing component frameworks such as Microsoft's OLE/COM, Apple's OpenDoc, and Netscape's LiveConnect. End users will be able to combine JavaBeans components using application builders. More information about JavaBeans can be obtained in Section 9.3.

Overcoming Performance Limitations

At the early stage of the development of the Java language, the goal of Java's creators was to build a system that could manage "a large, distributed, heterogeneous network of consumer electronics devices, all talking to each other." Until June 1994, when they retargeted it at the Internet, the priority on the creators' agenda was to achieve architecture neutrality. However, after Java took the Web by storm, the issue changed. People no longer just play around with Java. Serious developers are looking at Java for application development. Java is expected to be able to do more. The issue of performance now has taken the spotlight.

There are many factors that may affect the performance of Java. Some of them are:

- Interpreter: An interpreted language is always slower than a fully compiled language.

- Dynamic linking: Java resolves all symbols when a new class is loaded into the environment and prepares it for execution.

- Bytecode verification: Before a class loader may permit a given applet to execute, Java validates the code to prevent it from doing anything dangerous.

- Reliance on pointers for objects: Each Java object access needs a pointer dereference, which adds a level of indirection.

The larger an application is, the more severely these factors will affect the performance.

While Java is making distributed computing a real practice, the issue of performance is becoming more and more important. At first, many people believed that Java is likely to be always slower than C++ for typical application. ("A range of 50% to 300% slower than C++ has been suggested as the practical limit of Java performance improvements.") But, with the emergence of JavaOS and the JavaChip Family, or by using Just-In-Time compilation, we already see a huge improvement in performance for Java applications.

To greatly improve the performance and portability of the Java Platform, JavaSoft has implemented an optional Just-In-Time compiler in the Java Virtual Machine, and made available the JavaOS and picoJava (a specification for a microprocessor for running Java bytecode).

Both the JavaOS and the JavaChip Family eliminate the overhead of a host operating system and therefore improve application performance. The performance improvement achieved by JavaOS will be discussed in Section 8.4. The performance improvement gained by using a JavaChip is addressed in the next section. Also, because the JavaOS and JavaChip Family can be adapted to embedded devices where hardware resources are much more restricted, the Java Platform can penetrate into places where other platforms can not. This certainly improves the portability of the Java Platform and makes it available in a wider range of OS and hardware.

The JIT (Just-In-Time) compiler greatly improves performance by directly turning the bytecodes into machine code. Reports of comparisons with and without JIT are available. For example, a CaffeineMark test with the Symantec JIT (Windows NT) compiler gave Loop test scores that were 19 times faster than with the Sun JDK (Windows 95), which does not have a JIT. More details are available in *The Java Performance Report—May 1996* [25].

In the next section we will take an overall look at the Java platform and try to show which way it is headed.

8.3 The Java Platform

For understanding the fundamentals of the Java platform, let us first understand what we mean by a "platform." Most of the time, computer applications are developed using a particular programming language, and compiled for a particular platform of computation. A platform of computation refers to the actual hardware, software, or combination of hardware and software, on which the application is run. For example, if an application written in the C programming language has been compiled to run on a computer with an Intel microprocessor, it can not be run on a machine with a different architecture, say, PowerPC. Software must be compiled separately to run on each platform. Java breaks away from this paradigm and introduces one extra layer of software framework in order to achieve architecture neutrality.

The Java platform is a new software platform different from many others, such as Microsoft Windows, Macintosh, OS/2, UNIX, and NetWare; it sits on top of these platforms (or sits directly on the hardware) and is designed to deliver and run highly interactive, dynamic, and secure applets and applications on networked computer systems. Applications written in the Java language compile to architecture-neutral bytecodes, and not machine-specific binary code. This bytecode can be executed by the Java Virtual Machine (JVM), which is at the core of the Java platform. The primary advantage of this approach is that it allows a Java application to run on any system, as long as that system implements the Java Virtual Machine, regardless of the underlying operating system or hardware architecture. Let's take a brief look at the components of the Java platform.

Platform Components

The Java Virtual Machine and the Java API are the two basic parts of the Java Platform, as shown in Fig. 8–2.

Java Virtual Machine: The Java Virtual Machine (JVM) is an abstract machine designed to hide the underlying operating system from Java-enabled applets and applications. It is a software processor that sits on the top of existing processors. The JVM can also be implemented directly in hardware. The Java Virtual Machine Specification [12] defines the exact interfaces and adapters required to port the JVM to any platform. This makes it very easy to port the JVM to any hardware architecture and operating system combination, without the need for rewriting it completely.

The JVM specification also defines a machine-independent format for compiled Java programs, called the class file format. Any JVM must be able to execute a compiled Java program which confirms to the class file format.

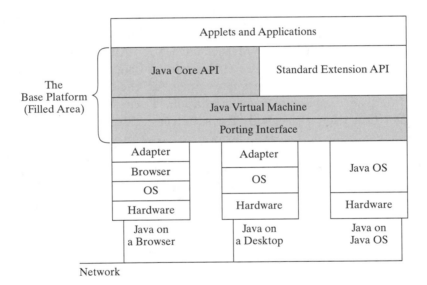

Figure 8–2 The Java Platform

Application Programming Interface (API): For any software framework, the application programming interface generally provides a higher-level abstraction to low-level system services, such as file I/O, process control, windowing system services, etc. The API provides a clean programming interface to developers and frees them from dealing with the low-level intricacies of system software. For example, the Java Abstract Windowing Toolkit (AWT, java.awt package) provides a set of high-level classes for creating windows and Graphical User Interface (GUI) components such as buttons and scroll bars. The programmer only has to define the layout of components in the window, rather than having to deal with how the actual components are drawn on the screen.

We gave an introduction to the existing and proposed Java APIs in the section on "Java API Categories" on page 147. In this section we will define the two different classes of APIs, as set forth by JavaSoft. To recap, the Java API consists of the classes and variables that can be used by programmers to develop applications with minimal coding. It provides a level of abstraction between Java applets (or applications) and the underlying operation system. Java APIs are organized into different packages (namespaces) by functions, with each package consisting of a related set of classes and interfaces. Further, JavaSoft classifies the various packages in the Java API as belonging either to the Core API or to the Standard Extension API [8].

- **The Java Core API:** The core API defines a minimal set of APIs for creating fully functional Java-enabled applets and applications. It includes the Basic Java APIs, as defined in the section on "Java API Categories" on page 147, and some additional APIs. JDK 1.1 has core support for the Java Security API, Java Remote Method Invocation API, JDBC API, and Java-Beans API. The main feature of the core API set is that any Java implementation on any platform must support all the core APIs in order to be certified as a complete implementation. Thus any Java application or applet that uses classes only from the core APIs will always run on any implementation of the Java platform.

- **The Java Standard Extension API:** The APIs in this category extend the capabilities of Java beyond the Java Core API and contribute greatly to making Java into a software framework for various types of computing tasks. Some of the Extension APIs will eventually migrate into the Java Core API. Currently, the Java Server API, Java Management API, and most of the Java Media APIs fall into this API category.

Java Application Environments

The Java platform is expected to be deployed in a variety of application scenarios, ranging from network-aware applications running on desktop computers and workstations, to smaller applications running on resource-constrained consumer devices such as set-top boxes, mobile phones, copiers, etc. In order to facilitate quick, orderly application development in different application domains, JavaSoft has defined different application environment specifications. Each Java Application Environment (JAE) caters to a different category of Java-powered applications, and has been defined keeping in mind the software requirements and hardware resources available for that particular category of applications. Currently, there are three different JAEs: The Java Base Platform, Embedded Java, and Personal Java.

Java Base Platform: The Java Base Platform contains the Java Virtual Machine and a minimal set of APIs (the Java core API) needed to run basic applets and applications. Programs written by using this minimal set can run on most of the Network Computers ("a new generation of affordable, easy-to-use information devices which are optimized for electronic communications, information access, entertainment and a host of applications"), desktop computers, and workstations without the need for additional class libraries. The Java Base Platform, as shown in Fig. 8–2 includes the Java core API, Java Virtual Machine, and the porting interface. The Java Base Platform along with the Java Standard Extension APIs provide the full range of Java features for application development.

Currently, the Java Base Platform is embedded in most of the popular Web browsers such as Netscape Navigator, MS Internet Explorer, and HotJava. It is available for all leading desktop, workstation, and network operating systems: Microsoft Windows, Macintosh, and various flavors of Unix such as Solaris, SunOS, Digital Unix, HP-UX, FreeBSD, AIX, IRIX, UnixWare, Linux, and some more. Most current information on the various operating systems supporting Java can be found at the JavaSoft Web site[1] [15].

EmbeddedJava: EmbeddedJava is an application environment for severely resource-constrained, high-volume, embedded devices (such as those with a small memory, no display, and/or no connection to a network). The EmbeddedJava API is the smallest API a low-function embedded device can have and still run. The EmbeddedJava specification is still under development. According to the *Java Platform White Paper*, this API will probably consist only of the java.lang and the java.util packages.

The EmbeddedJava API is designed to be easily portable to any real-time operating system, and to run on a wide variety of microprocessors. It has also been optimized to preserve the real-time support offered by the hardware. Developers will be able to use EmbeddedJava to create a variety of products including pagers, process control instrumentation, office peripherals, and networking routers and switches [14].

JavaChips: The Java Virtual Machine is a software processor that executes the Java bytecode instruction set. If this instruction set can be implemented in a hardware microprocessor, the hardware speed can work wonders for the performance of the JVM. A logical processor choice is one that directly implements the Java Virtual Machine. Sun is developing several chip-level Java engines: *picoJava* (low-cost implementation for low-cost consumer devices, such as phones), *microJava* (higher performance, adding application-specific I/O, memory, communications and control functions to picoJava), and *UltraJava* (high-performance implementation, for network computers, incorporating 2D and 3D imaging and graphics support, video compression and decompression,

---

[1] http://java.sun.com/products/jdk/jdk-ports.html

audio, networking, encryption). Sun has licensed the *picoJava* chip specification to other chip manufacturers who want to implement the Java VM in their own microprocessors.

The JavaChip instruction set is optimized for the unique demands of Java and enables Java to run in the most efficient, cost-effective manner. A JavaChip is expected to deliver up to 20 times the performance of Java on the x86 architecture. *picoJava I*, a small, simple configurable core supporting the Java VM, has shown outstanding performance on benchmarks, such as Javac (a Java compiler) and Raytracer (benchmark with substantial floating point activity). According to a *Sun Microelectronics* performance report, it is 15 to 20 times faster than a 486 and 5 times faster than a Pentium with a JIT compiler [27].

Besides the JavaChip family, JavaSoft has also developed the JavaOS—an operating system that implements the Java Virtual Machine, Java Embedded API, and the underlying functionality for windowing, networking and file system. JavaOS can also run in RAM on a JavaChip. We will give more details about JavaOS in Section 8.4.

PersonalJava: PersonalJava is a Java Application Environment for Java-powered networked applications running on personal consumer devices such as set-top boxes and smart phones. The PersonalJava 1.0 API is a subset of the JDK 1.1 API, supplemented by a small number of new APIs designed to meet the needs of networked embedded applications. It is much smaller than the JDK 1.1 API. The JDK 1.1 packages included in PersonalJava are:

- java.applet

- java.lang, java.lang.reflect

- java.awt, java.awt.datatransfer, java.awt.event, java.awt.image, java.awt.peer

- java.beans

- java.io, java.net

- java.util, java.util.zip

PersonalJava provides flexibility for dealing with the many input and output formats found in the consumer electronics market, such as remote controls, television output, and touch screens. PersonalJava will require less resources than JDK 1.1. It is expected that the PersonalJava VM and class libraries will fit into 2 megabytes of ROM, and 1–2 megabytes of RAM will be sufficient for application execution. PersonalJava may not support some of the features of the above-mentioned APIs, in which case, if an unsupported Java method is called, it will fail gracefully.

JavaSoft is planning to develop a set of specialized tools for developing embedded software confirming to the PersonalJava specification. Developers will be able to use these tools for placing the executable code in ROM, for configuring and compiling code, and for estimating application resource requirements. The PersonalJava specification is still under industry review at the time of writing this chapter. More current information on PersonalJava can be obtained from JavaSoft's Personal Java Web site [13].

We will end this section by listing out the benefits of the Java platform as compared to other existing paradigms of software development.

Benefits of the Java Platform

The computer world currently has many platforms. This has its pros and cons. On one hand it gives more choices to people; on the other hand it becomes more and more difficult to produce software that runs on all platforms. With its Java Virtual Machine and API, the Java platform provides an ideal solution to this. Being interactive, dynamic and architecture-neutral, the Java platform has benefits not only for developers and support personnel, but also for the end user [7].

- For end users, the platform provides live, interactive content on the Web, with just-in-time software access. Applications are readily available on all operating systems at once. Users do not have to choose operating systems based on the applications; they can run the applications on their favorite machines.

- For developers, the Java platform could provide "Write Once, Run Anywhere" capability. Developers can develop applications for one platform— the Java Platform, which is available on a wide variety of OS and hardware platforms. This reduces the development costs and makes Java a major contender also for stand-alone, non-networked applications.

- For support personnel, version control and upgrades are much simplified because Java-enabled applications can be kept in a central repository and served from there for each individual use. The number of platforms to support is reduced to one. This is a great incentive for developing enterprise intranet-based applications in Java.

How much the Java platform can benefit us depends on how widely it is deployed. According to JavaSoft's whitepaper [4], the Java Base Platform will soon be embedded in most of the widely used Internet browsers and in all leading desktop, workstation, and network operating systems. With the introduction of the JavaChip family, the platform will also be available in a wide range of industrial embedded devices. The presence of the Java platform will soon be felt almost everywhere, not just on the Web, but also on consumer electronics devices.

8.4 JavaOS

JavaOS is a small and efficient operating environment designed to run Java applications directly on hardware platforms without the need for a host operating system. It implements the Java Virtual Machine and the OS functionality needed for networking, windowing, and file system. JavaOS is currently targeted at systems such as Network Computers (NCs), intranet terminals for enterprise desktops and consumer electronics products. JavaOS is built from components and can be slimmed down to an appropriate size for embedded devices. For example, JavaOS can support devices having only 1–2 Mb of RAM and 1–2 Mb of ROM, such as set-top boxes, PDAs and even electronic devices without any graphical display.

In early March, 1997, Sun announced its first version of JavaOS—JavaOS 1.0—with more than 20 licensees. These include IBM, Toshiba Corp, Aplix Corp, and Advanced RISC Machines Inc. Versions of the JavaOS for the Sun SPARC and Intel x86 architectures can be directly licensed from Sun Microsystems. Other licensees are working on porting the JavaOS to other hardware platforms.

JavaOS is basically divided into 2 layers: the kernel and the runtime. The

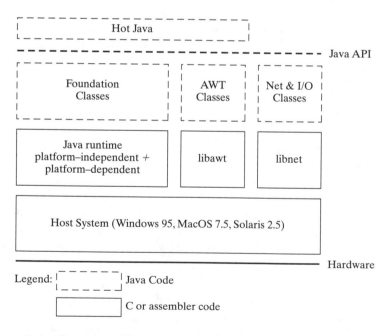

Figure 8–3   Java on a Host Operating System

kernel is the platform-dependent portion of the OS and the runtime is platform independent. This separation provides enough flexibility to product developers to customize their JavaOS-based products. For example, a smart phone may need a real-time kernel, but a network computer probably requires a full-featured kernel without any real-time constraints. The rest of this section is based on JavaSoft's white paper on JavaOS [16].

The Java Platform with and without JavaOS

To have a better understanding of JavaOS, let us make a comparison between the Java platform with a host operating system and the Java platform without an operating system.

Java with a Host Operating System: Fig. 8–3 illustrates the relationship between the Java platform and its host operating system. Everything above the line that defines the Java API is platform-independent; Java programs and applets are independent of the underlying host operating system. Java API does not rely on the host operating system and remains the same on all platforms.

The Java API is implemented in the language and utility classes, foundation classes, AWT classes, and the networking and I/O classes. These classes implement the major features provided in the Java platform and rely directly or indirectly on the host operating system. The Java runtime system consists of the Java bytecode interpreter and the garbage collector. The runtime consists mostly of platform-independent C code, and some platform-specific code which has to be ported when porting the Java runtime to another host OS. The platform-specific code includes the code for mapping the AWT classes, networking classes, and file-related I/O classes to the corresponding subsystems of the host OS, and also the platform-dependent part of the Java VM. The host OS is also responsible for providing primitive support for multithreading and memory allocation.

Java without a Host Operating System: To support the Java Platform, the JavaOS first needs to implement just enough kernel features to support the Java Virtual Machine. This includes support for booting, interrupts and exceptions, threads and synchronization, memory management, DMA, and file system. Then, it provides code to support the AWT, networking and file-related I/O classes. It also provides the drivers for controlling the display, network interface, mouse, and keyboard. The JavaOS ensures support for the full Java API, so that Java applications can be run without any change.

Fig. 8–4 shows a high-level view of the JavaOS architecture. What remains true of the Java platform with a host operating system is that everything above the line that defines the Java API is platform-independent. Java programs and applets are independent of the underlying host operating system. The Java API here is the same as the API of the Java platform with a host operating system.

Performance Issues

This section discusses some of the performance advantages of running Java applications on the JavaOS.

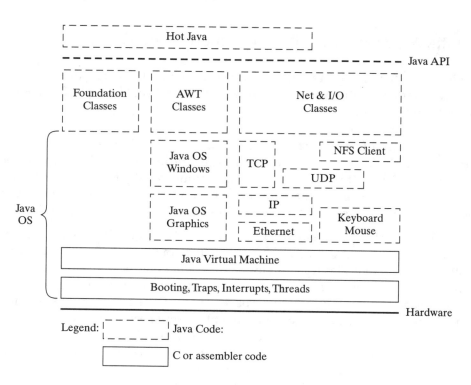

Figure 8–4   JavaOS Architecture

Speed: In its white paper on JavaOS, JavaSoft claims that benchmark tests on applications running on JavaOS have given even better results than some mature systems written in C or C++. They also claim that the TCP/IP throughput on JavaOS is much better than expected and is far more than adequate for Web browsing. Much of this performance improvement is because the JavaOS does away with the many software layers that traditional systems have for making programming in traditional languages less platform-independent.

Memory Requirements: A complete JavaOS needs a total of 4 Mb of ROM and 4 Mb of RAM. It can be slimmed down to fit smaller, low-function devices such as PDAs and even electronic devices without any graphical display. For example, if there is no display, the AWT classes and the windowing and graphics code could be removed. According to JavaSoft, the minimal memory for

JavaOS in its smallest possible configuration will be about 128 Kb of RAM and 512 Kb of ROM. This minimal memory requirement does not include additional memory that would be needed for applications.

Advantages of JavaOS

There are many advantages of using JavaOS. The biggest advantage is that JavaOS provides only enough functionality to support the Java platform. Thus, it is small in size and can run in minimal memory configurations. This allows smaller and simpler devices to be built that execute Java programs more efficiently than other systems. It can be stored in the device ROM also. Another advantage of using JavaOS is low system administration and maintenance costs. The most current versions of JavaOS can be kept in a central repository and made available for upgrade.

8.5 Java Development Tools

In this section we will give a brief introduction to the development and support tools available for Java.

Java Development Kit

The Java Development Kit (JDK) allows you to write applets and applications that confirm to the Java Platform. JDK Version 1.1 is the latest major release of the development kit for the Java Platform 1.1. Java 1.1 offers new capabilities which are included in the JDK 1.1: Internationalization, signed applets, JAR file format, AWT (window toolkit) enhancements, JavaBeans™ component model, networking enhancements, Math package for large numbers, Remote Method Invocation (RMI), Reflection, database connectivity (JDBC), new Java Native Interface, Object Serialization, Inner Classes, and performance enhancements.
    JDK 1.1 contains.

- Java Core Classes

- Java Source Files for Public Classes. The complete source code for Java can also be obtained from Sun for a license. A non-commercial free license can be obtained for educational, evaluation or research purposes. A commercial license can also be obtained for a fee. See the JavaSoft Web site for more details [18].

- Java Tools
    - Java Compiler (javac)
    - Java Interpreter (java)

- Java Runtime Interpreter (jre)
- Java AppletViewer (appletviewer)—For testing Java applets
- Java Debugger (jdb)
- Class File Disassembler (javap)
- Java Documentation Generator (javadoc)
- C Header and Stub File Generator (javah)—For programs with native methods in C
- Java Archive Tool (jar)
- Digital Signing Tool (javakey)—Manages entities, including their keys, certificates, and the trust associated with them
- Native-To-ASCII Converter (native2ascii)—Converts a native encoding file to an ASCII file that includes the \udddd Unicode notation.
- Java RMI Stub Converter (rmic)—For programs with RMI
- Java Remote Object Registry (rmiregistry)—For registering RMI objects
- Serial Version Command (serialver)—For resolving different class versions
- AWT 1.1 Conversion Tool (updateAWT)—To upgrade old AWT 1.0 programs to AWT 1.1
- Various C libraries and include files

- Java documentation and demos

More information on the latest release of the JDK can be obtained from the JDK Web site [17].

Java Runtime Environment

The Java Runtime Environment (JRE) is the smallest set of executables and files that constitute the standard Java Platform. It provides a minimum runtime environment for running Java applications. Once a Java application has been developed, the JRE can be bundled in as part of the final product. This is useful when the latest version of the Java runtime is not installed on the customer's machine, or if the runtime is not installed at all. It consists of the Java Virtual Machine, Java Core Classes, and supporting files. It does not include any of the development tools such as the compiler and debugger. The JRE tool (jre) can be invoked from the command line in a manner similar to invoking the Java interpreter.

Unlike the JDK, it is freely distributable, according to the terms of the license available from JavaSoft. Version 1.1 is the latest release of the JRE. JRE versions for Windows 95 and Solaris can be downloaded from the JavaSoft Web site. More information on the latest release of the JRE can be obtained from the JRE Web site [19].

Java Foundation Classes

The Java Foundation Classes (JFC) extend the original Abstract Windowing Toolkit (AWT) by adding a set of new components and services that are completely portable. Among other things, they add components and services for the following:

- High-level GUI Components that are lightweight and peerless, e.g., combo boxes, icons, tabbed panes, progress bars

- Drag and Drop

- Pluggable Look and Feel

- Images and Icons

- Undo Capabilities

More information on the latest release of the JFC can be obtained from the JFC Web site [20].

Other Java Development Tools

Many tools are available from third-party developers for Java development. A comprehensive list of existing Java tools can be obtained from the Gamelan Web site [1].

8.6 Summary

Only three years after its debut, Java has evolved into a sturdy platform for distributed computing. The Java Platform is now available in most of the leading desktop, workstation, and network operating systems, and is being readied for consumer and industrial embedded devices. Continuous improvements of the Java Platform in functionality, performance, and quality are winning it broader acceptance from the industry. Today, Java is leading the charge into a new era of distributed computing. It is fundamentally changing the architecture of today's computing systems and making distributed computing a real practice.

8.7 References

[1]   EarthWeb, Inc. "The Java Development Tools." *Gamelan.*
       <http://www.gamelan.com/pages/Gamelan.programming.tool.html> (9 Sept.
       1997).

[2]   Flanagan, D. *Java in a Nutshell.* 2nd Edition. O'Reilly and Associates, Inc.
       1997.

[3]   Hoare, C.A.R. "Monitors: An Operating System Structuring Concept." *Communications of the ACM*, Oct. 1974.

[4]   JavaSoft, "The Java Language: An Overview." May 1996.
       <http://java.sun.com/docs/overviews/java/java-overview-1.html> (9 Sept.
       1997).

[5]   JavaSoft. "The Java Language Environment Whitepaper." May 1996.
       <http://java.sun.com/docs/white/langenv/ > (9 Sept. 1997)

[6]   JavaSoft. "The 100% Pure Java Program Home Page."
       <http://java.sun.com/100percent/index.html> (9 Sept. 1997).

[7]   JavaSoft. "The Java Platform Whitepaper." May 1996.
       <http://java.sun.com/doc/whitePaper.Platform/CreditsPage.doc.html>
       (9 Sept. 1997).

[8]   Javasoft. "Java API Overview and Schedule."
       <http://java.sun.com/products/api-overview/index.html> (9 Sept. 1997).

[9]   JavaSoft. "Java Media and Communications Home Page."
       <http://java.sun.com/products/java-media> (9 Sept. 1997).

[10]   JavaSoft. "Java Server Product Family."
       <http://jserv.javasoft.com/products/java-server/> (9 Sept. 1997).

[11]   JavaSoft. "Java Management Home Page."
       <http://java.sun.com/products/JavaManagement/> (9 Sept. 1997).

[12]   JavaSoft. "Java Virtual Machine Specification." Sept. 1996.
       <http://java.sun.com/docs/books/vmspec/html/VMSpecTOC.doc.html >
       (9 Sept. 1997).

[13]   JavaSoft. "Personal Java."
       <http://java.sun.com/products/personaljava/> (9 Sept. 1997).

[14]   JavaSoft. "Embedded Java."
       <http://java.sun.com/products/embeddedjava/> (9 Sept. 1997).

[15] JavaSoft. "Operating Systems supporting Java."
      <http://java.sun.com/products/jdk/jdk-ports.html> (9 Sept. 1997).

[16] JavaSoft. "JavaOS: A Standalone Java Environment." May 1996.
      <http://java.sun.com/products/javaos/javaos.white.html> (9 Sept. 1997).

[17] JavaSoft. "The Java Development Kit."
      <http://java.sun.com/products/jdk/> (9 Sept. 1997).

[18] JavaSoft. "JDK Source Licensing."
      <http://java.sun.com/products/jdk/1.1/source.html> (9 Sept. 1997).

[19] JavaSoft. "The Java Runtime Environment."
      <http://java.sun.com/products/jdk/1.1/jre/index.html> (9 Sept. 1997).

[20] JavaSoft. "The Java Foundation Classes."
      <http://java.sun.com/products/jfc/> (9 Sept. 1997).

[21] JavaSoft. "Secure Computing with Java: Now and the Future." 1997.
      <http://java.sun.com/marketing/collateral/security.html> (9 Sept. 1997).

[22] Nombas, Inc. "CMM and Java Compared." 1995.
      <http://www.nombas.com/otherdoc/javavcmm.htm> (9 Sept. 1997).

[23] O'Connell, M. "Java: The Inside Story." *SunWorld Online Magazine.* July
      1995.
      <http://www.sun.com/sunworldonline/swol-07-1995/swol-07-java.html>
      (9 Sept. 1997).

[24] Orchard, D. "A detailed look at where Java's going this year and in the near
      future." July 1997.
      <http://www.javaworld.com/javaworld/jw-06-1997/jw-06-javafuture.html>
      (9 Sept. 1997).

[25] Pendragon Software. "JIT Compiler Results." May 1996.
      <http://www.webfayre.com/pendragon/jpr/jpr0596-article4.html> (9 Sept.
      1997).

[26] Shiffman, H. "Making Sense of Java."
      <http://reality.sgi.com/shiffman/Java-QA.html> (9 Sept. 1997).

[27] Sun Microelectronics. "picoJava I Microprocessor Core Architecture." Nov.
      1996.
      <http://www.sun.com/sparc/whitepapers/wpr-0014-01/> (9 Sept. 1997).

[28] Sun Microelectronics. "Java Computing in the Enterprise." July 1996.
      <http://192.9.9.100/javacomputing/whpaper/about_the_author.html>
      (9 Sept. 1997).

[29] Sun Microelectronics. "Sun Microelectronics' picoJava I Posts Outstanding Performance." Nov. 1996. <http://www.sun.com/sparc/whitepapers/wpr-0015-01/> (9 Sept. 1997).

World Wide Web and Object Technology

by Ashish B. Shah

The Web is a large-scale distributed system based on client/server computing. For most part, the Web is a static medium of computing and is document-centric. It provides little support for connecting interactive services or for interacting with "intelligent content." Recently, there has been much focus on applying distributed object technology to make the Web more interactive and to provide a Web interface to enterprise client/server applications. Distributed object-based systems can provide the necessary framework for creating interactive services on the Web. The building blocks are provided by component technology. Components are smart objects that are put together into compound documents. Compound documents can support many different data types and provide a uniform interface to each type. Component technology can turn static Web documents into active, multimedia-rich compound documents.

Many efforts at enabling interoperability between the Web and distributed object systems are based on the Object Management Group's Common Object Request Broker Architecture (CORBA) standards and a set of new APIs announced by JavaSoft for building distributed object-based applications in Java. A few are based on Microsoft's Distributed Component Object Model. In terms of compound document technology, the Object Management Group has adopted Apple's OpenDoc specification as a compound document standard. Microsoft's Object Linking and Embedding (OLE), which is based on the proprietary Component Object Model (COM), is also a competing compound document standard. Finally, Sun's JavaBeans API promises to provide a platform-independent component model for building distributed object systems on the Web. In this chapter we provide an introduction to the aforementioned

technologies for integrating distributed objects and component technology with
the Web and compare and contrast them.

Chapter Content

1. Introduction
   - Web Technology Today
   - Identifying and Defining the Key Technologies
   - What Can Object Technology Do for the Web?

2. Paradigms for Distributed Computing and Mobile Code
   - Common Object Request Broker Architecture (CORBA)
   - Java
   - Distributed Component Object Model (DCOM)
   - Comparing Paradigms

3. Compound-Document Frameworks
   - OpenDoc
   - Object Linking and Embedding
   - JavaBeans
   - Who Will Win the Battle?

4. Putting It All Together
   - Integration of Technologies
   - Current Implementations and Developments
   - Future Architectures

5. Conclusion
6. References

9.1 Introduction

There are two important issues to notice about existing Web technology. First of
all, the Web is essentially a huge distributed system, but more like a distributed
file system rather than a distributed computing system. Although client/server
applications based on the Common Gateway Interface (CGI) protocol and Java

exist on the Web, for the most part the Web still remains document-centric. Second, Web browsers are fast becoming the universal front-end. Today's desktops will soon be replaced with webtops. We have started expecting more and more capabilities from our favorite browsers. We want to be able to buy merchandise through the browser, listen to music, and even watch movies through the same magical browser. In short, we want to perform all our computing tasks through our browser. Isn't it true that the browser is one of the first applications we launch when we start a session with the computer?

It is possible to have commerce on the Web, have large-scale digital libraries that store multimedia information and access them from the Web, and much more. Yet, making all this possible requires a paradigm shift, a technological leap, in the way we program distributed client/server applications in general, and applications for the Web in particular. In this chapter we discuss some key technologies that can turn the Web into a more intelligent medium for communication and information dissemination and convert static Web documents into active compound documents with rich multimedia content. First of all, let's review the current status of Web technology.

Web Technology Today

When we talk about the Web today, we tend to glorify the benefits of Web technology and overlook the many shortcomings that can put a damper on the growth of the Web itself. Along with the increase in the popularity of the Web, the list of limitations imposed by the current Web technology is also on the rise. The following lists outline some of the major capabilities and shortcomings of the current Web technology:

Web Positives

Largest repository of information: The Web has become one of the largest repositories of information available to people. It's attractive because it is totally unregulated; anyone can publish anything of their choice.

Huge installed base: The number of Internet hosts serving Web documents is increasing at a very high rate. Thus, it provides a very large installed base for Web-based utilities and applications.

Interoperable standards: Web technology is largely based on interoperable standards such as the HyperText Transfer Protocol (HTTP), HyperText Markup Language (HTML) and Common Gateway Interace (CGI). The TCP/IP protocol suite, on which HTTP is based, has emerged as the dominant worldwide networking standard. These standards enable interoperability between Web applications and make them independent of the underlying hardware architectures and network protocols.

Browser interface: As mentioned earlier, the Web browser is becoming the interface of choice and has the potential to change the entire desktop paradigm.

Add-ons and plug-ins: Many plug-ins are available which enhance the basic capabilities of the Web browser, for example, plug-ins such as RealAudio and QuickTime.

Helper applications: Browsers support the use of helper applications which can be called upon to process some data that cannot be handled by the browser itself. This gives a lot of flexibility in the variety of data that can be published on the Web.

Java and the ability to download code: The Java programming language has provided Web users with an ability to download code from a server on the fly and execute it on the local machine. This has opened up a whole new array of possibilities for the Web, as we will see in a later section.

Support for simple applications: Protocols such as CGI provide sufficient support for creating simple applications that don't require extensive state management and can be controlled through an HTML forms-based interface.

Web Limitations

Limitations of protocols: Protocols such as HTTP and CGI severely constrain the Web communication model. The lack of persistent state management in HTTP is a major limitation for Web application designers.

Overloaded networks and servers: Web traffic, which is increasing at an exponential rate, can severely overload HTTP servers and existing network links. The average document-retrieval time is increasing constantly. The Internet backbone is not overloaded as much as are the links between the users and the Internet service providers (ISPs). Statistics show that the final link is usually the one that takes the most time to cross.

Increasing size of browsers: As vendors try to pack more and more features into Web browsers, the size of browsers is increasing steadily. Browser software needs to be converted from a monolithic application into a set of independent software modules that can be called upon whenever necessary.

Lack of interaction: CGI-based applications provide very little support for active interaction between the browser and the Web server. Even though Java applets have helped in making Web documents more interactive, until now there has been little support in Java for interaction between independent applets in an HTML page.

Lack of database support: The Web can provide a very elegant interface to existing relational and object-oriented databases, but the current communication model for the Web does not provide the necessary framework for creating such dynamic interfaces with ease.

Lack of secure application framework: Although many efforts are underway to create a standard secure framework for electronic commerce on the Web, there is no standard facility that allows companies and users to buy or sell goods on the Web freely, with minimal security risks.

Identifying and Defining the Key Technologies

Most of the limitations of existing Web technology mentioned in the previous section can be overcome by employing distributed objects and component technology for building Web-based applications. What are distributed objects and components, and how do they differ from normal software "objects"? Well, let's try to define and differentiate these.

Objects: Object-oriented programming differs a lot from classical procedural programming. The functions or procedures in procedural programs describe only behavior. The data which they operate on has to be passed to them as parameters. This is not the case in object-oriented programming. To understand the principles behind object-oriented programming let's define an "object" and its properties.

An object is a piece of code that owns things called attributes (data) and provides services through methods (also called operations or functions). Typically, the methods operate on private data—also called instance data or object state—that the object owns. A class acts as a data type for an object, and conversely, an object is an instance of a class.

Thus, the object describes both behavior and information associated with a software entity. Objects can easily model real-world entities and are inherently self-managing pieces of software. They have the classical object-oriented properties of encapsulation, inheritance, and polymorphism, which make them very useful.

- **Encapsulation:** It allows you to change an object's implementation without affecting the system that uses it. The object's implementation is *encapsulated*—that is, hidden from public view. The object has a public interface which defines how other objects or applications can interact with it. Thus, by limiting the visibility of what others can see, an object becomes more self-contained and manageable.

- **Inheritance:** It allows you to extend the functionality provided by existing objects and to build new systems that are independent of the original implementation of the object. This allows you to create new child classes from existing parent classes. Child classes inherit the parent's methods and data structures. You can add new methods to a child class or override methods inherited from the parent class by redefining them in the child class. The parent's method is not affected by this modification. It is also possible for a child class to have more than one parent class, which is called multiple inheritance.

- **Polymorphism:** Polymorphism is a way of saying that the same method can do different things depending on the class that implements it. Objects in different classes receive the same message yet react differently. The sender doesn't know the difference, each receiver interprets the message in its own way and provides the appropriate behavior. Thus, polymorphism lets you view two similar objects through a common interface and eliminates the need to differentiate between the two objects. It is the underlying principle behind object-style user interfaces. For example, you can click on any visual object and select it or drag and drop it.

Thus, an object-oriented program consists of a set of classes that define various types of objects. At runtime you instantiate a set of objects of these classes and operate on them using their public interface methods. There are a lot of different dimensions to this, but the length of this chapter doesn't allow us to cover them in detail. For now, the important thing to know is that object technology makes software faster to develop for programmers, easier to use for users, and easier to manage for system administrators. More information on object-oriented programming and object technology can be found in the books *C++ Programming Language* [20] and *Object Oriented Software Design and Construction* [13].

Distributed Objects and Components

Distributed objects have all the above-mentioned properties that objects have and much more. These are software components that have self-contained intelligence and are independent of the language, operating system, and hardware architecture used for implementation. They may be located anywhere on the network and can provide services to remote as well as local clients via method invocations. Clients do not need to know where the server object resides or what operating system it executes on. All the functionality required for local/remote transparency, platform independence, locating server objects dynamically at runtime, and finding out their properties is provided by a software framework which is called a **distributed object architecture.**

A **component** is a stand-alone object that is not bound to a particular program, computer language, or implementation. It does not constitute a complete application by itself but can be used to build cheap, personalized applications. Components reduce the cost and complexity of software development. Different components interact using language-neutral, client/server interaction models such as event notifications. Component technology is, by origin, a desktop technology, whereby different applications on the desktop can access and modify data objects created by peer applications regardless of the data content and format. Remember Microsoft Office. The underlying software framework that enables this functionality and provides the facilities required for it is called a **compound document framework.**

Now, we can identify the two key technologies for overcoming the current shortcomings of the Web: **Distributed Object Architectures** and **Compound Document Frameworks**. Distributed object architectures help in building client/server applications using "distributed objects" and provide services such as security, transactions, state management, licensing, etc. Compound document frameworks act as containers in which heterogeneous "components" can be placed to build customized applications. They can provide a front-end to applications that use distributed objects. *The Essential Distributed Objects Survival Guide* [18] is an excellent reference on distributed object architectures and compound document frameworks.

Before we get into the nitty-gritties of these technologies, let's take a short look at what they can do for the Web.

What Can Object Technology Do for the Web?

Distributed objects and components can enhance the capabilities of the Web in many ways. Following are some of the benefits object technology can provide to the Web:

- Turn static Web documents into **active compound documents** that can interact with users just like applications on the desktop.

- Provide a **seamless integration of various information media** like video, audio, text and images.

- Support **secure, long-lived transaction**s that execute over a long period of time, as they travel from server to server.

- Support **roaming agents.** Roaming agents are electronic agents which may work for consumers to buy things and for businesses to sell their wares; they can be sniffer agents which collect information and statistics or perform system management.

- Enable server and network **load balancing** by building hierarchies of interoperating proxy cache servers.

- Bring some order to the content on the Web, by providing interfaces to object-oriented and relational **databases**.

- Turn the Web into a **huge parallel supercomputer** capable of solving traditional time-consuming problems in a fraction of a second.

In the following sections we will take a look at some existing distributed object architectures and compound document frameworks and compare and contrast them. We will also see how these can be integrated into a uniform whole to benefit the Web and will look at the current developments taking place in this field.

9.2 Paradigms for Distributed Computing and Mobile Code

As the Web continues to evolve, its role as a means of delivering information and entertainment content is expanding to include delivery of interactive services. Examples of these services include stock trading, home shopping, home banking, package delivery, reservation systems, Internet search services, and interactive chat services. The common thread that runs among all these applications is that they require a sequence of interactions between the user and a server (or servers). In the simplest case, all interactions are via HTTP with a Web server. More sophisticated applications involve highly interactive client-side processing (such as a fully functional GUI interface), as well as a medium for the client to communicate with the server over the Internet. Distributed objects provide a particularly useful mechanism for this client-server communication.

Distributed object architectures are the software frameworks required for building and using client/server applications that use distributed objects. Distributed objects, as defined earlier, are packaged as independent pieces of code and can be accessed by local or remote clients via method invocations. Clients do not need to know where the object resides or what operating systems it executes on. The framework also provides an infrastructure for supporting a large number of servers and applications that can spawn any number of transactions.

A common set of services and capabilities provided by existing distributed object architectures is as follows:

- **The Object Bus:** It provides the basic messaging mechanisms needed by distributed objects to communicate with one another across heterogeneous languages, tools, platforms, and networks. It also provides an environment for managing these objects, advertising their presence, and describing their metadata. Using the object bus, a client object can transparently invoke a method on a server object, which can be on the same machine or on a remote network.

- **Static and Dynamic Method Invocations:** The framework should support both static and dynamic method invocation mechanisms on local as well as remote server objects. Static invocations are method calls which have been fully defined at compile time. In contrast, dynamic invocations allow you to add new classes to the system without requiring changes in the client code. They are very useful for tools that discover what services are provided at run time.

- **Object Repositories:** There should be a mechanism for uniquely identifying objects and storing them in a repository. The repository can be accessed by client objects to find out which server objects they can access, and what are the services provided by these server objects.

- **Distribution Services:** The architecture should provide basic services for naming objects, for defining key events for objects, and for creating, destroying, and transporting objects. It should also provide services for security, atomic transactions, concurrency, persistence, licensing, etc.

In this section we will talk about three existing distributed object architectures, viz. CORBA, Java, and DCOM, and try to compare and contrast them.

Common Object Request Broker Architecture (CORBA)

CORBA is a product of an industry consortium of 500-odd companies called the Object Management Group (OMG). It is a set of specifications for providing **interoperability and portability** to **distributed object-oriented applications**. CORBA-compliant applications can communicate with each other regardless of location, implementation language, underlying operating system and hardware architecture. Chapter 10 covers CORBA in detail, so this section will only give a brief introduction.

CORBA is composed of five major components which map nicely to the four attributes of a distributed object architecture defined above:

- **Object Request Broker (ORB):** The ORB is the object bus. It provides the middleware that mediates the interactions between client applications needing services and server applications capable of providing them.

- **Interface Definition Language (IDL):** IDL provides architecture and implementation independence to CORBA-compliant applications. It is a declarative language in which object interfaces are defined and advertised. The interface definition is independent of the actual object implementation.

- **Interface Repository:** It is an on-line database of object definitions that can be queried at run-time for dynamic method calls, for locating potentially reusable software components and for type-checking of method signatures.

- **Object Adaptor:** It provides the run-time environment for the server application and handles incoming client calls.

- **CORBA Services:** These augment the functionality of the ORB. CORBA defines services for persistence, transactions, concurrency, database queries, licensing, etc.

CORBA supports static method invocations as well as dynamic method invocations on remote objects through its Dynamic Invocation Interface (DII). CORBA 2.0 also defines a standard for inter-ORB communication, called the Internet Inter-ORB Protocol (IIOP). IIOP is basically TCP/IP with some CORBA-defined message exchanges that serve as a common backbone protocol. Thus, we can see that CORBA provides all the services outlined in the common set of services for a distributed object architecture. For more information on CORBA please refer to the next chapter. *The Essential Distributed Objects Survival Guide* [18] is an authoritative reference on CORBA.

Java

In this section we will talk about Java in the context of distributed computing. First of all let's discuss some basic facts about Java. More information on Java can be found in Chapter 8.

Java is a simple, object-oriented, architecture-neutral, portable, interpreted, and high-performance programming language and provides a distributed, robust, secure, multithreaded and dynamic execution environment.

Java specifies a "bytecode" representation for compiled Java programs rather than a binary representation. Java bytecode is platform independent and is transportable over a network. It can be interpreted and executed by a "Java Virtual Machine" (JVM)—a run-time executable available on an ever-growing number of platforms. The implication is that behavior, and not just data, can be downloaded to a client and executed locally without any sort of setup or compilation.

The main advantages of Java for distributed computing come from this capability to download behavior. Java enables three fundamental capabilities:

- It allows clients to dynamically gain an intelligence they did not originally have by downloading classes. This intelligence can be added to pre-existing client behavior without need for cumbersome recompilation and setup procedures.

- It simplifies software upgrade issues in large distributed systems. Upgrading client software becomes a lot easier, because it only involves downloading Java code over the network to the local machine and substituting it for the old code. There are no cumbersome recompilation and linking stages involved.

- The canonical bytecode and JVM interpreter simplify software development for heterogeneous platforms. A single application can run on multiple platforms. Thus, developers can concentrate on the actual application and still support a large number of operating platforms for their components.

In terms of a full-fledged distributed object architecture, the current implementation of Java (JDK 1.1.2) provides quite a few options, which are as follows:

- **Client/server method invocation paradigm:** The Java Remote Method Invocation Specification (RMI) is an API that lets you create objects whose methods can be invoked from a different Java Virtual Machine (JVM). The client JVM may be running in the same physical machine or a remote server. Thus, RMI basically provides the capability for calling methods on remote objects. This maps to the object bus component in a distributed object architecture.

- **Object registry:** RMI provides an object registry mechanism where distributed objects can be registered. Client programs can contact this registry and find out what objects are currently registered and active.

- **Object persistence and streamable storage:** The Object Serialization API provides a persistence mechanism for Java objects.

- **Distribution services:** Java does offer some distributed services which are not as explicit as provided by CORBA.

  - It provides a security API which can be used for distributed security via code-signing and certificates.
  - It also provide the Java Database Connectivity (JDBC) API for querying SQL databases.
  - JavaSoft is working on providing a service for transactions and concurrency management in distributed Java applications known as JavaSpaces.
  - Java IDL provides a way for transparently connecting Java clients to network servers using the industry-standard Interface Definition Language. It allows a Java client to transparently invoke a CORBA object on a remote server. Similarly, it allows a Java server to define objects that can be transparently invoked from CORBA IDL clients.

A Short Introduction to Related APIs

The new APIs in Java 1.1 make Java a more suitable medium for distributed computing, and a better, more robust distributed object architecture. What follows is a short introduction to these new APIs.

- **Remote Method Invocation Specification [5]:** RMI enables the programmer to create distributed Java-to-Java applications, in which the methods of remote Java objects can be invoked from other Java virtual machines, possibly on different hosts. A Java program can make a call on a remote object once it obtains a reference to the remote object, either by looking up the remote object in the bootstrap naming service provided by RMI or by receiving the reference as an argument or a return value. A client can call a remote object in a server, and that server can also be a client of other remote objects. RMI uses Object Serialization to marshal and unmarshal parameters and does not truncate types, supporting true object-oriented polymorphism.

- **Object Serialization Specification [7]:** Object Serialization extends the core Java Input/Output classes with support for objects. It supports the encoding of objects, and the objects reachable from them, into a stream of bytes and the complimentary reconstruction of the objects from the stream. It can be used for storing Java objects in a persistent state and reviving them whenever necessary. It can also be used for communication via sockets or RMI. The default encoding of objects protects private and transient data and supports the evolution of the classes. A class may implement its own external encoding and is then solely responsible for the external format.

- **Java Database Connectivity API [4]**. JDBC is a standard SQL database access interface. This API provides Java programmers with a uniform interface to a wide range of relational databases and provides a common base on which higher level tools and interfaces can be built. The JDBC API defines Java classes to represent database connections, SQL statements, result sets, database metadata, etc. It allows a Java programmer to issue SQL statements and process the results.

- **Java IDL [8]:** Java IDL provides standards-based interoperability and connectivity with CORBA (Common Object Request Broker Architecture), which is the open industry standard for heterogeneous language-independent computing. It specifies the mapping from IDL to Java and includes a tool named *idltojava* which automatically generates stub code for specific remote interfaces. The generated stubs are independent of any specific ORB and call into ORB-specific modules for data marshalling or any other ORB-specific operations. Java IDL also supports the CORBA naming service with the tool *nameserv*. The portable Java ORB core which supports IIOP version 1.0 is structured to make it easy to plug in new ORB protocols.

- **Java Security API [10]:** It is a framework for developers to easily and securely include high- as well as low-level security functionality in their applets and applications. It includes APIs for cryptography with digital signatures and message digests, data encryption, key management, and access control. Specific APIs support X.509 v3 certificates and other certificate formats.

JDK 1.1 also provides a tool named *javakey*, which is used to sign Java ARchive (JAR) files. The appletviewer allows any downloaded applets in JAR files signed (using the tool) by a trusted entity to run with the same full rights as local applications. This feature will be available very soon in the most popular Web browsers too.

Distributed Component Object Model (DCOM)

DCOM is Microsoft's standard for distributed computing. It is a third important standard to consider in the world of distributed objects. It is an extension of Microsoft's Component Object Model which forms the foundation for the Windows platform. It is also called Network OLE, as it supports distributed OLE controls. DCOM is based on Open Software Foundation's DCE-RPC specification for providing distributed services. It also forms the basis for the ActiveX[1] technology.

Comparing Paradigms

Let's take a short look at the relative merits and demerits of CORBA and Java as platforms for distributed computing.

Architecture Neutrality vs. Communication Transparency: Java provides architecture neutrality, while CORBA provides communications transparency and local/remote transparency. Local and remote invocations are syntactically and functionally equivalent for CORBA objects. CORBA also provides platform dependence, but CORBA applications can suffer from a new type of dependence, namely ORB dependence. Two applications using two different commercial CORBA ORBs might have problems in communicating with each other if the ORB implementations are not compatible with each other.

- **Single Language vs. Language Independence:** Java is a single language, while CORBA was designed to bridge language differences as well as other system differences. CORBA simplifies mixed language programming.

- **Distributed Services:** CORBA defines a much richer set of distributed services than Java does currently. However, new Java APIs that are being designed take a concrete step towards providing many of these services in Java.

- **Commercial Availability and Industry Support:** Commercial availability of CORBA-compliant ORBs is limited. Even the ones that exist are slow and inefficient. Java, on the other hand, is a complete implementation and

---

[1] http://www.microsoft.com/activex

is freely available. CORBA is an industry standard supported by over 500 companies while Java is a company standard.

- **Complexity**:   CORBA requires too much machinery for simple client/ server applications that are relatively easy to develop in Java.

Although Microsoft's DCOM is a relatively new standard, it has the potential to offer a tough fight to CORBA and Java, because of the wide popularity of the Windows desktop and the large number of applications available for it. More information on DCOM can be obtained from Microsoft's DCOM Web site [15].

9.3 Compound Document Frameworks

Compound document frameworks is the second important paradigm to consider for making Web documents more interactive with active multimedia content. So let's define a compound document framework. A compound document framework acts as a **container** in which a continuous stream of **various kinds of data** can be placed. Each form of content has **associated controls** that are used to modify the content **in-place**, and with **uniform user interfaces**.

It is important to understand the meanings of the different keywords in the above definition. In a sense, a Microsoft Word document is a partial compound document. You can put text, tables, images and drawings in it and Word provides the controls to manipulate each of these. Let's try to define the different functionalities that a compound document provides.

Compound documents:

- provide an intuitive way to group together related objects
- display seamlessly in a window
- are stored in a shared file
- can be shipped across networks to other desktops or to servers
- maintain persistent client/server links that allow those embedded components extract data from servers anywhere in the enterprise

Compound document data can be any of the following:

- Movies, sounds, and animation
- Text documents and spreadsheets
- Database access components
- Networked calendars
- Statistical data
- URLs

Thus, the document becomes the universal client—the ultimate front-end to servers. The desktop itself is becoming a giant compound document that integrates in a "borderless" manner applications and operating system services. Instead of switching between applications, you manipulate parts of a document. Different types of data in a compound document are contained in different types of "components." As defined in the first section of the chapter a "component" is a smart object that is independent of any applications and can by shipped anywhere and put into a container to co-exist with other components. As we will see, the functionality provided by the compound documents is not enough. Some more support is needed from the underlying framework.

The framework provides:

- an **organized environment** for running a collection of components and protocols for interaction between them.

- a **structured storage capability** that enables storage of various types of components in a single document file.

- a **scripting and automation facility** through which appropriate actions can be specified for specific events.

- a **uniform data transfer** mechanism that can be used with a variety of protocols—including clipboard, cut-and-paste, drag-and-drop, and linking.

In this section we will look at three existing compound document technologies, viz OpenDoc, Object Linking and Embedding, and JavaBeans. It is not possible to explain all of them in detail in such short space, but we will try to give an intuitive idea about each. Again, [18] is an authoritative reference on compound document frameworks.

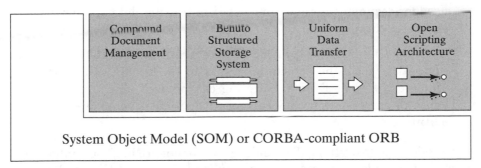

Figure 9-1   OpenDoc Architecture

OpenDoc

OpenDoc is the compound document standard proposed by Component Integration Labs (CI Labs) formed in 1993 by Apple, IBM, and other companies. The Object Management Group (OMG) has adopted OpenDoc as the official compound document standard for CORBA-compliant systems. OpenDoc provides all the facilities and capabilities provided by a compound document framework as mentioned previously. Fig. 9–1 shows OpenDoc architecture.

The components in an OpenDoc document are called "parts." A part consists of data stored in compound documents, including text, graphics, spreadsheets, and video, and a "part editor" that manipulates this data. OpenDoc parts can support almost any kind of data. The good thing about parts is that they are not constrained to be rectangular; a part can be any shape. From a client-server point of view, OpenDoc acts as a central integration point for multiple sources of data that reside on different servers. Let's look at the different components of the OpenDoc architecture.

- OpenDoc uses IBM's **System Object Model** (SOM) as the underlying object bus. SOM is a CORBA-compliant ORB and provides local and remote interoperability for OpenDoc parts. It allows OpenDoc developers to package their parts in binary format and ship them as Dynamic Link Libraries (DLLs).

- OpenDoc provides a structured storage facility called **Bento**. Bento defines a container format that can be used in files, network streams, clipboards, etc. It allows applications to store and retrieve collections of objects in a single structure file, along with their references to other objects. The Bento container format is platform-neutral; it can store any type of data. Thus it is a carrier for exchanging compound documents between applications running on different platforms.

- OpenDoc provides a **uniform data transfer** mechanism for data transfer across and within the same application. The same method invocations used for document storage can be used to transfer data and parts via drag-and-drop, cut-and-paste, and linking.

- OpenDoc specifies the **Open Scripting Architecture (OSA)** for defining semantic events and attaching scripts to them. OSA is an extension of Macintosh's Apple Events. Scripting can be used for giving more intelligence to parts, so that they can react to specific events such as creation, editing, etc.

In addition, Novell is distributing "ComponentGlue," an interface and library that provide seamless interoperability between OLE and OpenDoc for Windows.

Thus, parts can be linked to corporate databases, work-flow managers, image repositories, e-mail, or the local spreadsheet. The document acts as a repository of client-server relationships or "links" to external data sources and remote functions. More information on OpenDoc can be found at Apple's Open-Doc Website[2] [1].

Object Linking and Embedding

OLE is the object-based foundation of the Windows platform. It is an integral part of Windows 95. It consists of a number of interfaces that define a set of related functions. OLE architecture is very similar to OpenDoc architecture. There are significant differences, which we will see in a later section. Fig. 9–2 illustrates the OLE architecture.

OLE supports two types of compound-document objects: linked or embedded. The difference is in the how and where the actual source of the object's data is stored.

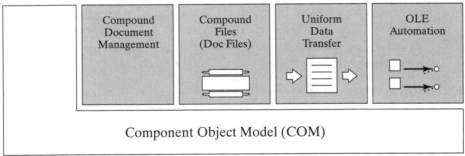

Figure 9–2   OLE Architecture

- **Linked Objects:** When an object is linked, the source data, or link source, continues to reside wherever it was initially created. Only a link to the object and the appropriate presentation data is kept within the compound document. Linked objects cannot travel with documents to another machine, unless they are copied explicitly.

- **Embedded Objects:** A copy of the original object is physically stored in the compound document, as is all the information needed to manage the component. You can edit embedded objects in-place.

---

[2] http://opendoc.apple.com/index.html

OLE provides a complete environment for components and a set of common services that allow these components to collaborate intelligently. Eventually Windows will evolve into a giant collection of OLE interfaces, with COM providing the underlying object bus and services. Let's look at the individual components of the OLE architecture.

- **Object Bus:** Microsoft's Component Object Model (COM) provides the object bus for OLE components. It separates interface from implementations and provides a local Remote Procedure Call (RPC) facility. It is called Lightweight RPC, as it does not support remote method invocations. The recently announced Distributed COM model does support remote method calls. COM's object model does not support multiple inheritance. Instead, a COM component can support multiple interfaces.

- **Automation and Scripting:** OLE's Automation and Scripting services allow server components to be controlled by automation clients (also called "controllers"). An automation controller is typically driven by a scripting language or from a tool such as Visual Basic.

- **Structured Storage**: OLE provides a structured storage facility similar to OpenDoc, called compound files. Compound files create a "file within a file" by introducing a layer of indirection on top of existing file systems. Compound files break a file into a collection of storages (or directories) and streams (or raw data values).

- **Uniform Data Transfer:** Like OpenDoc, OLE provides a generalized intercomponent data transfer mechanism that can be used in a wide range of situations and across a variety of media. Data can be exchanged using protocols such as the clipboard, drag-and-drop, links, or compound documents. The actual transfer can take place over shared memory or using storage files.

- **Compound Document Service:** It defines the interfaces between a container application and the server component that it controls. In this case, a server is a visual component that "serves" a container.

OLE Tools and Foundation Classes

Several visual tools are available for developing OLE-compliant applications. These tools include a C++ class framework called the Microsoft Foundation Classes (MFC), Visual C++, and Visual Basic. Additional tools are available from Borland and other vendors. MFC is a C++ class library for Windows development. Most of this code simply encapsulates the OLE interfaces with C++ classes. MFC supports OLE automation, compound documents, and controls.

The language of choice for OLE development is C++ because it nicely maps to the way OLE interface pointers are implemented. Visual C++ provides a graphic environment for creating OLE applications on top of MFC 3.0 and the OLE Custom Control Development Kit (CDK). The Visual C++ AppStudio lets you create and edit views, dialog boxes, bitmaps, icons, menus, and other resources. Extensive information on the internals or OLE/COM can be found at Microsoft's OLE development Website [16].

JavaBeans

The third important player to consider in the compound document market is JavaBeans. JavaBeans is a new API for the Java platform, to provide a software component model for Java. The main goal is to enable developers to write re-usable components once and then run them anywhere.

The Java Beans API was first included in JDK 1.1. According to the Java-Beans API specification, a JavaBean is a reusable software component that can be manipulated visually in a builder tool. The builder tools may include Web page builders, visual application builders, GUI layout builders, or even server application builders.

There are a range of different kinds of components that can be built as JavaBeans:

- Some JavaBeans will be used as building blocks in **composing applications**, e.g. buttons, lists, etc.

- Some JavaBeans will be more like regular applications, which may then be composed into **compound documents,** e.g., a JavaBeans spreadsheet.

The design center for Beans ranges from small controls such as buttons, up through simple compound documents such as Web pages. JavaBeans provides APIs that are analogous to an OLE control or ActiveX APIs, but does not provide the full range of high-end document APIs provided by OpenDoc. However, Java-Beans can be embedded in platform-specific containers such as an OpenDoc document, Netscape Navigator, or even a Word document by using a bridge to the native document framework.

Some of the other goals of the JavaBeans APIs are as follows:

- **It provides a platform neutral component architecture.** When a JavaBean is nested inside another JavaBean it will provide a full-functionality implementation on all platforms. However, at the top level, when the root JavaBean is embedded in some platform-specific container, then the JavaBeans API should be integrated into the platform's local component architecture (e.g., COM for Windows).

- **It provides a uniform, high-quality GUI API for different platforms.** Platforms will vary in their ability to support the full JavaBeans APIs. However, whenever a platform is unable to provide the full functionality it must provide some reasonable, harmless default instead.

- **It provides simplicity to component development.** It focuses on making small lightweight components easy to implement and use, while making heavyweight components possible.

The JavaBeans API makes heavy use of the other APIs in Java, such as RMI, object serialization and others. The API provides following services:

- **Component interface publishing and discovery:** The publishing system allows components to locate other components and to communicate with them. JavaBeans can make use of the RMI specification for remote method calls and Java IDL for interfacing with CORBA-based systems. JavaBeans also supports component introspection so that it becomes possible to find out the component's properties. It makes use of the Java Core Reflection API for this.

- **Event handling:** Events are a way for one component to notify other components that something of interest has happened. For example, a click of a button in one component can trigger the update of a graph in another component. The AWT Event model has been updated for JavaBeans.

- **Object persistence:** It allows JavaBeans to be stored away as part of the state of their parent container or as a stand-alone component having a specific state. The stored component can be retrieved at a later time and its state restored from its serialized state. It uses the object serialization mechanism for serializing and deserializing the object. Object serialization is also used by RMI to marshal and unmarshal the parameters for remote method calls.

- **Layout and properties management:** It is possible to define the layout of a component in relation to the other components in the container. Properties are named attributes associated with a bean that can be read or written by calling appropriate methods on the bean. Properties of a bean can be changed to customize it.

- **Application builder support:** Beans are capable of running inside application builder tools and provide custom component editors known as customizers.

- **Structured storage:** The JavaBeans API also specifies a structured storage mechanism called JAR files (Java ARchives), which are basically compressed files in which an entire compound document can be stored along with its state and restored at a later time.

- **Uniform data transfer:** The Java Abstract Windowing Toolkit (AWT) has been enhanced to provide support for data transfer through drag-and-drop and cut-and-paste.

Many vendors have announced that they will support JavaBeans in their products and application builder tools. Apple Computer and IBM Corporation are working with JavaSoft to ensure two-way interoperability between Java-Beans and OpenDoc applications, providing an invisible migration to client/ server applications.

In addition, JavaSoft will ensure that JavaBeans runs seamlessly inside ActiveX containers on Microsoft Windows platforms, as well as inside Netscape Navigator's LiveConnect containers.

Along with the JavaBeans API, JavaSoft also provides a Beans Development Kit (BDK) which can be used as a reference container for developing Beans and other similar bean containers. The current version of the BDK can be downloaded from the JavaBeans Website [12].

Who Will Win the Battle?

Let us first look at the comparative merits and demerits of the OpenDoc and OLE compound document frameworks.

Object Models

- OpenDoc follows the classical object model and extends it to components. An OpenDoc component supports inheritance while an OLE component does not. An OLE component is essentially a black box object.

- OpenDoc uses CORBA as the underlying bus for communication between distributed objects. Distributed OLE is still in the developing stages and is not mature yet. OLE does not support remote method invocations.

System Services

- OpenDoc supports all the CORBA distributed services such as RDBMS integration, transactions, concurrency, and security, while none of OLE services are distributed.

Compound Documents

- OpenDoc supports irregularly-shaped parts that help create very seamless-looking documents.

- OpenDoc scripting facilities are also superior, in the sense that they let you operate on a part's contents via semantic messages.

- Bento is more portable than DocFiles.

Supported Platforms

- OLE—Windows, Mac

- OpenDoc—Windows, Mac, OS/2, and various Unixes

From the above list we see that the combination of OpenDoc/CORBA is much superior technically to OLE/COM. Still, OLE leads OpenDoc in the marketplace because of the market share claimed by the Windows platform. Also most of OLE's shortcomings come from the fact that is it does not support distributed objects, which might change very soon with the announcement of the Distributed COM by Microsoft.

This is definitely not the end of the battle of compound documents. Java Beans is coming out as the third major contender in the field, with its promise of architecture neutrality, component reuse, and application builder tools. Although it is not a complete compound document framework like OpenDoc and OLE, it holds a lot of promise. No one can say which compound document standard will win or lose the battle, but it will be an interesting game, where the user has only to gain, rather than to lose anything.

9.4 Putting It All Together

In this section we will try to condense the material covered in the previous sections into a comprehensive whole. We will see how various technologies can be integrated to complement each other in functionality and to provide a better environment for developing Web-based, distributed client-server applications. We will also look at the current developments taking place in this wide field and what their impact can be on the Web. Finally, we will try to visualize what the Web might look like in the future and how it can change the desktop metaphor.

Integration of Technologies

The best way to understand how compound document technology can be integrated with distributed objects is to look at some possible application scenarios.

1. **Database access and charting**: You have an application that can access a remote database on the Web and show you different views of the database. It also contains a component that can take the data obtained from the database and chart it for you in the format you want. All this is controlled by incorporating GUI elements like buttons and lists in the application. For example, the click of a button may activate the database viewer component to send a request to the remote database, get the most recent set of data, and simultaneously instruct the charting component to update the chart on screen.

2. **Real estate agent**: You create a software agent and send it out on the network to query real estate information servers and find out the lowest price of a piece of real estate in a particular area. The agent moves from server to server and, after collecting the information it wants, returns to the home server. It then passes the information it collected to a display component that summarizes the results and presents them to you in a comprehensible manner.

3. **Distributed spell checkers**: Consider a word-processing plug-in in your browser that uses distributed spell checkers and thesauruses on the Web. You don't have to store the huge dictionaries on your machine and you can also spell-check multiple languages. All your spell checker needs to know is the location of the desired language dictionary on the Web.

Thus, compound documents on the user's desktop will contain links to remote compute engines and will access remote databases in real-time. Similarly, it will become possible to integrate Web-based applications with desktop applications in a way that brings the best out of both application domains. The Web will turn from an information warehouse to an application warehouse, with most of the information structured around the applications using it. It is quite possible that today's desktops may be replaced with webtops, with the Web browser providing the front-end for all applications, local as well as remote.

Current Implementations and Developments

Let's take a look at some of the existing products and major developments taking place in the field of distributed objects for the Web. The links point to the Web sites for the respective products.

- **Java Development Kit 1.1**:[3] JDK version 1.1 includes a lot of new APIs for developing commercial corporate applications. Some of the most

---

[3] http://www.javasoft.com/products/JDK/1.1/designspecs

important new features of this release are the JavaBeans API, JDBC API, Java Security API, the Java Electronic Commerce Framework, enhancements to the AWT, and APIs for remote connectivity.

- **Microsoft ActiveX[4] and Visual J++:**[5] ActiveX is a set of technologies from Microsoft that enable interactive content for the Web. ActiveX controls are the interactive objects in a Web page that provide interactive and user-controllable functions. ActiveX documents enable users to view non-HTML documents, such as MS-Excel or Word files through a Web browser.

  Visual J++ is an integrated development environment for building Java applications. It includes a visual debugger, an applet wizard, support for ActiveX controls, a class viewer and a Just-in-Time (JIT) compiler. It also contains a debugging tool that lets you view the internals of an object.

- **IBM's Arabica:**[6] Arabica is IBM's solution to supporting Java applets in an OpenDoc environment. Arabica components will be delivered as a set of JavaBeans. Arabica is a rapid assembly tool for developing platform-independent applications for the corporate world.

- **Apple's Cyberdog:**[7] Cyberdog is Apple's new approach to the Web using OpenDoc technology. It provides you with the ability to browse the Web, read and write e-mail, follow newsgroups, use ftp, telnet, and gophers, and even view text, movies, sounds, pictures, and QuickTime VR files on the Web. All of these services are included without the need for any helper applications.

- **Netscape LiveConnect:**[8] LiveConnect is a set of software development kits offered by Netscape for developing plug-ins for the Netscape Navigator. It also offers facilities for integrating plug-ins with Java applets and JavaScript. This allows plug-ins to be controlled by Java applets, and also by JavaScript routines contained in the HTML page.

- **Iona's Orbix:**[9] Orbix is a complete implementation of CORBA for developing distributed object-oriented client/server applications. Orbix provides C++, Ada95, and Java language bindings for CORBA and is supported on more than 10 UNIX platforms, Windows 3.1, Windows 95, OS/2, Mac,

---

[4] http://www.microsoft.com/activex

[5] http://www.microsoft.com/visualj

[6] http://ncc.hursley.ibm.com/javainfo/latest/javacomponents.html

[7] http://cyberdog.apple.com

[8] http://home.netscape.com/comprod/development_partners/plugin_api/

[9] http://www.iona.com/Orbix/

VMS, and some others. The first version of Orbix was released in June 1993.

- **IBM Aglets Workbench**:[10] Aglets are active agents programmed in Java using the Java RMI API. Aglets are objects that can move from host to host and return to their original host after collecting some useful information or doing some useful work. The Aglets Workbench is a visual environment for building network-based applications that use agents to search for, access, and manage corporate data and other information.

- **Spyglass's Enhanced Mosaic Toolkit**:[11] The Enhanced Mosaic Kit is similar in concept to Apple's Cyberdog. Spyglass licenses Enhanced Mosaic to software developers; it is the core of several commercial Internet clients, including Microsoft's Internet Explorer and Oracle's Power Browser. It is available for the Windows platform, Mac and UNIX, as well as operating systems, such as those used in PDAs and smart phones.

Future Architectures

There is a lot more to the Web than just surfing through hypertext information. It has the capability to transform the way in which we carry out our computing tasks as well as our daily business. Let's look at some scenarios that can become possible in future if the Web and Object technology successfully merge together [18].

- The Web will be an electronic market of planetary proportions. There will be boutiques, department stores, bookstores, banks, and travel agencies on the Web. Electronic currency and round-the-clock shopping will become a common thing.

- Electronic agents will be roaming around the networks looking for bargains and conducting negotiations with other agents. There will be sniffer agents which will collect information and statistics and do system management.

- Massive amounts of multimedia data will be stored in digital libraries and will be moved and stored on the network. People will be able to watch movies on the Web, and pay-per-view will become common for material on the Web.

- The desktop metaphor will have changed entirely to subsume the facilities provided by the Web. Microsoft will couple Internet Explorer 4.0 with the user interface in Windows 98.

---

[10] http://www.ibm.com.jp/trl/aglets

[11] http://www.spyglass.com/products/index.html

All these might seem to be wishful thinking at present, but if Web technology moves at the same pace as it is now, creating the above scenarios will not take much time.

9.5 Conclusion

Web users are demanding more and more sophistication from Web browsers for applications such as electronic commerce and on-line digital libraries. There is a strong need for a new programming model in which Web browsers become interactive clients containing application logic, while Web pages become behavioral servers. The popularity of Java attests to this demand.

Distributed objects can provide the required model. Compound document frameworks provide the capabilities of converting static Web pages into multimedia-rich interactive clients, and distributed object architectures provide the client-server capabilities required for servicing applications on millions of servers.

This chapter is only an overview of the different types of technology available and emerging in the field of distributed objects. Considering the rate at which new developments are taking place in this field, it is quite possible that some of the content of this chapter may become out of date very soon, or there might be a need to add new content. The references provided at the end of the chapter should be helpful, if you find that to be the case. In fact, why shouldn't that be the case? After all, we are trying to make the Web a more dynamic medium for communication and information dissemination by using all the technology available to us.

9.6 References

[1]   Apple Computer, Inc. "Apple OpenDoc."
       <http://opendoc.apple.com/index.html> (9 Sept. 1997).

[2]   JavaSoft. "Java API overview."
        <http://www.javasoft.com/products/apiOverview.html> (9 Sept. 1997).

[3]   JavaSoft. "JDK 1.1 API Documentation."
       <http://www.javasoft.com/products/JDK/1.1/docs/index.html>   (9   Sept.
       1997).

[4]   JavaSoft. "The JDBC database access API."
      <http://splash.javasoft.com/jdbc/index.html> (9 Sept. 1997).

[5]   JavaSoft. "Java RMI Documentation."
      <http://java.sun.com/products/jdk/1.1/docs/guide/rmi/index.html> (9 Sept.
      1997).

[6]   JavaSoft. "RMI Frequently Asked Questions List."
      <http://chatsubo.javasoft.com/current/faq.html> (9 Sept. 1997).

[7]   JavaSoft. "Java Object Serialization."
      <http://chatsubo.javasoft.com/current/serial/index.html> (9 Sept. 1997).

[8]   JavaSoft. "Java IDL."
      <http://www.javasoft.com/products/jdk/idl/index.html> (9 Sept. 1997).

[9]   JavaSoft. "Java Electronic Commerce Framework."
      <http://www.javasoft.com/products/commerce/index.html> (9 Sept. 1997).

[10] JavaSoft. "Security and Signed Applets."
      <http://www.javasoft.com/products/JDK/1.1/docs/guide/security/> (9 Sept.
      1997).

[11] JavaSoft. "JDK 1.1 AWT Enhancements."
      <http://java.sun.com/products/JDK/1.1/docs/guide/awt/> (9 Sept. 1997).

[12] JavaSoft. "JavaBeans Specification."
      <http://java.sun.com/beans/index.html> (9 Sept. 1997).

[13] Kafura, D. "Object Oriented Software Design and Construction."
      <http://actor.cs.vt.edu/~kafura/cs2704/Book/TOC.html> (9 Sept. 1997).

[14] Microsoft Corp. "Component Object Model: Technical Overview." 1996
      <http://www.microsoft.com/oledev/olecom/Com_modl.htm> (9 Sept. 1997).

[15] Microsoft Corp. "DCOM for Windows 95, Developer Beta." April 1997
      <http://www.microsoft.com/oledev/olemkt/oledcom/dcom95.htm> (9 Sept.
      1997).

[16] Microsoft Corp. "OLE Development: Technical Articles."
      <http://www.microsoft.com/oledev/articles.stm> (9 Sept. 1997).

[17] Object Management Group. "OMG CORBA Resources."
      <http://www.acl.lanl.gov/CORBA/index.html> (9 Sept. 1997).

[18] Orfali R., D. Harkey, and J. Edwards. *The Essential Distributed Objects
      Survival Guide.* New York: Wiley, 1996. ISBN 0471-12993-3.

[19] Resnick, Ron I. "Bringing Distributed Objects to the World Wide Web."
1996.   <http://www.interlog.com/~resnick/javacorb/index.html>   (9   Sept.
1997).

[20] Stroustrup, B. *C++ Programming Language*, 2nd Ed. Reading, MA:
Addison-Wesley, 1992.

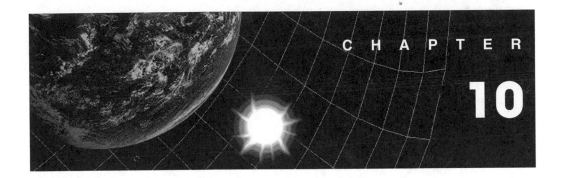

Common Object Request Broker Architecture (CORBA)

by Ashish Shah and Padmapriya Vasudevan

The Common Object Request Broker Architecture, or CORBA as it is better known, is a multivendor standard developed by the Object Management Group (OMG). It is a set of specifications for providing interoperability and portability to distributed object-oriented applications. CORBA-compliant applications can communicate with each other regardless of location, implementation language, underlying operating system and hardware architecture. Communication mainly occurs through method invocations from a client object on a server object.

CORBA is part of the Object Management Architecture (OMA) proposed by OMG. CORBA connects objects, not applications. More support is needed from the underlying software framework in order to connect applications. This support is provided by the rest of the OMA, which consists of *CORBAservices* and *CORBAfacilities*. CORBAservices provide the low-level functionality needed by objects, such as persistence, naming and directory services, transaction services, and so on, while CORBAfacilities provide a high-level framework that can be used by applications to invoke user-level facilities such as compound document management, help facilities, and system administration.

In this chapter we will primarily talk about CORBA and give details about the various components of the CORBA architecture. We will also look at the various method invocation paradigms supported by CORBA. We will briefly touch upon CORBAservices and CORBAfacilities.

Chapter Content

1. Introduction
2. CORBA Components
3. OMG Interface Definition Language

- IDL Structure

- Language Mappings and IDL Compilers

- IDL Stubs and Skeletons

4. Object Request Broker

- Object References

- ORB Interface

- Interface Repository

- Object Adapters

5. Dynamic Method Invocations

- Dynamic Invocation Interface

- Dynamic Skeleton Interface

- Pros and Cons

6. CORBA Interoperability
7. CORBAservices and CORBAfacilities
8. Summary
9. References

10.1 Introduction

Software development is an extremely complex process. In order to reduce the inherent complexity of software construction, more and more people have started adopting object-oriented software design and development. Object-oriented software is easy to build, understand, and maintain, and better supports application development for large enterprises. A second major revolution which is occurring in the computer industry is distributed computing. Distributed client/server computing is becoming very common with the increasing popularity of the Internet, the Web, and corporate intranets as platforms of deployment. A major issue in developing distributed client/server systems is coping with the heterogeneity of systems and achieving interoperability at the application level. Although connectivity between most types of operating systems is available at the network protocol level, interoperability at the application level still remains an issue. Key problem areas include the inherent difficulty of distributed application programming and the lack of standard interfaces between applications.

The Object Management Group (OMG) is an industry consortium of over 700 companies, which includes most major computer companies (e.g., Sun, IBM, HP, DEC), the only notable exception being Microsoft. The goal of the OMG is to develop and promote standards for the deployment of object-oriented applications in heterogeneous distributed environments. Towards this end the OMG has created the Object Management Architecture (OMA). CORBA is a major component of the OMA, the other two components being CORBAservices and CORBAfacilities. CORBA defines standards for a distributed object architecture. A distributed object architecture is defined in Section 9.1. The same section also gives a short description of classical and distributed objects. To recap, distributed objects are objects that can live anywhere on the network and can be accessed by client objects running on any machine across the network as well as on the local machine.

CORBA provides interoperability and portability to distributed object-oriented applications. It enables application-level interaction in the form of method invocations by client objects on server objects. It also provides facilities for creating and deleting objects, accessing them by object IDs, and storing them in databases. It also hides all the low-level details of distributed computing like traditional TCP byte-streams. It simplifies application interworking and provides the foundation for collaboration among applications at a much higher level using distributed objects.

10.2 CORBA Components

There are various ways in which applications can interact in a distributed, networked computing environment. Examples are low-level sockets, remote procedure calls, CORBA, Java RMI, and some others. Any such mechanism must support interaction between applications which run on various operating systems and hardware architectures and have been developed using different languages. This is becoming even more important with the increasing popularity of the Internet and the Web.

CORBA allows software running on different machines to communicate, without being aware of the underlying hardware or software systems or the relative location of the other application. Distributed, object-oriented applications generally consist of client objects that call upon server objects for performing some services. In order for objects to plug and play together in a useful way, clients have to know exactly what type of services are provided by the server object and the exact mechanism for invoking those services.

In CORBA, the services an object provides are expressed in a contract that serves as the interface between it and the rest of the system. The **interface** informs the clients of services available, tells them how to invoke each service, and also tells the **communication framework** about the format of messages it may have to send and receive. This helps the communication framework in translating data formats whenever necessary in order to provide a transparent connection. In addition to the interface, an object also needs a unique identifier that is location-independent. This identifier is referred to as an **object reference**. Even if the server object moves from its original location, its object reference must remain the same; it's the responsibility of the communication framework to figure out the exact object location from the reference. Thus, each server object has a well-defined interface and is identified by a unique object reference. Messages between objects identify the target object with its identifier, and the message format is defined by the object's interface that is known to the system. The framework takes care of the rest.

Now we can define the two major CORBA components: **OMG Interface Definition Language (IDL)** and the **Object Request Broker (ORB)**. IDL is the declarative language in which all interfaces are expressed, and the ORB provides the underlying communication framework that takes care of the transparent interaction between the client and server objects.

Fig. 10–1 shows a very simplified view of the CORBA architecture. It shows the steps involved in passing a request from a client object to a server object. The request is basically a method invocation on the server object.

Clients see only the server object's IDL interface, never the implementation. All communication between the client and the ORB and the implementation and the ORB is through IDL interfaces. An invocation request always passes through an ORB. Invocation is transparent to object location; the client or the server sees no difference in a local or remote method invocation.

Besides the ORB core and the OMG IDL the other components of CORBA are as follows:

- Interface Repository

- Language Mappings

- Dynamic Invocation Interface (DII)

- Object Adapters

- Inter-ORB Protocols (e.g., IIOP)

We will explain each of these components in the remaining sections of this chapter.

10.3 OMG Interface Definition Language

In order to make requests on a server object, the client must know the types of

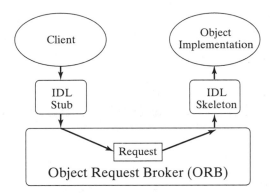

Figure 10-1 Basic CORBA Architecture

services provided by the object and the mechanism to invoke those services. The server object's interface specifies the types of operations it supports and defines how to invoke those operations. These interfaces are defined using the OMG Interface Definition Language (IDL). Interfaces are similar to C++ classes and Java interfaces.

IDL is language-independent. It is a declarative language, which means that it does not specify any implementation details. It forces interfaces to be defined separately from object implementations. IDL-defined methods can be written in and invoked from any language that provides CORBA bindings (C, C++, Smalltalk, COBOL, and Java at present). It basically acts as an intermediate neutral interface which allows client and server objects written in different languages to interoperate across networks and operating systems. IDL grammar is a subset of C++ with additional keywords to support distributed concepts. It supports a C++ like syntax for constants, type and operation declarations. IDL is a **strongly typed** language.

IDL Structure

The following code shows a typical IDL representation of a component [4].

```
module <module_name>
{

   <user-defined type declarations>;
```

```
<constant declarations>;
<exception declarations>;

interface <interface_name> [:<parent_interface_name>]
{

    <user-defined type declarations>
    <constant declarations>;
    <exception declarations>;
    <attribute declarations>;


    [<operation_type>] <operation_name> (<parameter_list>)
        [raises exception_name, ...][context(context1, ...)] ;

    ...
}

interface <interface_name> [:<parent_interface_name>]

...
}
```

Different elements of the above interface structure can be explained as follows:

- **Modules** are a set of interfaces (class descriptions) grouped together under a common name. A module is identified by the keyword *module*.

- **Interfaces** define a set of operations (methods) that a client can invoke on an object. An interface may also have attributes (private variables), and each of these attributes have implicit *get* and *set* methods for retrieving and setting values of these attributes.

- An important feature of IDL interfaces is that they can **inherit** from one or more other interfaces. Thus, existing interfaces can be reused and their functionality can be extended and built upon. IDL defines inheritance relationships using a syntax similar to the C++ syntax.

- An **operation** is a method and the operation's *signature* consists of the return type, the operation name, and the list of parameters required to invoke the operation. Every parameter has a *mode* which gives the direction of passing of values from server to client (out) or client to server (in) or both (inout). The *operation_type* is the type of the return value. Every operation can also optionally raise **exceptions**. IDL allows you to declare a **context** for an operation. A context is a list of name-value pairs and is the CORBA equivalent of UNIX or DOS environment variables.

- **Data Types** describe parameters, attributes and the return values that CORBA supports. CORBA supports two categories of data types: *basic* and *constructed*. CORBA's basic types include `short`, `long`, `long long`, `unsigned short`, `unsigned long`, `unsigned long long`, `float`, `double`, `long double`, `char`, `wchar`, `boolean`, and `octet`. CORBA's constructed types include `enum`, `string`, `struct`, `union`, `sequence` and `any`. The `struct` and `union` types are similar to the corresponding constructs in C/C++. The `sequence` type represents a variable-size array of objects. The `any` data type represents both basic and constructed data types dynamically.

- Definitions of types, constants, exceptions, interfaces, and modules are **scoped**; that is, they are in effect only within the section in which they are defined. The scoping operator (::) can be used to import a definition from an external scope.

- IDL has a special case of interface inheritance. All IDL interfaces inherit implicitly from the predefined **Object** interface defined in the pre-defined **CORBA** module (CORBA::Object). This is similar to all Java classes implicitly inheriting from the Object superclass.

Language Mappings and IDL Compilers

IDL is not a full-fledged programming language and does not provide features like control constructs. Instead, OMG-defined standard language mappings determine how IDL features get mapped to a real programming language. Till now, OMG has standardized language mappings for C, C++, Smalltalk, Ada, COBOL, and Java. Nonstandard language mappings for other languages such as Perl, Eiffel, and Modula-3 have been written by other interested parties. Table 10–1 shows the IDL language mapping for C++, as standardized by the OMG.

In object-oriented languages CORBA objects are directly mapped to programming language objects, but in other languages such as C, objects are mapped to abstract data types, such as struct definitions. The language mapping also specifies how the ORB interface and other predefined pseudo-objects within the CORBA specification are accessed from the given programming language.

The language mapping is embedded into the corresponding IDL compiler for that particular language. Given an IDL interface definition for a server object, the job of the IDL compiler is to use the standard language mapping and generate the corresponding **IDL stub and skeleton** files. Stubs are used on the client side and skeletons are used on the server side.

IDL Stubs and Skeletons

Fig. 10–2 shows the process through which IDL stubs and skeletons are generated and the role they play in transparently passing an invocation from the client object to the actual implementation of the server object. Stubs act as proxy objects from the client's viewpoint and skeletons act as proxy objects from the ORB's viewpoint. The response from the server object traces the same path back to the client.

Table 10–1 IDL to C++ Mapping

OMG IDL Type	C++ Type
module	namespaces
interface	class
operations	class member functions
object reference	pointer or object
long, short	long, short
float, double	float, double
enum	enum
char	char
boolean	bool
octet	unsigned char
any	Any class
struct	struct
union	class
string	char *
wstring	wchar_t *
sequence	class
fixed	Fixed template class

The stub works with the ORB to marshal the request, that is, to convert it from its programming language representation to one that is suitable for transmission over the connection to the target object. Once the request arrives at the target object, the ORB and the skeleton unmarshal the request from its trans-

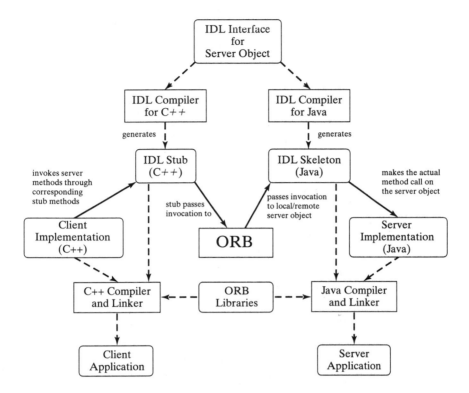

Figure 10–2   IDL Stubs and Skeletons

missible form to the programming language representation and dispatch it to the object.

Static Method Invocation

Calling server methods through stubs and skeletons is often called static method invocation because the stubs and skeletons are directly built (linked) into the client and server applications. Thus, the applications know of the objects and methods being invoked at compile-time itself.

10.4 Object Request Broker

The Object Request Broker (ORB) is the CORBA component that delivers client requests to server objects, and returns any response to the client. To the client, the request looks like a local method call; the ORB provides local/remote transparency and hides the details of the underlying communication framework. The

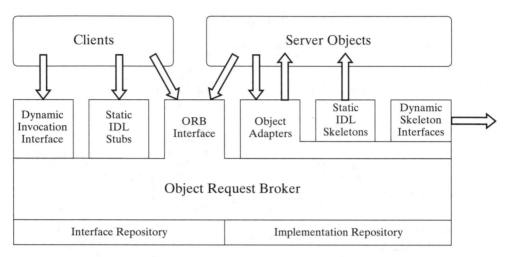

Figure 10-3   ORB Components

target object could reside in a different process on another machine across the network (with a completely different hardware architecture and operating system), on the same machine in a different process, or within the same process. It could be implemented in the same language as the client or in any other language that has CORBA bindings. The client does not have to know the execution state of the server object, that is, whether it is running and ready to receive requests or not. If the object is not ready (activated) the ORB transparently activates it before passing the request.

As shown in Fig. 10–3, the various components of the ORB Core are as follows:

- ORB Interface and ORB Core
- Client Stubs and Static IDL Skeletons
- Dynamic Invocation Interface (DII) and Dynamic Skeleton Interface (DSI)
- Interface Repository (IR)
- Object Adapters (OA)
- CORBA 2.0 Interoperability (GIOP and IIOP)

As shown in Section 10.3, IDL stubs and skeletons are used during static method invocations on the target objects. CORBA uses OMG IDL to separate interface from object implementation. The client and server implementations are isolated by at least three components: IDL stub on client side, ORB (or several ORBs), and IDL skeleton on implementation end. Stubs define the method by which clients invoke services on servers. A client has an IDL stub for each interface it uses on the server. CORBA also allows dynamic method invocations by discovering objects and services at run-time. We will talk about the two ORB components that facilitate dynamic method invocations, DII and DSI, in Section 10.5.

Object References

Every CORBA object is uniquely identified by an object reference. The object reference is assigned by the ORB at object creation and remains valid till object deletion. An object reference is not just a network or memory address. An object can move around on the network, and the reference to it will still be valid. Besides, the client does not have access to any internal details of the object reference; only the ORB can manipulate references. An object reference can be passed as a parameter of a method invocation or returned from an invocation.

In order to obtain the services from a server object, a client has to obtain an object reference to it from the ORB. Clients can obtain object references in a variety of ways.

- An object reference to a newly created object is returned when a client invokes a creation operation on the ORB interface.

- A client can also invoke a lookup service of some kind in order to obtain object references. The CORBA **Trader service** and the **Naming service** allow clients to obtain references by name or properties of objects. These services do not create new objects, they just store references of existing objects and supply them upon request.

- The ORB can convert object references to strings and vice versa. These strings, representing the references, can be stored in persistent storage, retrieved later, and converted into object references. These retrieved references will be valid if the object still exists.

ORB Interface

The ORB provides services for:

- creating and deleting objects
- accessing them by name
- storing them in persistent storage
- externalizing their state
- defining relationships among objects

These services are provided through the **ORB interface**. The most important part of the ORB interface is the initialization component. Since the only way of creating a new object in CORBA is by making requests on other objects, the ORB provides a way to obtain the initial set of object references. When the client starts up, it needs object references to a Naming service and to the Interface Repository. These are obtained by passing service names to the `resolve_initial_references` operation of the ORB interface. Service names are obtained by invoking the `list_initial_services` operation of the ORB interface. The ORB interface also provides operations to convert object references to and from strings.

The object interface, which is implicitly inherited by every IDL interface, is a part of the ORB interface. This interface defines operations that are valid on all CORBA objects, such as duplicating and deleting the object, creating a dynamic invocation request for the object, and accessing the implementation and type information for the object.

Interface Repository

An operation supported by the `object` interface, and hence all object references, is the `get_interface()` operation. This operation returns an object reference to an `InterfaceDef` that describes the object's interface. This interface definition is stored in the Interface Repository (IR). The IR allows navigation of an object's inheritance hierarchy and provides descriptions of all the operations it supports. Definitions can be retrieved, modified, and deleted. The services of the IR can be accessed directly through the standard IR IDL interface or through custom libraries provided by the ORB vendor.

The IR can be used in a variety of different ways by the client, the ORB, and the server object. Since the IR allows clients to programmatically discover type information at run-time, its main utility is in supporting dynamic method invocations (see Section 10.5). It can be used by clients to manage installation and distribution of interface definitions and by IDL compilers to compile stubs and skeletons directly from the IR. The IR can be used by the ORB for type-checking of request signatures for dynamic invocations and to check correctness of object inheritance graphs.

Object Adapters

The CORBA philosophy has been to keep the client side as simple as possible. To the client, it looks as though every object is running and active all the time, even though it may not be. The client only has to send a request, the ORB takes care of the rest. The **Object Adapter (OA)** is responsible for much of this activation transparency. It serves as the intermediate software layer that connects the ORB and the object implementation. It prepares the object to receive a request, and allows objects to notify the ORB that they are ready to process requests. The main duties of the OA include:

- **Object Registration**—Object adapters allow actual programming language implementations to be registered as CORBA objects in the implementation repository. Exact details of the registration vary by each programming language.

- **Generation of Object References**—The OA is responsible for assigning unique object references to each object implementation.

- **Object Activation**—When a request for an inactive object arrives, the OA is responsible for creating and activating the object.

- **Activation of Server Process**—If necessary, the OA can also start up the server processes in which the objects can be activated.

- **Request Handling**—The object adapter interacts with incoming client calls and maps the object reference to the corresponding implementation. It identifies the method requested and invokes the corresponding method on the interface skeleton, which in turn invokes the actual object method. It receives the return value and passes it on to the ORB for sending it back to the client.

A different OA is normally necessary for each programming language supported by the ORB, because many of the functions of the OA are specific to the object's implementation. Though multiple object adapters are allowed, currently CORBA supports only one: the Basic Object Adapter (BOA). The BOA is a flexible adapter designed primarily for server objects that reside in their own processes separate from their clients and the ORB. The BOA can accommodate several different kinds of implementations:

- *shared* implementations in which several objects reside in the same program

- *unshared* implementations consisting of one object implementation per program

- *persistent* implementations that are activated outside the BOA

- *server-per-method* implementations in which the BOA starts a separate server for each different object operation

In the next section we will look at CORBA's dynamic method invocation capability.

10.5 Dynamic Method Invocations

CORBA supports two types of method invocation paradigms: static invocations via stubs and skeletons, and dynamic invocations via a couple of interfaces provided by the ORB. As explained in Section 10.3, for static invocations, the client has to call and be statically linked to the stub corresponding to the object's implementation. The developer determines the stubs that a client contains, so this invocation mechanism cannot access new object types that are added to the system at run time. On the other hand, CORBA's Dynamic Invocation Interface (DII) enables a client program to discover new objects at run time and to construct and dispatch dynamic invocations to these objects. It does not require the client-side stub of the object to be statically linked into the client code. This allows clients to access objects as soon as they are added to any ORB on the network. The information for constructing the method invocation is obtained from the interface repository (IR). The Dynamic Skeleton Interface (DSI) handles the server-side component of a dynamic method invocation.

Dynamic Invocation Interface

The DII can be used by client applications to invoke requests on any CORBA object without having compile-time knowledge of the object's interfaces. An invocation request is represented by the `Request` pseudo-object. The `create_request` operation provided by the base object interface returns an object of type `Request`. Since the `object` interface is the base interface for every IDL interface, every CORBA object automatically supports the `create_request` operation. The following is a step-by-step guide on invoking methods on server objects dynamically:

1. The client obtains an object reference to a CORBA object located on any ORB on the network. This reference may be obtained as a return value of a method invocation on some other object or from the IR.

2. The client then invokes the `create_request` operation on the object reference and obtains a `Request` pseudo-object. Information on operations supported by the target object's interface can be obtained from the IR.

3. Argument values have to be provided before invoking the request. The client obtains the argument types by making method calls on the IR. It then provides the argument values for the request by invoking operations on the `Request` object obtained in the previous step.

4. Once the `Request` object has been completely created, the client can invoke the target method on the target object using one of the three possible invocation mechanisms:

- **Synchronous Invocation**: This is the most common invocation mechanism (also used for static invocations) where the client blocks till it receives a response. It is equivalent to a Remote Procedure Call (RPC).
- **Deferred Synchronous Invocation**: The client dispatches the request, continues other processing, and collects the response later on. This invocation method is useful if the request takes a long time to complete and the client has to invoke a number of such requests. Requests can thus be issued in parallel and responses collected as they arrive.
- **Oneway Invocation**: This is a request where no response is expected. The client fires the request and continues processing. It never receives a direct response for the request. It is also possible to make static oneway invocations.

The DII offers a great deal of flexibility in invoking methods on server objects; flexibility that comes at a cost (see the section on "Pros and Cons" on page 211). The CORBA invocation mechanism is completely transparent—so that the server object never knows whether a method was invoked through a statically compiled stub or through the DII.

Dynamic Skeleton Interface

The Dynamic Skeleton Interface (DSI) is the server-side counterpart of the DII. Just as the DII allows clients to invoke requests on objects for which it does not have statically linked stubs, the DSI allows the ORB to access server object implementations without the need for statically linked skeletons. The ORB invokes a single routine, called the Dynamic Invocation Routine (DIR), for each DSI request. The actual object implementation that receives the invocation is required to support the DIR explicitly. The DSI was originally included in the CORBA 2.0 specification in order to support implementation of bridges between ORBs utilizing different communication protocols. It is also useful for certain types of applications that bridge CORBA systems to non-CORBA implementations.

Pros and Cons

Dynamic invocation provides a more flexible environment. It allows the addition of new classes at run time without requiring any changes to the client code. It is very useful for tools that discover the services provided at run time.

On the other hand, static invocation also has its merits. It provides robust type-checking which is enforced by the compiler at build time. It improves performance, since it involves only a single API call to the stub. Dynamic invocations are inherently expensive because the ORB may have to transparently access the IR several times in order to build the invocation, and each access could in theory be a remote invocation. Static invocations are generally easier to program, since the remote method is invoked by its name and passing the parameters, as is done in any object-oriented programming language.

10.6 CORBA Interoperability

CORBA interoperability deals with ORB-to-ORB communication. A CORBA client object can invoke a request on a server object that is implemented in a totally different location and runs on a totally different ORB than the client. The client does not have to worry about these underlying differences; all it really cares about is getting the desired service from the server object. On the other side, the server does not have to know whether the request it received was from a client on the local ORB or from a client on some remote ORB. Since these are the requirements set forth in the CORBA specification, ORBs from different vendors and running on different platforms have to have a standard way of communicating. There are two ways in which ORBs can communicate:

- Direct ORB-to-ORB communication: This is possible when the ORBs are in the same *domain*, by using a common communication protocol understood by both. In this case the ORBs share common object reference formats, IDL type systems, and security information.

- Bridge-based communication: This is done by using a bridge to translate between the different communication protocols used by the two ORBs. This is necessary when the two ORBs are from separate domains and a mapping is required between the two domains.

The CORBA 2.0 specification supports both types of interoperability. The General Inter-ORB Protocol (GIOP) specifies transfer syntax and a standard set of message formats for ORB interoperation. It is simple and scalable and is designed for implementation on any reliable, connection-oriented protocol such as TCP/IP. The Internet Inter-ORB Protocol (IIOP) specifies how GIOP is implemented over TCP/IP. As shown in Fig. 10–4, GIOP can be built over any reliable transport mechanism. The CORBA 2.0 specification only mandates support for GIOP and IIOP for a CORBA-compliant ORB. Implementations over other transports may or may not be provided by the ORB vendor.

As shown in the figure, the ORB architecture also provides for other Environment-Specific Inter-ORB Protocols (ESIOPs). Every ESIOP can be a different protocol as long as it meets the requirements for ORB-to-ORB communication of object requests and responses. ESIOPs allow ORBs to be built for interoperation with existing distributed computing systems. For example, the first ESIOP to be standardized by OMG utilizes the Distributed Computing Environment (DCE) and is called the DCE Common Inter-ORB Protocol (DCE CIOP). It specifies ORB-to-ORB communication based on DCE's RPC mechanism. It allows for easy integration of CORBA and DCE applications.

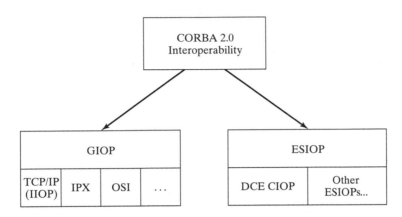

Figure 10–4   CORBA Interoperability Components

10.7 CORBAservices and CORBAfacilities

The CORBA component of the Object Management Architecture (OMA) connects objects, not applications. More support is needed from the underlying software framework in order to connect applications. This support is provided by the rest of the OMA, which consists of CORBAservices and CORBAfacilities. CORBA-services provide the low-level functionality needed by objects, such as persistence, naming and directory services, transaction services, and so on, while CORBAfacilities provide a high-level framework that can be used by applications to invoke user-level facilities such as compound-document management, help facilities, and system administration.

CORBAservices are system-level services which can be accessed through standard IDL interfaces. They augment and complement the functionality of the ORB. The OMG has currently defined standards for fifteen different services, which are listed below:

- Naming Service
- Event Service
- Life Cycle Service
- Persistent Object Service
- Transaction Service

- Concurrency Control Service

- Relationship Service

- Externalization Service

- Query Service

- Licensing Service

- Property Service

- Time Service

- Security Service

- Object Trader Service

- Object Collections Service

CORBAfacilities are collections of IDL-defined interfaces that provide services directly to application objects. CORBAfacilities are also known as common facilities. There are two types of common facilities: horizontal and vertical. Vertical facilities are services specialized for particular market segments such as medicine, manufacturing, finance, etc. Any service that is common across multiple vertical facilities becomes a horizontal common facility. Horizontal facilities include areas such as user interfaces, information management, task management, and systems management. Common facilities are built on top of CORBAservices.

10.8 Summary

The CORBA standards provide a mature software framework for creating truly distributed, client-server applications in heterogeneous object-oriented computing environments. The use of OMG IDL and the corresponding IDL-to-programming-language mappings allow CORBA-compliant systems to be written in a variety of programming languages, such as C, C++, Java, Smalltalk, COBOL, etc. CORBA-compliant applications do not have to worry about the details of the underlying network environment. CORBA is not a programming technology, it is basically an integration technology.

The CORBA specification is flexible enough to allow ORBs to integrate and incorporate existing protocols, applications, and distributed computing technologies such as DCOM and DCE. It allows for integration with legacy applications without any loss in investment. The CORBA strategy is becoming more and more important with the explosive growth of the Internet and Web. As more and more companies are trying to integrate their distributed client-server applications and provide them with a uniform Web interface, CORBA provides a very robust framework for handling the underlying heterogeneity and communication complexity.

On the other hand, we should also look at some of the current limitations of the CORBA technology. For example, standard CORBA does not address key "inherent complexities" of distributed computing, such as latency, fault tolerance, and deadlock. CORBA does not allow objects to be passed by value; although the OMG has recently issued an RFC to include this capability in the CORBA environment. Current implementations of CORBA lack efficient support for bulk data transfer. Also, CORBA does not take care of garbage collection and issues of memory leaks. Many of these limitations are currently being addressed by RFCs issued by the Object Management Group.

With these things in mind, we can definitely say that the distributed computing community only stands to gain by using the CORBA standards to the fullest possible extent.

10.9 References

[1]   Advanced Computing Laboratories. "OMG CORBA Resources."
       <http://www.acl.lanl.gov/CORBA/index.html> (2 Oct. 1997).

[2]   Mowbray, T. J., and R. Zahavi. *The Essential CORBA: Systems Integration Using Distributed Objects*. New York: Wiley, 1995.

[3]   Object Management Group. "OMG CORBA Resources."
       <http://www.omg.org> (2 Oct. 1997).

[4]   Orfali, R., D. Harkey, and J. Edwards. *The Essential Distributed Objects Survival Guide*. New York: Wiley, 1996.

[5]   Orfali, R. and D. Harkey, *Client / Server Programming with Java and CORBA*. New York: Wiley, 1997.

[6]   Orfali, R., D. Harkey, and J. Edwards. *Instant CORBA*. New York: Wiley, 1997.

[7]   Siegel, J., *et al.*, *CORBA Fundamentals and Programming*. New York: Wiley, 1996.

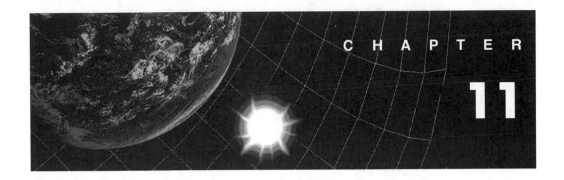

C H A P T E R

11

Java Security

by Vijay Sureshkumar

The Java programming language allows Java-compatible Web browsers to download code fragments dynamically and then to execute those code fragments locally. These code fragments are called *applets*. Information servers can customize the presentation of their content with server-supplied code. But this increased power for Web applications is also a potential security problem.

Born out of the popularity and the convenience offered by the Internet, the Java programming language has made distributed computing a practical reality. With the tremendous potential also comes the need for a sound security architecture. The Java security model, and flaws arising from implementation errors, loopholes in the security model, and unintended interaction between browser features, are examined in this chapter. The language features for security, the low-level security mechanisms through compile-time checking, and the Class-Loader and SecurityManager classes are described. The different types of attacks on security—namely denial-of-service attacks, second-party and third-party attacks, annoyance attacks, and disclosure attacks—are presented. Some simple examples of hostile applets are shown to illustrate attacks.

The chapter concludes with a discussion of some recent initiatives, including the Capabilities-based security model and the Gateway extension for electronic commerce. These accommodate the openness desired by Web application writers and the security needs of their users.

Chapter Content

1. Introduction
2. Security Issues

- Security
- Achieving Security
- Common Security Problems
- Java Security Model

3. Security Threats

- Denial-of-Service Attacks
- Trojan Horses
- Covert Channels
- DNS Weaknesses
- List of Security Holes

4. Java Security Features

- Language Features
- Memory Allocation and Layout
- ClassLoader
- Bytecode Verification
- SecurityManager

5. Extending Java Security

- Man in the Middle
- Java Security API
- The New Security Models

6. Summary
7. References

11.1 Introduction

The Internet is changing the landscape of computing. The monolithic approach to computing is slowly giving way to a distributed, component-based approach.

Since its release in May of 1995, Java has enjoyed a lot of hype as an ideal candidate for distributed computing. With its promise of truly network oriented computing and a nearly universal system for distributing applications, Java is widely seen as a solution to many of the most persistent problems in client/server and Web computing. However, the power and expressiveness has a cost. The distribution of executables automatically over the network raises concerns about Java's effect on network security.

The essence of the problem is that running a program on a computer typically gives that program access to certain resources on the host machine. In the case of executable content, the program that is running is untrusted. If a Web browser downloads and runs Java code and is not careful to restrict the access that the untrusted program has, it can provide a malicious program with the same ability to do mischief as a hacker who had gained access to the host machine. For example, downloaded code might need to write a temporary file to the disk on the machine running the Web browser; however, such a file might contain a virus. This chapter discusses some common security attacks and shows how Java addresses them.

Security is closely coupled with Java's design. The sandbox consists of a number of cooperating system components and language features that make security achievable. The sandbox ensures that untrusted malicious applications cannot gain access to system resources. On the other hand, real-world applications often must go "outside" the sandbox to be able to do something useful (e.g., to write a file to disk). Sun's Protection Domain and Netscape's Capabilities-based model and applet signing address this issue (Section 5.3). They allow a flexible security model for the Java platform.

This chapter discusses the features that make Java a good choice for secure computing on the Internet. Some security holes that arise due to implementation errors, unintended interactions between browser features, and weaknesses in the Java language and bytecode semantics are described. Finally, future extensions to the Java security model are discussed. For details on the Java programming language, refer to Chapter 8.

11.2 Security Issues

While applets solve many important problems in client/server and network-centric computing, they also raise new concerns about security. In traditional environments, companies could protect themselves by building a firewall between the Internet and the company's intranet, obtaining software only from known and trusted sources, and using antivirus programs to check all new software.

Use of applets adds a new security vulnerability. An employee searching an external Web site for information might inadvertently load and execute a malicious applet which could potentially steal or damage information stored in the user's machine on a network file server. Also, since this software is already behind the company's firewall, the applet could attack other unprotected machines on a corporate intranet. A home PC user who is banking online might download a malicious applet that transfers account information over the Internet to another server.

The meaning of security, typical security problems, and Java's security model are presented in the following sections.

Security

The following are key attributes required for good security practices:

- *Authentication*: A very important task is to authenticate remote users, systems and resources. The clients should know that they are connected to the host they wanted and not to an imposter, and that the applet they have downloaded has not been altered or replaced. Digital signatures (see the section on "Digital Signatures" on page 248) for applets and X.509 certificates address this.

- *Authorization*: Client-side administrators should be able to decide what levels of rights to offer to an authenticated principal. The Java `Security-Manager` class and Protection Domains implement authorization.

- *Confidentiality*: This is to ensure that the data being exchanged is private and there is no eavesdropping. Protocols like SSL (see the section on "Secure Sockets Layer" on page 251) and other encryption schemes can be used to achieve confidentiality.

- *Containment*: Given an authenticated applet, its compliance with the authorization granted should be verified. The sandbox achieves this through the `ClassLoader` and the Bytecode Verifier.

- *Auditing*: If a security breach should occur, an audit trail often helps developers and administrators isolate and remedy the problem to avoid future attacks. There are no auditing features available with Java yet.

- *Non-repudiation*: The security system should be able to prove that a party took part in a transaction. Digital signatures and message digests (see the section on "Digital Signatures" on page 248) ensure that each party in a transaction can prove the other's participation.

Achieving Security

Given the previously mentioned attributes of security, the objective of a good security strategy is "to minimize the potential cost of a breach and its impact on users and maximize the difficulty of potential attacks" [4]. Effective security involves constantly reinforcing security mechanisms and policies by training and periodically adapting to account for new threats. Security protects and extends competitive advantage. But there are costs associated with all security procedures. These costs must be weighed against the value of the assets protected by those measures and the potential harm which could be caused by the loss of those assets. A company that wishes to advertise on the Web may be satisfied with a simple firewall to discourage electronic vandals. But a large financial institution with billions of dollars at stake could justify much more elaborate security measures, possibly including public key encryption, dedicated private networks, and regular security audits. For applications like air traffic control and military and intelligence systems, the risk of connecting these systems to the Internet may outweigh the benefits of being on the Internet.

The cost of implementing security mechanisms is also a crucial factor. If a new technology makes it easier or cheaper to obtain the same level of security as an existing system, it would be very attractive. On the other hand, if a new technology increases security with a corresponding increase in cost, the organization must weigh the cost against the risks being averted. Therefore there is a trade-off between security and cost: achieving more security becomes increasingly expensive (see Figure 1 in [4]).

When calculating security costs, usability is an important factor. If security mechanisms are too time-consuming or difficult to use, they can decrease the productivity. Users who find the policies difficult to follow may ignore the policies or implement them haphazardly.

Java is able to provide transparent security mechanisms, which do not require any knowledge or action on the part of the end user. This is possible because Java's security model is meant to protect the end-user from hostile applets from untrusted sources.

Common Security Problems

Risk Avoidance
The most common security fallacy is that the goal of security is to eliminate all risk and vulnerabilities from a system. This is an unrealistic goal. A company with a "zero tolerance" approach will not survive on the Internet. As discussed in the previous section, there is a trade-off between cost and degree of security achieved.

System Security
Piecemeal security is a tendency to look at small pieces of a system or network in isolation from the system as a whole. Since computer networks are extremely complex, it is of little importance to examine the individual aspects of the system. Piecemeal security often results when several departments are responsible

for different aspects of security. If these departments do not work closely together, each can set policies without regard for how those policies affect security as a whole. This can create vulnerabilities at the borders. An example is the Domain Name System (DNS), which can be misused by a Java applet to break a firewall (see the section on "DNS Weaknesses" on page 226).

Eradicating the Root Problem

A flaw found in a new technology often prompts an organization to expend great effort patching the vulnerability, without first checking to see if this same vulnerability exists undetected in existing systems. Like steel doors on a grass hut, these patches, produced at great expense, close one possible hole but ignore other potential security holes in other parts of the system. So they do little to increase the security of the system as a whole. Each breach should be followed by a thorough investigation to eradicate all traces of the problem.

One of the most important parts of the security process is staying informed of new attacks and vulnerabilities of computer and network systems (e.g., by visiting the Secure Internet Programming Web site [8]), which are found regularly.

Java Security Model

Java's security allows a user to download and run applets from the Web or an intranet without undue risk to the user's machine. The applet's actions are restricted to its "sandbox," an area of the Web browser dedicated to that applet. The applet can do anything within the sandbox, but cannot read, write, or alter data outside of the sandbox. The sandbox ensures that even if a user downloads a malicious applet, it cannot damage the local machine. The sandbox is made up of the following components operating together [4]. (Each of the following Java security mechanisms is discussed in later sections in detail.)

- *Java Language Features*: Java has many language features which protect the integrity of the system. The language prevents pointer abuse and illegal type casts.

- *Class Loader*: ClassLoader is the first link in the security chain. It fetches executable code from a server on the network to the client machine and enforces the namespace hierarchy.

- *Bytecode Verifier*: The verifier checks that the applet conforms to the Java language guarantees and that there are no violations like stack overflows, namespace violations, and illegal data type casts.

- *Security Manager*: The SecurityManager class enforces the boundary of the sandbox. Whenever an applet performs an action which is a potential violation, the security manager decides whether it is approved or not.

- *Capabilities-based security*: This is the latest extension to Java. It allows trusted applets to run outside the sandbox. The level of trust decides the capabilities that the applet can be offered.

The next few sections present some security breeches that have been found since Java's release. It should be noted that very few of them are due to language weaknesses. The main weakness with the Java language is that it has neither a formal semantics nor a formal description of its type system, yet the security relies on the soundness of the type system. Most of the security holes are due to implementation errors, unexpected interaction of browser features, and differences between Java semantics and bytecode semantics.

11.3 Security Threats

An untrusted applet poses many potential security threats. Some of those identified by different research groups are presented in this section. Some of these holes that have been described have already been fixed. The purpose of presenting these examples is to describe the general nature of Java security threats. An important part of creating a safe environment in which a program can run is to identify resources used by the program and then to somehow limit access to these resources. Malicious applets attacks are categorized below.

- Integrity Attacks

    - Deletion or modification of files
    - Modification of memory currently in use
    - Killing processes and threads

These attacks are prevented by the Java sandbox approach. Web browsers can implement their own SecurityManager. Versions of Netscape Navigator using only the sandbox for security do not allow any modification of files. Hot-Java allows a more flexible scheme where the SecurityManager can allow some applets to write to the client's disk. Eventually, when applet signatures become prevalent, the SecurityManager will selectively allow access to client resources based on the signature.

- Availability Attacks

    - Allocating large amounts of memory
    - Creating high-priority threads

This type of attack is not avoidable because some genuine applets might need a lot of memory. The client can control this by fixing a ceiling on the amount of resources an applet can use.

- Disclosure Attacks

    - Mailing information about the client machine
    - Sending personal or company files across the network

Disclosure attacks are handled by Java by restricting socket connections to other sites on the Internet. Current implementations of browsers allow an applet to communicate only with the source of the applet. Browsers like HotJava allow the use of a configuration file to specify a list of hosts with which an applet can communicate. However, there are some implementation errors and weaknesses with existing systems (e.g., DNS) which allow applets to communicate with any host on the Internet. An example is presented on page 226.

- Annoyance Attacks

    - Displaying obscene pictures on the screen
    - Playing unwanted sounds on the client computer

This attack has more to do with netiquette than with Java. Thus classifying an applet as performing an annoyance attack is a matter of judgment.

Table 1 in [1] provides an example of the types of problems associated with a given resource.

Denial-of-Service Attacks

Java does not have many provisions to identify denial-of-service attacks. The common attacks are busy-waiting to consume CPU cycles, allocating memory until the system runs out, and starving other threads and system processes. The memory and CPU attacks are very difficult to handle because many genuine applications might need large amounts of resources. As an example of denial of service (from [2]), the code segment below can lock the status line at the bottom of the HotJava browser, effectively preventing it from loading any more pages.

```
synchronized (Class.forName("net.www.html.MeteredStream")) {
            while(true) Thread.sleep(10000);
        }
```

The `synchronized` construct acquires a lock on the class that maps a name into a reference, and the `while` loop never releases the lock. In Netscape, this attack can lock the `java.net.InetAddress` class, blocking all hostname lookups and hence all new network connections. This attack could be prevented by using wrappers around the class and preventing access to locks.

There are two variations of denial-of-service attacks. An attack can be made to occur after a time delay, probably causing failure to occur when the user is viewing some other page, thus masking the source of the attack. Another attack related to denial of service is the *degradation-of-service* attack. In this attack, there is no outright denial of service, but the performance of the Web browser is significantly reduced.

Trojan Horses

A Trojan horse is any program that has an overt function and a covert function. As a typical example, imagine a program that plays Solitaire, while secretly e-mailing interesting files to the program's creator. This attack works because a program usually inherits its access rights from the invoking user based on the way the `SecurityManager` is configured. Examples of Trojan Horses follow:

- An applet displays an animation but also discreetly searches the user's local file system and sends back interesting files across the network connection.

- An applet allows a user to play a game, but on a client running X windows, the applet also covertly opens an X terminal across the network, with the display at the remote site and the process running locally. The perpetrator can now execute arbitrary commands on the user's machine.

- An applet captures keystrokes intended for other applets and transmits them back over the network connection.

Though the security wall excludes rogue applets, inter-applet security is weak. Since applets can persist after the Web browser leaves the page which contains them, it becomes important to separate applets from each other. Otherwise, a hostile applet can sabotage a third party's applet. If an applet gains access to the top-level `ThreadGroup`, it can enumerate every thread and use the `stop()` or `setPriority()` methods to make them look slow and buggy. Most browsers implement this by putting applets from different sources and applets in different frames in separate `ThreadGroups`. Applets can communicate across frames using static classes and within a page by the `getAppletContext()` methods.

Covert Channels

Various covert channels exist in browsers which allow applets to establish two-way communication with arbitrary third parties on the Internet [2]. A two-party attack requires that the Web server on which the applet resides participate in the attack. A three-party attack can originate from anywhere on the Internet, and might spread if it is hidden in a useful applet that is used in many Web pages. Three-party attacks are more dangerous than two party attacks because they do not need the collusion of the Web server.

The three-party attack works as follows (see Figure 2 in [2]). Party A wants to steal information from other computers on the Internet, and thus writes a Java applet that looks useful to others (e.g., an applet to display a calendar), but is actually a Trojan horse. Party B, an innocent Web page designer, uses Party A's applet on a Web page. Party C visits Party B's Web page, which starts the Java applet. Unknown to parties B or C, the Java applet opens a covert channel from Party C's computer to another computer of Party A's choice. The Java applet then transmits information found on Party C's computer to Party A.

Even worse, if the applet is popular enough, then it may be used on many Web pages, allowing Party A to collect information from computers throughout the world.

Although Netscape and HotJava allow network connections only to the host from which the applet was loaded, the restriction is not enforced properly through a number of implementation errors.

First, the `accept()` system call, used to receive a network connection initiated on another host, is not protected by the usual security checks in HotJava. This allows an arbitrary host on the Internet to connect to a HotJava browser as long as the location of the browser is known. For this to be a useful attack, the applet needs to signal the external agent to connect to a specified port. Even a low-bandwidth covert channel is sufficient to communicate this information.

Second, if the Web server which served the applet is running an SMTP mail daemon, the applet can connect to it and transmit an e-mail message to any machine on the Internet.

Third, a covert channel can be created with the URL redirect feature. Normally, an applet may instruct the browser to load any page on the Web. An attacker's server could record the URL as a message, then redirect the browser to the original destination.

Fourth, DNS can be used as a two-way communication channel to an arbitrary host on the Internet. This is discussed next.

DNS Weaknesses

A significant problem arises in the Java Development Kit (JDK) and browser implementation of the policy that an applet can open a TCP/IP connection back to the server it was loaded from. While this policy is sound, it is not uniformly enforced. The policy is enforced as follows:

1. Get all the IP addresses of the hostname that the applet came from.
2. Get all the IP addresses of the hostname that the applet is trying to connect to.
3. If any addresses match, allow connection.

The problem is in the second step: the applet can ask to connect to any hostname on the Internet, so it can control which DNS supplies the second list of IP addresses; information from this untrusted DNS server is used to make an access-control decision. There is nothing that prevents an attacker from creating a DNS server that lies.

For example, suppose the attacker's computers are in domain attack.org. The attacker runs a DNS server. An innocent person on the Internet might visit a Web page containing a Java applet written by the attacker. The applet could then try to connect to a fictitious machine named X.attack.org. The name X.attack.org must be mapped to an IP address in the second step above. Because the name is fictitious, the authoritative DNS server that is asked to translate the name is the one run by organization attack.org. DNS requires the server to return one or more IP addresses that correspond to X.attack.org; however the attacker's DNS server could simply return arbitrary 32-bit quantities. Therefore DNS provides a low-bandwidth covert channel between the innocent user's computer and the attacker's DNS server: The Java applet sends a message to the attacker as the "X" in name X.attack.org; the attacker replies by sending a message as a sequence of 32-bit quantities that are misrepresented as IP addresses. The only disadvantage of this method of creating a covert channel is that it has very low bandwidth, because domain name lookups are slow. Figure 4 in [2] illustrates the attack.

Unfortunately, using DNS as a channel is so effective, that it even works across firewalls. Firewalls normally allow DNS lookups to pass between a private enterprise network and the Internet. So if the private network allows users to load Java Web pages from outside the enterprise, DNS can be used to create a covert channel through the firewall. There are several known network security problems that allow the Java applet to then break into other nearby machines. See [2] for further discussion.

List of Security Holes

Given below are the major security holes discovered thus far with the Java programming language design, virtual machine implementations, and bytecode semantics. Some of these flaws allow full system penetration, meaning an attacker could exploit them to do literally anything on the client machine, including corrupting data, reading private data, injecting a virus into the system, or leaving a trapdoor in order to enter the client machine at will. The list was compiled from the security pages at JavaSoft [9] and Netscape [7].

February 96

- Drew Dean, Edward Felten, and Dan Wallach at Princeton University's Secure Internet Programming group [8] discovered a flaw in Java's networking software, affecting Netscape Navigator 2.0. The flaw was in the method used to determine whether two machine names corresponded to the same machine. This flaw was also postulated independently by Steve Gibbons. The flaw could be exploited to launch security attacks on other machines on a private network.

March 96

- David Hopwood at Oxford University found a flaw that allows an attack that tricks Java into treating the attacker's applet as trusted. The attack exploited an error in the way Java processed file path names. This flaw allowed full system penetration.

March 96

- The Princeton team (Dean, Felten, and Wallach) found a bug in the Java bytecode verifier and a flaw in the class-loading mechanism. Together, these allowed full system penetration. This problem affected Netscape Navigator 2.01 and was fixed in Netscape Navigator 2.02.

April 96

- URL name resolution attack: For a specific firewall-protected network configuration, an applet downloaded from a client inside the firewall would be able to connect to a single specific host behind the firewall.

May 96

- New twist on previous `ClassLoader` attack: The 18 May 1996 edition of the *New York Times* reports that Felten, Dean and Wallach have found a new way to get past system restrictions on creating a `ClassLoader`. This attack builds on work done by Tom Cargill. The applet sandbox security model states that an applet is not allowed to create its own `ClassLoader`. If an applet could create its own `ClassLoader`, the applet could use it to define and execute classes that would otherwise be barred from execution.

- Independent consultant Tom Cargill, working with the Princeton team (Dirk Balfanz, Dean, Felten, and Wallach), found a flaw in the implementation of the Java interpreter. Cargill discovered a complex sequence of type-casting operations that, taken together, amounted to an illegal type conversion. This flaw allowed full system penetration.

June 96

- Hopwood found another flaw in the interpreter that again allowed full system penetration. This flaw was an error in the way Java compared two types to determine whether they were equal.

- Balfanz, Dean, and Felten found a flaw in Java's implementation of array types that allowed full system penetration. The flaw allowed an attacker to redefine Java's built-in array types.

July 96

- Cargill, Balfanz, Dean, and Felten found another implementation flaw in the Java interpreter. Like Cargill's earlier attack, this relied on a complex sequence of type-casting operations. This flaw allowed an attacker to mount some attacks on network services on other private-network machines.

August 96

- Balfanz and Felten found a flaw in Microsoft's Java implementation. The flaw involved the way Java checked whether a class was allowed to be a member of a particular package. The flaw allowed code in an attack applet to become a member of a security-critical Java package, thus gaining the ability to change various security parameters and hence to gain full access to the victim's files and the network. This flaw was fixed in Explorer 3.0.

December 96

- Princeton University researchers published a technical report describing an Internet security attack they term *Web spoofing* [3]. In this scenario, an attacker creates a shadow copy of a Web page, funnels all access to the Web page through the attacker's machine, and tricks the unwary consumer into revealing sensitive or private data, such as PIN numbers, credit card numbers or bank account numbers. Web spoofing requires that the attacker be able to interpose his machine between the server and client, in a man-in-the-middle attack (see the section on "Man in the Middle" on page 236). Web spoofing does not require and does not exploit Java technologies.

If consumers are using a browser that does not have JavaScript (Live-Script) enabled, they will be able to tell that they are being spoofed when they notice either of these visual cues in the browser status line:

- When a connection is made, the status line shows which host the browser is connecting.

- When you hold the mouse over a link, the address you will be taken to when you click on the link is displayed in the status line.

If consumers use a browser with JavaScript (LiveScript) enabled, then even these rudimentary and subtle alerts can be hidden by a malicious script. Recall that such scripts are not written in Java and are not subject to the Java security model. In that case, consumers would have no way of noticing the spoofing. For this reason, people concerned about Web spoofing attacks might consider disabling scripting languages.

Note that in any case, some novice Internet consumers will not be sensitive to visual cues, even if they aren't obliterated by scripting languages. However, it is often the case on the Internet that Web spoofing attacks are noticed quickly and given wide publicity. Given the nature of the Web and how quickly e-mail bounces around the net, there is strong likelihood that a spoofed Web site will be found out quickly and publicized widely.

April 97

- JDK 1.1.1 Signing Flaw: The Secure Internet Programming team at Princeton University notified JavaSoft of a flaw in the way the Java runtime managed identities of signers. JavaSoft tested the fix and shipped it to licensees.

May 97

- University of Washington Verification System: A team of researchers at the University of Washington independently developed a Java verification system that led to the discovery of a bug in the JDK 1.1.1 verifier. There are no known security attacks based on exploiting the bug, but JavaSoft has issued a fix to licensees in the JDK 1.1.2 release.

In the next few sections, we will examine the Java security model in detail.

11.4 Java Security Features

Many computer and network systems try to maintain security by hiding the inner works and policies of the system. This practice is called security through obscurity. It assumed that if the system were presented as a black box, then no one would expend the effort needed to discover the hidden vulnerabilities. The existence of a number of well-publicized attacks in the past demonstrates that this assumption is wrong; the box is never black enough. For widely used systems, too many people know the internal workings of the system for the details to remain secret, and the rewards for breaking into the system are too great.

Sun has chosen the exact opposite approach and has published all the details of the Java security model upon its release. This includes the design specifications, the sandbox model, and the full source implementation. This approach is called security through openness. It is intended to encourage security researchers to examine the model and report security flaws before attacks based on it become endemic. This allows an organization to study the Java security model in detail and make an informal assessment of the potential risks versus the benefits of the Java platform.

Language Features

Java has several language features which protect the integrity of the security system and which prevent several common attacks. The following are some such features:

- Security through being well-defined: The Java language is strict in its definition of the language:

    - All primitive data types in the language have a specific size.
    - All operations are defined to be performed in a specific order.

- Security through lack of pointer arithmetic: The Java language does not have pointer arithmetic, so Java programmers cannot forge a pointer to memory. All references to methods and instance variables in the class file are via symbolic names. The user cannot create code that has magic offsets in it that just happen to point to the right place. Users cannot create code that bashes system variables or accesses private information.

- Security through garbage collection: Garbage collection makes Java programs more secure and robust. Two common bugs in C/C++ programs are listed below:

    - Failing to free memory once it is no longer needed.
    - Accidentally freeing the same piece of memory twice.

- Security through strict compile-time checking: The Java compiler performs extensive, stringent compile-time checking so that as many errors as possible can be detected by the compiler. The Java language is strongly typed, meaning the following:

  - Objects cannot be cast to a subclass without an explicit run-time check.
  - All references to methods and variables are checked to make sure that the objects are of the same type.
  - Integers and objects are not interconvertible.

Strict compilation checks make Java programs more robust and avoid run-time errors. The bytecode verifier examines the bytecode generated by the compiler when an applet is loaded and makes security checks. The compiler also ensures that a program does not access any uninitialized variables.

Memory Allocation and Layout

One of the Java compiler's main lines of defense is its memory allocation and reference model. Memory layout decisions are not made by the Java language compiler, as they are in C/C++. Rather, memory layout is deferred until run time, and will potentially differ depending on the characteristics of the hardware and software platforms on which the Java system executes. Therefore it is hard to design Java attacks that are portable across systems.

Second, Java does not have pointers. The compiled code references memory via symbolic handles that are resolved at run-time. Java programmers cannot forge pointers to memory, because the memory allocation and referencing model is completely opaque to the programmer and controlled entirely by the underlying run-time platform.

Very late binding of structures to memory means that programmers cannot infer the physical memory layout of a class by looking at its declaration. These features lead to more reliable and secure applications.

However, there are some implementation errors that disclose storage layout. Although Java does not allow direct access to memory through pointers, the Java library allows an applet to learn where in memory its objects are stored. All objects have a hashCode() method which, unless overridden by the programmer, casts the address of the object's internal storage to an integer and returns it.

The use of garbage collection rather than relying on explicit user deallocation of memory eliminates some security holes. If Java had manual deallocation, this could provide a roundabout way of illegally casting. For example, an applet creates a malicious object of type MyFile and then deallocates the memory used by that object, keeping the pointer. Then, the program creates an object of type File. Using knowledge of how allocation and deallocation is done, the new pointer to the File object is the same as the original MyFile pointer. The private methods of the File object are now accessible through the MyFile pointer.

ClassLoader

The Java run time has two distinct ways of loading a new class. The default mechanism is to load a class from a file on the local machine. This mechanism does not need a `ClassLoader`. Loading a class over the network requires an associated `ClassLoader`, which is responsible for converting the raw data of a class into an internal data structure representing the class.

The environment seen by a thread of execution running Java bytecodes can be visualized as a set of classes partitioned into separate namespaces. There is one namespace for the local file system, and a separate namespace for each network source.

When a class is imported from across the network, it is placed into the private namespace associated with its origin. When a class references another class, a search is first made for the class in the namespace for the local system (these are built-in classes). If the class is not found, a search is then made in the namespace of the referencing class. There is no way that an imported class can "spoof" a built-in class. Built-in classes can never accidentally reference classes in imported namespaces—they can only reference such classes explicitly. Similarly, classes imported from different sources are separated from each other.

The Java language and bytecode semantics are different, which leads to some security problems. The Java language requires that all constructors call either another constructor of the same class, or a superclass constructor as their first action. The system classes `ClassLoader`, `SecurityManager`, and `File-InputStream` all rely on this behavior for their security. These classes have a constructor which throws a `SecurityException` if they are called from an applet. Unfortunately, while the Java language prohibits the following code, the bytecode verifier readily accepts its bytecode equivalent:

```
class CL extends ClassLoader {
    CL()  {
        try { super(); }
        catch (Exception e) {}
    }
}
```

This allows us to build (partially uninitialized) `ClassLoader`, `Security-Manager`, and `FileInputStream` classes. `ClassLoader` classes do not have instance variables. If the constructor is executed once, it will always run before the first applet is loaded. The result of this attack is a fully initialized, customized and possibly malicious `ClassLoader`.

Java packages are normally named `java.io`, `java.net`, and so on. The run-time system replaces each "." with a "/" to map the package hierarchy onto the file system hierarchy. It has been found that if the first character of a package name is "/", the Java runtime system attempts to load code from an absolute path. Thus, if an attacker could place compiled Java in any file on the victim's system (either through a shared file system or via an incoming FTP directory), the attacker's code would be treated as trusted, since it came from a local file. Trusted code is permitted to load dynamic link libraries which can ignore the Java run time and directly access the operating system with the full privileges of the user [2].

Bytecode Verification

Even though the Java compiler performs thorough type checking, there is still the possibility of attack via the use of a hostile compiler. The browsers that download the class files do not know if the bytecodes were produced by a trustworthy Java compiler. So all class files brought in across the network are subjected to verification. The verifier ensures that the class files have the correct format. The bytecodes are verified using a simple theorem prover which establishes a set of "structural constraints" on the bytecodes. Following are some checks that are made:

- Bytecode does not forget pointers.

- Bytecode does not violate access restrictions.

- Bytecode accesses objects as the type they really are.

- Stack overflows do not occur.

- Method calls have appropriate argument types.

The bytecode verifier enhances the performance of the interpreter. Runtime checks that would otherwise have to be performed for each interpreted instruction can be eliminated. The interpreter assumes that these checks have been already made [10].

The bytecode is in linear form, so type checking requires global dataflow analysis similar to the back end of an optimizing compiler; this analysis is complicated further by the existence of exceptions and exception handlers. The verifier must show that all possible execution paths have the same virtual machine configuration—a much more complicated problem and prone to error. Finally, the present type verifier cannot be proved correct, because it does not have a formal description.

SecurityManager

Each Java application can have its own security manager object that acts as a full-time security guard. The SecurityManager class in the java.lang package is an abstract class that provides the programming interface and partial implementation for all Java security managers. By default an application does not have a security manager. That is, the Java run-time system does not automatically create a security manager for every Java application. So by default an application allows all operations that are subject to security restrictions. To change this default lenient behavior, an application must create and install its own security manager. (Table 2 in [1] lists the intent of the public methods of the `SecurityManager` class.)

The `SecurityManager` provides an extremely flexible and powerful mechanism for conditionally allowing access to resources thus allowing an application to customize its security policy.

Using the `ClassLoader` attack described earlier (see the section on "ClassLoader" on page 233), an attacker can change any variable in the system, including `SecurityManager`'s private variables. The attacker can also change the variable used by the `SecurityManager` to determine where the class was loaded from, thereby tricking the `SecurityManager` into believing that the class is trusted.

11.5 Extending Java Security

While many experts agree that the Java Security model is basically sound, there is concern that the model has not been examined in sufficient detail to ensure that the sandbox model is as secure as is claimed. There could be implementation errors which malicious applets might exploit. There could be unexpected interactions between applets and other parts of the network which could be exploited.

Sun has initiated an independent, third-party security modeling effort. A third party will first produce a Security Reference Model which will document the Java Security Model in rigorous detail. The second step is to implement a compatibility test suite to ensure that the implementations comply with the Java standard. The final step is to commission an independent, third-party assessment of Sun's reference implementation of the Java standard.

Java originally defined an all-or-nothing "sandbox" model for security, in which Java classes loaded from the network were granted extremely limited privileges and classes loaded from the local disk were given free reign to do virtually anything. Under this binary trust model, many interesting Web applications could not be written to run from the network, while unrestricted local classes could inadvertently open up arbitrarily bad security holes that could be exploited by malicious applets, even if the malicious applets were not trusted.

Microsoft's Authenticode signing technology and Sun's JDK 1.1 and Netscape's Object signing add the ability to sign applets loaded from the network, so that they can enjoy the same privileges as local applications based on the amount of trust associated with the applet. This gives fine-grained control over access to resources on the client machine. One of the most important changes is the separation of policy configuration from the applets. In the future, there would be a configuration file for security on the client machine which might look like this (example based on [5]):

```
codebase "http://www.cs.vt.edu/"
signedBy "aabbccddeeffgghh00112233445566"
permission java.io.File "/home/vijay/.checkbook"
action "read,write"

codebase "http://www.cs.vt.edu/"
signedBy "*"
permission java.net.Net "www.cs.vt.edu:8000-9000"
action "connect"
```

The first codebase specifies that the subsequent attributes apply to applets loaded from http://www.cs.vt.edu. Next, `signedBy` requires the Java applets to have the specified signature. An asterisk for a signature allows applets to be loaded regardless of signature. The fine-grained access control is specified by `permission` and `action`. In the first case, Java applets can read and write a specified file, and in the second case, applets can connect to ports 8000 to 9000 on www.cs.vt.edu.

In the following sections, the new Java Security API and the new grayscale security models are presented.

Man in the Middle

All networked systems are potentially vulnerable to the "man-in-the-middle" attack. In this attack, a client contacts a legitimate server on the network and requests some action. The attacker, or man in the middle, notices this request and waits for the server to respond. The attacker then intercepts the response and supplies a bogus reply to the client. For example, an attacker might watch an Internet-based banking site. As clients visit the page which provides the bill-paying services, the attacker diverts the bank's responses and provides a malicious applet which mimics the bank's service, but also steals a copy of the user's credit card and bank account numbers.

The Java Security API is a new Java Core API, built around the `java.security` package. It is designed to let developers incorporate both low-level and high-level security functionality into their Java applications. This includes digital signatures, data encryption, key management and access control. Brief descriptions are given below; see Chapter 12 for details:

- *Digital Signatures*: Digital signature algorithms like DSA or MD5 with RSA are available. The functionality includes generating public/private key pairs as well as signing and verifying arbitrary digital data.

- *Message Digests*: Cryptographically secure message digests, such as MD2, MD5, or SHA, are included. These algorithms, also called one-way hash algorithms, are useful as "digital fingerprints" of documents. They are used as the basis of digital signatures and other applications that need unique identifiers for digital data.

- *Key Management*: A set of abstractions for managing principals (entities such as individual users or groups), their keys, and their certificates are provided. The abstractions allow applications to design their own key management system and to interoperate with other systems at a high level.

- *Access Control Lists*: A set of abstractions for managing principals and their access permissions are offered.

Java Security API

The Java Security is built around several important design principles:

- *Implementation and Format Independence*: Java Security will provide interfaces to various algorithms, such as DSA, MD5 and SHA. It does this while making it possible for applications to request an algorithm without regard to implementation details. For example, JDK 1.1 includes the Sun-Security Provider, which implements DSA entirely in Java.

- *Interoperability Across Implementations*: This feature is the by-product of JavaSecurity's implementation independence. A simple example of this is that keys generated by an implementation of a given algorithm should work with any other similar implementation. To achieve this, Java-Security defines standard encoding rules based on existing international standards such as X.509, PKCS#8.

- *Implementation-Specific Security*: JavaSecurity takes advantage of Java's type system to allow its implementations to design their own security policies while adhering to a set of common semantics.

Here are some extensions to the Java security model [9]:

- *Signed applets*: To sign an applet, the producer first bundles all the Java code and related files into a single file called a Java Archive (JAR). The producer then creates a string called a digital signature based on the contents of the JAR. JAR files also allow clients to download all related files with a single request. Signed JAR files are included in Java release 1.1. To sign code, a developer must first take two basic steps:

  - generate a private/public key pair, and
  - obtain a certificate attesting the authenticity of the public key.

After obtaining a private key and a certificate, an application may sign
code using them.

- *Flexible Policies*: Since digital signatures will allow one to assign applets
  some amount of trust, it may be useful to relax the Java security restrictions for authenticated applets. The `SecurityManager` could enforce different levels of control based on how much a particular publisher is
  trusted.

- *Auditing*: Auditing is another important feature. Auditing software maintains a record of everything which happens on the system. When something goes wrong, through an accident or through a bug, the audit trail
  allows system administrators and security personnel to figure out what
  has happened. Efforts are underway to define what standard auditing features should be supported by all implementations of Java.

- *Encryption*: The channel on which there is communication between servers
  and clients is still vulnerable. So the Security API is being developed.
  These will allow applets to select the type of encryption used, to negotiate
  with the server to create keys, and do the actual encryption of the data.

New Security Models

The original "all-or-nothing" sandbox model for security has turned out to be too
restrictive for writing real Web-based applications. While classes loaded from the
network were not allowed to do much, local classes could accidentally open bad
security holes through downloaded classes. There is a need for gray levels of
trust in the model. The following section presents the new security models from
the key players of the Java industry: Sun, Microsoft and Netscape. Because the
descriptions are from whitepapers, they are continually changing.

Sun: Protection Domains (4)

The Java Protected Domain is a component whose scope is defined by a set of
objects that are accessible by a principal. A principal is any entity to which
authorizations may be granted or revoked. The Java sandbox can be considered
the most restrictive Protected Domain.

Protected Domains interact only through trusted system code or when
explicitly permitted by both interacting domains. They fall into two classes: system and application. All system resources (e.g., files, network connections,
screen, keyboard) are accessible only through system domains. For example, a
program that tries to print something interacts with the domains responsible for
the file system and the printer. If code within a system domain invokes a method
within an application's method, the effective permissions are that of the application. Conversely, the application does not acquire less-restrictive permissions

when it invokes service within a system domain. However, surrogate code, or trusted code that executes on behalf of an application, is an exception.

The features proposed by Sun are summarized below:

- Table-based configuration: Security policy will be separated from programming.

- Secure communication: Encryption plug-ins will be available in Java including Sun's Simple Key Management Internet Protocol (SKIP).

- To allow remote code to be trusted for cross-machine authentication, IDs can be assigned to protection domains.

- There will be API support for X.509 certificates.

Microsoft: Trust Based Security (6)

Trust Based Security adds gray levels of trust to the existing security model. There are new administrative options for the Virtual Machine for fine-grained control over the capabilities granted to Java code, such as access to scratch space, local files, and network connections. Applications can be offered some of the available capabilities based on the trust level. The following are the features offered:

- *Capabilities-based model*: A capability is an access permission that can be used to determine a code path's authorization to access specific resources. A principal is anything that has a unique identity for security purposes. It could be a thread, a class, or a person or a company.

- *Zones*: Defines groups that share the same level of trust. Active security has predefined zones for typical categories such as (in increasing order of restriction) the local machine, intranet, trusted Web site, Internet and untrusted sites.

- *Capability Signing*: This allows an applet's signature to include a list of capabilities requested by it. The main advantage is that the user is not burdened with the task of making security-related decisions leading to authorization fatigue (e.g., the user blindly clicks "OK" to any security-related dialog box appearing on the computer screen).

- *Package Manager*: Allows the installation of local class libraries that are not fully trusted, using capability signing. This would allow local libraries that are not fully trusted.

- *Trust User Interface*: Defined by Active Security, and helps end users make trust decisions.

Netscape: Capabilities-Based Security (7)

In the Netscape model, a principal represents the "who," a target represents the "what," and the privileges associated with a principal represent the authorization (or its denial) for a principal to access a specific target. With its Communicator product, Netscape is introducing the Java Capabilities API, a powerful security model for Java code. In designing this security model, Netscape had to fulfill these user requirements:

- Using digital signatures, provide users with strong confidence in the identity of a software vendor and belief that software has not been tampered with.

- Allow users to restrict the capabilities of a Java executable, with fine-grained control over both *which* executables get access, and *what* each executable can do.

- Avoid "authorization fatigue."

In addition, the Communicator Java security model addresses these developer requirements:

- Allow developers to leave the sandbox, so that they can write powerful applications on top of Java (given permission from the user, of course).

- Make security reviews easy, by ensuring that extraordinary privileges are enabled only when needed.

All of these approaches are variants of the common idea of devising a model for allowing applets to operate outside the sandbox in a controlled environment.

11.6 Summary

The Java platform strives for a Write-Once/Run-Anywhere property. This, combined with the easy code-distribution mechanisms provided by the Web and intranets, makes Java a powerful tool for many network based systems. The mobile applications which Java enables solves many persistent problems in application distribution and systems management.

Java also opens up many security issues involved with mobile applications. Java uses the sandbox model to restrict security breeches. This model gives users the advantage of easy, ad-hoc application distribution while it protects them from potentially malicious applications.

Several efforts are underway to further enhance the sandbox model. Future releases of Java will provide applet signing, support for flexible policies, encryption, and auditing. This will allow operating outside the sandbox in a controlled environment to offer more power and flexibility for real applications.

Any organization which is considering adding Java applications or Java enabled software to its network should carefully consider how Java will affect their security policies. While no security policy can ever eliminate all risks from a networked environment, understanding how Java's security model works and what sorts of attacks are possible, keeping current with new developments, and evaluating Java in light of the organization's overall security policy can reduce risks to an acceptable level.

11.7 References

[1]   Bank, Joseph A. "Java Security." Dec. 1995.
      <www-swiss.ai.mit.edu/~jbank/javapaper/javapaper.html> (23 Sept. 1997).

[2]   Dean, Drew, Edward W. Felten, and Dan S. Wallach. "Java Security: From
      HotJava to Netscape and Beyond." in *Proc. 1996 IEEE Symp. on Security
      and Privacy*, May 1996.
      <http://www.cs.princeton.edu/sip/pub/secure96.html> (23 Sept. 1997).

[3]   Felten, Edward W. , Dirk Balfanz, Drew Dean, and Dan S. Wallach. "Web
      Spoofing: An Internet Con Game." Technical Report 540-96, Department of
      Computer Science, Princeton University, December 1996.
      <http://www.cs.princeton.edu/sip/pub/spoofing.html> (23 Sept. 1997).

[4]   Fritzinger, J. Steven, and Marianne Mueller. "Java Security." *Sun Microsys-
      tems White Paper,* 1996.
      <http://www.javasoft.com/marketing/collateral/security.html>   (23   Sept.
      1997).

[5]   Gong, Li, "Java Security: Present and the Near Future." Presentation at
      JavaOne, San Francisco, April 1997
      <http://java.sun.com/javaone/sessions/slides/TT03/slide07.htm>   (23   Sept.
      1997).

[6]   Microsoft. "Trust Based Security."
      <http://www.microsoft.com/java/security/jsecwp.htm> (23 Sept. 1997).

[7]   Netscape. "Capabilities-based Security."
      <http://developcr.netscape.com/library/documentation/signedobj/trust/
      index.htm> (23 Sept. 1997).

[8]   Princeton University, Secure Internet Programming. "Secure Internet Pro-
      gramming: News." <http://www.cs.princeton.edu/sip/News.html> (23 Sept.
      1997).

[9]   Sun Microsystems. "Applet Security FAQ."
       <http://java.sun.com/security/index.html> (23 Sept. 1997).

[10]   Yellin, Frank. "Low-level Security in Java." in *Proc. WWW4 Conference*. Dec.
       1995. <http://www.javasoft.com/sfaq/verifier.html> (23 Sept. 1997).

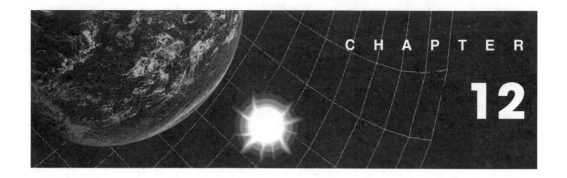

Cryptography

by Calin Groza

*I*nformation privacy on the Internet and Web has become an important issue in recent years. Individuals, companies, and governments are concerned that sensitive information has become more vulnerable to unauthorized access and use. Several solutions have been proposed over the years. This chapter discusses how cryptography can be used to increase the security of information on the Web. The chapter starts with an introduction to cryptography. It then presents a protocol for safe communication in a client-server application, and concludes with an example of how this protocol is used for buying a book through the Web. Throughout the chapter, technological and social issues related to cryptography are brought to the reader's attention.

Chapter Content

- SSL Application Data Protocol

- Application—Buying a Book through the Web

5. Summary

6. References

12.1 Introduction

The expansion of the Internet and the Web has allowed more people to have access to more and more information. At the same time, the ability to keep information private has become an important issue. Privacy is vital for businesses that want to protect proprietary and other sensitive information, and for individuals who engage in electronic commerce. Encryption is one of the most effective tools for keeping information secure.

Cryptography has a long history, but until recently only the government and the military were the users of cryptographic systems. Today, many civil organizations and individuals are using cryptography to protect information. There are several reasons for this. First, the equipment for encryption/decryption (i.e., powerful computers) has become more affordable. Second, an increasing amount of information is stored on computers, changing the way information is stored, transmitted and accessed in society. Next, because of the complexity of communication systems, users do not have complete control over the transmission channels. This is why users are looking for tools that allow secure communication over insecure channels. Finally, cryptography as a science has received the attention of the civilian sector, and important theoretical results and products are now available to the public.

There are many security challenges in building safe communication and collaboration. Typical security problems include the following:

1. *Authentication*:

- How to know, when connecting to a site, who operates the site?
- How to perform authentication without sending the user name and the password over the Internet?

2. *Eavesdropping*:

- How to protect the privacy of a communication?
- How to ensure that the messages have not been modified between the sender and the receiver?
- How to verify that the message received is an identical copy of the original document?

3. *Authorization*:

- How to ensure that the documents are read only by the people who have the authorization to do so?

The topic of Internet security is a very large one. Because the Web operates at the highest level (application) in the OSI model of communication networks (see Fig. 16–4 on page 310), all the security problems in the lower levels of the OSI model (data link, network, transport) are potential sources of security risk in the Web, too. For example, the fact that the Internet's protocol (Domain Name System) to map human-readable host names (e.g., cs.vt.edu) into IP addresses (e.g., 128.13.40.24) is insecure makes the Web system vulnerable to the same attacks. (The section on "DNS Weaknesses" on page 227 exemplifies such an attack.) The extent to which this chapter covers security is limited. The goal is to present the basic elements of cryptography used in achieving security in the Internet in general, and in the Web in particular. This chapter also presents an example (the Secure Sockets Layer) of how these algorithms are applied.

12.2 Cryptography

Cryptography is one way to solve the security challenges raised in the introduction. The basic idea is that, using some secret information, it is possible to protect the confidentiality and the integrity of the information that flows in the Web. This section aims to introduce the basic elements of cryptography so that one can understand how they are used in providing secure services in the Web.

Terminology

Consider the case when Alice wants to send a message to Bob so that another person (Eve) cannot find out the original information from the message. The message that Alice wants to send is the cleartext or plaintext. To assure the secrecy of the message, Alice encrypts the cleartext into an encrypted message. When Bob gets the message, he decrypts the encrypted message and retrieves the cleartext. Even if Eve has access to the encrypted message (that is, she eavesdrops the transmission channel) she cannot find the cleartext. In the previous example, Alice and Bob are using cryptography to achieve confidentiality: the message sent by Alice is understood only by Bob. In addition to confidentiality, cryptography can be used for the following purposes:

- *Authentication*: the receiver of the message can ascertain its origin.

- *Integrity*: the receiver can verify if the message was modified during the transmission.

- *Non-repudiation*: the sender cannot deny that she sent the message.

Secret-Key Encryption Algorithms

An entire family of cryptographic algorithms has been designed to encrypt messages when Alice and Bob share a common secret—the *key*. These algorithms are called *secret-key encryption algorithms* because they are based on the fact that only Alice and Bob know the secret key. We start with a simple example of a secret-key encryption algorithm. Let us suppose that Alice wants to send a message to Bob and they both know a key. To encrypt, Alice computes the XOR (exclusive or) operation between the characters from the message and the characters from the key. At the end she gets the encrypted message which is sent to Bob. To decrypt, Bob applies the operation XOR between the characters of the encrypted message and the characters of the key. This simple-XOR algorithm is an example of a polyalphabetic substitution cipher. It is considered a weak encryption algorithm because there are methods to derive the key and the clear text from the encrypted text.

There are secret-key encryption algorithms that are considered strong. The rest of this section will enumerate the most often used algorithms. The algorithms are complicated, and the reader can find details in [10].

- *DES* (Digital Encryption Standard): In 1977, this algorithm was adopted by the U.S. government as the federal standard for the encryption of commercial and sensitive-yet-unclassified government computer data. DES is a block cipher (encrypts data in blocks of 64 bits) and relies on a key of 56 bits. Many people unknowingly use DES, because the standard UNIX operating system authenticates users with a variation of DES. Some cryptographers consider that the key is too short and a brute force attack (the attacker tries all the possible keys) can break a message. To address this problem a more secure variant called Triple DES (TDES) has been proposed, which applies DES three times with different keys.

- *IDEA* (International Data Encryption Algorithm): The algorithm is a block cipher algorithm with blocks of 64 bits and a key of 128 bits. The algorithm is used in the popular Pretty Good Privacy (PGP) program.

- *RC2 and RC4*: These are two secret-key algorithms developed by Ron Rivest at RSA Data Security Inc. The algorithms have not been published (although a routine claiming to be RC4 was posted anonymously on the Internet) but are considered strong. The RC4 algorithm with a key of 40 bits is used in many Web browsers and other software products available in the U.S. and on the international market.

- *Skipjack*: The algorithm was proposed by the U.S. National Security Agency (NSA) to replace DES in the future. There is not much information about the algorithm, which is intended to be implemented only in hardware (in the Clipper chip). The algorithm is considered strong but has raised controversy because of the way it is used. Besides implementing the Skipjack algorithm, the chip contains a key-escrow mechanism to allow law enforcement agencies to decrypt messages.

A general problem with secret-key algorithms is the need for *key management*: the communication partners must use another (secure) channel to agree on a common key. **Key-exchange protocols** are designed to solve this problem. For example, the Diffie-Hellman algorithm can be used to create a common (secret) key as follows:

1. Alice and Bob agree on a large prime number n and another number g. These numbers are not necessarily secret.

2. Alice generates a random number x and sends to Bob the value $X = (g^x) \bmod n$.

3. Bob generates a random number y and sends to Alice the value $Y = (g^y) \bmod n$.

4. Alice receives the value of Y and computes $K_x = (Y^x) \bmod n$.

5. Bob receives the value of X and computes $K_y = (X^y) \bmod n$.

The algorithm ensures that the values of K_x and K_y are equal and can be used as the key in a secret-key encryption algorithm. A third party (Eve) cannot determine the value of the secret key by eavesdropping. The reason is that it is difficult to determine $K_x (= K_y)$ given the values X and Y.

Public-Key Encryption Algorithms

In an attempt to solve the problem of key management for secret-key algorithms an entire new family of cryptographic algorithms, called public-key algorithms, has been developed. The basic idea in these algorithms is to use different keys for encryption and for decryption. Bob has two keys: a *public key* that is known by any other party that wants to communicate with Bob and a *private key* that is known only to Bob. If Alice wants to send a secure message to Bob, she encrypts the message with Bob's public key and sends the message to Bob. Bob receives the message and decrypts it with his private key.

The advantage of public key algorithms is that they do not require a secret shared by both partners or a secure channel to exchange the key. One disadvantage of these algorithms is that they are slower than the secret key algorithms. Because of that, in practice, the communication is done using a hybrid protocol:

the partners use the public-key protocol to exchange a secret key that is used subsequently in a secret-key-based communication.

The "de facto" standard in public key encryption algorithms is the RSA algorithm (designed by Ron Rivest, Adi Shamir and Leonard Adleman) [9]. The algorithm has two phases. In the first phase, Bob generates two keys (a public and a private one) and makes public the public key. In the second phase, Alice encrypts a message and Bob decrypts it:

1. Bob generates two large numbers p and q, and computes the modulus, n = pq.

2. Bob chooses a public exponent, which is a number e that is smaller than n and relatively prime to $(p-1)(q-1)$. In practice the value of e is 65337.

3. Bob computes a private exponent $d = e^{-1} \bmod (p-1)(q-1)$.

4. Bob sends the pair (n, e) as a public key to Alice. Bob keeps the pair (n, d) as a private key.

5. Alice encrypts a message m with Bob's public key: $c = m^e \bmod n$ and sends the encrypted message c to Bob.

6. Bob decrypts encrypted message c with the private key to recover message m: $m = c^d \bmod n$.

For two-way communication, Alice also generates her pair of keys and publishes the public key so that Bob can use it to encrypt messages he sends.

The RSA algorithm is used in many applications. It has received more public attention since it has been used in Web browsers. For example, Netscape Navigator uses it for secure transactions over the Web, as we will see later in Section 12.3.

Digital Signatures

The algorithms presented so far are used to preserve the confidentiality of messages. As mentioned in the beginning of this chapter, other issues related to security are integrity and non-repudiation. These goals can be accomplished by using public key algorithms and one-way hash functions. The basics of public key algorithms have been presented in the section on "Public-Key Encryption Algorithms" on page 247. In this section we describe one-way hash functions and how they are used in the verification of integrity.

The purpose of the hash functions is to create a digest of a message that has the following properties:

• The digest is relatively short (typically between 128 and 256 bits).

• Given a message it is easy to generate the hash value.

- Given the hash value, it is difficult to reconstruct the message.

- Given a hash value, it is difficult to find a message which has the given hash value.

The algorithms for computing secure hash functions are intricate. We refer the reader to [10] for several examples. The most popular algorithms are Message Digest 5 (MD5), designed by Ron Rivest, and Secure Hash Algorithm (SHA), designed by the U.S. National Institute of Science and Technology (NIST) and NSA and proposed as a standard. Consider the following situation: Alice sends a message to Bob and Bob wants to verify the integrity of the message. In order to do so, the following protocol is used between Alice and Bob:

1. Alice computes the SHA digest of the message and encrypts the digest with her private key. The encrypted digest is called the *digital signature* of the message.

2. Alice sends the message and the digital signature to Bob.

3. Bob receives the message and the digital signature. He decrypts the digital signature using Alice's public key. After that, he computes the digest and compares it with the value decrypted. If the two digests are the same, Bob is sure that the message has not been altered during transmission, and that Alice is the person who signed the message.

Using one-way hash functions and public-key cryptographic algorithms, it is possible to verify the integrity of the message and also to ensure non-repudiation.

Public-Key Certificates

The algorithms presented in the sections for public-key encryption and digital signatures raise the following question: How does Alice know that the key she has is Bob's public key? This is part of a more general issue in security: authentication, or how to ensure that a certain public key belongs to a person. The solution is to use a trusted third party (called in cryptography slang "Trent"). The rest of this section presents the solution to authentication using public-key certificates. The basic idea for the authentication protocol used in the Web is the following: Bob goes (physically) to a Certificates Authority and presents his ID and his public key. The Certificates Authority issues a certificate that contains the following:

1. Bob's distinguished name (DN) (e.g., C=US, O=Virginia Tech, CN=Bob Smith),

2. Bob's RSA public key,

3. issuer's distinguished name (e.g., C=US, O=AuthorityOrg, CN=Authority),

4. validity period,

5. serial number, and

6. issuer's digital signature.

The term "distinguished name" is used twice in the certificate definition. This term is used in the X.500 standard to denote a unique name for a person. A person's distinguished name contains the name of the person's country (C), their organization (O), their name (CN), and other information required to identify the person. The issuer of the certificate "signs" the certificate with his private key, using the procedure presented above in the section on "Digital Signatures" on page 248. The signature ensures that the certificate itself has not been altered after the issuer sends it. This structure of the certificate is defined in the X.509 standard.

With a public key certificate, communication between Alice and Bob proceeds as follows. When Alice wants to send a message, she needs Bob's public key, so she asks Bob for his certificate. Bob sends the certificate. Alice verifies the validity of the certificate (explained below) and extracts Bob's public key. Then Alice generates a random key and sends it to Bob using the public key encryption algorithm. From this point forward, Alice and Bob can communicate using a secret key algorithm. Note that Bob can also ask Alice to present her public key certificate for a two-way communication.

This description of the communication between Alice and Bob omitted the detail of how to verify the authenticity of the certificate. (If Alice gets a phony certificate from a person imitating Bob, then that person can supply their own public key in the certificate, which Alice would use to encrypt the message, permitting the imitator to decrypt the message with their own private key.)

To verify the certificate, Alice needs the public key of *the issuer* of the certificate. There are two ways to get it: either the issuer is well known and has publicized the public key in the media, or there is another Certificate Authority that can certify the public key of the issuer with a public key certificate. This can go on until Alice knows, and trusts, the public key of an authority. This process of certification is called a certificate chain, and the entire system that supports the process of certification and verification is called the "public key infrastructure."

Many books and papers describe, to various levels of detail, the cryptographic algorithms presented in the section. The reader interested in this topic can find more information in [10, 6, 7, 11].

12.3 Secure Sockets Layer

The Secure Sockets Layer is an intermediate layer between the application and the transport protocol (see Fig. 16–4 on page 310) with the purpose of creating secure and reliable communication. The current version of the protocol (3.0) is defined in [5]. The SSL Protocol provides connection security with three basic properties:

1. The connection is private. Encryption is used after an initial hand-shake to define the cryptographic protocol. Secret-key cryptography is used for data encryption (e.g., DES, RC4).

2. The peer's identity can be authenticated using public-key cryptography.

3. The connection is reliable. Message transport includes a message integrity check using secure hash functions (e.g., SHA, MD5).

The Secure Sockets Layer Protocol has two parts. First, the SSL Hand-shake Protocol establishes the secure channel. Next, the SSL Application Data Protocol is used to exchange data over the channel.

SSL Handshake Protocol

The goal of the protocol is to create an agreement between a client and a server on a set of cryptographic protocols, algorithms and parameters used for communication between them.

The protocol consists of a sequence of steps:

1. Client Hello: In this step the client sends to the server a message that contains two lists, naming the cryptographic and compression algorithms implemented in the client:

```
ClientHello(CypherSuite[], CompressionMethod[])
```

Argument CypherSuite defines three encryption protocols to constitute a suite:

    a. the key-exchange protocol (e.g., Diffie-Hellman),

    b. the secret-key algorithm (e.g., null, RC4, RC2, DES, DES40), and

    c. the one-way hash algorithm (e.g., null, MD5, SHA).

2. Server Hello: After receiving the message from the client, the server chooses the first suite of cryptographic algorithms that was in the client's list and is also implemented by the server. It also takes the first option provided by the client for the compression algorithm. After

that, the server sends to the client a message that contains the server's decisions:

```
ServerHello(CypherSuite, CompressionMethod)
```

After these steps, the server and the client have agreed on the suite of cryptographic and compression algorithms. The next step is to decide on some parameters for the algorithms, of which the most important is the key used in the secret-key encryption. There are two alternatives for how the protocol continues, depending on whether or not the server has a public key certificate.

In the first alternative (e.g., the server has a public key certificate), the server sends the certificate to the client:

```
ServerCertificate(Certificate)
```

Then the client generates a master secret and sends it to the server, encrypted with the public key of the server:

```
encrypt(ClientMasterSecret, ServerPublicKey)
```

The master secret is the basis from which the partners derive the keys used in the cryptographic algorithms. It has 48 bytes (i.e., the current time plus random digits) and is used for one secure session.

In the second alternative (the server does not have a certificate), the server initiates a Key Exchange Protocol using, for example, the Diffie-Hellman protocol. After the exchange of three messages, the server and the client have a master secret. Based on the master secret, both parties create the keys used in communication.

3. Finished: This is the final step in the handshake protocol. Both the client and the server send to each other the digest of the messages sent so far, encrypted with the key generated from the master secret.

The client sends to the server

```
hash(AllMessagesSentByClient+MasterSecret).
```

The server sends to the client

```
hash(AllMessagesSentByServer+MasterSecret).
```

At the end of the handshake protocol both the client and the server are ready to communicate information in a secure way. They agree on the cryptographic and compression algorithms and the parameters for the protocol.

SSL Application Data Protocol

When the client wants to send to the server a message, he computes the digest, encrypts the message and the digest, and sends them to the server:

`encrypt(ClientRequest + hash(ClientRequest+MasterSecret),ClientWriteKey);`

When the server receives the messages, it decrypts the message using the agreed key and verifies the integrity using the same hash function. Then, the server responds to the client using the same cryptographic procedure:

`encrypt(ServerResponse + hash(ServerResponse), ServerWriteKey);`

This concludes the description of SSL. A number of aspects that were not presented above are worth mentioning:

- SSL is flexible. It does not specify a cryptographic algorithm, but rather defines a framework in which to apply existing algorithms to create a secure session.

- SSL allows multiple forms of authentication. Probably in most cases the server will present a certificate. In some cases the server can ask the client for a certificate. It is also possible to communicate without authentication at all.

- SSL has been implemented in most popular Web browsers as a method to provide secure transactions. It has been successfully used in the Web because it does not require much user intervention and the level of security provided is high.

The SSL Protocol is described in several documents available on the Internet. The reader can find out more details about SSL in [5, 1, 6].

12.4 Application—Buying a Book through the Web

The previous section has shown the details of how SSL works. In this section we present how to configure and use SSL for buying a book using a common Web browser. The purpose is to show how the elements involved in a secure communication appear in the user interface and the configuration and troubleshooting of the security system. Suppose that Alice wants to buy a computer book from a bookstore that sells books through a Web site. Let us call the vendor Bob's Online Bookstore (BOB). Alice uses a browser that supports SSL. The following steps are required for a secure transaction:

1. Alice sets up the security preferences of her Web browser. Generally this involves configuring the following:

- *The cipher suite on the client*: The browsers allow the user to choose from a set of possible cryptographic algorithms. A minimum for an economic transaction would be RC2, RC4 or DES with a key of at least 40 bits.

- *The list of public keys trusted by Alice*: This is a bit confusing because Web browsers do not actually store the public keys, but rather the public-key certificates of trusted parties contain the public key. For example, Netscape Navigator comes preloaded with a list of public key certificates for important Certificate Authorities in the U.S. and Canada.

- *Personal public key certificate*: Although rare today, it is possible for individuals to have their own certificates that can be used in transactions. These certificates are useful for the situation when the client has to be authenticated before accessing a server.

- *General preferences*: Alice can set the alert conditions such as whether to get a warning when she communicates through an insecure connection, when the session starts to be secure, and when the secure session is closed.

2. After browsing through Web pages to select a book to purchase, Alice must fill in a Web form on the bookstore's site and provide her credit card number to pay for the book. There are now two alternatives.

   a. If Alice's browser and the vendor's server both support SSL, Alice views the form by visiting an address whose URL starts with `https` instead of `http`. In this case, when the browser downloads the form, it first starts the SSL Handshake Protocol (see page 251) with the server. When the negotiation ends, the browser displays on Alice's computer screen an alert window indicating that the secure channel has been opened. Alice's browser then receives and displays the form.

      Alice can check optionally the security features of the document. In a separate window Alice's browser will display information about the form, such as the public key certificate of the server. This also contains information about who is the issuer, and Alice can check the validity of the certificate using the public key of the issuer. The following excerpt shows the information from a form from www.amazon.com, a bookstore on the Internet:

```
Amazon.com: Finalizing Your Order has the following structure:
     https://www.amazon.com/exec/obidos/order2/1560-1716296-170014
   Form 1:          Action URL:
                    https://www.amazon.com/exec/obidos/
```

```
                    order-form-page1/1560-1716296-170014
                 Encoding: application/x-www-form-urlencoded
                    (default)
                 Method: Post
       Netsite: https://www.amazon.com/exec/obidos/order2/
                    1560-1716296-170014
File MIME Type: text/html
   Source: Currently in memory cache
 Local cache file: none
  Last Modified: Unknown
  Last Modified: Unknown
 Content Length: 2699
       Expires: No date given
       Charset: iso-8859-1 (default)
      Security: This is a secure document that uses a medium-grade
                 encryption key suited for
                 U.S. export (RC4-Export, 128 bit with 40 secret).
   Certificate:This Certificate belongs to:
                 www.amazon.com
                 Amazon.com, Inc.
                 Washington, US
                     This Certificate was issued by:
                     Secure Server Certification Authority
                     RSA Data Security, Inc.    US
                 Serial Number: 02:78:00:06:72
                 This Certificate is valid from Sun Jun 02,
                    1996 to Tue Jun 03, 1997
                 Certificate Fingerprint:
                    93:1D:1A:C6:2B:7F:60:2C:77:46:72:EB:1B:B4:4F:65
```

b. If Alice does not have SSL support, she cannot connect to the SSL port on the server. If she fills in a form and tries to send it, her Web browser should alert her to the fact that the credit card number will be sent over an insecure channel and may be compromised.

Further information on how to use SSL in browsers can be found in [8] and the user manual of browsers supporting SSL.

12.5 Summary

The purpose of this chapter is to present how cryptography can be used to implement security in the Web. It starts with a list of challenges for protecting information, continues with the presentation of the basic cryptographic algorithms and protocols, presents the Secure Sockets Layer protocol, and concludes with an example of how cryptography is used in a commercial transaction on the Internet.

From a technical point of view, cryptography is the solution to many of the security challenges that are present in the Internet. The technology exists to solve most of the problems. However, there are several issues that have obstructed the widespread use of cryptography in the Internet. First of all, cryptography, as a science, faces a difficult problem. Most of the algorithms cannot be proven secure. For this reason, there is suspicion around many of the cryptographic algorithms. Another aspect is related to the intellectual property associated with the algorithms. Most algorithms are patented, and only some companies have licensed them for use.

Finally, cryptography can be used to harm society. Governments are concerned that encryption will make law enforcement and national security goals more difficult to achieve. For example, terrorists could communicate information over the Internet using encryption that law enforcement agencies could not decrypt. Therefore some governments, such as the U.S., have regulated the export of software containing encryption algorithms. This is a topic of debate, pitting governments against the right to free speech (see Chapter 19). For example, U.S. export regulations can prevent the publication of cryptographic research. In one court case, in March 1996, Phil Karn filed suite over whether he could export some source code from [10]. A District Court ruled that "export controls on encryption software are constitutional under the First Amendment" to the U.S. Constitution [2].

However, the following year a different District Court made an opposite ruling in a different case. Daniel Bernstein, while a PhD candidate at the University of California, was told by the U.S. government that he had to register as an arms dealer under the International Traffic in Arms Regulation in order to publish a cryptographic program. Bernstein sued. In August 1997 the Federal District Court in San Francisco ruled that export restrictions on encryption are "an unconstitutional prior restraint in violation of the First Amendment" [3, 4]. According to the Justice department, the larger issue of exporting cryptographic algorithms remains unresolved .

The current trend in society indicates that cryptography is gaining importance. One day cryptography may be widely used throughout the Internet: for electronic mail, for sending documents that are sold over the Web, and even perhaps for all network communication between routers or switches in the Internet. The use and debate on cryptography promises to be prominent for many more years.

12.6 References

[1]   Consensus Development. "Secure Sockets Layer Discussion FAQ." 1996.
      <http://www.consensus.com/security/ssl-talk-faq.html> (19 Sept. 1997).

[2]   Department of Justice. "Justice Department Still Reviewing District Court Decision on Export Controls on Encryption Software." 26 August 1997. <http://www.eff.org/pub/Privacy/ITAR_export/Bernstein_case/ 19970826_govt.pressrel> (20 Sept. 1997).

[3]   Electronic Frontier Foundation. "EFF 'Privacy—Crypto—ITAR Export Restrictions' Archive." <http://www.eff.org/pub/Privacy/ITAR_export/> (20 Sept. 1997).

[4]   Electronic Frontier Foundation. "EFF 'Legal Cases—Crypto—Bernstein v. US Dept. of State' Archive." <http://www.eff.org/pub/Privacy/ITAR_export/Bernstein_case/> (20 Sept. 1997).

[5]   Internet Engineering Task Force. "SSL 3.0." 1996. <ftp://ietf.cnri.reston.va.us/internet-drafts/draft-freier-ssl-version3-01.txt> (1 Nov. 1996).

[6]   Netscape. "Secure Communication on the Intranet and over the Internet." July 1996. <http://home.netscape.com/newsref/ref/128bit.html> (19 Sept. 1997).

[7]   Netscape. "Using RSA Public Key Cryptography for Internet Security." 1996. <http://home.netscape.com/newsref/ref/rsa.html> (19 Sept. 1997).

[8]   Netscape. "Netscape Data Security." 1996. <http://home.netscape.com/newsref/ref/netscape-security.html> (19 Sept. 1997).

[9]   RSA, Inc. "RSA Labs FAQ—Question 8: What is RSA?" <http://www.rsa.com/rsalabs/newfaq/q8.html> (20 Sept. 1997).

[10] Schneier, Bruce. *Applied Cryptography*. John Wiley and Sons, 1996.

[11] VeriSign, Inc. "VeriSign Digital ID Center FAQs." <http://digitalid.verisign.com/id_faqs.htm> (19 Sept. 1997).

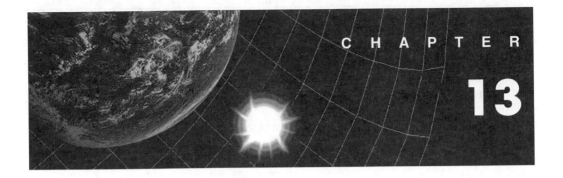

Electronic Commerce

by Patrick N. Brooks

When the Web was in its infancy, commercial use of the Internet was limited. When these restrictions were lifted, commercial use of the Web exploded. In less than half a decade, the Web has brought innumerable changes to the ways companies do business. The major issue restraining the commercial use of the Web is the lack of a de facto standard system of paying for products or services. Another issue looming in the future of the Web is how users pay for access to Web content. One proposal is the use of "microcents"—transactions on the order of $0.0001. This chapter discusses these and other issues in the development of commerce on the Web.

Chapter Content

1. Introduction
2. Secure Payment Systems

- First Virtual
- NetBill
- DigiCash's ecash
- IBM's Cryptolope
- MasterCard's Secure Electronic Transactions (SET)
- CyberCash
- Against Secure Payment Systems
- Summary and Conclusions

3. Microcent Transactions

- Digital's Millicent Proposal

- Arguments Against Microcent Transactions

- Arguments For Microcent Transactions

4. Other Commerce Issues

- Paying for Network Traffic

- Pricing as Congestion Control

- Shareware as a Marketing Tool

- Web as a Public Relations Tool

5. Conclusions

6. References

13.1 Introduction

In the early years of the Internet, commercial use was prohibited. As restrictions were lifted, commercial use of the Web exploded. Instead of periodically printing new catalogs, companies could update online catalogs for a fraction of the cost. Instead of shipping computer diskettes across the country, companies could allow software to be downloaded from the company's Web page. Company policies, product descriptions, career opportunities, and financial sheets were all made immediately available through the Web. In less than half a decade, the Web has brought innumerable changes to the ways companies do business.

The major issue restraining the commercial use of the Web is the lack of a trusted, secure system of paying for products or services. Many payment systems are in use, but no system has gained widespread acceptance. This chapter discusses the major systems and the prospects for future payment systems.

Currently the Web follows a model of advertising borrowed from television: The user only pays to connect to the network—companies and advertisers foot the bill for developing the content and making it available. Soon this may change to a pay-per-view model, where the user pays a per-access fee to view content. One idea for this per-access fee is microcent transactions—transactions on the order of $0.0001. Prospects for the future of microcent transactions will also be discussed.

13.2 Secure Payment Systems

Widespread use of secure payment systems will be the next big step in the evolution of the Web. In this section, several approaches to Web payments are discussed.

The development of secure payment systems has led to much discussion in
the financial and regulatory arenas. By providing electronic financial services,
are these system providers acting as a financial institution? If so, should they be
subject to the same regulations as existing financial institutions? The Computer
Law Association[1] has published "The Internet and Business: A Lawyer's Guide to
the Emerging Legal Issues" [24], which addresses these issues.

In the United States, the main Federal regulation that may apply to electronic commerce is the Electronic Fund Transfer Act (EFTA) and its implementing regulation called Regulation E. In Chapter 8 of the aforementioned book, the
author states, "One of the most hotly debated questions arising from the possible
applicability of Regulation E to electronic cash transactions relates to its
requirement of delivery of a physical receipt, a requirement that would make
electronic cash transactions unworkable" [24].

Two approaches that provide secure electronic cash transactions are Secure
Socket Layer (SSL) and Secure HTTP (SHTTP). SSL and SHTTP encrypt all Web
network traffic, thereby allowing credit card numbers to be safely transmitted.
Secure transactions are a by-product of these systems, so they are not discussed
with systems designed from the ground up to provide secure transactions. Chapter 12 discusses SSL in more detail.

In the following sections, many different secure payment systems are discussed. To compare them, keep the following questions in mind:

- How does the system interact with financial institutions?

- How much does each transaction cost?

- How complex is the system to set up and use?

- Does the system allow anonymous transactions?

- Does the system distribute some cash equivalent?

- What is the relationship between the system, vendor, and user?

- What is the financial risk to the system, vendor, and user?

---

[1] http://cla.org

First Virtual

Summary of First Virtual

First Virtual [12] was the first to provide a secure payment system to the Internet in October, 1994. Their system does not require any user software (except e-mail), uses no encryption, and does not require a special bank account. When a user sets up a First Virtual account, the application is done over the Internet. To activate the account, the user must call a 1-800 number, and input their assigned account number and their credit card information. In this manner, the credit card information never travels on the Internet. At First Virtual, all credit card information is stored on machines not connected to the Internet to enhance security. Currently, a First Virtual account costs a user $2 per year. Each transaction costs a vendor $0.29 plus 2% of the cost of the transaction.

A First Virtual transaction

When the user creates an account at First Virtual, he receives an account number called a VirtualPIN. This account number is in no way related to the user's credit card number. When the user finds a product he wants to buy, he sends the VirtualPIN to the vendor. The vendor verifies the VirtualPIN and e-mails it to First Virtual. First Virtual sends an e-mail to the user confirming the purchase. When the user replies, First Virtual debits the user's credit card, deposits the correct amount (minus fees) into the vendor's account, and confirms the sale via e-mail with the vendor. The vendor then forwards the product to the user. This system also supports the idea of shareware/demo periods. In this case, the user could download the product, and later initiate payment. More information about buying and selling using FirstVirtual is available [13].

NetBill

Summary of NetBill

NetBill [22] is a secure payment system designed to support the online purchase of electronic information goods. A user creates a NetBill account that is linked to an existing account at a financial institution. Users can deposit and withdraw money from this account as needed. NetBill software installed on the user's computer as a plug-in to Netscape 3.0 manages transactions between the user and NetBill. NetBill uses two encryption schemes to maintain security: RSA public-key encryption and Kerberos tickets. Chapter 12 discusses public-key encryption in more detail. NetBill has been used on the campus of Carnegie Mellon University.

An interesting aspect of NetBill is that when the user purchases a product, the vendor sends an encrypted version of the product to the user's machine. After the financial transaction has been completed through NetBill, a decryption key is sent to the user's machine to decrypt the product.

A NetBill transaction

When a user wants to purchase an item using NetBill, he clicks on the item in his Web browser. The vendor sends an encrypted version of the item to the user's machine. When the user's machine verifies correct reception of the encrypted version, the vendor sends the user's payment information and the decryption key to NetBill. NetBill handles the financial transactions (withdrawal from the user's account, deposit to the vendor's account) and sends a report back to the vendor. The vendor then forwards the decryption key to the user to allow use of the product. If the vendor fails to forward the decryption key, the user can retrieve it directly from NetBill. More detailed information about how NetBill works is available [21].

DigiCash's ecash

Summary of DigiCash's ecash

DigiCash [6], founded in 1990 by Dr. David Chaum, has been in the electronic payment arena from the start. Their first product was a road toll system. Since that time, they have been involved with smartcard technology, modular encryption hardware, and cross-border electronic wallet systems. DigiCash's approach to secure payment systems is based on patented advances in public key cryptography.

Where the previous systems have relied on communicating transactions to a financial institution, DigiCash takes the different approach of creating an electronic, encrypted form of cash called "ecash." This ecash has many properties of physical cash, including anonymity. Additionally, person-to-person payments can be easily made with ecash, whereas other systems have distinct roles of buyer and vendor.

Nearly 30,000 people participated in a trial of ecash which started in October, 1994 [7]. This trial used "cyberbucks," which could not be exchanged for any real currency. This trial has since been closed to further applicants, and ecash has moved on to using real currency. Four banks have issued ecash in five different currencies.

An ecash transaction

A user obtains ecash from an issuing bank—typically the bank debits the user's account and returns to the user the correct amount of ecash. The ecash is an encrypted form that actually has value, and is stored on the user's machine. Software acquired from DigiCash allows transactions to be made to any other entity that accepts ecash. DigiCash provides a detailed explanation of how their system works and how to use ecash software [8].

IBM's Cryptolope

IBM's Cryptolope [17] technology allows a user to encrypt an electronic product for transport over the network. Two features distinguish this approach from other payment methods: usage tracking and unencrypted abstracts. A cryptolope container has built-in abilities to track its usage regardless of when it is opened. This enables the owner to track the usage of a product after the product's first owner. For example, if user A buys a video clip contained in a cryptolope, and passes a copy to user B, when user B opens the cryptolope to get the video clip, the originator of the cryptolope is notified. The Cryptolope Web site[2] is not exact about how this notification is accomplished.

The second distinguishing feature is the availability of an abstract on every cryptolope. The abstract contains a description of the contents, the price to open the contents, and instructions for using the contents. Users on the network can look at the abstract to decide if they want to purchase the key to the cryptolope. IBM touts this technology as the best method of collecting payment for copyrighted information. No matter where the cryptolope travels, it is still only available to users who pay for access.

IBM also claims that cryptolope technology allows the creation of a unique digital object. This leads to the idea of a "digital collectible" [16]—an object that has been reproduced by its owner into a limited number of copies. Each of these copies can be authenticated as one of the original copies. This idea potentially leads to genuine trade of original work on the Internet.

MasterCard's Secure Electronic Transactions (SET)

MasterCard, in conjunction with GTE, IBM, Microsoft, Netscape, Visa, and others, is developing a standard for secure on-line credit card transactions. Their goal is to develop "a single method that consumers and merchants will use to conduct bankcard transactions in cyberspace as securely and easily as they do in retail stores today" [20]. Creating a standard would speed the acceptance of commerce on the Internet, but may inhibit the development of other better-suited payment systems.

CyberCash

Summary of CyberCash

CyberCash, Inc. [3] was founded in August 1994 with the goal of providing secure financial transactions over open networks. In April 1995 they began providing secure credit card transactions. Their payment system used 1024-bit RSA encryption to protect transactions on the Internet.

---

[2] http://www.cryptolope.ibm.com

On October 7, 1996, CyberCash announced a partnership with Netscape to become the first product that implements the Secure Electronic Transactions credit card payment protocol. CyberCash's software will be included in Netscape's LivePayment server software. Additionally, CyberCash announced on October 30, 1996 that it would support Microsoft Merchant Server [4].

CyberCash recently introduced CyberCoin technology to support micropayments in the range of $0.25 to $10.00 and up. In the next section of this chapter, we will see that CyberCoins are one interpretation of micropayments.

A CyberCash transaction

After the user locates an item she wants to purchase, CyberCash software forwards encrypted payment information to the vendor. The vendor can decrypt the order information, but cannot decrypt the user's account numbers or other personal information. The vendor forwards the order information to CyberCash. CyberCash takes the information off the Internet, decrypts it, and sends the payment transaction across existing financial networks. When the appropriate financial institution approves the transaction, CyberCash returns approval to the vendor, and the vendor then delivers the product to the user. The CyberCash Web site describes the six steps in a secure Internet credit card payment [5].

Against Secure Payment Systems

In the April 10, 1995 issue of *PC Week*, Ben Rotheke argues that using a credit card over the Internet is as safe as using a credit card at a retail store [23]. In retail stores, shoppers are typically not concerned about the security of their credit card information. They write their credit card numbers on checks, allow the carbon copies to be thrown in the trash where they could later be retrieved, and give their cards to merchants. Any of these habits allow credit card information to be intercepted. Even if the consumer is vigilant, a dishonest clerk or accountant could photocopy the store's copy of a credit card slip.

Additionally, credit card agreements limit a consumer's liability for misuse of their credit card if the misuse is reported within a reasonable amount of time. Credit card companies also go to tremendous lengths to detect dramatic changes in a card's usage. If a card is stolen and a thief goes on a shopping spree, or if a card is used in two geographically distant locations within a short period of time, the credit card company may detect the misuse and suspend the card number.

These factors lead to the conclusion that secure payment systems may be overkill compared to conventional credit cards, and in the end, unnecessary. However, the mere existence of companies competing to create the first accepted payment systems indicates the above reasons are not sufficient to comfortably perform credit card transactions on the Internet.

Summary and Conclusions

The previous sections described many different approaches to providing a system for secure payments to the Web. These systems can be divided into two groups based on their transaction style. Most systems perform transactions by issuing commands to make a credit card or bank account transaction. For example, First Virtual performs a credit card transaction after confirmation from the user. In contrast, DigiCash's ecash (and Digital's Millicent, discussed in the next section) use an electronic representation of cash that physically exists on the user's machine in electronic form. The two groups offer contrasting advantages and disadvantages.

By using an electronic representation of cash, true anonymous transactions are possible. This is more like physical cash, and provides many advantages to users concerned about some Orwellian "Big Brother" knowing about their financial transactions.

A major problem with electronic representation of cash is the potential for double spending. If the issued coins are not kept track of efficiently, or they can be somehow duplicated, then the same coins could be spent twice with two different vendors. This problem adds to the complexity of electronic representation-based systems.

The use of encryption technology in these payment systems is a double-edged sword. Encryption provides security but demands processing time. The processing required for each transaction determines the processing power necessary to run the system, and thus partially determines the cost to run the system. The cost to run the system is charged to users for each transaction made. If this transaction cost is significant, it prohibits the idea of microcent transactions discussed in the next section.

One final point is that the average consumer will not shop on the Web until a de facto standard emerges. This emergence could easily be brought about by a big name company (MasterCard, Microsoft, Netscape, etc.) coming forward and convincing the public that using their system is safe enough. Until this happens, the average user will continue to believe that putting their credit card on the Web in any way is essentially asking someone to steal it.

13.3 Microcent Transactions

The idea behind microcent transactions is that users would pay something like $0.0001 to view different items on the Web. Online services that provide web pages, news articles, stock prices, horoscopes, and so forth could charge this small amount for online items. This would allow users to view content without needing to set up an account with a service provider and potentially pay for services the user may not use. It allows content providers to receive income when a user accesses their pages, without the overhead of administering user accounts.

For example, on a particular day an issue of *USA Today* had roughly 126 articles, and cost $0.50 from a newsstand. This works out to about $0.004 per article. If the user only wants to read a few articles, then purchasing the entire paper may be too costly. If the newspaper company gives their newspaper away on the Internet, then they give up a source of income. Microcent transactions represent a middle ground between paying for access and giving content away.

Digital's Millicent Proposal

Millicent [9] is a payment system designed for microcent transactions by Digital Equipment Corp. It uses the idea of "scrip," which is currency valid for only a certain vendor. Instead of users trying to keep track of many different kinds of scrip for many different vendors, Millicent uses "brokers" to buy many different types of vendor scrip and sell broker scrip to users. Thus users buy a few kinds of broker scrip which can be paid to the broker, who then exchanges it for a specific vendor scrip.

The main goal of Millicent is to lower the cost of each scrip transaction. By lowering the cost of each transaction to the broker and vendor, the minimum payment can be lowered. If the cost per transaction is extremely small, then microcent transactions can be supported. An initial implementation of Millicent has transaction costs consistent with microcent transactions (handling about 1000 Millicent requests per second [14]).

In a later section, a discussion of usage-based pricing leads to the conclusion that microcent transactions may be inevitable.

Arguments Against Microcent Transactions

Arguments against microcent transactions include the difficulty of maintaining records for thousands of microcent transactions, the lack of technology that currently supports transactions of this small magnitude, and the general resistance to users' paying for content.

Currently, Web content providers receive the majority of their income from advertisers who pay for prominent advertising space on the provider's Web site. It is easier to keep up with a limited number of advertisers than with hundreds of thousands of microcent transactions.

The payment systems described in Section 13.2 are designed for transactions with a minimum worth of between $0.25 and $1.00. No current available technology exists to support microcent transactions. Additionally, most also include some form of encryption, which requires significant processing power for each transaction. For microcent transactions to be feasible, the cost of processing for each transaction must be extremely small. No current payment system has this level of cost per transaction.

Only in the past couple of years have some Web sites charged their users for access. Most Web users are accustomed to paying a single fee for access to the Internet and then paying nothing for the accessed content. Charging users on a widespread basis may meet with resistance.

Arguments for Microcent Transactions

Arguments for microcent transactions include the fair allocation of costs to users, the deterrent to theft and fraud, the ease of creating a payment relationship, and the incentive of income to Web content providers.

Currently, most Web content providers charge a fixed fee to all users that access their system, regardless of the amount of traffic each user generates. Thus two users pay the same amount for access to an online newspaper, even if one user reads every single article every day of the week, and the other reads only one article a month. By charging for only what a user accesses, microcent transactions allow users to pay for exactly what they use.

When a Web item costs $0.0001, there is extremely little incentive for users to steal the item. Even if a first user purchases the item, and wants to pass the purchased copy on to a second user, it may be easier to purchase the original, virus-free, up-to-date copy from the original source.

Some users would be very wary of paying an unknown content provider $10 or $30 for access to a certain Web site. The user would be vulnerable to the content providers defaulting on his obligation in some way. Microcent transactions allow a pay-as-you-go structure that does not expose the user to significant financial risk.

Finally, if the content providers receive income from frequently accessed content on the Web, then they have an incentive to provide quality content that will draw in users. Potentially, any user that can effectively filter the vast amount of information on the Web into well-defined lists could provide those lists to other users for a microcent charge.

13.4 Other Commerce Issues

Paying for Network Traffic

To this point, this chapter has discussed payment systems that handle purchases of one sort or another using the Web. They do not handle transactions for such low-level activities as passing communications packets across a network. The Digital Silk Road [15] proposes including a money field in some packets that can be used to pay for the transit of the packet across the network. In a sense, the packets are cars and the links in the networks are toll roads. The companies that maintain links on the network receive income from the packets that use their links. Per-packet pricing for international network traffic has already been implemented in Chile [1] and New Zealand [2].

This approach to paying for network access has advantages. Instead of paying a set amount each month, a user pays only for what he uses. This could save a light-traffic user money if the user transmits only a small amount of traffic. This approach also subsidizes companies for maintaining network links. The companies' income is related to their quality of service, reliability, and toll rate. The major (and potentially prohibitive) disadvantage is that current protocols must be rewritten to use this approach.

Pricing as Congestion Control

In "Economic FAQs About the Internet" [19], the authors consider different methods of congestion control for Web traffic that are not based on the details of communication protocols. To date, most attempts at congestion control on the Internet have been voluntary in nature. With increasing demands for network bandwidth, pricing-related congestion control may become a necessary reality.

The authors [19] propose a "smart market" where users place a "bid" representing their willingness to pay to get their traffic through a congested network. If the network is not congested, then no charges would be assessed to the users. If the network is congested and all the users are bidding, then the lowest-bid packets could be dropped from the network. Users are only charged the bid of the lowest-bid packet that was allowed through the network. This allows users to be charged only what is necessary for their desired level of service.

Shareware as a Marketing Tool

In her speech "Slaves of a New Machine: Exploring the For-Free/For-Pay Conundrum" [11], Laura Fillmore, President of the Online BookStore, describes her first publishing experience on the Internet. *The Internet Companion: A Beginner's Guide to Global Networking* by Tracy LaQuey was the first popular book about using the Internet. Fillmore describes how the book was made available for free over the Internet, which paradoxically spurred the sales of the book in retail stores.

After this experience, Fillmore made an attempt to sell Stephen King's story "Nightmares and Dreamscapes" over the Internet for $5 a copy. The sales over the Internet from this effort were minimal, but again the retail sales were boosted.

In a similar situation, id Software distributed the first level of their computer game "Doom" as shareware over the Internet. The remaining levels were only available through mail order from the company. Shareware is software distributed for free for a trial period. At the end of the period, the user is expected to send payment for the product. Doom went on to sell 2 million copies. However, as many as 20 million copies exist around the world, legally distributed as shareware. "By releasing chunks of their games as shareware, id's marketing strategy turns every player into a potential distributor…." [18].

These stories lead to the practice of using the Web as a marketing tool. If sales of an electronic product can be enhanced by giving away some controlled part, then this kind of marketing will only become more prevalent.

Web as a Public Relations Tool

In late 1994, Intel's Pentium processor was discovered to have a division bug. Dr. Thomas R. Nicely was one of the first people outside of Intel to discover the bug, and his e-mail to his colleagues was the start of an avalanche of public outcry on the Internet. Dealing with a public relations problem on the Internet is inherently different, and Intel had difficulty limiting damage to their corporate image.

In "A Learning Experience: The Pentium Chip Story" [10], Vince Emery describes the lessons to be learned from Intel's difficulty. These lessons include:

- monitor the Internet and respond to criticisms and complaints quickly,

- contact by telephone any particularly harsh critic (people act differently on the Internet than in person),

- continually respond to complaints in a crisis (don't make a statement and then disappear), and

- remember that the Internet is a growing source for reporters for traditional media.

13.5 Conclusions

The issues and systems discussed in this chapter will become part of mainstream Web usage in the near future. Secure payment systems will allow the Web to change from an online mail-order catalog to an online store. Microcent transactions will lead to greater access and to more worthwhile content. Other issues affecting the commercial use of the Web will continue to appear. It will be interesting to return to this chapter in five years to see how quickly and radically these issues have changed the use of the Web.

13.6 References

[1]   Baeza-Yates, R., J. Piquer and P. Poblete. "The Chilean Internet connection, or, I never promised you a rose garden." In *Proc. INET '93*, 1993.

[2]   Brownlee, N. "New Zealand experiences with network traffic charging." *ConneXions*, 28 April 1995.
<http://www.auckland.ac.nz/net/Accounting/nze.html> (accessed 22 Nov. 1996).

[3]   CyberCash. "CyberCash Home." 4 Nov. 1996.
<http://www.cybercash.com/> (accessed 22 Nov. 1996).

[4]   ——. "CyberCash and Industry Press Releases" 15 Nov. 1996.
<http://www.cybercash.com/cybercash/news/news3.html> (22 Nov. 1996).

[5]   ——. "The Six Steps in a Secure Internet Credit Card Payment." 7 Aug. 1996. <http://www.cybercash.com/cybercash/info/sixsteps.html> (22 Nov. 1996).

[6]   DigiCash. "DigiCash home page." 22 July 1996. <http://www.digicash.com/> (accessed 22 Nov. 1996).

[7]   ——. "The ecash trial." 20 June 1996.
<http://www.digicash.com/ecash/trial.html> (22 Nov. 1996).

[8]   ——. "An introduction to ecash." 08 May 1996.
<http://www.digicash.com/publish/ecash_intro/ecash_intro.html   (22 Nov. 1996).

[9]   Digital Equipment Corp. "Millicent—Digital's Microcommerce System."
<http://www.research.digital.com/SRC/millicent/> (22 Nov. 1996).

[10] Emery, V. "A Learning Experience: The Pentium Chip Story." 14 Feb. 1996.
<http://owi.com/netvalue/text/v1i3c1.html> (accessed 22 Nov. 1996).

[11] Fillmore, L. "Slaves of a New Machine· Exploring the For-Free / For-Pay Conundrum." 15 July 1994.
<http://cism.bus.utexas.edu/ravi/laura_talk.html> (accessed 22 Nov. 1996).

[12] FirstVirtual. "The First Virtual Internet Payment System." 22 Oct. 1996.
<http://fv.com/> (22 Nov. 1996).

[13] ——. "Payment System Summary (Buying and Selling)." 16 September 1996. <http://fv.com/info/intro.html> (22 Nov. 1996).

[14] Glassman, S. M. Manasse, M. Abadi, P. Gauthier, and P. Sobalvarro. "The Millicent Protocol for Inexpensive Electronic Commerce."

   <http://www.research.digital.com/SRC/millicent/papers/millicent-w3c4/
   millicent.html> (22 Nov. 1996).

[15] Hardy, N. and E. Tribble. "The Digital Silk Road." 14 Sept. 1996.
   <http://www.agorics.com/~agorics/dsr.html> (22 Nov. 1996).

[16] IBM. "Digital Collectibles Are Here!" 5 Nov. 1996.
   <http://www.cryptolope.ibm.com/digital.htm> (22 Nov. 1996).

[17] ——. "Welcome to the Cryptolope Showcase!" 05 Nov. 1996.
   <http://www.cryptolope.ibm.com/> (22 Nov. 1996).

[18] Laidlaw, Marc. "The Egos at Id," *Wired* v.4 n.8, Aug. 1996.
   <http://www.wired.com/4.08/id/features/id.html> (10 Dec. 1996).

[19] MacKie-Mason, J., and H. Varian. "Economic FAQs About the Internet." 1
   July 1995.
   <http://www.spp.umich.edu/ipps/papers/info-nets/Economic_FAQs/FAQs/
   FAQs.html> (22 Nov. 1996).

[20] MasterCard. "Secure Electronic Transactions." 18 Oct. 1996.
   <http://www.mastercard.com/set/> (22 Nov. 1996).

[21] NetBill. "How NetBill Works." 06 Nov. 1996.
   <http://www.netbill.com/netbill/works.html> (22 Nov. 1996).

[22] ——. "Welcome to NetBill." 06 Nov. 1996. <http://www.netbill.com/> (22 Nov.
   1996).

[23] Rothke, B. "Shopping the Internet is safe as buying at the mall." *PC Week*.
   v.12 n.14, Apr. 10, 1995).

[24] Ruh, Joseph F., Jr. "The Internet and Business: A Lawyer's Guide to the
   Emerging Legal Issues." 18 July 1996. <http://cla.org/RuhBook/index.htm>
   (22 Nov. 1996).

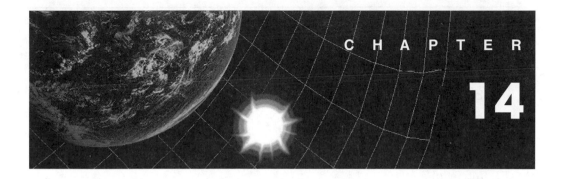

C H A P T E R

14

Searching for Documents on the Web

by Aixiang (I Song) Yao and Marc Abrams

Search systems for the Web can be viewed as consisting of four functional modules: gatherer, indexer, search, and retrieval. This chapter discusses Web searching by examining each of these four functional modules in detail. A second way to view Web search systems is as database queries. Essentially all search services are variations of database searches. The chapter concludes by surveying several popular search systems for the Web, and discusses criteria to select a search system.

Chapter Content

4. Search

- Search Language

- Search Engine

- Vector-based Search

5. Retrieval

- Direct Retrieval

- Client-Server Retrieval

6. How to Select a Search System

- Search Systems on the Web

- Selecting a Search System

7. References

14.1 Introduction

One weakness of the Web is our limited ability to find documents of interest. As the Web grows in popularity, so does the difficulty of searching for documents. In recent years, many search systems have become available. But how do they work? How can we select the search service that best satisfies our needs? These questions are addressed in this chapter.

Suppose that we were to build a search system for the Web. One way would be to create a catalog of Web pages, analogous to a catalog of holdings available in a library. In the case of a library, the collection of books grows slowly, and cataloging is done by humans. In contrast, Web pages are created quickly by many people worldwide, and a mechanical human cataloging can only include a fraction of the world's Web pages. Several catalogs, directories, or "subject hierarchies" are offered that cover a subset of the Web's documents (see the section on "Search Systems on the Web" on page 284).

In contrast to the human judgment in constructing a library catalog, universal search systems in the Web are based on automatically constructed indexes, using database technology for searching. To do this, Web search systems first collect information about Web documents over the Internet itself. This step is called the gathering process. They then determine which terms should be indexed, and create a record for each document. The record is then inserted into a database. This step is called the indexing process. The indexing process builds a database. Each record is a brief description of a document. Whenever Web users use a search system to find documents containing certain terms, a database search process is initiated.

To search or to query the database, a specific query language and search engine must be used. The query language transforms a question from the user into a formal query that search engine can process. The search engine applies the query to the database and finds records that are most likely to satisfy the user's question.

Finally the search system should have capability of giving the user access to the original document. In this retrieval process, the system transfers the original document from a Web server to the user's computer so that the user can view, save, or print the document. Search systems typically provide an HTML document to the user that contains hypertext links to the original documents on other Web servers.

To summarize, a Web search system can be viewed as consisting of the following four functional modules [25]:

- Gatherer (Section 14.2): Collects information about documents to be indexed.

- Indexer (Section 14.3): Creates index records and enters them into a database.

- Search (Section 14.4): Takes questions from the user, searches the records in the collection, and returns the information about the documents that may answer the user's question. The search module consists of two components: a query language and a search engine.

- Retrieval (Section 14.5): Provides the original documents to the user.

Subsequent sections examine how each of the four modules in detail.

14.2 Gatherer

A gatherer traverses the Web as a spider traverses a spider web. It collects information about documents to be indexed. A gatherer starts from a single document, usually the home directory of a Web server, then selects the next document to index by following a hypertext link.

The names "robot," "bot," "robot gatherer," "crawler," and "spider" are often used to describe a gatherer. The reference to "robot" refers to the fact that a gatherer is a computer program that runs without human intervention, visiting Web sites and collecting Web pages for indexing. Only a few gatherers, operated by the major Web search systems (Section 14.6), visit sites worldwide, owing to the large network bandwidth required to gather the world's Web pages.

Documents on the Web are complex, widely distributed, and dynamic. Someone might be adding, modifying, or deleting the documents on a Web server while a gatherer is retrieving the server's page. Furthermore, some Web documents are dynamically generated by a CGI-bin script (Chapter 7), and thus the content might vary each time the URL of the script is visited. In fact, it is impossible to gather every document on the Web for the reason that there are just too many documents.

Robot gatherers locate Web severs and retrieve a set of documents on each server. Each retrieved document is passed to the indexer, which extracts words from the document that might be used later on in a user's search query (see Section 14.3).

This leaves the question of how a gatherer chooses which pages to retrieve from a Web server. Typically gatherers start with a list of one or more known URLs on the Web server (at least http://S, where S is the name of the Web server), and then traverse the hypertext links in the documents named by these URLs. The links lead to other documents on the Web server, which themselves contain more hypertext links, and so on. There are two policies used to control the order of documents visited, and to limit the number of pages traversed: *breadth first* and *depth first*.

Breadth First

A *breadth-first* policy, starting with a document D, will first traverse all the hypertext links in document D, and will next consider the hypertext links in each document to which D links, recursively applying to each linked document the breadth-first policy. A maximum number of times that the recursion is applied may be defined, to prevent the traversal from taking excessive time.

Breadth first can be visualized as a spider traversing a path starting from the center of its web. It first traverses all the threads in the closest circle (first-level breadth), then searches the threads in the second circle (second-level breadth), and so on. In this case, it uses breadth-first policy. A gatherer using a breadth first policy does a wide and shallow traversal.

Depth First

The *depth-first* policy, starting with a document D, will traverse the first hypertext link in D, then recursively apply the depth-first policy to that first document, and so on, either until a document without any links is reached, or until some maximum number of levels is traversed. This maximum number or limit on links to follow is often used to prevent the gatherer from following links down forever. At this point gathering continues with the second and subsequent hypertext links in D in a similar manner.

Depth first can be visualized as a spider that follows a thread from the center of its web all way out to the outermost circle, then returns to the center and follows another thread from the center out to the outermost circle. A gatherer using a depth-first policy does a narrow but deep traversal.

Breadth first tends to gather Web pages on a variety of topics on a Web server. It is well matched to hierarchical page structures, such as a top level Web page with links to articles on subtopics, and thus is preferred by several search systems. The Web-site version of this book is such an example. On the other hand, a gatherer using a breadth-first policy will tend to bombard the same Web server with rapid requests, possibly overloading the server. In contrast, depth first tends to locate a variety of Web servers quickly, and tends to spread successive page requests by a gatherer over multiple servers.

Other Gatherer Issues

A gatherer often constructs a map of Web sites that it visits. These maps are used to prevent the gatherer from revisiting Web sites it has already gathered. A gatherer may also maintain information on which documents should not be indexed (e.g., executable binaries), and which sites were difficult to reach and should be skipped when gathering is repeated on another day [25]. Site maps could store the time of last modification of visited pages, so when the gatherer starts again to update the index, it can avoid fetching pages that are unmodified since the last time the gathering ran.

A set of guidelines have been developed for gather behavior [15]. If gatherers were run by too many organizations, and if they revisited Web pages too frequently, then a significant fraction of the world's Internet and server capacity would be consumed by gathering. The guidelines propose use of a file named /robot.txt in the root document of a Web server to request certain behaviors of Web robots visiting the site. These include listing pages that should not be indexed, such as pages the author prefers to keep out of Web search systems, and pages that lead to infinite loops in gathering (e.g., a URL of a script that returns a page that is always one level down in the hierarchy [15]).

Another issue in using gathering robots is that they must be carefully designed to avoid creating problems for Web-site and network operators. A poorly designed robot can bombard a Web site with requests, making the server unresponsive or even crashing the server. Poor design can also cause repeated retrievals of the same document in a short span of time.

A larger issue for gathering robots is what Koster refers to as ethics [15]: "Is the cost to others of the operation of a robot justified"? The result of running a robot is to provide a service to someone (e.g., a Web search system), but the cost is less network bandwidth and slower servers for everyone using the Web. The trade-off between cost and benefit must be evaluated. For example, if you create a new Web page, how long will it be before gathers automatically discover your page and add it to Web search systems? You might prefer that search systems add the page to their index within a few days, but to do that the gatherer must rescan the world's Web pages every few days—possibly causing too high a load on the Internet and Web servers.

Efficient, Shared Gathering: Harvest

Results of gathering can also be shared to eliminate redundant gathering by multiple organizations. This is accomplished by the Harvest system [4].

Harvest is an alternative architecture to today's world in which each search service runs its own robot gatherer. Harvest can coordinate gathering from a set of Web search services to provide shared gathering. In Harvest, gatherers run on a "provider" site, rather than being initiated from the indexing organization. The provider's gatherer alone scans pages at the provider's site, and exports summaries of the content of those pages. The gatherer maintains a cache of content summaries. The gatherer also incrementally updates its information.

A Web search service that wishes to build an index would be a "broker" in the Harvest system. Brokers remotely access providers' gatherers through the Internet, rather than accessing raw Web pages themselves. The brokers obtain content summaries from the gatherer cache, thereby not placing additional load on individual Web servers. Harvest also defines a broker/indexer interface that accommodates a variety of search engines.

Harvest is a more efficient architecture for Web searching, but it requires the cooperation of Web site or ISP operators worldwide to implement. The Internet may migrate toward a Harvest-like approach as the size of the Internet makes intractable redundant gathering of Web pages by multiple organizations.

14.3 Indexer

An indexer takes information collected by the gatherer, creates index records, and enters them into a database. This process is called indexing. In some search systems, the gatherer and indexer are combined into one module, in which case the gatherer creates index records while it traverses the Web.

Indexing is the key component of the search system. An effective indexing process will produce high-quality records that accurately represent a collection of documents. Searching a high-quality index leads to precise identification and correct retrieval of documents. A high-quality index also can reduce the time required for searching.

In fact, the principle of indexing for a search system is almost the same as creating a traditional database. In a traditional database, a record is a set of values treated as a unit. For example, a record for a book may consist of the title, author, publisher, subject, and so on. The following example shows three sample records in a database:

```
Record: 012
------------
Author:    Lincoln D. Stein
Title:     How to Set Up and Maintain a World Wide Web Site
Publisher: Addison-Wesley Publishing Company, Inc. (1995)
Subject:   Web, Netscape, HTML
ISBN:      0-201-63389-2


Record: 345
------------
Author:    David Flanagan
Title:     Java in a Nutshell
Publisher: O'Reilly & Associates, Inc. (1996)
Subject:   Java
ISBN:      1-56592-183-6


Record: 678
------------
Author:    W. Richard Stevens
Title:     TCP/IP Illustrated, Volume 3
Publisher: Addison-Wesley Publishing Company, Inc. (1996)
Subject:   TCP/IP, Networks, HTTP, NNTP
ISBN:      0-201-63495-3
```

Similarly, for a Web search system, a record of a Web document is a set of attributes that describes the document. The term Uniform Resource Characteristic (URC) is used to refer to the attribute set. For example, the simplest type of URC is that used as the elements of a hotlist or bookmark list (e.g., a list of interesting links maintained by the user of a Web browser) supported by many Web browsers. In a hotlist, the URC consisting only of a document title and document location (URL). The example below illustrates records containing URCs:

```
Record: 210
Title: Table of Contents
URL:   http://www.netscape.com/search/


Record: 543
Title: Virginia Tech Computer Science Department Home Page
URL:   http://www.cs.vt.edu/


Record: 876
Title: CS6204: WWW:Beyond the Basics
URL:   http://ei.cs.vt.edu/~wwwbtb/
```

An important characteristic of a database is its ability to let a user locate information without knowing the details of how the database stores its records.

Primary Index

A database consists of a set of records. A document record is a set of attributes that describes the document. Each record in a database can be uniquely identified by a key value, called the *primary key*. If a database has primary keys, it may also be called a *primary index*. We then could search the primary database on the primary key to retrieve individual documents. For example, the URL could be used as the primary key in a database of Web documents.

Inverted Index

Searching only on the primary key, however, limits the capability of the database. A user may not know the primary key, or may want to search for words in a document that are not contained in the primary key. For example, we want to search for job information on the Web either by a position title, by a skill, or by a degree. Alternately, we might search for a Web document that matches a certain title. Searching records on an alternate key other than the primary key can be done by creating a second index organized by that alternate key. Databases support searching via an alternate key through an *inverted index*. The alternate key is called the *secondary* or *inverted* key. For example, to support searching via document title in a database, an inverted index is created that uses document title as a secondary key. The inverted index then would map document titles to database records.

A database may include several inverted indexes to speed up the search process. Many criteria or strategies on indexing differ in the ways of creating inverted indexes. In fact, an inverted index is the union of all possible searches according to the strategy.

Inverted indexes may be created for some or all of the terms in the database. When all the terms are indexed, the index is called a *fulltext index*. A fulltext index is fast and effective, especially when the user wants to search using only one piece of information.

Fulltext Index

A fulltext index is built from all the words in each document. Because an entire document is scanned to derive the information that makes up the record, this indexing technique allows the user to search for any words, phrases, or combinations of words and phrases in a collection of documents.

Documents on the Web vary greatly in both their type, size, and location (i.e., the Web server on which the document resides). Many data types and formats, such as words, pictures, audio, video, multimedia, and news groups, exist on the Web. In addition, some Web documents are small files, and some are huge databases containing thousands of entries. Thus new challenges arise in indexing the Web. Practically speaking, a wide variety of classification schemes are used. An advantage of fulltext indexing is that it avoids the need for such classification.

The practical disadvantage of a fulltext indexing is the great amount of storage and indexing time it requires: scanning entire documents and pulling out all the words creates a huge volume of data and takes much time.

To solve these problems, some reduction operations may be applied to the documents. For example, to create a URC describing the document, a parser can be used to derive only the most important keywords, such as the document title, heading, subheadings, the most frequently occurring words, clickable hypertext links, and so on. The reduction operation depends on what strategies or criteria are chosen by the designers of the search system. For example, Lycos uses as the URC the document title, heading, subheadings, 100 most weighted words (derived via fulltext indexing), first 20 lines, size in bytes, number of words. To obtain the most weighted words, the weight of a term is the ratio of the term frequency to the document frequency, where term frequency is the ratio of frequency of occurrence of that word to all documents in the document collection. The document frequency is the ratio of the frequency of occurrence of that word in a given document [25, pp. 238–239].

14.4 Search

The search module contains two parts: a search language and a search engine. The search language transforms a user's search query into a formal representation in a database query language. The search engine then applies the formal to the database, finding all records that meet the criteria specified by the query.

The capabilities of the search language depends on the database. The more sophisticated the technology used to produce the database, the higher the level of sophistication is of the search language.

Search Language

There are two popular types of search languages on the Web: *keyword matching* and *boolean search*.

Keyword matching is a search language that can directly combine terms specified by the user into a search query. It is the most common search capability and is supported by almost all search systems for the Web. If a search system supports keyword matching, a user can use any word or even part of a word in a query to the search engine.

Keyword matching works by pattern matching the characters in the keywords to characters in the database records. A query of a string of characters results in all records that contain the string.

Boolean search is a more sophisticated search language that serves to narrow and refine keyword-matching searches. Boolean search language allows the user to combine keywords using the boolean operators AND, OR, and NOT. If a search system supports boolean search language, then the user could input words, phrase, or combinations of phrases as a search query. If we want the set of results to better match what we are looking for, then boolean search may yield better results than keyword matching search.

A variation on boolean search is fuzzy boolean [5]. The user provides a list of terms, and the items retrieved must match at least one of the terms. However, they are ranked by the number of terms matched: records matching all terms are ranked first, followed by those matching all but one term, and so on.

Search Engine

A search engine applies a formal query to the database and then returns matched records to the user. The search engine finds matches between the value of attributes in database records and the attribute specified by the query. The set of matched records then is transferred to the user.

Wide Area Information Server (WAIS) is one of the popular indexing and searching methods currently used on the Web. WAIS is a client-server Internet service and was developed independently of the Web. WAIS offers a sophisticated search language and search engine. It uses keyword search with optional use of boolean operators.

Although WAIS doesn't have a gatherer, it has most of the components of a search system: an indexer, search, and retrieval. Combining WAIS with a gatherer robot makes it a complete Web search system.

Vector-based Search

We referred earlier to "weighted words." Weight refers to an indexing strategy called vector-based search [5]. The frequency of occurrence of a particular word in a particular document is compared to the frequency of occurrence of the word in all documents in a collection. If a word occurs with higher frequency in a document than the whole collection, then the document is judged more important.

An advantage of a vector-based search is that it represents matching records from a database search as points in a multidimensional geometric search. The outcome from a search may produce clusters of points in the space, which allows automatic characterization documents of similar in ranking the outcome of a search.

14.5 Retrieval

After gathering, indexing, and searching are complete, the retrieval module gives the user access to original documents located by searching. There are mainly two models for retrieval: direct retrieval and client-server retrieval.

Direct Retrieval

If the original document is stored in the database, then retrieval is trivial. In this case, the user can retrieve the original document directly from the database. In the searching and retrieval process of a traditional database, the database service and interface are closed protocols and reside on a single computer, often a mainframe. The search engine accepts a query from the user in a query language and searches the database, then retrieves documents from the database and returns them directly over the Internet to the user.

Client-Server Retrieval

More typically on the Web the user obtains from the query a set of records containing information about the original documents, or a list of URLs. For Web search services, the database and its records normally reside on separate servers from the Web servers containing the original documents. In this case, the user has to retrieve the original documents named in the URLS returned by searching by contacting the Web servers named in the URLs. This is the client-server retrieval model.

In the client-server retrieval process, the client (the user's Web browser) sends a retrieval request to the server (an HTTP GET—see Chapter 23). The server then locates the document in its file system and returns it to the client via an HTTP response message. The client then can display, save, or print the document.

An alternative to using the Web's HTTP is the network Information Retrieval Service and Protocol standard, ANSI/NISO Z39.50, which is officially recognized by the American National Standards Organization (ANSI) and National Information Standards Organization (NISO) [16]. The protocol allows a user (or client) to access remote database records, to transmit a query, and to receive in response database records matching the query. The Z39.50 standard is used in WAIS.

14.6 How to Select a Search System

Search Systems on the Web

There are many popular search systems available on the Web. Listed below are search services that index the entire world's Web pages. Internet World has published a comparison of six of the services [8]; the comparison ranks HotBot followed by AltaVista in achieving the highest recall for a set of test queries.

- *AltaVista* [2]: Developed in 1995, uses the AltaVista search engine. Optionally displays a graph or topic map to organize results of searches returning many documents. Drop-down menus and check boxes in the graph allow refinement of the search. AltaVista has a 60-Gb index of more than 8 billion words from 31 million Web pages found on 627,000 servers, and 4 million articles from 14,000 Usenet newsgroups. AltaVista uses a Web spider called Scooter to collect about 6 million Web pages per day. A fulltext index is built, including instances of different capitalization. Web pages with non-Latin characters are converted to English-equivalent letters before being indexed [3].

- *Excite* [6, 5]: Indexes full text. Uses a proprietary search algorithm called "Intelligent Concept Extraction," which adds to your search request synonymous terms. Allows sorting of results by Web site. Search time for most queries is constant, regardless of database size. Similar in performance to latent semantic indexing, which, like vector-based indexing, creates a geometric representation of search results, but reduces searches to a matrix and performs mathematical computation to determine matches. Users can search the whole Web or sites reviewed by Excite.

- *HotBot* [9]: In addition to a conventional search for Web pages, also permits searches of all Web pages that link to a particular URL. Permits search based on last modification date of Web pages. Also contains a catalog of Web sites. HotBot is the first site to use multimachine parallel computing for Internet searching. Indexes full text of more than 50 million documents.

- *Infoseek* [13]: Users can search the entire Web or Usenet newsgroups for words and phrases. In addition to Web pages, Infoseek allows searching of images on the Web, shareware, news and sports, stocks, and maps. Also offers a directory of Web pages, as well as a natural language query interface. A patent was granted for Infoseek's algorithm to rank retrievals from multiple databases [12]. Typical search methods rank documents returned by a search higher if a search term occurs more rarely. By this method, documents found in a database that is inherently more related to the search term wind up ranked lower than documents found in other databases, which is contradictory to the behavior a user desires. Instead, the Infoseek algorithm also takes into account the total number of documents in each database to generate a correct ranking. Indexes more than 50 million documents.

- *Lycos* [17]: Includes both subject and word searches. The gatherer used by Lycos can visit up to 10 million Web pages a day [18], and as of September 1997 cataloged over 100 million URLs. Also offers a catalog of the Web's pages, updated weekly. In addition to Web pages, Lycos allows searching of people, stock quotations, yellow pages, classifieds, guides to cities, and a driving-directions database that generates maps for locations within the U.S. Lycos originated as a research project at Carnegie Mellon University, and the university is in the process of patenting the heuristic method originally developed by Michael L. Mauldin and used today in Lycos' gatherer robot [19].

- *Open Text Index* [21]: Indexes Web pages, representing the document title, URL, first heading, and a summary in the index.

- *WebCrawler* [7]: This was the first world-wide search engine and is one of the oldest in the Web. Like Lycos, it is an outgrowth of a university project. WebCrawler has a "natural language" search engine with an index that is updated daily, including WebCrawler Select site reviews.

The following search systems index selected Web pages:

- *Electric Library* [14]: Searchable database of 800 full-text magazines, 150 full-text newspapers, and thousands of books and over 28,000 photos, TV and radio transcripts, maps. The Electric Library also supports natural language searches and allows purchase of information from online providers. Unlike the other services, Electric Library requires users to pay for access after a free trial period.

- *infoMarket* [10]: Provides free search followed by purchase of documents over the Web. Searches multiple commercial and Internet databases, including "75 newswires, 300 newspapers, 819 newsletters, 6882 journals, and 11 million companies in a variety of areas including: Business & Finance, News, Computers & Telecommunications, Health & Biotechnology, Sciences & Engineering, Environment, Law & Government, Entertainment & Leisure, Travel, and Industries" [11].

- *Magellan* [20]: Offers reviews of selected Web sites, assigning a rating using a certain number of stars. Can search either reviewed Web sites only or the entire Web. Operated by a subsidiary of Excite.

- *Starting Point* [23]: Performs metasearch via ideas instead of words. Also provides a directory of Web sites.

- *Yahoo* [24]: This pioneering Web directory of selected Web sites is now integrated with Alta Vista's search engine. It is updated daily for collecting Web information. In addition to gathering by a robot, Yahoo also allows Web site operators to add their sites to the list indexed by Yahoo. It supports keyword search, substring or all keys (boolean) as well as complete word searches. In addition to Web pages, Yahoo allows searching for people, stock quotations, sports scores, yellow pages, classifieds, news, and maps.

Selecting a Search System

Which search system is the best? It is difficult to answer this question universally. Every search system for the Web is unique. Different search systems satisfy different needs. There is not an absolute answer for everyone. Different people may have different judgments or different opinions on the search systems.

However, there are three objective measures that can be used to quantify the performance of a search system:

- *Recall*: the fraction of documents in a collection of documents that a search locates in response to a user's query.

- *Precision*: the fraction of recalled documents that the user judges to be relevant.

- *Speed* (latency): the time required to search and retrieve documents.

Recall and precision must be considered together in judging the effectiveness of a search system [5]. One system might recall 50% of the documents in the database in response to a query, but only have a precision of 1%. Consider a second system with lower recall—namely 10%—but with a precision of 90%. For a database with 1000 documents, the first system locates 50 relevant documents, but the second, despite its lower recall, out performs the first by locating 90 relevant documents.

As for performance, Web search systems vary in search and retrieval time. A key issue is whether the system performance scales as the Web grows larger (both in number of documents that need to be indexed, and in number of users of a search service). A scalable system would perform a search in a constant amount of time, even as the number of Web documents grows. For example, to provide this characteristic Excite uses a constant-time search algorithm [5] and

HotBot uses scalable hardware. In a system that does not scale, query time grows with the database size.

Finally, there is an alternative way to offer a simple search engine for one's own Web site using a Web server with a CGI script (Chapter 7). A CGI script can invoke the UNIX system call "grep 'search_string' $*" to search a string pattern in a set of documents in the script's current directory. We refer the reader to an example of CGI script called WWW_search in Powell's book [22, Chapter 28]. No indexing or search engine is required. All of the work is handled by the CGI search script. This is a fast and simple solution for searching a small set of documents in a single directory.

14.7 References

[1]   Ackermann, Ernest. *Learning to Use the World Wide Web*. Franklin, Beedle & Associates, Inc., 1996.

[2]   Digital Equipment Corp. "AltaVista Search: Main Page." <http://www.altavista.digital.com/> (11 July 1997).

[3]   Digital Equipment Corp. "About AltaVista Search." <http://www.altavista.digital.com/av/content/about_our_technology.htm> (19 Sept. 1997).

[4]   C. Mic Bowman, Peter B. Danzig, Darren R. Hardy, Udi Manber and Michael F. Schwartz. "The Harvest Information Discovery and Access System." Computer Networks and ISDN Systems 28. 1995. pp. 119–125 <ftp://ftp.cs.colorado.edu/pub/cs/techreports/schwartz/Harvest.Conf.ps.Z> (19 Sept. 1997).

[5]   Excite. "Information Retrieval Technology and Intelligent Concept Extraction." <http://www.excite.com/Info/tech.html> 1996. (18 Sept. 1997).

[6]   Excite. "Excite." <http://www.excite.com> (19 Sept. 1997).

[7]   Excite. "WebCrawler Search." <http://www.webcrawler.com/> (16 Sept. 1997).

[8]   Haskin, David. "The Right Search Engine." *Internet World*. Sept. 1997. <http://www.iw.com/1997/09/report.html> (19 Sept. 1997).

[9]   HotBot. "HotBot." <http://www.hotbot.com/> (19 Sept. 1997).

[10] IBM. "InfoMarket Search Page." <http://www.infomarket.ibm.com/> (19 Sept. 1997).

[11] IBM. "IBM infoMarket Service Information."
      <http://www.infomarket.ibm.com/ht3/info.shtml> (19 Sept. 1997).

[12] Infoseek. "Illustration of Traditional vs. Infoseek Patent Approach."
      <http://software.infoseek.com/patents/dist_search/patent_diagram.pdf> (19
      Sept. 1997).

[13] ——. "Infoseek." <http://www.infoseek.com/> (18 Sept. 1997).

[14] Infonautics Corp. "Welcome to the Electric Library."
      <http://www.elibrary.com/id/2525/> (19 Sept. 1997).

[15] Koster, M., "Robots in the Web: Threat or Treat?" Updated version of paper
      appearing in *ConneXions*, Vol. 9, No. 4, April 1995. Updated 1997.
      <http://info.webcrawler.com/mak/projects/robots/threat-or-treat.html>
      (19 Sept. 1997).

[16] Library of Congress. "Z39.50 Maintenance Agency Home Page."
      <http://lcweb.loc.gov/z3950/agency/> (18 Sept. 97).

[17] Lycos, Inc. "Welcome to Lycos." <http://www.lycos.com/> (18 Sept. 1997).

[18] Lycos, Inc. "All-New Lycos Offers Most Advanced Search Technology."
      16 Sept. 1997. <http://www.lycos.com/press/allnew.html> (18 Sept. 1997).

[19] Lycos, Inc. "Significant Patent To Be Issued for Lycos' Intelligent 'Spider'
      Technology" 2 Sept. 1997. <http://www.lycos.com/press/spidertech.html>
      (18 Sept. 1997).

[20] The McKinley Group. "Welcome to Magellan!" <http://www.mckinley.com/>
      (19 Sept. 1997).

[21] Open Text Corp. "The Open Text Index." <http://index.opentext.net/>
      (19 Sept. 1997).

[22] Powell, James E. *HTML Plus!* Wadsworth Publishing Company, ITP., 1997.

[23] Starting Point. "Welcome To Starting Point." <http://www.stpt.com/>
      (19 Sept. 1997).

[24] Yahoo. "Yahoo!" <http://www.yahoo.com/> (18 Sept. 1997).

[25] Yeager, Nancy J. and Robert E. McGrath. *Web Server Technology*. San Fran-
      cisco, CA: Morgan Kaufmann Publishers, Inc., 1996.

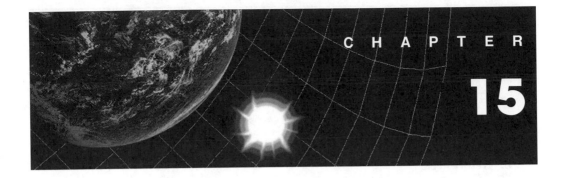

C H A P T E R

15

Real-time Audio and Video

by Shaohong Qu

Audio and video signals are analog signals by nature. Those signals must be converted to digital form before they are transmitted through computer networks. Transfer of real-time audio and video information requires a large network bandwidth and low data latency. In this chapter we provide an inside look at the theory of audio and video digitization. We also introduce two real-time applications: telephony and videoconferencing.

Chapter Content

4. Applications

- Telephony

- Videoconferencing

5. References

15.1 Introduction

Real-time audio and video are two important multimedia applications on today's computer networks. These applications enable efficient communications through computer networks. For example, videoconferencing enables a face-to-face meeting between groups of people at two or more different locations. It can be used for distance learning and collaborative work with remote teams.

Real-time Audio and Video in the Web

The Web was designed to focus on static document retrieval. These documents may include text files, images, audio and video files. The current Web technology is unsuitable for real-time applications (i.e., telephony and videoconferencing). The main reason is that Web uses HTTP as the transfer protocol. HTTP is a request/response protocol, which is inherently unsuitable for real-time applications. Furthermore, HTTP is run over TCP, and TCP is optimized for large-file transfer. With the rapid growth of real-time audio and video applications, more and more Web technologies are being developed that support real-time audio and video applications. For example, Chen [3] discusses a protocol called VDP that is specialized for handling real-time video over the Web.

Chapter Guide

First we discuss the fundamentals of transmitting audio and video. Audio and video signals are analog signals by nature. To be transmitted, these signals must be first converted to digital form. In Sections 15.2 and 15.3, the concept of digitization is introduced. To reduce the transmission bandwidth, audio and video files are often compressed before transmission. The compression formats are also introduced in these two sections. Using these fundamentals, Section 15.4 describes the telephony and videoconferencing systems. References are provided for readers who have deeper interests in these areas.

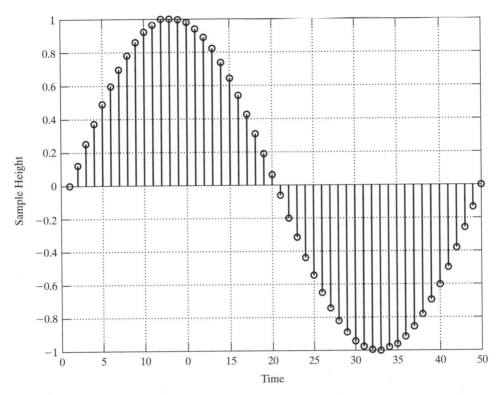

Figure 15–1   Sampled Waveform

15.2 Digital Audio

Sound is produced by the vibration of matter. Audio refers to sound within the human hearing range. An audio signal in the natural world is analog, which is continuous in both time and amplitude. To be stored and processed by computers and transmitted through computer networks, the analog signal must be converted to digital form. First, the audio signal is converted to an analog electric signal through a microphone. Then, this analog electric signal is digitized by an Analog-to-Digital Converter (ADC). The analog-to-digital conversion comprises two steps: (1) sampling, and (2) quantization. Digital audio may be quantized using different encoding schemes to compress the byte stream being sent.

Sampling

To sample a signal means to examine it at some point in time, as shown in Fig. 15–1. Sampling usually happens at equally separated intervals; this interval is called the sampling interval. The reciprocal of sampling interval is called the sampling frequency, or sampling rate. The unit of sampling interval is a second. The unit of sampling rate is Hz, which means cycles per second.

In Fig. 15–1, the sampling interval is 1 μsec (10^{-6} sec), or in other words the sampling frequency is 1 MHz (10^6 Hz). This means that the analog/digital conversion samples this sine wave every 1 μsec.

If the highest frequency of the analog signal is f, then to reconstruct the original analog signal faithfully, the sampling rate must be at least 2f. This is also called the sampling theorem. In Fig. 15–1, the frequency of this sine wave is 2×10^4 Hz, and the sampling frequency is 10^6 Hz, which is much greater than $2 \times 2 \times 10^4$ Hz. So this sine wave will be faithfully reconstructed back to an analog signal.

Because human hearing is limited to a range of 20 Hz to 20 kHz, the minimum sampling frequency used to obtain CD quality is typically 44.1 kHz. Since human speech is only limited to 20 to 3000 Hz, an 8000-Hz sample frequency is high enough for telephony-quality audio.

Quantization

To quantize a signal means to determine the signal's value to some degree of accuracy. Fig. 15–2 shows the same analog signal being quantized. The digital signal is defined only at the points at which it is sampled. The height of each vertical bar can take on only certain values, shown by horizontal dashed lines, which are sometimes higher and sometimes lower than the original signal, indicated by the dashed curve. In Fig. 15–2, 11 quantization levels are used, and hence 4 bits are needed to encode each sample.

If the height of each bar is translated into a digital number, then the signal is said to be represented by pulse-code modulation, or PCM.

The difference between a quantized representation and an original analog signal is called the quantization noise. With more bits for quantization of a PCM signal, the signal sounds clearer.

Using higher sampling frequency and more bits for quantization will produce better-quality digital audio. But for the same length of audio, the file size will be much larger than for low-quality audio. For example, the CD-quality audio uses a 44.1 kHz sampling rate and a 16 bits amplitude. The resulting aggregated bit rate (bits per second) of a stereophonic (2 channels) CD-audio stream is thus $44.1 \times 16 \times 2 = 1,415.2$ kbps. On the other hand, the telephony quality audio uses 8 kHz sampling rate and 8 bits amplitude. The file size of one second of speech is only $8 \times 8 = 64$ Kbits.

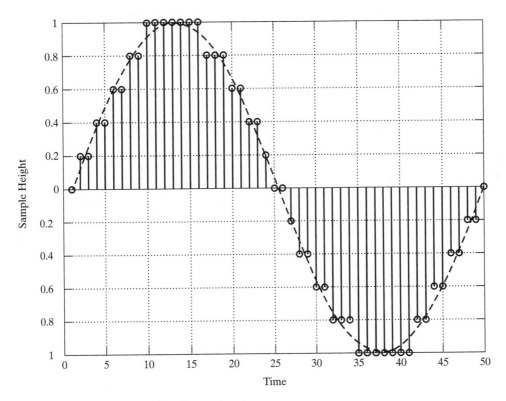

Figure 15-2 Four-bit Quantization

Other Encoding Schemes

PCM audio encoding method is an uncompressed audio format. Real-world requirements may make it impossible to handle the full bit stream of, for example, CD-quality audio. In the following we will introduce some other audio encoding methods that are used to compress digital audio.

A-law and μ-law Encoding

For speech signals, a system which works with a quantization step size that increases logarithmically with the level of the signal is widely used. This allows a larger range of values to be covered with the same number of bits. The International Telecommunication Union—Telecommunication Standardization Sector (ITU-T) Recommendation G.711 codifies the A-law and μ-law encoding scheme. For A-law encoding, the formula is

```
y=Ax/(1+lnA), where (0<=x<=1/A), and

y=(1+Ax)/(1+lnA), where (1/A<=x<=1).
```

For μ-law transmission, the signal is encoded according to

`y=ln(1+ μx)/ln(1+ μ), where (0<=x<=1).`

In standard telephone work, μ is set to 255. The result is an 8-bit-per-sample signal that produces the dynamic range approximately associated with 12-bit PCM.

Delta Modulation and Adaptive Delta Pulse Code Modulation

Delta modulation method is to encode not the value of each sample, but the difference between one sample and the next. In most cases, the difference between one sample and the next is much smaller than the sample itself, so fewer bits are needed to encode the difference compared to using the complete sample value. Its variation, *adaptive delta pulse-code modulation*, or ADPCM, is often used to handle both signals that change quickly as well as signals that change slowly. The step size encoded between adjacent samples varies according to the signal itself. In other words, if the waveform is changing rapidly, large steps can be quantized. ADPCM typically achieves compression ratios of 2:1 when compared to μ-law or A-law PCM.

There are also many other encoding schemes that compress digital audio (see [4] for details). Table 15–1 summarizes the main formats used for real-time audio.

Table 15–1 Typical Formats for Real-Time Audio

Name	Encoding Method	Bits per Sample	Sampling Rate (kHz)	Bandwidth (kbps)
G.711	A-law PCM	8	8	64
G.721	ADPCM	4	8	32
G.722	SB-ADPCM	14	16	64, 56, 48
G.728	LD-CELP	14	16	16

15.3 Digital Video

A video signal is also analog. Before a video signal can be processed by a computer or transmitted through a computer network, it needs to be digitized. Because digital video data is often too large to be transmitted through a computer network, compression techniques become crucial. In this section, the concepts are presented to develop an understanding of motion video. These include the moving picture theorem, the color-encoding theorem, and the compression formats for real-time video.

Moving Picture

A moving picture may be represented using a discrete sequence of still pictures (frames) as long as they are presented rapidly enough to the human eye. This property is used in television and motion pictures. To represent visual reality, two conditions must be met. First, the rate of repetition of the images or frame rate must be high enough to guarantee smooth motion from frame to frame. Second, the rate must be high enough so that the persistence of vision extends over the interval between successive images. The unit of frame rate is frames per second, or fps.

It is well known that the human eye perceives a continuous motion at any frame rate faster than 15 fps. Video motion seems smooth when frame rate is achieved at 30 fps.

There are two widely used standards for motion video signals: the National Television System Committee (NTSC) standard and the Phase Alteration Line (PAL) standard. NTSC is used in the Americas and Japan. It specifies the frame rate to be 30 fps. PAL is used in Europe, China, and Australia. PAL uses 25 fps as the frame rate.

Color Encoding

The human eye has three types of photoreceptors: one is sensitive to red, one to green, and one to blue. Any color perceived by the human eye is the mixture of those three. The 3-dimensional color space whose axes correspond to those three colors are called the RGB color space. The color encoding systems used for video are derived from this color space. The following is the summary of all approaches of encoding schemes used for video:

1. RGB signal

2. YUV signal

3. YIQ signal

RGB signal consists of separate signals for red, green, and blue colors. Any color can be coded as a combination of these primary colors.

As human perception is more sensitive to brightness than to color information, a more suitable coding distinguishes between brightness and color. Instead of separating colors, the YUV signal separates the brightness information (Y) from the color information (U and V). The component division for YUV signal is:

```
Y=0.30R+0.59G+0.11B
U=0.493(B-Y)
V=0.877(R-Y)
```

The resolution of luminance is more important than that of the color. Therefore, the brightness values can be coded using more bits than the color values; for example, the YUV encoding can be specified as (4:2:2) signal.

YIQ signal is similar to the YUV signal, which builds the basis for the NTSC format.

```
Y=0.30R+0.59G+0.11B
I=0.60R-0.28G-0.32B,
Q=0.212R-0.52G+0.31B
```

Compression Formats

To transmit the analog video signal just described over the Internet, it must be converted to digital form in order to be processed in a computer. Each frame of video becomes a two-dimensional array of picture elements (pixels). A full-color picture is composed of three such 2-D arrays. The most common array sizes are 640×480 and 320×240, and each pixel is quantized to 256 gray levels. For example, The Sun Video Digitizer from Sun Microsystems captures the NTSC video signal with a frame resolution of 320×240 pixels, quantization of 8 bits/pixel, and a frame rate of 30 fps.

The transmission of uncompressed video data over a computer network requires very high bandwidth. The video data must be compressed before transmission. In applications, the speed of compression and decompression is very important. If the compression or decompression consumes too much computational resources, this will slow down the frame rate. Compression can be performed either in hardware or in software. Software compression is more flexible, but hardware compression is faster. For large frame sizes and high frame rates, using hardware compression/decompression may be the only viable option.

Summarized below are two commonly used compression formats for real-time video. (See [1] for the details of the compression schemes.)

ITU-T Recommendation H.261: H.261 was developed for processing the encoding/decoding of real-time audio and video. The recommendation is intended to be used at video bit rates between 40 Kbps and 2 Mbps.

The MPEG Motion Video Compression Standard: The Moving Picture Expert Group (MPEG) standard was developed to cover motion video as well as audio coding according to the ISO/IEC standardization process. MPEG-1's image size is either 160×120 or 320×240, 24-bit per pixel (color). The frame rate is 30 fps. It delivers acceptable video quality at compressed data rates between 1.0 and 1.5 Mbps, yet maintains audio/video synchronization. This data rate is feasible for network use; for example, a T1 line can carry 1 MPEG at a time.

For more information, see *Multimedia: Computing, Communications and Applications* [13], and *Standards Related to Desktop Videoconferencing* [12].

15.4 Applications

In this section we introduce two popular real-time audio and video applications: telephony and videoconferencing.

Telephony

Telephony enables people in different places in the world to talk to each other through computer networks. The appeal of the Internet today is that Internet connections are generally priced by flat fee, not by volume, so the cost is lower than conventional long-distance telephone charges. However, the quality of voice over the Internet may suffer due to audio transfer delay caused by heavy traffic. This delay is typically a half second.

There are many different telephony software products available on the market today, but most of them work the same way. When one party starts talking, his or her speech signal is received by a microphone. The electric signal is then digitized through an analog/digital conversion board on the talker's computer and stored in computer memory in a binary form. The data is then compressed and transmitted through the computer network. When the listening party receives the data, it is decompressed and converted to an analog electric signal by a digital/analog conversion board. The speaker converts this electrical signal to sound.

Because different software products use different digital formats (i.e., sampling rate, quantization level), compression schemes, and transport protocols, the conversation quality is different. *A/V Streaming: Not Quite Ready for Prime Time* [7] evaluates eight programs that provide real-time streaming audio and video.

For more information, visit the *Internet Telephony Page* [8]. *Voice on the Net* [10] shows many telephony products.

Videoconferencing

Videoconferencing is a telecommunication facility that enables a face-to-face meeting between groups of people at two or more different locations through both speech and sight. Every party involved can see, hear and speak just as they would at a conventional round-the-table meeting. Videoconferencing can be used for:

- face-to-face meeting,

- distance learning, and

- collaboration on projects with remote teams.

When a video conference starts, the participants in each party may gather in an office or meeting room equipped with videoconferencing hardware. This may include a multimedia-equipped computer, a TV camera, etc. The video and audio information are recorded by TV cameras and microphones. After digitalization and compression, the information is sent to other parties through computer networks.

Videoconferencing usually involves more than two parties; thus, multi-casting is used for data transmission over computer networks. There are two technical methods of obtaining multicast functionality: (1) multiple point-to-point connections and (2) packet network multicast technology (e.g., MBone in IP). When multiple point-to-point connections are used, the number of participating parties is usually restricted to six or eight. For a big conference (involving more than eight parties), multicast may be the only viable option.

For more information on videoconferencing, visit *Videoconferencing FAQ* [5]. For more videoconferencing products information, visit *The Desktop Video-conferencing Products Survey* [6].

15.5 References

[1]   Borko, F., W. S. Stephen, and Z. Hongjiang. *Video and Image Processing in Multimedia Systems*, 1995.

[2]   Buford, J. *Multimedia Systems*, 1995.

[3]   Chen, Z., S. Tan, R. Campbell, and Y. Li. "Real Time Video and Audio in the World Wide Web." <http://choices.cs.uiuc.edu/Papers/New/vosaic/vosaic.html> (8 Oct. 1997).

[4]   Fluckiger, F. *Understanding Networked Multimedia*, 1995.

[5]   Hendricks, C. E. and J. P. Steer. Videoconferencing FAQ. <http://www.bitscout.com/faqtoc.htm> (8 Oct. 1997).

[6]   K. Hewitt. The Desktop Videoconferencing Products Survey. May 1996. <http://www3.ncsu.edu/dox/video/> (8 Oct. 1997).

[7]   B. Hurtig. "A/V Streaming Brings the Web to Life... Almost." *NewMedia*. 28 Oct. 1996. <http://www.newmedia.com/NewMedia/96/14/td/ AV_Streaming_Web.html> (8 Oct. 1997).

[8]   Internet Telephony Consortium. Internet Telephony Interoperability Consortium. <http://itel.mit.edu/> (8 Oct. 1997).

[9]   Luther, A. *Using Digital Video*, 1995.

[10] Pulver.com. Voice on the Net. <http://www.von.com> (8 Oct. 1997).

[11] Rettinger, L. A. "Desktop Videoconferencing: Technology and Use for Remote Seminar Delivery." M.S. thesis. North Carolina State University. July 1995. <http://www2.ncsu.edu/eos/service/ece/project/succeed_info/larettin/thesis/ > (8 Oct. 1997).

[12] ——. "Standards Related to Desktop Videoconferencing." Aug. 1995. <http://www3.ncsu.edu/dox/video/Other/std.html> (8 Oct. 1997).

[13] Steinmetz, R. and Nahrstedt, K. "Multimedia: Computing, Communications and Applications," 1995.

Other On-line Resources

[14] ACM SIGMM. Guide to Multimedia Educational Materials. <http://www.cs.cornell.edu/Info/Faculty/bsmith/mmsyl.htm> (8 Oct. 1997).

[15] Cornell University: Multimedia Systems <http://www.cs.cornell.edu/Info/Courses/Fall-95/CS631/>

[16] Dept. of Electrical Engineering and Computer Science, George Washington University. EECS Multimedia Suite. <http://www.seas.gwu.edu/seas/projects/multimedia/> (8 Oct. 1997).

[17] Kurose, J., Dept. of Computer Science, Univ. of Mass. "CMPSCI 691: Multimedia Networking.," Fall 1995. <http://gaia.cs.umass.edu:80/cs691/> (8 Oct. 1997).

[18] UC Berkeley. "CS 294-3: Multimedia Systems and Applications." <http://bmrc.berkeley.edu/courseware/cs294-3/fall95/> (8 Oct. 1997).

[19] Univ. of Texas, Austin. "CS384M: Multimedia Systems." <http://www.cs.utexas.edu/users/vin/cs384m.html> (8 Oct. 1997).

[20] ——. "CS395T: Multimedia Communication and Databases." <http://www.cs.utexas.edu/users/vin/cs395t.html> (8 Oct. 1997).

[21] UIUC: Topics in Multimedia Communications <http://nahrstedt.cs.uiuc.edu:5000/pub/cs497mm.html>

[22] UIUC: Multimedia Computing Systems
      <http://nahrstedt.cs.uiuc.edu:5000/pub/cs397mm.html>

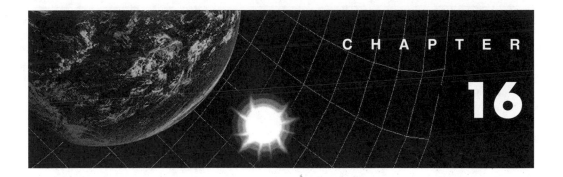

C H A P T E R

16

Wireless Connectivity

By Farhood Moslehi

Traditional networking technologies offer tremendous capabilities from an office or home via the Web. Limitations to networking through the use of wired-based systems exist, however, because you must be physically connected to the system. As mobile computing becomes more prevalent, systems and applications must deal with scarcity of resources such as bandwidth. Mobile devices and wireless workstations should handle some of the work that has been traditionally carried out by the network through techniques explained in this chapter, such as document partitioning. Dynamic documents can also be used to cache and prefetch documents while the network connection is not being utilized fully.

Meanwhile, the need for higher-speed wireless connections is growing with multimedia rich content on the Web. The IEEE 802.11 protocol and the Medium Access Control part of the protocol (DFWMAC) will allow wireless networks to operate at high data rates (1 to 20 Mbps). Furthermore, the 802.11 only effects the bottom two layers of the OSI's seven-layer architecture; hence, through an access point (router), wireless packets are routed to the Web.

Chapter Content

1. Introduction
2. Operation
3. Wireless Application Design
4. Data over Cellular Links
5. Radio-Based Wireless Connectivity

6. IEEE 802.11 Protocol

- Protocol Description

- Internetworking Units

7. Internet Mobile Host Protocol

8. References

16.1 Introduction

Wireless LANs will provide the first layer of connectivity between mobile users and the global information infrastructure. Wireless devices, such as cellular phones with displays, personal digital assistants (PDAs) and notebook computers, can become extensions to the Web (also see the section on "Mobile Network Computer Reference Specification" on page 50). The user can be completely unaware of whether the information travels over a wire or a radio frequency. Depending on the power of the transmitters and the sensitivity of the receivers, wireless devices may become the first truly universal form of virtual LAN. By mixing wireless networks with other wireless communication technologies, such as cellular and satellite, the user can have full connectivity at all times and, more importantly, in all places on the globe.

Wireless connectivity to the Web can also be achieved through the use of existing cellular telephone links. Spread Spectrum Technologies (SST), such as time-division multiple access (TDMA), code-division multiple access (CDMA), and extended time-division multiple access (ETDMA), have allowed cellular links to carry more information and are thus well suited for data transmission. Caching and prefetching techniques are often used to reduce the large overheads created by data transmissions over cellular links.

With the introduction of PDAs, the desirability of integration of wireless technology into mobile devices became evident. However, presently these devices have limitations on several fronts, such as computational power, bandwidth, display size and power usage. Nevertheless, such devices running on operating systems such as Microsoft's Windows CE are running a variety of Web browsers and Web clients with efficiency and success. The device that Apple computer introduced in 1992 as a PDA has taken a life of its own in variety of shapes such as palmtops and pen-based devices. These devices have become an essential part of the Web expansion into the wireless world.

Personal communication, accessing on-line real-time information, and freedom to physically move with the information are several reasons for wireless Web connectivity. Storage limitations would make it almost impossible to store information ahead of time into a handheld device, since the data of interest is not known. Furthermore, data can change dynamically, such as weather forecast or stock market activity. [6]

Current applications are not designed to run on the wireless Web. The wired Web squanders a fair amount of bandwidth through inherent inefficiencies that are built into its infrastructure, but users only perceive these inefficiencies as adding a fraction of a millisecond to their waiting time when retrieving documents. However, because bandwidth is lower over wireless links, those milliseconds delays can grow to seconds and, worse, lead to time-outs by the underlying protocols, such as TCP/IP. As a result various groups have proposed a new HTML or new protocols such as HTTP+. But these avenues of solutions are rigid and the need for standardization is greater than that for a temporary increase in throughput for a particular scheme.

16.2 Operation

Similar to any transmission system, a wireless system needs a transmitter, a receiver, and a transmission medium. In a wireless system, the transmission medium is air rather than the cables used by conventional wired systems. The use of air as a transmission medium utilizes two major spectra: infrared and radio frequency.

The key difference between the use of infrared and radio frequency is the support of roaming. Infrared is a line-of-sight technology. There has to be a direct line of sight or at least a surface to bounce the waves from the transmitter to the receiver. On the other hand, radio-frequency systems can penetrate through objects such as walls and doors in most office buildings; hence their popularity in present wireless systems. FCC rules allow only small sections of the electromagnetic spectrum (Fig. 16–1) to be used for wireless data networks; thus techniques are needed to avoid interference from other devices that share the space or perhaps from multiple stations using the same frequency.

A technique developed by the military in the 1970s to help secure transmissions offers a way around this problem. This technique is called Spread Spectrum Technology (SST). It is designed to transmit across a wide range of frequencies, and not just over one frequency continuously.

One approach, known as Frequency-Hopping Spread Spectrum (FHSS), divides a range of the radio spectrum into multiple channels, with each single channel using a specific preknown frequency. A transmitter can hop from one channel to the next, sending a portion of a message on each channel. A receiver that follows the hopping pattern of the transmitter can recover the message. The second method of spread spectrum is Direct Sequence Spread Spectrum (DSSS). Halsall explains DSS as follows: "The source data to be transmitted is first exclusive-ORed with a pseudorandom binary sequence; that is, the bits making up the sequence are random but the same sequence is made much larger than the source data rate. Hence when the exclusive-ORed signal is modulated and

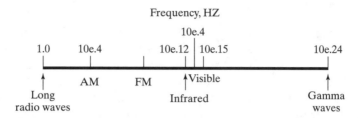

Figure 16–1   Electromagnetic Spectrum

transmitted, it occupies—and is said to be spread over—a proportionately wider frequency band than the original source data bandwidth, which makes the signal appear as (pseudo) noise to other users of the same frequency band" [2]. Thus, all receivers first search for the known preamble sequence, and once it has been recognized, the receivers start to interpret the bit stream.

FCC rules for DSSS transmission require 10 or more redundant data bits to be added to each signal. This limits the maximum throughput of DSSS transmitters to approximately 2 Mbps when using the 902-MHz band, and approximately 8 Mbps in the 2.4-GHz band.

16.3 Wireless Application Design

Designing a Web application for a wireless node is different from designing a Web application for a workstation. Bandwidth is a precious resource in the wireless domain, and it must be utilized in the most efficient fashion. Research focuses on streamlining applications to make the best use of the available bandwidth. These options include using dynamic documents, which use the resources of the mobile node itself to generate parts of a document, or partitioning the application between a client and the server.

Dynamic documents can address the variable resource requirement of mobile computers accessing the Web. Dynamic documents are programs executed by Web browsers in order to generate the actual information displayed to the user. Execution of a dynamic document causes the client to perform any number of actions in order to generate a final presentation to the user. Dynamic documents can be tailored for individual needs based upon resources that are available at a particular node [3].

Application partitioning can be used effectively over a wireless link. Much like a client/server application design, the application and its functionality are divided into two separate interacting parts. How much of the application is run on the client side versus the server side can be decided dynamically, based upon available bandwidth. Much like the object-oriented paradigm, the data and data functionality are packaged into hyperobjects. The purpose of hyperobjects is to present application structure and semantics in a manageable and uniform fashion. The system will use this hyperobject structure, along with observations of access patterns, to make informed decisions. [7]

Partitioning of documents is combined with several other well-known techniques to increase the effectiveness of wireless clients such as browsers. These are explained next.

Caching: Watson explains the use of caching: "Applications specify the caching attributes of an object or a number of objects. The default is to optimistically replicate objects on the mobile device. Explicit synchronization can be used to make the cache consistent with the wired network if the wireless link is up" [7].

Prefetching: As a document is being loaded and displayed on a wireless device, the links are used to prefetch and cache the information in anticipation of the user's using the links to access information. In some models, such as the hyperobject model, the system uses its knowledge of object positions and their relevancy to the present document to prefetch information. Prefetching can be done if the system resources are not fully utilized at any given point in time. For example, as a user is viewing the contents of a particular page, objects and links on the page are being used to prefetch and cache the relevant documents. Prefetching hides the latency of the link, and it will also filter the burstiness by spreading the traffic over a longer time.

Data Reduction: Data reduction can be dynamically decided by the user for various high-bandwidth applications, such as video transmissions. A video stream delivers a certain number of frames per constant unit of time. As the number of frames is reduced, it adversely affects the quality of the video, but the bandwidth needed is also reduced. Hence, the user can dynamically find a balance between the available resources and the desired video quality. The same principle can be applied to the sound, and also to any real-time stream of data over the wireless link.

Mobile Web Browsers: The Web infrastructure as it is presently designed can not accommodate mobile clients. The information that the Web supports presently resides in static HTML documents and databases. Most of the dynamic information on the Web today is user input via information forms that require direct input by the user. Extensions to the Web have to be created to update mobile computing contexts within a pre-defined client domain. Furthermore, automatic callback mechanisms must be created to notify the Web clients as the user roams from one computing environment to the next. Finally a syntax for referencing dynamic information in URLs and documents is needed [5].

Active Documents: Active documents are HTML documents that allow the Web client to automatically react to changes in the mobile computing

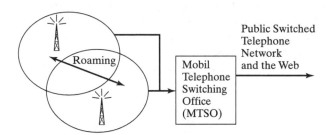

Figure 16–2   General Circuit Switched Cellular Telephone System

environment. If the information in an active document that the client is displaying becomes invalid, then the client can be notified of that change so that more
relevant information can be displayed. Variables such as location can be updated
as the mobile user roams from one cell area to the next. Active documents are
written just like any other HTML file with only a minor addition. A subscribe
command is embedded in an HTML comment line. Thereby backward compatibility can be preserved, thus allowing regular Web browsers to view the documents [5].

Dynamic URLs: Ordinarily URLs are links to static documents on the
Web. Dynamic URLs will refer a user to a different document based upon other
variables, such as the location variable. Dynamic URLs exist in active documents
in order to receive variables from the client. When a user selects a dynamic URL
in a document, the client browser is responsible for resolving all references to
dynamic variables within the URL. When all variable references have been
resolved, the result is a standard URL that the client then sends to the server. [5]

16.4 Data over Cellular Links

The analog cellular telephone network is based upon radio-wave signals to
transmit/receive voice quality signals (Fig. 16–2). Radio waves in the FM section
of the electromagnetic spectrum are used to transmit and receive these signals.
The quality and strength of these signals are proportional to their distance from
cellular sources (towers). The effective range of a cellular tower is called a cell,
and as users of the network roam, the cellular network passes them from one cell
to the next. The towers are owned and operated by cellular carrier telephone
companies, and through their Mobile Telephone Switching Office (MTSO) the
users are connected to the public telephone networks that act as gateways to the
Internet.

Most modems that operate over wireline telephone services will also interface and interoperate with cellular phones; however, cellular modems and their

optimized software would further tax the limited supply of power (usually batteries). There are more fundamental problems with modem communication over cellular links. One problem is the hand-off, or roaming, problem. As a mobile user moves from one service area to the next, a hand-off occurs. The hand-off disrupts the call for 100 to 200 ms. This is just long enough to disrupt the carrier-detect (CD) cycle; hence, the modem assumes that one of the callers has disconnected, and it hangs up. This problem can be overcome in a similar manner to that used for fax modems over cellular links. The modem will delay 400 ms before hanging up, giving the hand-off enough time to take place. Some data may be affected, but error-detection and error-correction procedures (e.g., cyclic redundancy codes) will detect and correct the data bits that have been corrupted. All these techniques lower the effective throughput of a communication system. The effective throughput achieved with cellular modems hovers around 19200 bits/s [1].

In order to establish a nationwide wireless data network for wireless users, major wireless companies in the U.S. agreed on the Cellular Digital Packet Data (CDPD) standard. CDPD uses the same portion of the electromagnetic spectrum as the conventional analog cellular telephone system. Techniques such as channel hopping (previous section) are utilized to transmit data in short bursts during idle times in a cellular channel. CDPD operates in full duplex, permitting simultaneous transmission in both directions in the 800 and 900 MHz frequency bands. Since CDPD uses digital signals, it can easily and with a high degree of robustness carry digital information. Digital information and data can be encrypted with private and public authentication keys for privacy. CDPD is a connectionless protocol, and thus can handle error correction on one side of the transmission without requiring a retransmission of a corrupted packet.

Other wireless digital transmission techniques presently being tested and utilized by the carrier companies are

- time-division multiple access (TDMA),

- extended time-division multiple access (ETDMA),

- code-division multiple access (CDMA), and

- narrowband advanced mobile phone service (N-AMPS).

These techniques could one day provide significantly enhanced wireless data communication. For example, ETDMA promises to increase bandwidth by a factor of 15, which will open up wireless communication to a broader range of Web application needs.

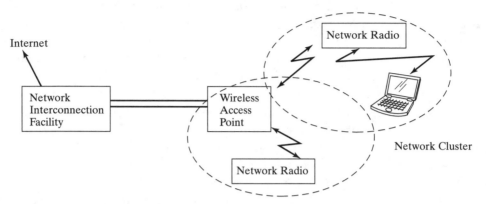

Figure 16–3   Two-Way Radio Based Multiuser System

16.5 Radio-Based Wireless Connectivity

The most widely sold wireless LAN products use radio waves as a medium between computers and the Web or each other. An advantage of radio waves over other forms of wireless connectivity such as infrared and microwaves is that they propagate through walls and other obstructions with little attenuation. Even though several walls might separate the user from the server or an access point to the Web, users can maintain connections to the network, thus supporting true mobility. The disadvantage for radio frequencies is that governments manage the region and not all the spectrum can be used everywhere; hence, techniques such as FHSS and DSSS (defined in Section 16.2) must be used.

Three regions of the E-M spectrum are utilized by these waves:

- 902–928 MHz

- 2.4–2.484 GHz

- 5.725–5.850 GHz

Presently two-way radio based multi-user systems are being used for data and voice communications in several major metropolitan areas. The architecture is shown in Fig. 16–3.

The concept is to use wireless access points and radio relays placed strategically in a metropolitan area to facilitate connectivity between the users and the network. The radios operate in the license-free 902–928 portion of the radio spectrum using FHSS. The underlying network protocol is TCP/IP, allowing it to interact with the Internet seamlessly.

An important goal for wireless communications has been to make the application layer transparent to the underlying protocol (TCP/IP) in order to gain acceptance by the Web users. To understand the kind of standards developed for wireless networks, it helps to see the affected layers in an OSI (Open System Interconnect) model. The bottom two layers are the ones of interest to us. At the very bottom is the Physical Layer. This layer defines the electrical characteristics of the actual connection between network nodes. For wired networks, it covers topics like voltage levels and type of cabling. But for wireless networks, it addresses areas such as frequencies used and modulation techniques, including spread-spectrum technologies.

The next layer up is the Data Link Layer. It deals with how the network is shared between nodes. The Data Link Layer defines rules such as who can talk on the network and how long they can occupy network resources. This layer can be further divided into two separate layers (see Fig. 16–4):

- The Medium Access Control (MAC) layer.

- The Logical Link Control (LLC) layer.

The first five layers of the OSI model remain unchanged; hence TCP and IP can be implemented unchanged in their respective layers.

16.6 IEEE 802.11 Protocol

Protocol Description

The wireless network interface manages the use of the broadcast medium through the operation of a communications protocol. For synchronization, wireless networks employ a carrier sense protocol similar to the common Ethernet standard. This protocol enables a group of wireless computers to share the same frequency and space.

Lack of speed in developing a standard protocol for wireless networks has been a major issue. Therefore, the Institute for Electrical and Electronics Engineers (IEEE) developed the IEEE 802.11 wireless protocol. The IEEE 802.11 exists as another member of the IEEE 802 family, which includes the popular 802.3 (Ethernet) and IEEE 802.5 (Token ring) protocols. This enables seamless integration of wireless networks into the existing wired networks.

As with other 802 standards such as Ethernet and token ring, the primary service of the 802.11 standard is to deliver Media Access Control (MAC) Service Data Units (MSDUs) between Logical Link Control connections to the network. In other words, the 802.11 standard will define a method of transferring data frames between network adapters without wires. In addition, the 802.11 standard includes the following:

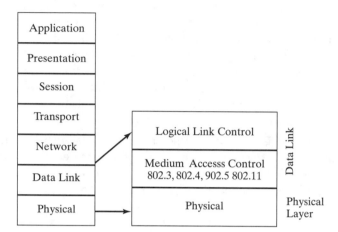

Figure 16–4   OSI Model. The first five layers of the OSI model remains
                  unchanged; hence, TCP and IP can be implemented
                  unchanged in their respective layers.

- Support of asynchronous and time-bounded delivery service

- Continuity of service within extended areas

- Accommodation of transmission rates between 1 and 20 Mbps

- Support of most market applications

- Multicast service

- Network management services, registration and authentication services

    The IEEE 802.11 standard supports operation in two separate modes, a dis-
tributed coordination (DCF) and a centralized point-coordination mode (PCF).
The IEEE 802.11 MAC is called Distributed Foundation Wireless MAC (DFW-
MAC), Fig. 16–5, and the access mechanism is based upon the principal of
CSMA/CA (Collision Sense Medium Access with Collision Avoidance), which is a
variation of the CSMA/CD (CSMA with Carrier Detection) protocol underlying
Ethernet networks.

    Stations and devices that operate under the CSMA/CD protocol listen for
idle times in a network to send their data packets. If the medium is busy, the station has to wait until an idle period occurs. It is entirely possible for two or more
stations to transmit at the same time, thus resulting in packet collisions. After
collisions occur, a jamming signal is sent throughout the network to notify the
other stations of the collision. Stations will then wait for a predetermined
amount of time before attempting to retransmit the collided packets. In a wired
network like Ethernet with relatively high bandwidth, collisions do not waste as

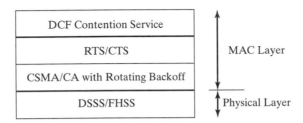

Figure 16–5 DFWMAC Structure

high a fraction of the available bandwidth as in wireless networks, because wireless networks have lower bandwidth.

Under the CSMA/CA technique, as in CSMA/CD, stations continuously monitor the communication medium. A station that is ready to transmit a frame will sense the medium. If the medium is busy, the transmitter starts a *contention procedure*. First the transmitter waits for a predetermined time period, known as the DCF Interframe Space (DIFS) length. Then, based upon a random calculation, the transmitter picks a future time slot from the next 31 slots (the set of 31 slots is a *contention window*). The transmitter will send the frame in that future time slot unless another station starts a transmission. If there are transmissions by other stations before the future time slot begins, the station will freeze a count of the number of slots left until the picked slot and will continue decrementing the count where it left off after the other station has completed its frame transmission. The random back-off calculation reduces the risk of packet collisions between stations that are ready to transmit packets. The collisions can now occur only when two or more stations select the same time slot to transmit. These stations will have to reenter the contention procedure (roughly doubling the contention window size each time the procedure is reentered) to select new time slots in which to transmit the collided frames.

In case of collisions, this procedure results in multiple stations deferring and entering into a rotating back-off procedure; then the station selecting the lowest time slot will transmit first. This method tends toward being fair across the network ona first-come, first-served basis.

Fig. 16–6 illustrates the DFWMAC access scheme.

Interworking Units

Similar to IP routers in wired networks, the interworking unit (IWU) provides protocol manipulation to connect networks with different protocols together. To connect a wireless network that is using the 802.11 protocol to the Internet, IWUs are needed at access points. Access points are nodes that allow traffic flow in and out of a wireless network. Alternatively, IWUs (IP routers) control the in

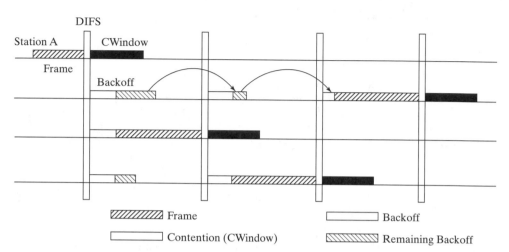

Figure 16–6   DFWMAC Access Scheme

and out of the Internet thus routing wireless packets into and out of the Internet as shown in Fig. 16–7. In this figure, the IWU, or router, connects a wireless network using 802.11 over the Direct Sequence Spread Spectrum to the conventional (wired) Internet, running another data-link protocol over a wire.

IWUs act as access points between wireless stations and the Web. They address issues such as

- correcting delivery of data to its destination,
- controlling congestion, and
- handling differences in maximum packet sizes.

The 802.11 protocol can support data rates of 20 Mbps, thus making it an attractive wireless protocol for Internet connectivity.

16.7 Internet Mobile Host Protocol

An important part of wireless connectivity is mobility. Mobile computers must be able to move between adjacent cells or across multiple network domains without disturbing the application-level process. Mobile users and mobile protocols must not make any changes to the existing TCP/IP Internet protocol to insure connectivity and usability of the Internet as it exists today.

A mobile host is the Internet Mobile Host Protocol (IMHP) entity that roams through the Internet. Each mobile host has a home agent on its home network. Each home agent maintains a list known as a home list. The home list is a

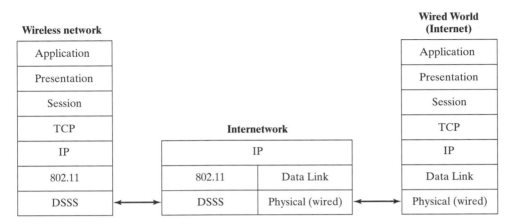

Figure 16–7   OSI Model and Routing of Wireless Packets

list of mobile hosts that the home network will serve, and it also maintains the location of each mobile host as the network becomes aware of their locations. As mobile hosts roam from one network to the next, they have to register with foreign agents on new subnets as they try to connect to that network. Foreign agents are much like a home agent except they interact with visiting home agents from other networks. Each foreign agent maintains a list known as the visitor list, which identifies the mobile hosts that are currently registered with it. The combination of the foreign agent's address for a particular home agent (in-care-of address) along with its home address is known as a binding. A binding defines where to send packets for a particular home agent at any given time [4].

The registration protocol, which is part of the IMHP management protocol, notifies all the concerned parties of the new mobile host's location. Those include the previous foreign agents and the host's home agent. It is the responsibility of the IMHP management protocol to keep a forwarding pointer from the previous foreign agents until all information about the new location has been updated with the new network and the home network. Time stamps are used to keep visitor lists current and to delete the home agents that have left the network. Fig. 16–8 demonstrates a possible simplified registration process.

Any node may function as a cache agent by caching the bindings of one or more mobile hosts. All of these cache agents are under the umbrella of the IMHP management protocol, which is running on all IMHP agents as long as they are not on their home networks. The IMHP management protocol manages the cache agents in a distributed fashion. This allows packets to travel to their destinations without having to be routed to a home network first. Cache agents actively attempt to reconform bindings in their location caches using the IMHP management protocol, and they also periodically send out notifications to update caches when agents move in and out of networks.

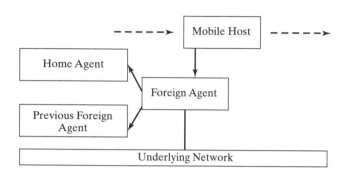

Figure 16–8   Possible Simplified Registration Process

IP Tunneling

Tunneling is a technique by which IMHP entities can direct data frames to a mobile host's present location. In the IMHP management protocol tunneling takes the form of encapsulation. If the sender has a location entry for the host destination in its cache, it adds 8 bytes of data to each packets header; otherwise it needs to add 12 bytes to compensate for extra addressing requirements. The tunneling header is inserted into the packet immediately following the existing IP header. In the IP header, the protocol number is changed to indicate the IMHP encapsulation tunneling protocol. The destination address is the mobile host's care-of address, and the source address is set to the IP address of the encapsuling entity [4].

Much like IPV6, encapsulation in the above procedure can ensure operation and coexistence of the IMHP with the present underlying architecture of the Web. The intermediate routers will see a normal IP packet. It is only the IMHP network that can recognize the packets by seeing the protocol number and deliver them to their final destination.

16.8 References

[1]   Bates, Bud, and Donald Gregory. *Voice & Data Communications Handbook*. McGraw-Hill, 1996. pp. 572–573.

[2]   Halsall, Fred. *Data Communications, Computer Networks and Open Systems*. 4th Ed. Reading, MA: Addison-Wesley, 1996. pp. 325–326.

[3]   Kaashoek, M. Frans, Tom Pinckney, and Joshua A. Tauber. "Dynamic Documents: Mobile Wireless Access to the WWW," 1994.
<http://snapple.cs.washington.edu/library/mcsa94/kaashoek.ps> (22 Oct. 1996).

[4]   Perkins, Charles, Andrew Myles, and David B. Johnson. "IMHP: A Mobile
         Host Protocol for the Internet," 1994.
         <http://www.neda.com/mobileIpSurvey/html/mobileIP.html> (15 Nov. 1996).

[5]   Voelker, Geoffrey M. and Brian N. Bershad. "Mobisaic: An Information Sys-
         tem for Mobile Wireless Computing Environment." Department of Com-
         puter Science and Engineering. University of Washington, Seattle, WA.
         Sept. 1994.
         <http://www.cs.washington.edu/homes/voelker/mobisaic/abs-mobile94.html>
         (15 Sept. 1997).

[6]   Watson, Terri. "Wit: An Infrastructure for Wireless Palmtop Computing."
         1994. <http://snapple.cs.washington.edu:600/papers/wit.ps> (24 Oct. 1996).

[7]   Watson, Terri. "Effective Wireless Communication Through Application
         Partitioning." 1995. <http://snapple.cs.washington.edu/papers/hot_os.ps>
         (22 Oct. 1996).

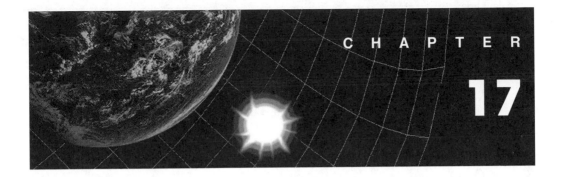

C H A P T E R

17

Imaging with Photo CDs

by Dan Haim

The development of the Photo CD by Kodak [1], in conjunction with N.V. Philips [2] of the Netherlands, represents a quantum leap in electronic imaging. It provides consumer and commercial users alike the benefits of electronic manipulation with the high quality of silver halide imaging. Now, this technology is making its way into the Web. To date, still imagery on the Web has been limited to GIF and JPEG files. Recently, Kodak has added a new choice: Photo CD imaging, which can serve Photo CD images natively, without first converting them to some other format. Currently there are four leading application areas for Photo CD: printing and publishing, presentations and training, image archiving and distribution, and desktop color compound documents. This technology empowers Web authors to create pages which allow their audiences to interact with images by zooming, enlarging, cropping, and rotating.

Chapter Content

1. Introduction

2. Digital Imaging and Photo CD

- Digital Imaging

- Photo CD—Usability

- Color-Coding Compatibility

3. Photo CD on the Web

- Functionality
- Procedure
- Technical Notes

4. Summary

5. Acknowledgments

6. References

17.1 Introduction

In the past few years the Web has seen a lot of progress. However, not until recently did people start viewing this powerful tool as more than merely a large database. In particular, "real life" applications began to emerge, many of which are discussed in this book. One of the more recent applications is the addition by Kodak [1] of Photo CD capability on the Web.

In general, the Photo CD system offers a powerful tool for viewing, storing, and working with images that is fast becoming a computer industry standard. Launched in 1992, the original Photo CD format enables photographers to take standard 35 mm film pictures and have them scanned onto a CD by a photo finisher or service bureau. They can then view their pictures on television using a Photo CD player [1].

More recently, with the big advances in personal computers, the Photo CD system is able to bridge from consumer and professional photography to the desktop computer. It combines the quality, convenience, and low cost of conventional picture-taking with the benefits of digital technology—the ability to display, enhance, store, and transmit images electronically. Perhaps more importantly, the same discs can now be read by practically any computer equipped with a CD-ROM drive [2].

Photo CDs offer many advantages for users which make them a convenient way for desktop users to work with images.

- Low-cost scans. People can bring their roll of 35 mm film scanned onto a Photo CD Master disc, which must be done at a local vendor, for under $10, which is very cheap compared to previously available scanning.

- Multiple resolutions. Photo CDs enable storage of each image at multiple levels of resolution. Users can work locally with smaller, lower-resolution images on-screen, then use the highest-resolution version for publication.

- High-quality images. On a Photo CD Master disc, the highest resolution level (2048×3072 pixels) captures all the image detail which a 35 mm film can contain. Lower resolutions are usually sufficient for applications such as professional photography and color pre-press operations.

- Consistent colors. Photo CD images are produced using scanning algorithms and color-management software designed to ensure consistent, high-quality color.

- Convenient storage. Each Photo CD Master disc provides long-term, low-cost storage of approximately 100 images; the Photo CD Portfolio II disc format can store more images at a lower resolution.

This chapter reviews the Photo CD technology, how describing it in a simple manner is incorporated into the Web. The simplicity brings the Web a step further in becoming a desktop interactive tool, rather than just a database browser.

17.2 Digital Imaging and Photo CD

Digital Imaging

The development of solid-state image capture devices for commercial use began in the mid-1970s. In 1986, Kodak scientists designed and fabricated the world's first megapixel sensor—a sensor capable of recording 1.4 megapixels, or 1.4 million picture elements. In 1994, Kodak introduced the KODAK Professional DCS 460 Digital Camera, containing a 6 megapixel sensor—capable of recording an image with six million picture elements [1].

Before going into the details of Photo CDs on the Web, let us describe the process of digitization of photographs, upon which Photo CD technology is based.

We start with the widespread 35mm camera. When a camera exposes an image on sensitized film, photochemical changes occur. Special developing and processing techniques then reproduce the recorded image as a photographic negative, from which prints can be made.

Digital imaging makes use of the fact that films are coated with extremely fine granular chemicals [1]. Using digitizing equipment, a photograph can be scanned, digitized to 18 million picture elements (pixels), stored, and then played back for television viewing. The average camcorder, on the other hand, records approximately 250,000 pixels per frame. Compact discs are natural storage devices for such a purpose, and can be accessed via CD players that play both Photo CDs and audio CDs. They can be viewed and manipulated on personal computers, transmitted via telephone lines, and printed. Thermal printers can print images from a Photo CD that approach photographic quality. In general, Photo CDs serve as a high-quality storage medium for photographs in much the same manner as an audio compact disc stores recorded music. Currently, Photo CDs can hold up to 100 photographs, but as compression improves, this number can be much higher. Since the images on a Photo CD originated on film, they have a much higher resolution than images recorded electronically.

Photo CD makes it possible for the first time to incorporate continuous-tone images into computing environments [2]. Kodak has created a new worldwide standard for reproducing color in digital form and has developed software to provide consistent color across computer platforms and peripherals. This standard has been supported by the industry's leading computer equipment and software manufacturers.

In addition to Photo CD, Kodak has introduced a number of other hybrid products that combine the high quality of silver halide imaging with the convenience of electronic manipulation [1].

Photo CD—Usability

Computer users were first to take advantage of digital imaging technology, helping to drive acceptance of the Photo CD format as a computer industry standard—supported by hardware operating systems, software applications, and CD-ROM drives. Based upon a multisession recording standard, every multi-session CD-ROM drive is capable of playing Photo CD discs. This has created an installed base of tens of millions of Photo CD-compatible drives. Once a disc has been loaded into a drive, additional software is needed to read and display Photo CD images. This capability is offered nowadays as a built-in feature of computer operating systems, allowing users to incorporate Photo CD images directly into any software application. Photo CD support is built into Apple Computer's QuickTime extension, the IRIX operating system from Silicon Graphics, and Sun Microsystems' Solaris. IBM's OS 2/WARP platform can read and write Photo CD discs, and IBM supports Photo CD technology in its AIX operating system (which runs on RISC System/6000 workstations) through Ultimedia Services, an optional package of multimedia tools [3].

Although Photo CD technology can benefit almost anyone who wants or needs to use pictures, there are four leading application areas: publishing suite, presentations and training, image archiving and distribution, and desktop color compound documents [4]:

- *Publishing Suite*: Photo CD scans offer low-cost and high-quality printing and publishing for professionals. Compared to traditional flatbed or drum scanners for many pre-press applications, Photo CD technology provides the most cost-effective way to scan and store color images in a standard format for later use on all computer platforms in high-quality, cross-media publishing.

- *Presentations and Training*: Professionals who support the creation of presentations, along with those who deliver large numbers of presentations, can use Photo CD images to communicate more effectively. Since Photo CDs are easy to use, they provide a more interactive presentation than is possible with either videotape or slides. Presentations are faster, easier, and cheaper to produce than with high-end multimedia authoring packages.

- *Image Archiving and Distribution*: Owners of large-scale collections, containing 500,000 images or more, can convert their current film images and photography to digital form using Photo CD technology. Once converted, these images can be used, managed, archived, and distributed in an online database. On a smaller scale, individual photographers can distribute on-disc portfolios, making it easy to show images to customers while controlling the use of their high-resolution images through Photo CD features such as encryption or watermarking.

- *Desktop Color Compound Documents*: There are over three million small office/home office multimedia computer users in the U.S., many of whom would benefit from adding images to their communications and presentations. Photo CD technology enables the incorporation of good-looking photographs quickly, easily, and inexpensively into documents. Photo Insert software makes adding pictures even easier.

Color-Coding Compatibility

Photo CD has a unique encoding scheme of color (luminance and chrominance). Photographic products which are currently being used for input to Photo CD are not specifically designed to be scanned and digitized. Instead, each is designed either for direct viewing by a human observer or for printing onto other photographic materials. Because each type of source is designed for a different purpose, each is physically (and colorimetrically) different from the others. As a result, unprocessed data from scanned images on different types of sources, such as negatives and transparencies, are not compatible with each other. Unlike Photo CD image data, this incompatible scanned image data from different sources cannot be adjusted or modified, merged to produce composite images, or processed by an output device, without requiring knowledge of the origin of each image [9].

In this section we will briefly discuss some of the aspects of color encoding by Photo CD. For a more comprehensive review please consult the Kodak literature.

Perhaps the most distinctive feature of Photo CD color encoding is that it allows each output device (such as a home player, a computer monitor, or a thermal printer) to produce images from any Photo CD data file, independently of the type of input imaging medium that was scanned to produce that file, such as negatives and positives. This feature results from the use of an input encoding technique that achieves input compatibility of Photo CD images scanned from a variety of different sources [5]. The fact that Photo CDs removes the dependency between input and output devices makes them even more attractive.

Without input compatibility, each output device requires multiple output data-processing paths (transforms) in order to properly produce images encoded from different types of inputs. With Photo CD's unique input compatibility, the data-processing path for each output device is independent of the original source of the Photo CD encoded image. Each output device therefore requires only a single transform to produce output images from any image encoded on any Photo CD disk.

Additionally, Photo CD input compatibility allows cutting-and-pasting of elements of Photo CD images that originated from different types of input media into composite images. For example, portions of images scanned from negatives can be readily edited together with images scanned from transparencies to form homogeneous-appearing composites. A composite image can then be sent to any output device, where the entire image will be reproduced in a way that has been optimized for that particular device. In addition, input compatibility allows all images to be adjusted and manipulated, during and after encoding, by the use of a common set of application software tools.

The color-encoding basis of the Photo CD system is the Reference Image-Capturing Device. All Photo CD images, regardless of their origin, can be regarded as having been captured and encoded by the Reference Image-Capturing Device. This conceptual device provides a consistent calorimetric definition for the Photo CD system. Moreover, it provides the basis for achieving compatibility among the various types of media that are input to the Photo CD system. Output values from the reference device then go directly to the Photo YCC color encoding (we will discuss Photo YCC in more detail in the next section) and are processed on the Photo CD Imaging Workstation (PIW) to produce values corresponding to those produced by the reference device. Compatibility is therefore achieved by the transformation of scanned image data from each input medium to a common meaning and a common numerical encoding [9].

One of the unique features that results, in part, from input compatibility is the flexibility that is created for output. Photo CD image data can be transformed in the output process to correspond to either of the above calorimetric objectives, or to virtually any other desired color-reproduction objective. But it is important that, during the encoding process, the basic original-scene-colorimetry interpretation is fundamentally maintained in order to ensure that all recorded images are consistent and compatible with all other Photo CD images.

The next section looks at how Photo CD makes use of the Web.

17.3 Photo CD on the Web

Functionality

To date, still imagery on the Web has been limited to GIF and JPEG files. Kodak has introduced another choice: Photo CD Image Pacs [10]. These are files that store all the information needed to reproduce a photograph on almost any medium. Each Image Pac includes the following options:

- index images

- image selection

- TV viewing

- small prints

- hardcopy prints

Each of the above has different resolution and can be delivered by using a simple recomposition scheme. Therefore, Photo CD images can now be served natively, without first converting them to some other format. Other options, such as large proofs/print, can be stored in a separate file, the Image Pac Extension (IPE), which is available on request.

When you choose to serve an image in Photo CD format, powerful new things are possible that cannot be done with GIF and JPEG images. First—and perhaps most exciting—is the fact that the images become interactive. You can zoom in on the image without its becoming pixelated. Few people realize the world of detail that is captured in a standard 35 mm film image. Photo CD can reveal all of it—on the Web. Once zoomed, you can pan around the high-resolution images. In addition to zooming, you can enlarge the images. This is analogous to enlarging a photograph in a real world darkroom. Photo CD brings the digital equivalent to the Web.

Second, Photo CD brings color management to the Web for the first time. Unlike GIF and JPEG, Photo CD images are stored in a well-characterized color space called YCC [10]. Based on international color standards, YCC promises to deliver the color of the original scene to your monitor, via color management software such as Kodak Color Management Software (KCMS). Essentially Photo-YCC is the color space that is used when storing Photo CD images. PhotoYCC is designed to retain all of the important scan information and permit the use of the stored image on any output device. In contrast, other scanning systems choose a more restricted color space (for example, various RGBs) that loses information. Once lost, information cannot be recovered. For the latest browsers with color management capability, the YCC data translates to the best possible color on your monitor or printer. In simple terms, you could visit a museum on the Web and see a Monet with the correct colors. Or you could visit a clothing store on the Web and be sure that the green shirt you view on your monitor will be the same shade of green when you order it and put it on.

All of this is possible, and easy to do. On the server side, images are simply referenced in pages using standard HTML. On the browser side, they simply appear in pages, along with functions that allow you to zoom, pan, crop, and rotate them. All of this is accomplished with standard Web technology and a Java applet. We now describe in more detail the mechanism used in making Photo CD available on the Web.

Procedure

In this section we will describe how the images are prepared for the Web. We will outline the steps in producing a Photo CD image on the Web. The steps are rather trivial, but they do involve a third party (a photo shop) which owns an imaging device needed to create the correct file format [6]. Currently the imaging device is rather expensive ($100K–$200K) for individuals to own.

1. Take pictures with your camera, or use existing negatives or slides.
2. Transfer the film/slides to Photo CDs. Bring the roll of film to your local photo finisher offering Photo CD services. The original 35 mm film or slides are first transferred to Photo CD using an imaging device, such as the Kodak Photo CD Imaging Workstation 2400 (PIW). The PIW is a Photo CD authoring system consisting of the following components:

   - High-resolution scanner
   - Data manager (workstation)
   - CD writer
   - Thermal printer
   - Software

   Exposure and focus are automatic. Color balance is set through the selection of "film terms"—special sets of data that interpret the color information collected by the PIW's scanner. Film terms take into account characteristics particular to various film types, and they play a vital role in optimizing scan quality.

3. Place your images onto the Web by copying the image pacs to your server's disk.

Technical Notes

Making Photo CD available for viewing on the Web involves the two ends of the network, the server and the client. The capabilities of the Photo CD depends on the server [6].

The heart of Photo CD on the Web is a set of CGI programs that are provided by Kodak. The Webmaster for the server configures the programs and stores them in the same directory as other CGI programs (usually the cgi-bin directory). Once that is done, the Photo CD image pacs to be served are copied to the directories indicated. At this point, they are ready to appear in pages. Standard HTML is used to do this, such as the IMG tag. Standard URLs are constructed to point to the images via the cgi-bin syntax. For example, to place an image on a page, the simplest tag might be:

```
<img src="/cgi-bin/pcd/image.pcd">
```

When a page with Photo CD images in it is requested from a server, the CGI program pcd is invoked. The program does three things: extracts the requested image from the image pac, JPEG-compresses it on the fly, and then sends the JPEG stream to the browser. It also has a smart caching mechanism: it stores the JPEG stream for a while in case you make a request for the same image again.

If just the name of the Photo CD file appears in the URL, then a default size version of the full image is served. However, a set of parameters can be included in the URL to define the subimage desired, the Photo CD resolution level to extract it from, the rotation and the compression level to use. Thus, a single Photo CD image pac can appear on lots of different Web pages in different guises.

To make the image interactive, the HTML should make use of the Java applet when referencing the image. An interactive instance of the image might be:

```
<applet code=PcdApplet.class width=192 height=153>
<param name=src value="/cgi-bin/pcd/image.pcd"> </applet>
```

On the other hand, the client must have the capability to display images with browsers that can recognize the newest technology. Image options vary for the three types of browsers that can display Photo CD images on the Web.

- Images for browsers which recognize only JPEG formatted images: In this option the only function that can be used is zooming on certain portions of the JPEG image. This is achieved by simple usage of the "Imagemap" option of HTML: each click on the mouse sends you to another image at higher zoom, depending upon where on the image you clicked. However, in each "new" page, the images remain static on the page, just like GIF and JPEG images. A demo is available [7].

- Images for Java-aware browsers: Here the control over the functions of the image is done using a Java applet which places the function keys (zooming, cropping, rotating and panning) below the image and allows the user to analyze the image. Readers with a Web browser that can run Java applets can find a demo in [7].

- Images for Photo CD-aware browsers: This option is similar to the Java option, except that a menu of new functionality is brought up by clicking on the image. On this menu are functions like zoom in, zoom out, enlarge, reduce, crop, and rotate. The Mosaic 2.1 Web browser is Photo CD-aware [11]. Some sample demos using the Mosaic browser are also available in [7].

In the latter two options, the browser simply edits the URL and issues another request, as needed. The image is then repainted in its new form— zoomed, or whatever was requested. One nice benefit of this architecture is that a new "page" is not created. Thus, ten requests to modify the image do not result in ten pages that you have to go "Back" through.

A good review on how to construct a Photo CD URL is available in [8].

17.4 Summary

The Photo CD imaging technology, developed by Kodak, has proven to be an important tool in many applications. There are many possible uses for this technology in the future, such as in police investigations, astronomy and other scientific curricula. It is only natural, therefore, that this technology is incorporated into the fast-developing Web. It was shown how easy it is to merge the Photo CD images into the Web to create one powerful tool that goes well beyond the scope of conventional photography.

There are still some obstacles, such as image loading time and browser availability, which need to be addressed. However, some solutions, which are discussed in other parts of this book, are being developed. For instance, increasing bandwidth and/or making the Photo CD format much more compressed are appropriate solutions in improving the image loading time (currently, a typical Photo CD file for a single photograph has a size of about 4–5 Mb, which needs to be accessed for each operation). It is anticipated that Photo CD-aware browsers eventually will be widespread; in the meantime recent versions of popular browsers can run the Java applet to view Photo CDs.

17.5 Acknowledgments

This chapter is based on extracts from several publications by Kodak. I wish to thank the Kodak Company for kindly supplying me with material on Photo CDs, as well as advising on the implementation of Photo CD technology on the Web. In particular, I would like to thank Paul Benati,[1] John Bulter,[2] and Wayne Neale[3]

[1] benatip@kodak.com

[2] bulter@kodak.com

[3] neale@kodak.com

of the Kodak Company for their invaluable help and information in preparing this chapter. Some portions of this chapter are copyrighted by the Kodak company. All of these materials are reprinted by permission. Kodak is not responsible for the accuracy of any material which was not originated by it, or is not directly linked to its site.

17.6 References

[1]   Eastman Kodak Company. "From Glass Plates to Digital Images." <http://www.kodak.com/aboutKodak/kodakHistory/kodakHistory.shtml> (17 Sept. 1997).

[2]   Eastman Kodak Company. "Photo CD Menu." <http://www.kodak.com/daiHome/products/photoCD.shtml> (17 Sept. 1997).

[3]   Eastman Kodak Company. "Digital Imaging Menu." <http://www.kodak.com/digitalImaging/digitalImaging.shtml>.   (17   Sept. 1997)

[4]   Eastman Kodak Company. "Photo CD Products and Features." <http://www.kodak.com/digitalImaging/aboutPhotoCD/aboutPCD.shtml> (17 Sept. 1997).

[5]   Eastman Kodak Company. "Technical Information for Digital Imaging Products." <http://www.kodak.com/daiHome/techInfo/techInfo.shtml> (17 Sept. 1997).

[6]   Eastman Kodak Company. "What Does Photo CD on the Web Mean?" <http://www.kodak.com/digitalImaging/cyberScene/whatIsIt.shtml> (17 Sept. 1997)

[7]   Eastman Kodak Company. "Photo CD on the Web: Demos!" <http://www.kodak.com/digitalImaging/cyberScene/demo/staticDemo.shtml> (17 Sept. 1997).

[8]   Eastman Kodak Company. "URL Construction for Photo CD on the Web." <http://www.kodak.com/digitalImaging/cyberScene/enableURLspec.shtml> (17 Sept. 1997).

[9]   Giorgianni, Ed, Steve Johnson and Bill O'Such, "Using Information Beyond 100% White." Eastman Kodak Company. 1996.

[10] Lawler, Brian. "Optimizing Photo CD Scans for Prepress and Publishing." <http://www.aols.com/colorite/optimizing.html> (17 Sept. 1997).

[11] National Center for Supercomputer Applications, "Mosaic 2.1." 1996.
     <ftp://ftp.ncsa.uiuc.edu/Web/Mosaic/> (17 Sept. 1997).

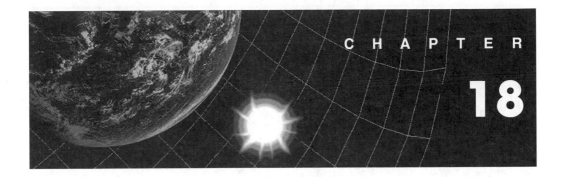

C H A P T E R

18

Intellectual Property on the Web

by Kelly R. Hanood

The amount of information and the number of places to visit on the World Wide Web have grown so rapidly that it is virtually impossible to keep up with every article, picture, idea, and piece of software published. Because of this, it is difficult to protect these components of intellectual property. This chapter will discuss what intellectual property is, who owns it and how it can or cannot be protected in the United States. Because the current intellectual property laws are becoming outdated by technology, President Clinton formed an Information Infrastructure Task Force (IITF) to investigate and review these laws. Their findings and recommendations are in a report entitled "Intellectual Property and the National Information Infrastructure." This chapter will explain their findings and how their recommendations might affect the Web as it is today.

Chapter Content

1. Introduction
2. Copyright Basics

- History

- Copyright Components

- Exclusive Rights

3. The Copyright Evolution

- Introduction
- Developments
- Court Cases

4. The Working Group on Intellectual Property Rights

- Background
- The Green Paper
- The White Paper

5. NII Copyright Protection Act of 1995

- Introduction
- Major Revisions
- Effects on the Web

6. Concerns and Related Issues

7. References

18.1 Introduction

In a few years the Web has grown from virtual nonexistence to an enormous library of newspapers, magazines, organizations, museums, government agencies, schools, personal pages and much, much more. Thirty million or more users tap into the Web and explore the endless realm of information. A user, according to the American Internet User Survey, is an individual who uses "at least one Internet application other than e-mail." E-mail ranks first in the use of the Internet with the Web coming in second. Forty-one percent of users say they use e-mail on a daily basis while only 27 percent use the Web daily. Regardless, the number of users more than doubled from 1995 to 1996.

The overwhelming growth of the Web has led to the explosion of information on the Internet. Because of this explosion the concern for copyright protection has also grown. Technology has made it possible to reproduce copyrighted works quickly and easily. Not only is it easy to reproduce the work, but also the quality of the copies approaches that of commercially published copies. In other words, a copy that one person pays for can look almost identical to a reproduced copy that another person gets without paying a royalty.

As technology has evolved, copyright law has been subject to constant scrutiny and investigation. Law makers cannot predict the future; therefore

Congress has the ability to revise the laws so that they are in accordance with current technology. The Web has quickly grown to 30 million users worldwide. That is 30 million people who potentially have the ability to look at your Web page, or see what your math class is doing, or read about the employment opportunities for your company. Or 30 million people who could download, modify, and transmit your work all over the Internet.

There are different points of view on this matter, and it will be left to the readera to form their own opinion. Intellectual property on the Web is not an issue to ignore. All Web users should be concerned because the law has the potential to change every aspect of the Web as it is known today.

18.2 Copyright Basics

History

The founding fathers of the United States of America had intellectual property in mind when they wrote in Article 1, Section 8 of the U.S. Constitution "The Congress shall have the Power... to promote the Progress of Science and Useful Arts, by securing for limited Times to Authors and Inventors the exclusive Rights to their respective Writings and Discoveries." It was left to Congress to develop this in detail. In 1789, the first bill relating to copyright was presented to Congress, and in 1790 the first law was put in place. This law went through a series of revisions, adding music, art and certain unpublished works to the list of protected works of authorship.

Eventually Congress established four components of Intellectual Property: Copyright, Trademark, Patents, and Trade Secrets. From the time the first law was accepted until the present day, copyright law has been constantly amended and changed. More recent revisions include the 1976 Copyright Act, which is the last major revision of copyright law. This act was the fourth generation of copyright law In 1980, computer programs became protected works, and in 1984, Congress enacted the Semiconductor Chip Protection Act. The United States became a member of the Berne Convention in 1989 which brought protection for all copyrights in the countries that were also members of the convention. The Computer Software Rental Amendment Act of 1990 gave software owners the right to control the rental and lending of their software. And finally there was the NII Copyright Protection Act of 1995, which will be discussed in detail later in the chapter.

Copyright law has undergone many changes and additions. This section will certainly need to be expanded in the future. Exactly what will happen is unclear, and only technology will tell.

Copyright Components

Each of the four components developed by Congress protects different types of intellectual property. A copyright protects literary works, art, music and items of a similar nature that are produced by authors and artists. Trademarks are symbols that help protect an object against mistaken identity [3]. For example, the golden arches are a trademark of McDonald's, not Burger King. Patents are usually obtained by inventors who desire protection for an invention or process. And trade secrets are simply the secrecy of a process, recipe, or any item that is to remain a secret. The recipe for Coca-Cola Classic is a trade secret.

Copyrights will be the main focus for this chapter, because the Web has had the biggest impact on this component of intellectual property as compared to the other three. A copyright begins on any work the minute that work is placed on a fixed medium. A fixed medium ranges from paper to audio or video tapes to CD-ROM. As soon as the work is recorded, the author owns a copyright and has the ability to reserve the rights of that ownership. There are, however, three basic requirements that a new work must meet in order to have a copyright. First, the work must be original. An author must produce something original, not copied or derived from some other work. Second, the work must also be creative. There is no strict definition for creativity; however, the work must be in some sense creative. And finally, the work must be on a fixed medium such as the ones described.

It is not required, but almost necessary, for an owner of a copyright to give notice of the copyright on the work. There are three parts of a notice of copyright: 1) the symbol, word or abbreviation of copyright, 2) the first year the work was distributed and 3) the name of the copyright owner. For example: Copyright © 1996 Kelly R. Hanood. In order to signify clearly to the public that your work is protected, the piece should contain notification. Otherwise, it may be forgotten that a copyright exists.

Exclusive Rights

Once a work meets the three basic requirements, the owner has the right to reserve five exclusive rights: the right to reproduce the work or make copies, the right distribute the work to the public, the right to modify the work or make derivative works, the right to perform the work in public, and the right to display a piece in public.

Despite the exclusive rights of a copyright the public has the freedom to reproduce a work for certain reasons. "Fair use" allows a person to make a copy of a work for purposes of criticism, news reporting, research, and others. If the copy is for personal, noncommercial use, the person who made the copy is not violating the copyright. In the circumstance of teaching or education, multiple (more than one) copies are allowed. There are certain items that are not protected by a copyright. The copyright on a work does not cover the title, ideas or concepts. A copyright also does not cover names, slogans, coloring, lettering, and speeches or performances not recorded in some way.

There are many sites on the Web that explain copyright law in more detail. This chapter is not meant to teach copyright law but to give an overview so that the readers will have a base of copyright knowledge to take with them as they read the following sections of this chapter.

18.3 The Copyright Evolution

Introduction

The copyright evolution began in the 1960s with concerns about how technology was affecting intellectual property law. New machines began appearing that enhanced the ability to violate copyrights. Photocopiers and VCRs have made it easier to copy television shows, movies and books. Computers, scanners and the Internet have made it just as easy to scan in a paper or article, make multiple copies of it and distribute the copies to many users on the Internet. All of this can be done in minutes and can create original looking or publisher-quality copies.

Computers and computer software also joined the realm of copyrightable material and raised many questions and concerns. As the number of patents and copyright applications increased, questions arose about the extent of copyright protection on computers and computer programs. Does a patent on a computer also protect the operating program for the operating system, are programs in ROM included in the copyright protection, and is object code also protected? As these issues were ironed out in a court of law the questions became deeper. Issues of "protectability of structure, sequence and organization ('SSO') of a computer program" [5], protection for screens and user interfaces, and decompilation and reverse engineering arose.

Developments

The Copyright Office has been accepting registration for computer programs since 1964; however, it was not until the Computer Software Copyright Act of 1980 that programs were legally declared copyrightable works. There were three stipulations placed on program copyrights in 1964. First, the program had to contain sufficient original authorship; second, the program had to be published; and third, the copies of the program submitted had to be human-readable. Between 1964 and 1976, only about 2000 programs were registered with the copyright office [5]. This period preceded the explosion in the number of personal computers, and there was little concern for protection.

By 1974, Congress saw a need for investigation into the effects of technology on copyright issues. The National Commission on New Technological Uses of Copyright Works (CONTU) was created and given the task to study problems that were arising. CONTU presented their findings and recommendations in 1978. Their suggestion was for the enactment of an amendment that would clarify the scope of copyright protection on computer software. This recommendation resulted in the Computer Software Copyright Act of 1980. This amendment added the definition of a computer program and a new section 117 concerning an owner's exclusive rights in computer programs [15].

By 1986, the Office of Technology Assessment (OTA) conducted a study and concluded that the advancement of technology could not be handled by the current legislature and recommended *sui generis* legislation. The current laws, at that time, did not adequately handle certain situations; therefore the courts had to handle these cases as best they could. On December 1, 1990, the Computer Software and Rental Amendment Act of 1990 was enacted. This gave the owners and copyright holders of computer programs control over the rental and lending of their work. The National Information Infrastructure (NII) and the Information Infrastructure Task Force (IITF) were created in 1993 to advance the development of technology and the intellectual property system. The NII Copyright Protection Act of 1995 was the result of the IITF's efforts.

Court Cases

Many court cases occurred during what this chapter calls the copyright evolution. This section will highlight a few in order to better explain the events that were actually occurring. The majority of these cases occurred before the Web's inception, and they demonstrate the effects of technological advancement.

Possibly the first computer-related case was **Telex Corp. v. International Business Machines, Corp. (IBM)** [5]. In 1973, IBM Corp. charged Telex Corp. with infringing on the copyright protecting IBM computer manuals. In 1979, **Data Cash Systems v. JS&A Group**, raised the question of whether or not object code in ROM is protected, given that it is not readable by humans. In a similar case in 1983, in **Midway Mfg. Co. v. Strohon**, the courts ruled that ROM was also protected because logically it was the same as code stored on tape or disk.

A case involving operating systems occurred in 1983 between Apple Computer, Inc. and Franklin Computer Corp. Franklin used Apple's exact operating system code so that applications for that operating system could run on their machines. The courts ruled in favor of Apple because operating system code and application programs have no logical distinction.

18.4 The Working Group on Intellectual Property Rights

Background

With the formation of the Information Infrastructure Task Force (IITF) in early 1993, President Clinton acted on the issues that were facing the policies and laws for intellectual property. The Administration envisioned creating a National Information Infrastructure (NII) that would combine the existing single infrastructures of radio, television, telephones, fax machines, and computers and create one information infrastructure of all communication mediums. Computers and communication tools would be merged to create an unlimited interaction between all media of communication. The NII was to become an "advanced, high-speed, interactive, broadband, digital communications system" [16].

The purpose of the IITF was to work "with the private sector, public interest groups, Congress, and State and local governments to develop comprehensive telecommunications and information policies and programs that will promote the development of the NII and best meet the country's needs" [16]. The IITF was organized into three committees: Telecommunications Policy Committee, Committee on Application and Technology, and Information Policy Committee. The third committee included a group called the Working Group on Intellectual Property Rights. Bruce Lehman, the Assistant Secretary of Commerce and the Commissioner of Patents and Trademarks, chaired this group. The Working Group was created to examine the existing intellectual property policies and determine how they were affected by the creation of the NII. Second, the group was to make recommendations on how the policies needed to be changed, amended or revised. The Working Group's main focal point was on copyright laws.

The Green Paper

The Working Group had a very difficult task ahead of them. They began by allowing many opportunities for individuals, companies and organizations to state their concerns and opinions on what should happen to the laws (e.g., [22]). Next the Working Group developed a preliminary draft of "Intellectual Property and the National Information Infrastructure." This is called the "Green Paper." The Working Group had to address many issues, a few of which are explicitly addressed in this report by Lehman and the committee. The "Background" section of the report reviews common suggestions made to them by involved parties and states the committee's position on these matters. Since these requests are common, it is important to go over them here.

One suggestion was made that copyright law should be less strict on the Web. The argument for this is that information should be "free and unencumbered on the NII," and "the law should reflect the public interest" [16]. The Working Group responds to this by stating that "creative works of authorship" will eventually disappear from the Web. Without protection on the NII authors will not have the incentive to make their works available. Hence, in the public's best interest, it is important to apply these laws to the NII in order to continue having creative work available.

Another suggestion was that copyright protection could be reduced because technology makes it so easy to violate copyrights. The Working Group simply responds that "this argument is not valid" [16] because the ability to do something does not mean that it should be allowed to be done.

The last common suggestion reviewed by the committee was that any law, regardless of what country, did not apply to "Cyberspace" because it is "a sovereignty unto itself that should be self governed by its inhabitants." [16] The idea behind this is that the inhabitants "will rely on their own 'netiquette' to determine what uses of works, if any, are improper." [16] The Working Group responds that "Cyberspace" is not a virtual world and is in fact in the jurisdiction of the law. Communications or transmissions, whether it be through satellite, broadcasts, or networks, are governed by the country from which they are coming and going. And once again, the Working Group suggests that if cyberspace were a law-free domain, authors would choose not to enter it with their contributions.

The members of the Working Group on Intellectual Property Rights feel that in order to have the NII reach its "full potential," copyright law must be applied and the laws must be effective. In order for the IITF to be successful in building and developing the NII there need to be "efforts in three disciplines: law, technology and education."

The White Paper

The Green Paper was subject to much review and was eventually developed into the White Paper in September of 1995. The hearings and testimonies before and after the Green Paper became recommendations for intellectual property policies and proposed legislation for copyright protection. "The Report of the Working Group on Intellectual Property Rights" covers the majority of questions that can be thought of concerning IP policies and issues that are related to today's technology. It is likely, however, that because of the rapid advancement of technology these answers and recommendations will become outdated quickly. Regardless, it is important to examine the issues addressed in the report.

It is best to review some of the major proposals rather than the White Paper as a whole. First (this is not necessarily in the order in the paper), it is suggested that the owner of a copyright have exclusive use of the digital form of that work. In order for any other person to legally own a copy of a work in digital format, the copyright owner must have given them a copy whether through a license or for free. Additionally, transmitting a digital copy of a work with a copyright is suggested to be a form of distribution. Hence, without the permission of the copyright owner, this is an illegal action. For a simple example, if you have a copy of a paper or article which you obtained by buying a license and would like to share it with a colleague and do so via e-mail, you violate a copyright law. Your colleague cannot benefit from this article unless they obtain the article in the same manner that you did.

The White Paper recommended eliminating fair use in the NII. By creating licensing systems throughout the NII, the only way to obtain articles would be to buy them. The only way to share a copy with another person would be to send the original copy from the first person's machine to the second person. This is the "first sale right." The Working Group compares this to utilizing first sale rights with a book. Once a person sells a book, either to a friend or to a used book store, he no longer has a copy of the book. Therefore, a person should not retain a digital copy of an article. Hence, if a person is prohibited from making a copy, fair use has been eliminated [4].

The White Paper also calls for Copyright Management Information. This is information about the author and copyright owner, license information and the terms of the license, distribution information, etc. The proposal suggests that it is not mandatory for this information to be included in a document, but that it should be illegal to provide false information or to falsify Copyright Management information provided.

Copyright Management Information might be information appended to a document and digitally signed (see the section on "Digital Signatures" on page 248). An example is digital watermarking [28], being developed by several U.S. and Japanese companies for audio recordings. Watermarks thwart Web sites that offer free and illegal downloads of music without royalty payment. A record company first uses watermark software to embed information into an audio file, including the name of the song title, recording artist, and the recording date. When the recording is sold, an online retailer that sells a copy of the recording then adds to the watermark the purchaser's name and date of sale. If the song were played on the radio or sent over the Internet, an electronic decoder could capture the watermark information as the song was being played. This allows the owner of a recording to be traced in order to detect illegal copies.

The Working Group also suggests adding a new section to the copyright law that would prohibit devices that are for the primary purpose of avoiding, or deactivating, protection on a work. For example, it is illegal to possess, manufacture or distribute a device for decrypting protected, encrypted files.

Finally, the Working Group suggests that On-line Service Providers (OSPs), such as America Online, become the enforcers of copyright law on the Web. The OSPs have the authority to watch and control activity that occurs in their domain. Therefore, they should be the police that serve to protect the copyright owner. OSPs have the ability to discover violations and punish users for inappropriate actions. Working toward a solution for the future, the Working Group suggests educating children to help set standards for the NII that is developing.

The Working Group on Intellectual Property Rights provided only proposals for new policies. It is within the discretion of the lawmakers to use these recommendations as they please. In November of 1995 Congress enacted the first of the accepted recommendations with the NII Copyright Protection Act of 1995.

18.5 NII Copyright Protection Act of 1995

Introduction

Laws are intended to be written with flexibility so that they can be adapted to changes in technology. This is not always possible, however, as we have seen occur with copyright law in general. The size and capabilities of the Web could not have been anticipated in 1909 when the first copyright laws were set in place. Therefore, the revisions in the NII Copyright Protection Act are necessary changes that follow suit with similar actions taken in the past [19, 20]. Laws must encompass and address all issues that might arise, and thus we are given a new amendment for copyright law.

Senator Hatch and Representative Moorhead sponsored the bills S. 1284 and H.R. 2441, respectively, which are now the NII Copyright Protection Act of 1995. The act follows the proposed legislation from the Working Group fairly closely. There are three important revisions that are explored in this chapter: 1) Transmission of Copies, 2) Copyright Protection Systems, and 3) Copyright Management Information.

Major Revisions

First, the forms, or methods, of distribution originally included in copyright law were "by rental, lease or lending." The new act adds "transmission" as a form of distribution. Second, the act calls for a new section entitled "Copyright Protection Systems." This section makes it illegal for anyone, be it an individual or a company, to "import, manufacture, or distribute any device, product or component" that enhances the ability to violate copyrights technologically.

Copyright Management Information for the NII Act is the same as described in the White Paper. It contains information about the author and the copyright owner and other pertinent information concerning a copyright. The act declares it illegal to remove or alter the information. It is also illegal to provide false information. The final section is about civil rights and how to take action against a copyright infringer and the types of damages that can be awarded.

Effects on the Web

For all practical purposes, users on the Web will not see any changes to the Web as a result of the NII Copyright Protection Act of 1995. For now, users do not need to worry about strict enforcement of copyright laws because of the difficulty of the actual enforcement. It is important, though, not to forget what is fair use of a document and what is not. Even though enforcement is difficult, users are not at liberty to do as they please simply because the law cannot catch them. Most likely, when someone has infringed on a copyright and the author knows this for a fact, the author will probably request a correction of the problem rather than asking a court of law to force a remedy.

The copyright act is most likely, in this author's opinion, a prelude to more laws in the future. Copyright owners will push for more enforcement in the future leading to laws and methods that will protect works more strictly. As shown with the copyright evolution, it is virtually impossible to predict the future for copyright law. The lawmakers attempt to pass legislation that will endure technological changes but, inevitably, they fail. Because of this trend, it is only predictable that more changes will come.

18.6 Concerns and Related Issues

There are many concerns to be expressed about how the Web might change as a result of new copyright laws. Certainly the Web is destined to change. It has been changing ever since its birth, mainly growing in size. As the Web expands into educational, governmental, and commercial use, questions and concerns regarding its growth, utility, and safety inevitably arise. Ironically, the efforts to make the Web a bigger and better place create bigger and worse problems for users, Web publishers and others.

Users are becoming concerned with keeping the Web a free world in which to do what, where, and how they please. Stricter laws pose a threat to a user's freedom to put on and take from the Web as they please. New laws mean new methods of enforcement that could jeopardize the aspects of the Web today. This ties in with freedom of speech and the Telecommunications Bill, which was strongly opposed through the Blue Ribbon Campaign that spread across the Web. More information on freedom of speech and how it relates to the Web can be found in Chapter 19.

It is also important to consider what will happen if new, stricter laws are enacted. How will these laws be enforced? Will our on-line service providers (OSPs) be responsible for our actions? This is a very likely scenario. OSPs have the capabilities to monitor and control what we do with our accounts. It is a possibility that OSPs will become the Internet Police. They will watch our activities and extend the necessary punishment to law breakers. Does this monitoring violate our right to privacy? Will laws be proposed to protect the user also?

If copyright laws become stricter and authors and Web publishers become more protective of their works, the availability of free information may diminish. Commerce on the Web may not be limited to catalog shopping in the future. One day articles might cost you a penny a page or a dollar per article. Or perhaps the user will have to pay for subscriptions to specific sites, and visitors without an ID and password will not be able to access the useful information that lies within. This scenario would be detrimental to educators who want their students to use this free domain for quick and easy research.

There are many possible results that can occur from strict copyright laws. For the immediate future, users probably will not see any effects from the recent copyright act. However, this may not be the case in the future. Just as there are users who would like the Web to be virtually lawless and free from the intrusion of police, there are also authors, publishers and commercial businesses who would like compensation for providing their information on the Web. It remains to be seen whom the law will ultimately answer. It is this author's opinion that we will see some changes, possibly drastic, in the future. It is inevitable that more laws will be proposed and passed.

18.7 References

[1]   Akdeniz, Yaman. "Cyber-Rights & Cyber-Liberties (U.K.)."
       <http://www.leeds.ac.uk/law/pgs/yaman/yaman.htm> (28 Aug. 97).

[2]   Bruce, Tom. "Legal Information, Open Models, and Current Practice." June
       1995. <http://www.droit.umontreal.ca/crdp/en/equipes/technologie/
       conferences/dac/bruce/bruce.html> (28 Aug. 1997).

[3]   Burk, Dan L. "Trademarks Along the Infobahn: A First Look at the Emerg-
       ing Law of Cybermarks." *Rich. J. of Law & Technology* 1, April 1995.
       <http://www.urich.edu/~jolt/v1i1/burk.html> (28 Aug. 1997).

[4]   Consortium for Educational Technology for University Systems. Working
       Group on Ownership, Legal Rights of Fair Use and Fair Use of the Joint
       CSU-SUNY-CUNY Joint Committee. "Fair Use of Copyrighted Works."
       1995. <http://www.cetus.org/fairindex.html> (28 Aug. 1997).

[5]   *Computers and Intellectual Property*. Hearings before the Subcommittee on
       Courts, Intellectual Property and the Administration of Justice of the Com-
       mittee on the Judiciary, 101st Congress, First and Second sessions, 1989-
       90.

[6]   Cyberspace Law Center. <http://www.cybersquirrel.com/clc/> (28 Aug.
       1997).

[7]   Lessig, Larry, David Post, and Eugene Volokh. "Cyberspace Law for Non-Lawyers: An Electronic Course." Cyberspace Law Institute, Social Science Electronic Publishing. <http://www.ssrn.com/cyberlaw/> (28 Aug. 1997).

[8]   Digital Future Coalition. "DFC Media Center."
       <http://www.dfc.org/dfc/newstand/media.htm> (28 Aug. 1997).

[9]   Franklin Pierce Law Center. "Intellectual Property Mall Pages."
       <http://www.fplc.edu/ipmall/> (28 Aug. 1997).

[10]   Michael Froomkin. "Law 745: Law and the Internet 1997." Univ. Miami School of Law. Fall 1997. <http://viper.law.miami.edu/~froomkin/sem97/> (28 Aug. 1997).

[11]   International Federation of Library Associations and Institutes. "Information Policy: Copyright and Intellectual Property."
       <http://www.nlc-bnc.ca/ifla/II/cpyright.htm> (28 Aug. 1997).

[12]   Internet Law & Policy Forum. <http://www.ilpf.org/> (28 Aug. 1997).

[13]   LawSource, Inc. "American Law Sources On-Line. (ALSO!)."
       <http://www.lawsource.com/also/> (28 Aug. 1997).

[14]   Lawyers Cooperative Publishing. "The Legal List."
       <http://www.lcp.com/The-Legal-List/TLL-home.html> (28 Aug. 1997).

[15]   Legal Information Institute. Cornell Law School. "Title 17—Copyrights, Section 117." <http://www.law.cornell.edu/uscode/17/117.html> (28 Aug. 1997).

[16]   Lehman, Bruce A., Chairman. *The Report of the Working Group on Intellectual Property Rights*. Intellectual Property and the National Information Infrastructure, Library of Congress. 1995.

[17]   Library of Congress. "U.S. Copyright Office Home Page."
       <http://lcweb.loc.gov/copyright/> (28 Aug. 1997).

[18]   Litman, Jessica. "Revising Copyright Law for the Information Age." Oct. 1995. <http://swissnet.ai.mit.edu/6805/articles/int-prop/litman-revising/revising.html> (28 Aug. 1997).

[19]   *NII Copyright Protection Act of 1995*. Joint Hearings before the Subcommittee on Courts and Intellectual Property of the House Committee on the Judiciary and the Senate Committee on the Judiciary, H.R. 2441 and S. 1284, 104th Congress, First Session, 1995.
       <http://thomas.loc.gov/cgi-bin/query/D?c104:1:./temp/~c104IZOA::>
       (28 Aug. 1997).

[20] *NII Copyright Protection Act of 1995*. Hearings before the Subcommittee on Courts and Intellectual Property of the Committee on the Judiciary (Part 2), H.R. 2441, 104th Congress, Second Session, 1996.

[21] O'Mahoney, Benedict. "The Copyright Website." 1997.
<http://www.benedict.com/homepage.htm> (28 Aug. 1997).

[22] Samuelson, Pamela. "Legally Speaking: The NII Intellectual Property Report." *Communications of the ACM*, 1994.
<http://www.eff.org/pub/GII_NII/Govt_docs/HTML/ipwg_samuelson.html>
(28 Aug. 1997).

[23] UCLA Online Institute for Cyberspace Law and Policy. "Cyberspace Law and Policy." <http://www.gse.ucla.edu/iclp/hp.html> (28 Aug. 1997).

[24] U.S. Congressional Internet Caucus. "U.S. Congress Internet Caucus."
<http://www.house.gov/white/internet_caucus/netcauc.html>   (28   Aug.
1997).

[25] U.S. Department of Commerce. "US Patent and Trademark Office Home Page." <http://www.uspto.gov/> (28 Aug. 1997).

[26] U.S. Patent and Trademark Office. "Intellectual Property and the National Information Infrastructure." 1995.
<http://www.uspto.gov/web/offices/com/doc/ipnii/> (27 Oct. 1996).

[27] Venable Law Firm. *The NII Reporter*. Vol. 1, No. 3, June 25, 1994.
<http://venable.com/oracle/oracle3.htm> (28 Aug. 1997).

[28] Veomett, Elizabeth. "Just Add Watermark." *Business Week*, 1 Sept. 1997, p. 35.

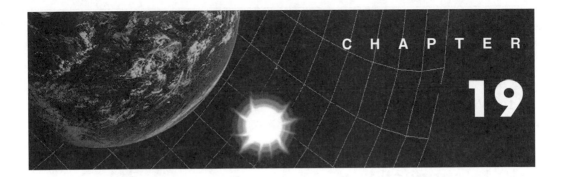

Freedom of Speech

by Mike McGee

The Internet is the latest battleground for the age-old human debate on freedom of speech. And is the battle ever raging! The Internet has been discovered to be a nearly ideal medium for mass populations to express opinion without censorship. But that situation may soon change. Governments around the globe are discussing legislation and implementing censorship of Internet content. Numerous human rights activist groups are countering, waging the war for the free speaker. What started as simply not letting children be subjected to obscene material has blossomed into a classic democratic struggle. This chapter tries to consolidate some of the information and opinions that exist on freedom of speech on the Internet.

The issue of freedom of speech also arises in the context of government restrictions on the export of cryptographic algorithms. This is discussed in Chapter 12.

Chapter Content

1. Introduction
2. Defining Freedom of Speech
3. The Internet: The Ultimate Medium for Freedom of Speech
4. General Opinions about Free Speech on the Internet
5. Let There Be Laws!
6. Opinions on the Communications Decency Act
7. Internet Freedom of Speech and Censorship Attitudes Around the World

19.1 Introduction

Obscenity, indecency, freedom of speech, rating systems, prurient interest, censorship, communications decency: what does it all mean? Specifically, what does it mean for the Web and the Internet as a whole? It means perhaps the greatest democratic movement in history, at least in pure numbers of people voicing their opinion on the matter. Freedom of speech may be the most revered human right in democratic societies. It is adamantly protected in the courts that rule on its behalf. However, it does have limits. As has been noted repeatedly and wisely, freedom of expression is not an absolute right. There are limits, both moral and legal, to which we must adhere.

The basic right to speak one's mind freely goes back to the days of the orating philosophers of ancient times. Advancing on the timeline, a defining moment of free speech came with the separation of the American colonies from Great Britain with the Constitution of the United States. More specifically, the First Amendment of the Bill of Rights granted citizens the ever-after contentious right to freely speak their minds. Today the U.S. continues to lead the rhetorical debate in defining freedom of speech for the Internet. The rest of the world intently watches the evolution of the discussion, both within the courts and the newsgroups. However, the rest of the world is not waiting passively for U.S. guidance. Governments around the world are already imposing restrictions on the Internet, censoring where some deem it unnecessary. Can the global uncensored Internet that is developing be stopped? Should it be censored at all? And if so, how?

These questions and more will be addressed in this chapter. Viewpoints for and against limits on freedom of speech on the Internet will be detailed, especially in terms of law. The most controversial of them all, the Communications Decency Act (CDA) [4], will be dissected. Methods for possible restriction on the Internet will be reviewed. Finally, a vision for the future of freedom of speech on the Internet will be enunciated. This all comes in an attempt to bring forth a clearer understanding on the issue of freedom of speech on the Internet.

19.2 Defining Freedom of Speech

The Bill of Rights First Amendment to the Constitution of the United States of America reads as follows [11]:

"Congress shall make no law respecting an establishment of religion, or prohibiting the free exercise thereof; or abridging the freedom of speech, or of the press; or the right of the people peaceably to assemble, and to petition the government for a redress of grievances."

Once again the important part (for this discussion):

"Congress shall make no law... abridging the freedom of speech..."

The United Nations Universal Declaration of Human Rights in 1948 defined what constitutes human rights for the citizens of the world [2]. Article 19 of that document addresses the right to freedom of expression:

"Everyone has the right to freedom of opinion and expression; this right includes freedom to hold opinions without interference and to seek, receive and impart information and ideas through any media and regardless of frontiers. "

The ability of U.S. citizens to speak freely is a right guaranteed by the document that defined the country over 200 years ago. The Universal Declaration of Human Rights has been written into the constitutions of numerous countries throughout the world and is commonly held as the standard for such issues. By these two major statements, societies around the world to one degree or another have similar provisions for their peoples to speak their mind.

So, theoretically, free speech is guaranteed to many of the world's people. If only it were so simple.

19.3 The Internet: The Ultimate Medium for Free Speech

"Free speech" has often been dictated by the voices of the few, the rich, and the powerful. The voices of the many, the not-quite-so-rich, and the not-nearly-as-powerful have heretofore not been given equal due. The Internet changes this tradition to a debate that allows many voices, many cultures, and many opinions. U.S. Supreme Court Justice John Paul Stevens said that "any person with a phone line can become a town crier with a voice that resonates farther than it could from any soapbox." In the Internet, no single person can dictate universal opinion. The resulting atmosphere is a democracy for the masses by the masses without any inherent control by central authorities. It is no wonder that government leaders and print and broadcast media owners are worried about the Internet.

The Internet has opened doors to freedom of speech that have never been accessible before. The ideal of free speech for all has only tacitly been achieved in the past. Control over communications media has always been in the hands of a few. The hands of the many were left to small rooms, discussion amongst family, friends and maybe neighbors, but oftentimes only to their diaries. Certainly such a grand scale of many speaking to many has never been achieved with such success. The Internet allows the "lowest," least privileged persons to engage in discourse on any subject of their choosing with any of the "highest," most privileged members of society.

Some people in high places agree that the Internet is a unique communication environment [8]:

> "The Internet may fairly be regarded as a never-ending worldwide conversation. The Government may not...interrupt that conversation. As the most participatory form of mass speech yet developed, the Internet deserves the highest protection from governmental intrusion."

The author of that quotation sounds like a staunch supporter of freedom of speech. The quotation above comes from the conclusion of Judge Dalzell, United States District Court for Eastern Pennsylvania, one of the ruling judges that found the Communications Decency Act (CDA) unconstitutional. The CDA is a bill that proposes restrictions on telecommunications in the U.S., including the Internet [4].

19.4 General Opinions about Free Speech on the Internet

At a symposium on free speech in the information age, Parker Barss Donham defined his own edict entitled "Donham's First Law of Censorship." This semi-serious precept states: "Most citizens are implacably opposed to censorship in any form—except censorship of whatever they personally happen to find offensive" [6].

Nothing could more accurately describe the free speech debate than that quotation. Everyone is fundamentally for the right to free speech; the issue resides in the limits to free speech, what the boundaries are, and how we should enforce them.

On one side of the argument are governments protective of their role in society, parents concerned about exposing their children to inappropriate Web pages and chat rooms, and federal agencies attempting to deal with illegal actions like terrorism. On the other side are citizen action groups desiring to protect every ounce of their freedom to speak, individuals concerned about their right to information on the Internet, and organizations seeking to empower the citizens of the earth.

All groups want nothing except what is best from their position. The disagreements deal with the exact methods selected to achieve this goal. The debate can become very heated indeed when attempts are made to enact these methods into law—such as when proponents of free speech and child rights advocates shouted at each other in the rain while the U.S. Supreme Court considered the free speech issue for the first time [5].

19.5 Let There Be Laws!

The legal battle on freedom of speech and its counterpart, censorship, is where the interesting commentary can be found on this issue. Given that freedom of expression is a human right for all persons, how that right is to be legally protected and interpreted has already proven to be a major judicial endeavor. Now that the Internet enters the equation, even more difficulties need to be overcome.

Numerous summaries exist on the development of the legal specifics of freedom of speech. Sifting through the various relevant cases (or accountings of these cases), one begins to think of the axiom that any point of view can be proven with statistics. It seems that the interpretation of past cases involving freedom of expression depends on the person reviewing them. A few excellent summaries have been found that will be highlighted here [10].

The basic legal foundation for freedom of expression was stated earlier in the First Amendment to the United States Constitution and the Universal Declaration of Human Rights by the U.N. It has also been stated that this definition of free expression does not give an individual or group the absolute right to say or express anything without limit. So what are the legal limits to free speech?

One note before continuing: All references to "laws" are attempts to generalize to the international interpretation of freedom of expression and its corollary issues. However, most comments will be based on U.S. court rulings. It is the intent that these generalizations are the common interpretations by governments around the globe (at least the democratic ones).

Generally there are provisions in law for two cases that limit free speech: obscene material and a compelling government interest.

The U.S. Supreme Court ruled that obscene material a) depicts sexual or excretory acts listed in state obscenity statutes, b) depicts those acts in a "patently offensive" manner, appealing to the "prurient interest," as judged by a reasonable person applying the standards of the community, and c) lacks "serious" literary, artistic, social, political, or scientific value. Furthermore, from a global perspective, 104 countries have adopted a 1911 treaty (Protocol to amend the Convention for the Suppression of the Circulation of, and Traffic in, Obscene Publications, concluded at Geneva on 12 September 1923) to prohibit obscenity trafficking.

The other limit to free speech, legally, is when there is a "compelling government interest" to limit free speech rights. This second restriction to freedom of speech has rarely been exercised and rarely been successfully defended in court. However, this has been implemented in limiting "indecent" exposure to children. A supplemental addition to the "compelling governmental interest" statement is that restriction must be exercised through the "least restrictive means possible." This extension is an important weapon to both sides of the freedom-of-speech debate.

All is relatively clear until the term "indecency" is thrown in the mix. The CDA, signed as part of a major telecommunications bill in the U.S. on February 1, 1996 defines indecency as: "any comment, request, suggestion, proposal, image, or other communication that, in context, depicts or describes, in terms patently offensive as measured by contemporary community standards, sexual or excretory activities or organs." Violators could be jailed for two years and fined $250,000 [4]. This definition of indecency and its interpretation in the CDA have been found unconstitutional by a three-judge U.S. Philadelphia federal district court. The case was appealed to the U.S. Supreme Court. In the court's first ruling on free speech on the Internet, it upheld the Philadelphia court's ruling in June 1997 by a vote of 7 to 2, with even the two dissenting judges agreeing that the CDA improperly limited communication between adults. Thus, with this rejection of censorship, the public argument on the true purpose and legal interpretation of "indecency" and the CDA commenced.

19.6 Opinions on the Communications Decency Act

The Supreme Court's ruling was written by Justice John Paul Stevens. He wrote that the desire to protect children "does not justify an unnecessarily broad suppression of speech addressed to adults." The CDA did have a provision to allow sexually oriented material to be put on the Internet if access to it were limited through a credit card number or an adult access code. Stevens wrote that "such systems were prohibitively expensive" [3].

Justice Sandra Day O'Connor, writing for the two dissenting judges, argued that the CDA did not impair free speech of minors, but acknowledged that the CDA was unconstitutional in its impairment of communication between adults.

The Court struggled with the question of whether other forms of communication could be used as a basis for ruling on communication over the Internet. Justice Stephen Breyer, during oral arguments preceding the decision, noted that "the Internet is very much like a telephone." Therefore why would "indecent" conversations between teenagers on the Internet be restricted, but not over the telephone? Further, O'Connor observed the "The Internet is much like a street corner or park." Therefore if children are protected on the Internet, should they be protected from "indecent" language in pubic places [5]?

Some of the arguments for and against the CDA by its supporters and opponents are summarized in Table 19–1. Long opinionated essays already fill many Web servers around the world.

The aftereffects of striking down the CDA vary. One approach, articulated by Sen. Daniel R. Coats, is to simply draft new legislation that uses the Supreme Court ruling as a "blueprint" to create a constitutional bill [7]. Another approach,

Table 19–1 Point-Counterpoint Arguments on the CDA.

Pro CDA	Con CDA
The CDA is solely intended to protect children from "harmful" material on the Internet.	"Harmful" material is already restricted from children by the obscenity laws. And furthermore, there are clear(er) judicial rulings on what is "harmful" to children as opposed to what is indecent. ("Harmful to children" terminology was removed from a draft version of the CDA and replaced with "indecency.")
Courts should rule on what is included in the "indecency" clause and what is not. They argue the court rulings would limit the scope of the "indecency" clause to harmful material exposed to children.	The judges that ruled the CDA unconstitutional argue that the language of the CDA left open the possibility of restricting content that had artistic, educational, and political merit.
The Internet is wide open to children who may unintentionally (or intentionally) come across indecent content.	The Internet is unlike broadcast media such as radio and television in that active use of the Internet must be made to encounter such indecent material.
There will be legal restrictions applied to the Internet in some form if the CDA is ultimately proven unconstitutional by the Supreme Court, just as there have been restrictions applied to every other communication medium that has evolved in the past. Why resist restrictions that will only make the world safer, and better for you and your children?	Unnecessary legislation imposed onto such a dynamic new medium could kill the very heart and soul of the medium itself. Protecting children from the indecent portions of the Internet can be achieved without hindering free speech with unnecessary laws. Why write new laws when proper ones already exist? What happened to the "least restrictive means possible"?

from the U.S. White House, is to find a solution "as powerful for the computer as the V-chip will be for the television and that protects children in ways that are consistent with America's free-speech values" [3]. Such an approach is discussed in Section 19.9. Part of the oral arguments about the CDA presented to the Supreme Court questioned whether the responsibility to protect children lies with parents (e.g., with a V-chip-like mechanism) or with providers of "indecent" material [5]. A third approach is self-regulation, used in the U.K. and described in the next section.

19.7 Internet Freedom of Speech and Censorship Attitudes Around the World

Having looked at freedom of speech in general and in regard to the Internet, and having examined the contentious CDA and reviewed some of the main arguments for and against it, we now make a brief survey of various free speech and Internet censorship attitudes around the world.

A comprehensive review of global Internet censorship can be found in "Silencing the Net" [9]. Some very interesting, and sometimes disturbing, approaches are being taken by governments around the world towards censorship, and consequently, freedom of speech. Information from the review is discussed below.

Asia

The Asian regions are active in general on the Internet, and action on censorship is no less significant.

Singapore openly advocates censorship. It licenses content providers and ISPs, so that they follow guidelines on acceptable content. It has disclosed that it searched user accounts to identify individuals that downloaded sexual content. Controlling access is the primary method of restriction, possible because only three Internet service providers are allowed to exist. Only certain Usenet newsgroups are carried. Singapore actively seeks to stop "misinformation," which includes political discussions not to the government's liking. Even religion is not exempt from the censorship.

Indonesia is a unique country. As of 1996, there were no laws or regulations governing the use of the Internet, even though regulation exists for other communication media. In fact, one news weekly, *Tempo*, was shut down by the government, but then was free to reopen and publish electronically via a Web site.

South Korea bans sexually explicit material, "subversive" information (bomb making, drug related, etc.), and even network access to some software such as computer games. The Information and Communications Ethics Committee of the Data and Communications Ministry has asked local computer networks to block access by users to banned sites.

China is seeking to control all incoming traffic into the country and implement restrictions. The reasoning is to stop any action initiated on the Internet that "hinders public order." Among other actions, Internet service providers must register with the authorities.

Middle East

Around the Middle East similar attitudes exist, plus some extra interesting ideas. The first priority seems to be to restrict sexual content on the Internet. Second, political and religious information is monitored, or outright censored.

In Saudi Arabia, access to the Internet is through a single, government-controlled gateway. Large segments of the population cannot use the Internet because its use is restricted to universities, to those who can pay "exorbitant" fees for access, and to hospitals. The official policy is to protect people from the harmful effects of pornographic material, and whatever other harmful items are on the Internet. Therefore local accounts automatically record what material is accessed by users, and the Ministry of the Interior can inspect these records.

Iran basically has an unregulated Internet; however, one communications company had its service lines cut for unknown reasons. Some private chat lines do maintain their popularity, along with their continued existence.

Iraq also is choosing to vastly limit Internet content. However, as in much of the Middle East, the infrastructure is still limited.

Europe

European Union commissions have proposed limiting sexual content and racist hatred on the net. France has banned specific literary works, particularly those with political leanings. In addition sites with controversial statements (e.g., the Holocaust did not happen) are banned.

In the U.K. there are no explicit Internet laws, yet. They have been using previously written obscenity laws to enforce respectable Internet publishing. Various U.K. organizations are attempting to initiate voluntary regulation of content on the Internet. The belief is that the only alternative to self-regulation is eventual government control.

In Munich, Germany, criticism by a federal prosecutor provoked CompuServe to remove over 200 newsgroups and picture databases. This resulted in embarrassment for the country while doing little to limit access to users, because instructions were circulated on CompuServe explaining how users could still connect to computers that carried the newsgroups. In defense of the officials that tried to impose the ban, they were only trying to comply with existing laws on censorship. This failed ban illustrated the difficulties with regulating the Internet on anything more than a very local level.

Latin and South America

Latin and South America is generally free from Internet law. Cuba, still without more than e-mail, is seeking to implement a full-scale Internet service with restrictions.

Africa

Africa must leap tremendous hurdles on issues of larger magnitude than censorship before Internet freedom of speech becomes important (e.g., infrastructure, poverty, and literacy). But the medium itself may help to propel Africa and its countries to greater heights. Government control and censorship are high in some countries that have managed a small measure of Internet infrastructure.

19.8 Achieving Restrictions on the Internet

It has been stated that the hardest issue to resolve for preserving freedom of expression on the Internet is how to feasibly restrict content. This is not an insignificant issue. For all the rhetorical discussion on the right to free speech and the need to implement restrictions upon certain materials, the actual difficulties of imposing these restrictions are now becoming known.

The crudest approach is to simply eliminate vast sections of the Internet from individual access, which was seen in many of the previous approaches being used around the world. Other relatively simple approaches are to filter e-mail, Web pages, and other Internet content based on keyword searches and pattern-matching algorithms. This broad-based censorship is non-discriminating and generally eliminates far more information than is necessary. Keyword searches have been implemented with search engines by several concerned organizations. In an oversimplification, for every "sex" site found that includes dirty pictures and graphic text, there is one that is about education or science.

Some other novel approaches include monitoring Web sites for content and providing a list of "kid"-approved zones for Internet content. Several large corporations have adopted this approach. One "kid"-approved service provider, as of this writing, included nearly 200,000 different Web pages in its portfolio. This is a labor-intensive effort, however, and the limitations are quite clear. Eventually a sniffer, such as search engines use, might be tailored to sniff sites for "decent" content.

The careful reader may have noticed in Section 19.7 that the U.K. is attempting to self-regulate the Internet without any explicit government involvement. This is the method that freedom-of-expression proponents are touting as the answer. It satisfies the legal "good faith" effort to preclude children's access to undesirable ("indecent") sites and it meets the "least restrictive means possible" clause without needlessly treading on "decent" sites. The development of a self-rating system is most refined in PICS, developed by the World Wide Web Consortium.

19.9 Platform for Internet Content Selection

The V-chip blocks television broadcasts based on ratings applied by various organizations. The Platform for Internet Content Selection (PICS) claims to be better [12]. PICS allows the supervisor of some organization (e.g., family, corporation, business, government) to choose what comes in and what doesn't. PICS operates on a methodology called flexible blocking, based on the supervisor, the recipient, and the context in the given situation. It can replace the current, mostly ineffective censorship methodology in place.

In 1997, several industry leaders announced support for rating and blocking systems. Netscape and Microsoft have pledged to adopt PICS. Several companies offering Internet search engines planned to work together towards adoption of ratings [1].

PICS is not software or hardware; it is a set of technical specifications that allow software and rating services to work together (PICS-compatible filtering software will work with PICS-compatible rating services). There already exists a whole host of PICS compatible software. It works with gopher, ftp, and http, but not e-mail.

PICS provides a common format for labels so that any PICS-compliant software can process any PICS-compliant label. PICS labels describe content. Different rating services can apply the ratings for the labels. The rating services provide the language of the label. Each rating service can choose its own labeling vocabulary. "Coolness" and "Boredom" could be included along with "Sexual Content" or whatever the service chooses to have in its vocabulary. Selection software will decide access, based on the labels and ratings. A simple pictorial example can be found on a set of pages describing PICS [13, 14].

Generally the Web page developers would choose a rating service for their Web sites. The author can, if so desired, devise a unique rating system, but then responsibility is assumed for legal measures ensuring honest representation of the site. Selection software can block any labeling scheme that does not conform to its settings. This would permit access to be restricted to any independently rated material, or any unlabeled documents. In addition, independent organizations can provide third-party ratings where necessary—if the content providers are unwilling to self-rate, or if the content providers have given dishonest ratings (reported by a customer to an unnamed authority).

Selection software can also limit access to specific sites. For example, a science teacher may want students to use only appropriate class Web sites and not to surf. PICS software could be configured to accept only sites with the school-specific label. Hospitals, businesses, and other organizations could use labeling the same way. This access-only-to-certain-sites paradigm, while appearing like another free-speech infringement, already exists legally in many areas. A paper chooses which articles to print and which ads to run. A cable company chooses which stations to carry in its repertoire. A radio talk show host chooses who gets to speak on the air, and for how long. Each of these entities has an owner, who is the "speaker" expressing his free speech (in essence selecting items that are approved and "censoring" items that are disliked). This viewpoint has been upheld in court numerous times.

However, not everyone supports content rating. The American Civil Liberties Union has argued that ratings and blocking based on ratings will, in the long term, limit free speech [1].

The ACLU argues that large organizations that produce content will hire staff to follow ratings guidelines and will be trained in how ratings software works to affix rating labels. However, individuals creating Web pages are unlikely to have the time or training to do these things. Thus content created by individuals effectively will become invisible on a rating-blocked Internet. Therefore every individual will have to rate every item of speech they personally post on the Internet, or risk having it blocked everywhere. Although in theory users can access unrated material, the default for Web browsers will be to use the one or two dominant rating services that will inevitably emerge. Their conclusion: "The Internet will become bland and homogenized."

Another implication, according to the ACLU, is that governments will make it illegal to mis-rate content. Legislation was proposed by Sen. Patty Murray that would make it a crime to mis-rate Internet content [1]. Thus, "We are moving inexorably toward a system that blocks speech simply because it is unrated and makes criminals of those who mis-rate."

Other problems exist with ratings: Chat room conversations will always be unrated. Further, ratings will inadvertently prohibit content from reaching its intended audience. One example cited is a Web site that contains information on safer sex whose intended audience is teenagers. The site might be categorized with pornographic sites by a rating system, thereby blocking access by the intended audience.

The ACLU recommends, instead, five principles for resolving the problem:

- The Internet users should be the primary persons who decide what is suitable for themselves or their children.

- Internet products should not require speakers to rate their own material, or/and products should not by default block unrated material.

- Industry should develop products that maximize individual control over blocking mechanisms.

- "The First Amendment prevents the government from imposing, or from coercing industry into imposing, a mandatory Internet ratings scheme."

- "The First Amendment prevents the government, including public libraries, from mandating the use of user-based blocking software."

19.10 Vision of the Future

Having reviewed material and opinions on the issue of censorship and free speech, this author now offers his own vision of the future for the Internet and freedom of speech.

We need to understand the medium, global society, and existing law concerning free speech before decisions can be made concerning the regulation of the net. The rising answer appears to be self-regulation coupled with passive government monitoring/responding to complaints. As government involvement warrants, existing laws, with judicial bent towards understanding the medium, can be used to ensure that legality and morality exist on the Internet.

Cyberspace is not a federal construction project needing exacting requirements to operate efficiently; it is a globally unowned mental playing field of the masses. It is controlled chaos, and chaos makes it strong. No physical or geographical borders should equate to no intellectual borders, and therefore, to absence of censorship.

And finally, it is important to remember the context of the issue of free speech, and free speech on the Internet. Illiteracy and poverty are the true barriers to free speech that cannot be overcome by ensuring that free speech is legal in the courts. Access to the Internet and speaking freely on it is ultimately limited by local infrastructure (e.g., phone lines, modems, computers) and economy. Until the entire world population can be hooked up, the millions of free-speaking Internet users will still be a very small minority to the billions without the opportunity to speak on the Internet.

19.11 References

[1]   American Civil Liberties Union. "Fahrenheit 451.2: Is Cyberspace Burning?" 1997. <http://www.aclu.org/issues/cyber/burning.html> (5 Sept. 1997).

[2]   Amnesty International. *Universal Declaration of Human Rights*. 1994. <http://www.smartdocs.com/~migre.v/APXIB/declaration.html> (Oct. 1996).

[3]   Associated Press, "Supreme Court Strikes Down Internet Law." *The Roanoke Times*. 27 June 1997, pp. A1–A2.

[4]   U.S. Congress. *Communications Decency Act. 1996*. H.R. 1555 and S. 652. <http://www.eff.org/pub/Alerts/s652_hr1555_96_draft_bill.excerpt>   (Oct. 1996).

[5]   Cox News Service. "Supreme Court Eyes Internet.porn." *The Roanoke Times*. 20 March 1997, pp. A1, A8.

[6]   Donham, P.B. "An Unshackled Internet." 1994.
      <gopher://insight.mcmaster.ca:70/00/org/efc/doc/sfsp/donham> (Oct. 1996).

[7]   Evans, James, "CDA, Act 2: ISPs May Need to Filter." *Internet World*. Oct.
      1997, p. 16.

[8]   FEED. "Decency Reconsidered." 1996.
      <http://www.feedmag.com/96.07cda/96.07cda1.html> (Oct. 1996).

[9]   Human Rights Watch. "Silencing the Net." *Human Rights Watch* 8, No. 2.
      10 May 1996. <http://www.eff.org/~declan/global/g7/hrw.report.051096.txt>
      (5 Sept. 97).

[10] Lappin, T. "The First Amendment, New Media, and the Supreme Court."
      1996.   <http://www.eff.org/pub/Censorship/lappin_obscen_indecen.article>
      (Oct. 1996).

[11] National Archives. "Transcription: The Bill of Rights."
      <http://clio.nara.gov/exhall/charters/billrights/billrights.html> (Oct. 1996).

[12] Resnick, P. and J. Miller. "PICS: Internet Access Controls without Censor-
      ship." *Communications of the ACM* 39 (10), Oct. 1996, pp. 87–93.

[13] World Wide Web Consortium. "Platform for Internet Content Selection."
      <http://www.w3.org/pub/WWW/PICS/> (Nov. 1996).

[14] World Wide Web Consortium. "Platform for Internet Content Selection."
      <http://www.w3.org/pub/WWW/PICS/951030/AV/StartHere.html>   (Oct.
      1996).

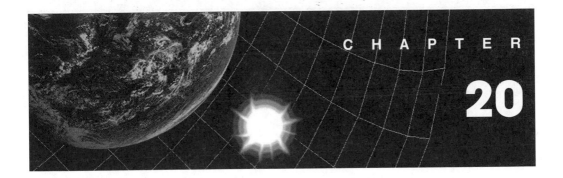

CHAPTER

20

Collaboration

by George Chin Jr.

The Web represents an expansive, pervasive medium for communications. As a communications infrastructure, the Web offers immense opportunities for users to collaborate on activities and work. In this chapter, we examine how users collaborate over the Web. First, we examine the various kinds of computer-mediated communications mechanisms, shared artifact mechanisms, and collaboration frameworks that are required to support collaborative interaction. Next, we survey the Web to identify various forms of collaboration in which Web users participate. We seek to identify the kinds of collaborative activities and work that users perform over a computer network. Finally, we present and examine some of the underlying social and organizational issues associated with computer-supported collaboration.

Chapter Content

357

3. Classes of Collaboration

- Professional Work

  - Meetings and Conferences
  - Collaborative Writing
  - Collaborative Research
  - Remote Equipment Operation / Remote Data Collection and Analysis
  - Project Management

- Education and Training

  - Lectures and Presentations
  - Situated Experience
  - Expert Advice
  - Collaborative Simulations
  - Collaborative Writing
  - Academic Expositions and Fairs

- Entertainment and Social Activities

  - Social Forums
  - Games and Roleplaying
  - Entertainment Reviews
  - Sports and Hobbies
  - Artistic and Literary Pursuits

- Commerce

  - Purchases
  - Reservations and Appointments
  - Expositions and Conventions
  - Advertisements

4. Social and Organizational Issues

- Development of Online Virtual Communities
- Social and Psychological Impact
- Breaking Social and Cultural Barriers
- Construction of Group Knowledge
- Telepresence

5. Future of Collaboration on the Web

6. References

20.1 Introduction

People work together on specific tasks and activities in their day-to-day lives. Whether we're toiling at work, going to school, or shopping at the mall, each of us comes into contact with numerous people on a daily basis. In our interactions with others, we often collaborate to achieve a joint goal or to serve a common purpose. For each of us, our acquisition and evolution of collaborative skills play a crucial part in our social being and development.

Computer systems are intended to support and enhance the activities and tasks that people perform. Unfortunately, most computer systems have been developed with the view that the user performs activities and tasks in isolation. Realistically, people perform many activities and tasks in collaboration with others. The design of computer systems should reflect, support, and enhance the natural ways that people collaborate to accomplish work.

In designing and developing collaborative systems, we must consider how people communicate and work together to accomplish objectives. How does computer technology enhance or degrade people's abilities to collaborate? What are the social and organizational impacts? Collaboration is an important aspect of work activity and it should be studied, supported, and incorporated into the enabling technologies that computer science provides.

Because of its ability to connect users from around the world, the Web provides a logical infrastructure from which collaborative work and activities may be spawned. We should take advantage of the Web's immense reach, connectivity, and popularity to introduce computer-mediated collaborative technology and to facilitate collaborative work among the masses.

To talk coherently about collaboration on the Web, we first need to define a few terms:

- **Collaboration**: the act of participants working as a group to strive towards a common purpose or to achieve a common goal. Implicit in group interaction is multiway communications and mutual awareness among collaborating group members.

- **Computer-Supported Cooperative Work (CSCW)**: "the sharing of software and hardware among groups working together so as to optimize the shared technology for maximum benefit to all those who use or are affected by it" [50].

- **Groupware**: "software designed to be used by more than one person" [50].

In a sense, any interaction over the Web is a form of collaboration. In the general case where a Web user locates and views a Web page, the collaboration is one where a Web developer publishes Web pages for general consumption and a Web user collects and assimilates the information for his/her personal benefit. This typical interaction, however, represents a very weak level of collaboration. The Web publisher and reader do not directly communicate. They are not necessarily cognizant of each other, nor do they necessarily share a common purpose or goal.

Our view of collaboration is one where multiple Web users share common objectives and collectively work to accomplish those objectives. Participants of a collaboration are aware of each other and they directly communicate. Relationships among the participants are clearly elucidated. Each participant has a defined role that carries particular duties, tasks, and expectations.

In this chapter, we examine how users collaborate over the Web. First, we examine the various kinds of computer-mediated communications mechanisms, shared-artifact mechanisms, and collaboration frameworks that are required to support collaborative interaction. Next, we survey the Web to identify various forms of collaboration in which Web users participate. We seek to identify the kinds of collaborative activities and work that users perform over a computer network. Finally, we present and examine some of the underlying social and organizational issues associated with computer-supported collaboration.

20.2 Technologies for Collaboration

Collaboration over the Web is made possible by different kinds of collaborative technology. One kind of collaborative technology is the computer-mediated communications (CMC) mechanism. CMC mechanisms allow users to communicate with each other over a network. Additionally, other software mechanisms have been developed to allow remote users to share objects during the course of their collaborations. Examples of shared objects include topics, documents, equipment, and data. We call these shared objects "shared artifacts." Often, CMC and shared-artifact mechanisms are integrated into larger systems that support specific types of collaboration. We call these systems "collaboration frameworks."

Computer-Mediated Communications Mechanisms

For collaboration to occur over a network, one or more forms of CMC must be available. Groupware applications have been traditionally supported by a number of synchronous and asynchronous CMC mechanisms. Synchronous CMC mechanisms provide a live, spontaneous exchange that occurs in real-time. They require that communicating parties are on the network at the same time. Asynchronous CMC mechanisms defer interaction and allow a time lag between correspondences. Using asynchronous CMC mechanisms, communicating parties are not typically on the network at the same time.

Forms of synchronous communications include

- **Inter-Relay Chat (IRC)**: A text-based CMC mechanism in which multiple users read, write, and post messages. Collaboration appears as a concatenated, chronologically ordered list of messages.

- **Synchronous Audio / Internet Phone**: An audio-based CMC mechanism in which multiple users talk to each other much as they would in a telephone conference call. Similar to real-life, if multiple users speak simultaneously, the received audio transmission is the combined effect of all audible voices.

- **Video Teleconferencing**: An audio- and video-based CMC mechanism in which multiple users communicate with each other much as they would in face-to-face interaction. Video teleconferencing combines a live video feed with a live audio feed. This mechanism is bandwidth-intensive. For reasonable performance, the video image may have to be limited in size, resolution, and/or frame rate.

Forms of asynchronous communications include

- **E-mail**: A text-based CMC mechanism in which a sender delivers a message to one or more receivers. Messages are persistent and may be saved by both sender and receiver.

- **Bulletin Boards**: A text-based CMC mechanism in which multiple users read, write, and post messages. A user may initiate new topics of discussion or reply to an existing topic. A bulletin board saves a topic with all its replies. In this way, the bulletin board maintains a history of discussion over a particular topic.

To a certain extent, CMC models the kinds of communications that occur in our day-to-day lives. For example, video teleconferencing simulates face-to-face interaction, synchronous audio resembles the use of telephones, and e-mail is an electronic version of the physical mail we send and receive on a daily basis. Like their real-life counterparts, synchronous and asynchronous modes of collaboration have varying applications and support varying needs. Both modes are essential for effective collaboration.

All the CMC mechanisms described above have been or are being integrated into Web applications to varying degrees. IRCs, e-mail, and bulletin boards are common communications channels available on the Web. Web-based synchronous audio systems such as CoolTalk [41] and Conference [40] are available but in limited use. Web-based video teleconferencing systems such as

LiveMedia [43] are in the latter stages of development and will be available in the near future.

Shared-Artifact Mechanisms

Collaboration requires a common, shared object to serve as the focus of work and/or discussion. In some cases, the shared object is simply an abstract topic or idea. In other cases, the shared object has a physical manifestation. Examples of shared physical objects are paper documents, equipment, and physical implements used in one's work.

For collaboration to occur over the Web, the shared objects or artifacts must be recognized by collaborating members. Shared artifacts may either be explicitly defined and delivered by the collaborative technology or implicitly maintained by collaborating members. In either case, collaborative technology is purposefully designed to share certain kinds of artifacts. Types of shared artifacts include

- **Topics of Common Interest**: Topics are implicitly shared among Web users. For example, when a user visits a topical IRC or bulletin board, s/he expects and participates in discussion over a particular topic.

- **Web Page Documents**: The viewing of Web pages may be shared among Web users. To support this, remote users must have the ability to navigate and browse through Web pages as a group. Shared Web page mechanisms such as EMSL TeleViewer [69] and EMSL WebTour [37] allow remote users to synchronize their viewing of Web page documents.

- **Physical Objects**: Real-world physical objects may be represented by simulated objects such as those found in virtual worlds. Shared-object mechanisms such as multi-user dungeons (MUDs) and Object-Oriented MUDs (MOOs) allow users to collaboratively create and manipulate virtual objects.

- **Physical Equipment**: The operation of equipment may be shared among operators at remote locations. Shared equipment control mechanisms enable operators at remote sites to collaboratively control a device or a piece of equipment.

- **Data**: Data sets may be shared among Web users. Mechanisms for dynamically sharing and analyzing data include shared electronic whiteboards and shared spreadsheets.

- **Web Applications**: Groupware applications may be shared among Web users. Web users may collaborate to control and execute different types of shared applications. The emergence of application servers such as Lotus Notes [32] and Netscape Suitespot [42] may spur this form of sharing.

With the exception of shared Web applications, all shared-artifact mechanisms described above have migrated onto the Web to varying levels. Shared Web application mechanisms are currently under research at companies such as Netscape [44] and Sun Microsystems [60] and research universities such as Rensselaer Polytechnic Institute [53] and Virginia Tech [66], but such mechanisms will not be available in the near future.

Collaboration Frameworks

A number of collaboration frameworks have been developed from CMC and shared-artifact mechanisms. Collaboration frameworks support specific kinds of high-level activities and tasks. More focused than pure CMC, collaboration frameworks structure and organize interaction in purposeful ways. More generic than groupware applications, they provide infrastructure that may be configured to support many specific applications and domains.

Collaboration frameworks provide an environment where users may discuss and/or manipulate shared artifacts. Some examples of collaboration frameworks include multi-user dungeons (MUDs) and MUDs object-oriented (MOOs), graphical virtual worlds, news and discussion groups, and review and annotation systems.

Multi-User Dungeons (MUDs) and MUDs Object-Oriented (MOOs)

MUDs and MOOs are collaboration frameworks that typically combine an IRC channel with shared objects. A user of a MUD or MOO is called a player. MUDs and MOOs simulate physical, two-dimensional (2D) or three-dimensional (3D) spaces. They may simulate real-world environments such as houses, city blocks, and convention halls, or fantasy environments such as mystical dungeons and space stations. MUDs and MOOs are often referred to as text-based virtual realities. Players imagine and pretend they live in a virtual world. They cast off their true identities and assume the identities of characters of the players' own designs.

Within a MUD or MOO, players move from place to place by issuing text-based commands. They may pick up and examine objects as well as communicate with other players in their travels. More sophisticated players may construct objects of their own and make them accessible to other players.

For the most part, the development of MUDs and MOOs has occurred independent of the Web. More recently, Web developers have constructed Web page front-ends to a variety of MUDs and MOOs. Through these front-ends, players can view graphical representations of the virtual world as well as access descriptive information on objects, players, and the simulated environment. Examples of Web-based MUDs and MOOs include Harper's Tale [22], Frontier City [23], and The Sprawl [55].

Graphical Virtual Worlds

Like MUDs and MOOs, graphical virtual worlds provide a virtual reality environment in which users move from place to place, pick up and examine objects, and communicate with one another. Unlike MUDs and MOOs, however, graphical virtual worlds are highly visual. They simulate the real world by providing a 3D graphical representation of it. Users appear in 3D space as "avatars." An avatar is a fictitious, graphical representation of the user. Typically, a user's avatar is selected from a palette of characters or graphically constructed using supplemented drawing tools.

Web-based graphical virtual worlds combine desktop virtual reality with text-based communications. These virtual worlds are constructed using the Virtual Reality Markup Language (VRML) and may be displayed using a number of Web-based VRML viewers. A common mode of communications in Web-based graphical virtual worlds is through text balloons. A user types a message into a text line and the message appears above the head of his/her graphical manifestation. An example of a VRML graphical virtual world is V_Expo [48].

VRML is an evolving technology on the Web. As a collaboration framework, Web-based graphical virtual worlds are severely limited by their restricted communications capabilities. Lengthy, sophisticated communications and interactions are difficult to conduct using only text balloons. As a result, graphical virtual worlds have limited support for collaboration in its current form.

Newsgroups and Discussion Groups

Web-based newsgroups and discussion groups are rapidly becoming popular. Newsgroups and discussion groups are essentially bulletin boards focused on specific topics. Under this collaboration framework, the shared artifact is simply the topic under discussion.

Prior to the introduction of the Web, Usenet [62] newsgroups were common collaboration mechanisms for sharing information and advice. Usenet is an Internet-based message maintenance and propagation system that allows users to subscribe to specific topical newsgroups and to read and post messages. Users may respond to specific messages by issuing replies. Reply messages are then connected or linked to the original message to create a network or hierarchy of messages. Usenet topics are extensive and cover a variety of issues including sports, recreation, science, sociology, and computers.

To take advantage of Usenet's existing base of collaborative technology and established users, a number of Web interfaces have been developed to access, display, and interact with Usenet newsgroups. Web systems such as HyperNews [38] and NetForum [64] establish a link between Web browsers and the Usenet software. In such hybrid systems, the input and output of the Usenet software are redirected to Web pages and forms.

Apart from Usenet, other kinds of newsgroups and discussion groups have also evolved over the Web. In some cases, a discussion group is maintained by a single individual or organization that collects e-mail messages from group participants and posts the messages on a Web page for others to view. Examples of this type of discussion group include Internet Vet Column [35] and JavaSoft Forum [29]. Other systems such as Newsstand [7] duplicate the hierarchical topical discussion capabilities of Usenet newsgroups but eliminate the overhead of maintaining the Usenet software.

Review and Annotation Systems

Review and annotation systems allow users to review and critique the work of others. Such systems may be used to evaluate the content of a written composition or technical paper. For example, the Virtual Mathematics and Science Fair [67] is a Web site where judges may review and evaluate Web-based science and mathematics papers written by middle and high school students.

Review systems may also be applied to more leisurely activities such as movie-going, dining, and travel. These systems allow users to rate the quality of movies, restaurants, airlines, hotels, etc. and to pass these evaluations on to other prospective customers. As an example, the Internet Movie Database [26] is a Web site where amateur movie critics review and rate various box-office movies.

The forms capability of the Web provides a natural way for users to attach ratings, scores, and comments to a particular piece of work. To conduct reviews over the Web, however, the work must somehow be created, transferred, represented, and/or reproduced in the form of a Web page. Thus, the medium of the work must be one that is supported by the Web. More specifically, the work must be in the form of supported Web multimedia types which include text, image, audio, video, and 3D virtual reality. Written work is easily transferred onto Web pages. Other kinds of work may be more problematic.

Web-based review and annotation systems allow users to review and critique Web documents. As part of the review process, reviewers may wish to annotate a Web document by attaching comments to it. To support this, some Web-based review systems are realized in the form of a bulletin board where each thread of discussion is comprised of a source Web document followed by reviewers' comments.

As discussed, the granularity of a Web-based review is at the level of the Web page. In many cases, the reviewer needs greater capability to identify and highlight specific portions of a Web page. For example, the reviewer may wish to reference and comment on a specific passage of the text or a specific area of a diagram. Most existing annotation systems cannot support this level of detail. As Web programmers are given greater control over the user interface with evolving features such as Java, we expect to see the capabilities and sophistication of Web-based review and annotation systems dramatically improve.

20.3 Classes of Collaboration

Collaboration is impacted by the roles that participants assume. Different kinds of roles and relationships will inherently induce different forms of collaboration. For example, the collaboration between a teacher and a student is much different than that between a salesperson and a customer.

Over the Web, a multitude of roles and relationships exist. Some of the most common relationships are:

- **Worker–Worker:** Workers collaborate to perform tasks associated with their professions. Ideally, workers partake in peer collaboration where each worker has the same power and ability to perform the work and to effect change.

- **Manager–Worker:** A manager and worker also collaborate to perform work. The collaboration, however, is supervisory rather than peer. The manager directs the actions and activities of the worker. Conversely, the worker takes direction from and performs under the supervision of the manager.

- **Student–Student:** Students collaborate to collectively construct knowledge and understanding. Ideally, students partake in peer collaboration where each student has the same power and ability to enter into discussion and to perform learning activities.

- **Teacher–Student:** A teacher and student collaborate to transfer knowledge. The teacher functions as the keeper or facilitator of the knowledge. S/he transfers the knowledge through lecture, instruction, and/or explanation. The student functions as the assimilator of knowledge. S/he captures knowledge by listening and seeks understanding and clarification through inquiry.

- **Hobbyist–Hobbyist:** Hobbyists share information and advice surrounding specific hobbies. A hobbyist wishes to share his/her experiences with others as well as solicit the expertise of other hobbyists.

- **Friend–Friend:** Interaction among friends is usually in the form of informal, personal conversation. The purpose of collaboration is to merely apprise one another of daily events and current feelings.

- **Courter–Courted:** Some collaborations may be best described as courting rituals where participants pursue romantic relationships. Such collaboration is often accompanied by signs of showboating, flirting, and "smooth-talking."

- **Salesperson–Customer:** Salesperson and customer collaborate to perform a business transaction. The salesperson provides product information and tries to persuade a sale. The customer assimilates information, compares features, and decides whether to buy the product.

- **Consumer–Consumer:** Consumers share information and advice on products. A consumer wishes to share his/her product experiences with others as well as solicit the opinions of other consumers.

Looking at the roles and relationships defined above, we may categorize them along general classes of collaboration that occur over the Web. Worker-worker and manager-worker relationships identify types of collaboration occurring in professional work. Student-student and student-teacher relationships occur in education and training. Hobbyist-hobbyist, friend-friend, and courter-courted relationships occur in entertainment and social activities. Salesperson-customer and consumer-consumer relationships occur in commerce.

The four collaboration classes that have emerged are professional work, education and training, entertainment and social activities, and commerce. As exemplified by the differing roles and relationships, these four classes represent distinctive forms of collaboration with unique goals, roles, relationships, interactions, requirements, and demands.

Professional Work

The most common application of collaborative technology is to support group activities in professional work. Various commercial companies such as Lotus Development Corporation [31] and Oracle Corporation [49] are in the business of developing corporate groupware solutions. Unfortunately, the Web is slow in being recognized and realized as a viable delivery vehicle for groupware applications. Consequently, the amount of collaboration over the Web in support of professional work is currently quite limited.

Nevertheless, Netscape Communications Corporation is pushing forward with a Web-based groupware suite known as Suitespot [42]. As the availability of professional groupware increases over the Web, corporations may find the Web to be a reasonable alternative to proprietary groupware suites that execute outside of the Web.

With the increasing capabilities and capacity of the Web to support collaboration, many existing professional groupware tools will eventually migrate onto the Web. Of course, some high-bandwidth groupware tools cannot fully migrate until the Internet is able to sustain greater bandwidths. Nevertheless, lower-bandwidth, professional groupware tools are already finding their way onto the Web today. We examine five different classes of Web-based groupware applications that professionals use to collaborate on their work. These five classes are meetings and conferences, collaborative writing, collaborative research, remote equipment operation/remote data collection and analysis, and project management.

Meetings and Conferences

A large portion of the typical workday of a professional is spent in meetings. Meetings inherently portray collaborative activities as workers discuss issues, organize activities, and make decisions. Web support for meetings may allow workers to hold and conduct meetings in the convenience of their individual offices. The minimum requirements for supporting virtual meetings are a multi-way communications channel and possibly a shared document system for distributing information. Examples of Web-based meeting and conferencing applications include:

- The wOrlds Project, an office workplace metaphor where workers may "warp" from "locale" to "locale" to meet and collaborate with other workers. A locale may be another employee's virtual office, a conference room, or simply a location where a particular project resides. The application allows a worker to gather specific documents and applications into his/her briefcase and to carry his briefcase from locale to locale. All workers within a locale have shared access to all applications and documents that are present at that locale [27].

- NetMeeting, a collaborative software suite built around a synchronous Internet phone. Workers participate in conference calls through their computers. During a conference call, workers may share Microsoft applications, pass data back and forth using an electronic whiteboard, and browse Web pages using Internet Explorer. Microsoft calls this form of collaboration "data conferencing" [33].

Collaborative Writing

A typical product of most office-based occupations is a written document or report. Often, such documents are collaboratively developed by a group of writers. When developing a physical report, writers often have difficulties in partitioning the work, since they must share a single, physical document. Collaboration is often asynchronous as writers take turns developing and editing the shared document. This is a case where groupware may provide significant benefit. Collaborative writing tools will allow writers to simultaneously work on different portions of the same document and/or to review and critique the written works of others. Writers are no longer restricted by the physical limitations of the shared document. Examples of Web-based collaborative writing tools include:

- Storyspace, a hypertext writing environment that allows multiple writers to compose different sections of the same document. Individual sections are referenced through hypertext links. Storyspace provides authors and editors with "multiple ways of viewing and mapping the hypertext, to see both the hierarchical structure and the links [13].

- CommonSpace, which supports the collaborative review of written documents. Reviewers critique written work by typing annotations along the borders of an electronic document or by attaching voice annotations to specific areas of the document. Furthermore, writer and reviewer may communicate in real-time using IRC while the document is being reviewed [56].

Collaborative Research

Time and distance often impede scientists and researchers from participating in joint research efforts. The Web potentially offers a pervasive medium that will allow researchers at different locations to collaborate on research activities. From sharing results to jointly running experiments, the Web currently offers or will soon offer the communications and shared application tools that researchers need to conduct research from geographically dispersed sites. An example of a collaborative research effort is:

- The EMSL Collaboratory, which allows environmental and molecular scientists to collaborate on research activities. Scientists may give on-line presentations to other researchers at remote locations using synchronous Web browsers. Furthermore, researchers may collaboratively analyze computer models and simulations by sharing and annotating snapshots of their computer screen [36].

Remote Equipment Operation/Remote Data Collection and Analysis

Video teleconferencing on the Web may be applied to support the collaborative, remote operation of physical equipment. Collaboration may occur in various forms. One possible collaboration would be between an operator at a remote site and a technician at the location of the equipment. The operator would remotely view the equipment and direct the technician in its operation. Another possible form of collaboration would have multiple operators at remote sites. The operators would collaborate to jointly operate the shared equipment. In many cases, the purpose of operating remote equipment is to collect data. Thus, collaboration may also occur in the form of shared data collection and analysis. An example of collaborative remote equipment operation and shared data collection and analysis is:

- LabSpace, a current research effort aimed towards supporting the collaborative operation of an analytic electron microscope. The project will provide a MOO-based environment where microscopists may meet, converse, organize research, and conduct experiments [59].

Project Management

Managing a project is a collaborative endeavor among a manager and his/her staff members. In any management situation, the manager ultimately controls the work and makes the crucial decisions. Good managers, however, elicit and consider input and feedback from his/her staff members. A manager and his/her staff members collaborate along the roles of a supervisor and his/her subordinates. Project management tools aim to facilitate these kinds of interaction.

Collectively, the manager and staff members must negotiate tasks and deadlines, organize activities and work, and evaluate progress. Commercial project management software such as Microsoft Project [34] allows managers to develop PERT charts, Gantt charts, and schedules to organize work. Most commercial project management systems, however, are not generally accessible by staff members. By providing project management support over the Web, both manager and staff members are better able to function in their respective roles and to contribute to the organization and management of the project.

Education and Training

The potential for the Web to serve as an information and collaboration infrastructure for education and training is tremendous (see Chapter 21). Large educational research projects such as the Networked Infrastructure for Education [39] program and the Collaborative Visualization [46] project are looking closely at the Web as an effective means towards delivering educational content and materials. Collaboration skills are important for students to obtain—particularly in science fields where students commonly perform experiments in working groups. We examine six different forms of education and training in which Web users collaborate. These are lectures and presentations, situated experience, expert advice, collaborative simulations, collaborative writing, and academic expositions and fairs.

Lectures and Presentations

In today's classroom, the most common teaching style is didactic teaching. The goal of didactic teaching is to transfer knowledge from the teacher to the student. The teacher acts as the keeper and disseminator of knowledge while the student acts as the assimilator of knowledge. Under this traditional form of pedagogy, the teacher typically gives lectures to relay and reinforce concepts and facts. The student learns by listening and absorbing information. Although the role of the student appears somewhat passive in didactic teaching, communication does flow in both directions between the teacher and student. For example, the teacher may call on students to give answers to questions. Alternatively, students may seek clarification from the teacher by asking questions of their own. A number of Web-based applications have been developed to support this kind of lecture-style approach. Examples of such Web-based applications include:

- KMi Stadium, which supports a collaborative lecture-based forum where teachers and experts give presentations. Students may ask questions by sending e-mail which is received by the speaker during the course of the presentation. During the presentation, students see a synchronized slide show and listen to real-time audio of the speaker. KMi Stadium attempts to mimic the mood and environment of a particular setting by augmenting the audio with sounds of clapping, laughing, shouting, and whispering. The simulated setting may either be a classroom, an auditorium, or a stadium [14].

- Virtual Summer School, which allows college students to remotely attend various cognitive psychology courses. The student selects a building and room from a graphical campus map. When attending class, the student may listen to a lecture from the professor and ask questions over a synchronous audio or video teleconferencing link [15].

- Diversity University, which represents another virtual college campus in which college students attend various classes. Unlike Virtual Summer School, Diversity University is self-contained within a MOO. Consequently, communications among students and teachers are strictly text-based via IRC [12].

Situated Experience

In contrast to didactic teaching, some educators believe that students learn best when they are engaged in activity. Rather than sitting passively and listening to a lecture, the student should learn by doing. Student engagement and hands-on experience represent the basis of a pedagogical approach known as "active learning." Web-based applications may support collaborative active learning by providing students a shared, situated experience. Collectively, students, teachers, and professionals may collaborate to experience a unique, once-in-a-lifetime encounter (e.g., solar eclipse, appearance of comet) or to relive a past historical event. Students are engaged in the activity since they take part as participants in the authentic or simulated experience. Examples of Web-based situated experience applications include:

- Telegarden, which allows students to collaboratively tend a living garden over the Web. Through Telegarden, users control a robot arm that can plant seeds, water plants, and monitor growth. Students are asked to relive the "post-nomadic" era where human survival depended on the ability of people to work together to grow and harvest food [20].

- The Mercury Project, which allows students to perform remote excavation of an archaeological dig. Students collaboratively control the movements and operations of a mobile robot. The robot is placed in a sand-filled terrarium where replica artifacts are buried. Students collaborate in attempts to find and excavate hidden artifacts [21].

- Project LINK, a collaborative exercise among atmospheric scientists and K-12 teachers and students. Together, scientists, teachers, and students performed experiments while flying at high altitudes aboard NASA's Kuiper Airborne Observatory airplane. Via an Internet video link, the airborne crew compared the results of their experiments with those of other scientists, teachers, and students who performed the same set of experiments on the ground [16].

- Night of the Comet, a collaborative project among NASA astronomers and K-12 teachers and students. The goal of the collaborative effort was to trace the path of the comet Hyakutake as it travelled past the Earth. Students were to keep an eye towards the sky and post sightings of the comet through a Web form. Students were encouraged to take photographs of the comet and to submit these as well. NASA collected the sightings and traced the path of the comet on a Web page [24].

- Oregon Trail On-line, a collaborative simulation that relives Lewis and Clark's historical journey from Missouri to Oregon. Students participate in the simulation as members of a wagon train. They vote on issues such as how much food to ration, what routes to take, and how to handle emergencies and unanticipated events. Majority vote determines course of action for the wagon train. Objectives for students in the simulation are to make wise, informed decisions and to safely arrive in Oregon [57].

Expert Advice

Didactic and active learning represent teaching approaches that promote continuous, long-term learning. In some instances of education and training, students may need shorter-term collaboration to seek specific information or advice. In such cases, the collaboration is often just a one-time occurrence. Examples of Web-based applications that are designed to provide professional or expert advice include:

- The Internet Vet Column, which allows pet owners to e-mail in questions concerning their pets. A professional veterinarian selects some questions and post answers and advice on a Web page [35].

- JavaSoft Forum, which allows students and researchers to ask renown computer scientists technical questions. Questions are submitted via e-mail. The computer science expert selects some questions and post answers and advice on a Web page [29].

- NetworkTA, which allows college physics students to ask their teaching assistant questions on specific homework assignments. Questions and answers are submitted to a bulletin board for all to see [28].

Collaborative Simulations

A computer-based simulation is one kind of educational tool that teachers employ to teach specific concepts and lessons. Most commercially-available simulations are not inherently collaborative. Students cannot manipulate the same simulation from different computers. The main drawback of such stand-alone simulations is that students fail to experience group interactions and to develop collaborative skills typically associated with more traditional learning activities such as with physical group experiments. Since the development of social and group skills is a vital part of a student's education and evolution, we desire collaborative simulations that allow students to practice and reinforce these collaborative skills. Examples of research projects that aim to study and develop collaborative simulations include:

- Collaborative Visualization (CoVis), a suite of scientific visualization tools that allow K-12 science students to collaboratively construct visualization models. Scientific visualization may be described as the graphical simulation of physical and natural processes [46].

- Learning in Networked Communities (LiNC), a research effort with the goal of developing a collaborative learning environment for K-12 science education. One feature of this environment is support for collaborative physics simulations that may be shared among students over the Web [2].

Collaborative Writing

Students working in groups are often required to collaborate on the composition of a group report. When developing a written report, students often have difficulties in partitioning the work, since they must share a single, physical document. Often, one student will develop the entire report while the other group members direct or observe. Unfortunately, some students will become disengaged because they do not actively participate in the writing. As a result, students may not develop comparable writing skills.

Collaborative writing is an area where groupware may provide significant benefit. Collaborative writing tools will allow students to simultaneously work on different portions of the same document and/or to review and critique the written works of others. Students are no longer restricted by the physical limitations of the shared document.

Various software systems are available for collaborative writing over the Web. For examples of Web-based, collaborative writing systems, see page 368.

Academic Expositions and Fairs

Academic fairs and expositions provide a unique form of collaboration among students, teachers, and parents. In this collaboration, students develop and display their work for others to see, teachers review, evaluate, and judge students' contributions, and parents keep abreast of the academic efforts and progress of their children. Collaboration is inherently asynchronous since students must develop the work first before teachers may judge students' contributions, and teachers typically evaluate and award prizes before the student contributions are made available to parents.

On the Web, some virtual academic fairs and expositions have been held. Often, student contributions at these fairs take advantage of the capabilities of the Web and are delivered as multimedia presentations. Virtual fairs may additionally be supported by review systems that allow teachers to evaluate and comment on student contributions, and by MUDs and MOOs that allow teachers and parents to navigate among the student presentations. An example of a Web-based academic fair is:

- The Virtual Mathematics and Science Fair, a MOO which simulates a middle and high school academic fair. The fair takes place in a school gymnasium. Students submit papers on various science and mathematics topics. Judges review and evaluate the papers from within the MOO and prizes are awarded to the highest-rated papers. [64]

Entertainment and Social Activities

Collaboration for the purpose of entertainment and/or social activity is probably the most popular form of collaboration occurring over the Web. According to a Web user survey [19], a majority of users access the Web from home rather than school or work. Thus, users may often access the Web during their hours of free time. We examine five different forms of entertainment and social activities in which Web users collaborate. These are social forums, games and roleplaying, entertainment reviews, sports and hobbies, and artistic and literary pursuits.

Social Forums

Many Web sites are organized as social forums where users come to meet and converse with others. Collaboration occurs not to perform group work, but rather to establish and develop personal relationships with other users. Some interaction appears in the form of flirting or courting. Most often, interaction occurs in the form of friendly conversation.

Today, most social interaction on the Web occurs over text-based IRC channels. The use of strictly text-based communications eliminates many of the social barriers that are present in face-to-face interaction [4]. The anonymity of text-based communications draws many introverts into social interactions and situations [30].

MUDs and MOOs are particularly well suited to support social functions. Players move from room to room looking for good conversation or move to more private rooms to hold more personal dialogues. Examples of Web-based social forums include:

- The Sprawl, a social MOO which is set in the downtown area of a large city. Players gather at different downtown locations such as Webster's Bar and URL, the Skyway Hotel, the Chiba Zoo, and the Chiba Museum of Natural History. Players who wish to meet many people may frequent the Visitors' Center, which tends to draw a large crowd. Alternatively, couples who want privacy may meet at more secluded locations such as the Night Flight Cafe [55].

- MOOtiny is yet another social MOO which is set on a group of small islands. Players move from island to island in search of companionship and conversation [63].

Games and Roleplaying

Some Web users collaborate to play games. As in video games, multiple players may compete against each other or work together to score the highest number of points. In either case, players must collaborate to set up and execute the shared game. Compared to home video and personal computer games, games played over the Web are far less interactive. Developing interactive Web-based games is difficult because current Web technology is generally stateless, provides minimal graphics, and supports a low level of interactivity. Nevertheless, as Internet bandwidth increases and Web technology further evolves, we will likely see an explosion in the number and kinds of interactive games available over the Web. Examples of current Web-based, interactive games include the following:

- Ppong is a version of the interactive game of "Pong" where players paddle a digital ball back and forth across a window [3].

- The Bingo Zone allows multiple Web users to play Bingo. Each player is given a set of Bingo cards on a Web form. Balls are drawn every twenty seconds. Players intermittently reload their screens to view the newly-drawn balls. When a new ball appears, players check off the corresponding cells of their Bingo cards. If a player gets a "Bingo," s/he hits a "Bingo" button on his/her form, and all other players are notified of the winner [45].

Other less resource-demanding forms of game playing such as Multi-User Simulated Environments (MUSEs) are available on the Web. MUSEs are thematic MUDs in which players act out fictitious characters that live on virtual, fantasy worlds. Commonly, a MUSE virtual world is derived from the setting of a book, movie, or television series. Examples of Web-based MUSES include the following:

- TrekMUSE is based on the "Star Trek" television series. Players take on various characters that have been developed on the television show or develop new characters that are consistent with the Star Trek setting. Together, TrekMUSE players participate in virtual space missions [9].

- Harper's Tale is another MUSE which takes place on a fictitious fantasy world known as "Pern." The MUSE is based on the "Dragonriders of Pern" novels written by Anne McCaffrey. In Harper's Tale, players act out various characters from McCaffrey's novels [22].

- Frontier City is a futuristic MUSE in which players work together to build a space colony in the far reaches of space [23].

Entertainment Reviews

Web users often collaborate to share opinions and reviews of various forms of entertainment such as movies, music, books, and dining. Some entertainment Web sites are dedicated as repositories or databases from which Web critics may add and edit review information. Reviews are then accessed by other Web users who may be looking for a video to rent, a compact disc to buy, a book to read, a restaurant at which to dine, or information for some other entertainment activity. The collaboration among Web users is essentially one of information pooling and sharing. Examples of Web-based entertainment review systems include:

- The Internet Movie Database, which contains movie reviews composed entirely by Web moviegoers. Among other capabilities, moviegoers rate movies from one to ten, submit personal reviews, submit descriptions of plots, and identify cast members. In essence, moviegoers collaborate to evaluate the quality and to supply comprehensive reviews of different box-office movies [26].

- rec.arts.movies.lists+surveys, rec.music.reviews, rec.arts.books.reviews, and rec.food.restaurants, all of which are Usenet newsgroups intended to collect and disseminate reviews of movies, musics, books, and restaurants. Review newsgroups are also available for many other forms of entertainment.

Sports and Hobbies

Sports and hobbies are also popular topics of collaboration over the Web. Sports fanatics collaborate to hold discussions over sports events, teams, and players. Conversations appear in various forms. For example, sports fanatics may root for their favorite teams, agitate the supporters of rival teams, debate over who are the best players and coaches, and compare team and player statistics. Reflecting the competitive nature of sports, discussions among sports fanatics tend to have competitive overtones.

Unlike sports fanatics, hobbyists collaborate towards more constructive ends. Hobbyists enter into discussions to provide and gather advice on their hobbies. Collaboration is more cooperative than competitive. Hobbyists collaborate to better their own individual knowledge and abilities.

The most common collaboration framework for sports and hobbies is a newsgroup or discussion group. Prior to the Web, Usenet provided numerous newsgroups representing a large variety of sports and hobbies. These Usenet newsgroups are also available through the Web today. Alternatively, IRC lines are also becoming a popular medium for discussing sports and hobbies. IRC lines allow the discussion to be more spontaneous and dynamic, but users have more difficulties in following a line of discussion or finding and gathering all related information on an ongoing topic. Examples of Web-based sports and hobby discussion groups are the following:

- ESPNET SportsZone[1] provides a set of IRC lines dedicated to the discussion of specific collegiate and professional sports such as NCAA college basketball,[2] NCAA college football,[3] National Basketball Association,[4] National Football League,[5] and Major League Baseball[6] [58].

- rec.sport.basketball.college, and rec.sport.football.college are Usenet newsgroups that have been established for group discussions of collegiate basketball and football. rec.sport.baseball, rec.sport.basketball.pro, and rec.sport.football.pro are Usenet newsgroups covering professional baseball, basketball, and football. Numerous other Usenet newsgroups are also available for a variety of different sports.

- rec.antiques, rec.gardens, rec.juggling, rec.kites, rec.skydiving are Usenet newsgroups for discussions on the hobbies of antique collecting, gardening, juggling, kite-flying, and skydiving.

[1] http://espnet.sportszone.com/

[2] http://chat-espnet.sportszone.com/chat/chat.dll?room=ncb1

[3] http://chat-espnet.sportszone.com/chat/chat.dll?room=ncf1

[4] http://chat-espnet.sportszone.com/chat/chat.dll?room=nba

[5] http://chat-espnet.sportszone.com/chat/chat.dll?room=nfl1

[6] http://chat-espnet.sportszone.com/chat/chat.dll?room=mlb

Artistic and Literary Pursuits

The computer is a modern medium for artistic and literary expression. Forms of computer art and literature are still largely experimental, as the computer art and literature culture has yet to fully take shape. Nevertheless, many writers and artists are employing the Web as a way to expose their talents to others and to collaborate on joint artistic and literary ventures.A number of Web sites are dedicated to collaborative artistic and/or literary pursuits. Through these Web sites, Web writers and artists collaborate to develop computer-based stories, music, and art. In another mode of collaboration, writers and artists display their works in virtual anthologies and galleries for others to see. Art and literary critics then visit these virtual sites to browse and critique the work. Examples of collaborative art and literature Web sites include:

- World Fiction is a Web site in which Web cartoonists work together to develop a comic strip. A cartoonist may draw cartoons, build frames, and insert frames into one of several ongoing comic strips. Furthermore, a cartoon critic may review and critique portions of a comic strip developed by others [47].

- Interactive Genetic Art supports the collaborative construction of genetic art. The Web site displays ten different images produced by varying the parameters to a genetic algorithm. The genetic algorithm is applied to define the RGB color values of each pixel of an image. Web art critics visiting this site vote for the image they like best. Votes are tallied and the parameters to the genetic algorithm are adjusted to reflect the preferences of voters. Ten new images are then constructed and subjected to additional votes [68].

- Interactive Genetic Music supports the collaborative construction of genetic music. A genetic algorithm is applied to define musical attributes such as note length, amplitude, frequency, duration, and spacing between notes [51].

- WAXWeb is a collaborative moviemaking venture where Web cinematographers jointly develop the script for a movie entitled, "WAX or the Discovery of Television among the Bees." Cinematographers provide snapshots of scenes as well as develop narration and dialogue for various passages of the script [6].

- The Global Clock Project is a collaborative effort in rendering an artistic image from natural phenomena. In this project, participants are recruited from all over the world. Each participant uses a physical, light-detecting device to determine the intensity level of the natural light at his/her location. The intensity values for all locations are collected to produce an image which is displayed on a Web page. The image represents an instantaneous, evolving art form that maps onto the naturally-changing physical characteristics of the Earth [18].

- Picasso and Portraiture is a virtual art gallery containing many digitized images of Picasso's paintings. Picasso's works of art are divided along several themes including self-portraits, family, friends, women, and children. The Web site also provides a calendar of events which lists dates and locations of various Picasso exhibits [8].

Commerce

One area that has great potential for an explosion on the Web is commerce (see Chapter 13). Many efforts are underway towards establishing the Web as a medium for buying and selling services and products. The emergence of security and encryption mechanisms (see Chapter 12) makes the Web a viable and safe medium for performing business transactions. In this section, we examine four different forms of Web-based applications that salespeople and customers employ to conduct business transactions. These are purchases, reservations and appointments, expositions and conventions, and advertisements.

Purchases

The most common form of a business transaction over the Web is the purchase of a product or service. In most cases, the purchase is a physical product that is delivered to the home of the customer. In other cases, the purchase is an electronic product or service that may be downloaded to the customer's computer. Common forms of electronic products or services include computer software, electronic documents, and subscription services to Internet magazines. The most common form of payment is through credit cards, although a number of Internet payment systems are actively being researched (see Chapter 13).

The typical collaboration that occurs is one between a customer who makes a purchase and a purchasing agent who eventually retrieves and processes the order. The collaboration is inherently asynchronous. In more automated systems, the purchasing agent may be replaced with a direct link to an order database which processes and stores orders. Examples of Web-based purchasing applications include the following:

- Computer Mall provides access to a number of personal computer mail order companies where a customer may purchase computer equipment directly from a Web page [10].

- ANET Virtual Mall is an Internet directory service that provides access to a variety of companies. Products available at the virtual mall cover everything from apparel to pets to automotive [1].

Reservations and Appointments

Another form of a collaborative business transaction is a Web-based reservation system. Travellers employ such systems to make travel accommodations. Typical events or accommodations that may be reserved include airline reservations, car rentals, and hotel reservations.

The typical collaboration that occurs is one between a traveller who makes a reservation and a reservation clerk who eventually retrieves and documents the reservation. The collaboration is inherently asynchronous. In more automated systems, the reservation clerk may be replaced with a direct link to a reservation database which processes and stores reservations. Examples of Web-based reservation systems include:

- Travelocity, a Web-based travel agency that allows passengers to make on-line airline reservations. The site also provides access to an IRC line where vacationers can communicate with travel professionals and special-event organizers [54].

- Best Day Mexico Travel Reservations, a Web-based travel agency that allows vacationers to make on-line hotel reservations [5].

Expositions and Conventions

Expositions and conventions are events where salespeople and companies display their wares. Customers attend expositions to gain exposure to a diverse range of products. By having convenient access to competing products, customers may easily compare product features. Similarly, virtual expositions and conventions on the Web serve these same purposes. Web-based expositions and conventions, however, are only collaborative if salespeople and customers directly interact. Examples of Web-based expositions include:

- V_Expo, a 3D virtual trade show developed using VRML. Customers may move from booth to booth and interact with different salespeople and customers. People in the virtual trade show appear as avatars. To communicate, a trade show participant types in a message and the message appears in 3D space as a balloon above his/her avatar's head [48].

- Virtual Campus, an academic technology trade show sponsored by Sun Microsystems. The trade show is organized around a graphical virtual campus in which customers can "fly" in 3D space from building to building. The site is developed using VRML. Each building houses information on an academic technology topic such as distance learning, K-12 teaching, scientific computing, administration, and high-performance computing. While in the Virtual Campus, customers may join IRC sessions with academic technology experts, execute product demos, and run movies or slide shows [61].

Advertisements

Commercial advertisements are common on the Web today. Many Web page publishers recoup their publishing costs by selling advertisement space to other companies. Typically, an advertisement is comprised of a banner image promoting a product or service. The image is usually linked to another site which has more extensive information on the product and company. Although Web-based advertising represents a somewhat impoverished level of interaction between a potential customer and a company, an advertisement may be a precursor to more extensive collaboration if it attracts interest and if users initiate further contact with the company to obtain additional information or to purchase a product.

- ESPN Sportszone [58], Infoseek [25], and USA Today [65] are all Web sites that sell advertisement space to outside companies.

20.4 Social and Organizational Issues

Social and organizational issues are active areas of current research among the CSCW community. Collaboration is largely a social and organizational endeavor. Understanding these issues may aid us in discovering more effective and efficient forms of collaboration. It may also lead us to better understand the underlying context in which work and collaboration take place. "For computer systems to be useful, they must be integrated within an existing network of humans and other technological artifacts" [50].

The social and organizational issues presented in this section are not exclusive to the Web. In fact, their origins precede the Web. Yet, as collaborative applications and activities grow on the Web, these social and organizational issues will become increasingly relevant and important to study. Social and organizational issues are sources of ongoing debate in CSCW. The aim of this section is to survey the kinds of social and organizational issues that collaborative technology has instigated, but not to make judgments or draw conclusions on these issues.

Development of Online Virtual Communities

In cases where the same members of a group consistently collaborate over time, members may perceive the emergence of an online, virtual community. Over time, a member develops a strong sense of loyalty and commitment to the computer-mediated group, much as a community member develops loyalties and commitments to real-world associations such as neighbors, friends, and workmates. Developing a sense of community further engages the member into the collaborative activity and shifts the focus of the collaboration away from personal agendas and toward the benefits to the community as a whole.

As an example of community behavior, Dibbell describes an incident where a MUD player repeatedly made obscene gestures to other members of the MUD

[11]. After weeks of being harassed, members of the MUD called an online town meeting to discuss how to deal with the obscene player. During this town meeting, members discussed the culprit's behavior, victims' individual feelings, and appropriate forms of punishment. The final verdict from the meeting had the obscene player banished from the MUD.

The actions of the MUD members portray a deep sense of community. The MUD as a whole developed moral and ethical policies and took action against one of its members. In the process, the MUD community addressed deep-seated social issues of law, order, and ethical forms of conduct. Collaboration was carried out and policies were enacted for the good of the community.

A sense of community evolves naturally from the effects of group dynamics. Yet, this sense may be induced or promoted through computer mediation. How important is it that collaborative applications establish a sense of community? Does a sense of community improve the work produced? If so, in what ways? In what ways do virtual communities compare to real-world, physical communities?

Social and Psychological Impact

CMC mechanisms inherently eliminate many of the physical and social cues that people rely on to communicate in their day-to-day activities. Cues such as eye contact, tone of voice, hand gestures, and head nods may or may not be supported by the various forms of CMC. Regardless of the CMC mechanism, the level of social interaction is often reduced.

The restricted interaction imposed by CMC has social and psychological impact. For example, people involved in bargaining situations depend heavily on physical and social cues in their negotiations. The loss or diminishment of such cues would adversely affect a person's ability to negotiate. On the other hand, the loss or diminishment of social and physical cues associated with status or position (e.g., leader sits at the front of a table, unempowered subordinates sit along the outer fringes of a room) may lead to more equitable and universal collaboration.

Asynchronous forms of CMC introduce other social and psychological effects. For example, newsgroups and discussion groups are well known for incidents of "flaming." Flaming occurs when argumentation over a topic evolves into personal attacks among discussants. "Flaming is impulsive, highly emotional, and often rude behavior that is rarely exhibited in a face-to-face setting" [4].

CSCW research has also shown that CMC may lead groups to make riskier decisions [4]. One possible explanation for this tendency is that the decision-making process is hampered by greater group conflict and confrontation as evidenced in flaming. A second theory is that virtual groups tend to consult more people online, and thus, produce a greater number of extraneous solutions. Third, those users who have the greatest capacity to make good decisions may not have as much influence as they would in real life owing to the equalizing effects of CMC.

The social and psychological impact of CMC poses many questions with respect to groupware and collaboration. What are additional social and psychological effects of CMC? To what extent should we manipulate collaboration to minimize or maximize social and psychological effects? Is such social or psychological manipulation ethical?

Breaking Social and Cultural Barriers

With computer-supported collaboration, the interaction that occurs among group members is modified or manipulated from its naturally occurring form. With this in mind, some CSCW researchers wish to apply CMC in ways that diminish social and cultural barriers. For example, some CMC systems may hide the identity of a group member such that his/her appearance, gender, and race are not revealed. In these systems, users develop and utilize other kinds of criteria to evaluate and form opinions of other collaborating users. Some preconceived biases and prejudices may be averted.

The use of characters in MUDs and MOOs is an example of hidden identity in CMC. In a MUD or MOO, players take on the name, description, and behavior of fictitious characters as they collaborate with others. Most often, players in a MUD or MOO do not know the true identities of the other players with whom they interact. In fact, the anonymity of a MUD or MOO often lures many introverts into a social setting [30]. Thus, MUDs and MOOs may provide socially timid users a social outlet to the outside world.

The controversy surrounding hidden identities is one of information or misinformation. Is it ethical to hide the identity of those with whom one collaborates? Are there situations where hidden identities are and are not appropriate? Do users have a right to know the true identities of those with whom they interact? These are the questions we must address if we choose to manipulate collaboration to break social and cultural barriers.

Construction of Group Knowledge

People collaborate in the performance of work. In the process of collaborating, knowledge is distributed and evolves among the members of the group. Each member holds a unique manifestation of knowledge. Yet, the combined knowledge of all members is needed to accomplish the work at hand.

In general, group knowledge is implicitly maintained by individual members and shared through communication. In this vein, the construction and evolution of group knowledge occurs naturally through collaboration. Alternatively, collaborative technology may also facilitate the construction and evolution of group knowledge. For instance, bulletin boards lay out individual pieces of user-created information in a hierarchical structure. In an abstract sense, the information hierarchy represents the evolving group knowledge of the discussion group as it struggles to understand and reason about the topic under discussion.

There are a number of issues surrounding the development of group knowledge among collaborating computer users. How is the group knowledge distributed among the users and machines? How is the knowledge constructed and accessed? Is the knowledge persistent or ephemeral? How can computers better support the construction of group knowledge?

Telepresence

Collaborative technology eliminates the requirement that people must be collocated in order to collaborate. With collaborative technology, users separated by large geographical distances may still work together on tasks and activities. In any collaborative setting, however, a sense of presence is important for effective interaction. People are used to communicating and collaborating with other people; they are not used to communicating and collaborating with computers. People want to sense the presence of living, human beings at the opposite ends of a collaboration.

Collaborative technology simulates presence in a variety of ways. This simulation of presence is known as "telepresence." Two types of telepresence are generally supported by collaborative technology: group presence and environmental presence. Group presence is related to the richness of communications among group members. The richer the communications channels, the more natural the interaction appears among group members. One stream of thought in CSCW is that groupware should simulate as closely as possible the level of interaction that occurs in face-to-face communications. This suggests the inclusion of higher-bandwidth communications mechanisms such as video teleconferencing.

Environmental presence is concerned with immersing the user in the environment of the activity and work setting. By simulating the context of work on a computer, the user ideally becomes more familiar and comfortable with the computer-mediated form of work. Kmi Stadium[7] is an example of environmental telepresence where the physical setting of a classroom, auditorium, or stadium is modeled [14]. Auditory cues such as clapping, laughing, shouting, and whispering are inserted into the stream of a presentation to simulate the presence of an active audience.

Telepresence support in groupware poses many interesting questions. How much telepresence is desirable in collaboration over the Web? Does it greatly enhance our ability to collaborate and work, or is it merely "window dressing" on collaborative activities and situations? Are there situations where too much telepresence hampers users' abilities to collaborate or to carry out work? For example, some CSCW researchers believe that a high sense of telepresence may actually lessen the level and equity of social interaction [4].

---

[7] http://kmi.open.ac.uk/stadium/aboutstadium.html

20.5 The Future of Collaboration on the Web

The collaborative technologies described in this chapter reflect various levels of integration with the Web. CMC mechanisms such as IRC, bulletin boards, and e-mail have been well integrated into Web browsers. These mechanisms have been incorporated into many Web groupware applications available today. Other CMC mechanisms such as synchronous audio and video teleconferencing are much less common on the Web. As for collaboration frameworks, newsgroups and discussion groups, graphical virtual worlds, and review and annotation systems have experienced moderate to high levels of integration with the Web while MUDs and MOOs have experienced minor levels of integration.

In the near future, we should see increased development and application of collaborative technologies over the Web. Asynchronous audio capabilities are rapidly becoming available on the Web today through CMC applications such as CoolTalk [41] and Conference [40]. Video-conferencing applications such as Live-Media [43] are in the midst of development. Fully integrated Web-based MUDs and MOOs are being explored in research projects such as Xerox's Jupiter project [17].

As collaborative technology evolves over the Web, we must shift our focus on the technology from its development to its use. We must consider how to best utilize collaborative technology to allow remote users to effectively work together. We must evaluate how computer-supported collaborative environments deviate from natural environments. Can we improve the level of collaboration over natural forms? Does collaborative technology inherently impose constraints that necessarily impede collaboration? How do users perceive collaborative technology? Do they find it natural or artificial? These are the types of questions that become important to answer as collaborative technology establishes a foothold on the Web.

From a social standpoint, we expect that the user's perspective of the Web will change. No longer will the Web be viewed just as the super-highway to massive amounts of information; it will be seen also as a gateway to real people with interconnected needs and goals. The Web will evolve from a massive information database to a dynamic, living organism that encompasses the knowledge and capabilities of its users. The human element of the Web will increasingly be emphasized.

Collaborative applications should not be developed for and installed on the Web merely for the purpose of advancing technology. Such applications have human consequences. As responsible scientists and technologists, we must come to understand the social and organizational impact of this technology, for it will forever change the way that people work, interact, and communicate.

20.6 References

[1]   The Atkerson Connection. "The Anet Virtual Mall—Mall Selection Page."
       1996. <http://aconnection.com/anet/mallcate.htm> (10 Dec. 1996).

[2]   Begole, James. "Leveraging Networks for Collaborative Education." 1996.
       <http://www.cs.vt.edu/~hci/nie/> (10 Dec. 1996).

[3]   ——. "Ppong!" 1996. <http://simon.cs.vt.edu/~begolej/Ppong.html> (10 Dec.
       1996).

[4]   Belson, David. "A Networked Nation Revisited." 1994.
       <http://www.stevens-tech.edu/~dbelson/thesis/thesis.html#sect5> (10 Dec.
       1996).

[5]   Best Day Tours. "Best Day Mexico Travel Reservations." 1995.
       <http://www.bestday.com/homepage.htm> (10 Dec. 1996).

[6]   Blair, David. "Waxweb Starts Here." 1996.
       <http://bug.village.virginia.edu/index.html> (10 Dec. 1996).

[7]   Chin Jr., George. "HCI Class Discussion." 1995.
       <http://ei.cs.vt.edu/cgi-bin/hci-discuss/discuss> (10 Dec. 1996).

[8]   Club Internet. "Picasso." 1996.
       <http://www.club-internet.fr:80/picasso/homepage.html> (10 Dec. 1996).

[9]   Craighead, Laura M. "TeleMUSE Home Page." 1995.
       <http://www.trekmuse.org/> (10 Dec. 1996).

[10]   Creative Computers Inc. "Creative Computers Home Page." 1996.
       <http://www.cc-inc.com/scripts/dbml.exe?template=/tables/cchomepage.dbm>
       (10 Dec. 1996).

[11]   Dibbell, Julian. "A Rape in Cyberspace or How an Evil Clown, a Haitian
       Trickster Spirit, Two Wizards, and a Cast of Dozens Turned a Database
       Into a Society." 1994.
       <http://lydia.bradley.edu/las/soc/syl/391/papers/rape_cyb.html> (10 Dec.
       1996).

[12]   Diversity University. "Diversity University East Campus—Web Gateway."
       1996. <http://moo.du.org:8000/> (10 Dec. 1996).

[13]   Eastgate Systems Inc. "Storyspace." 1996.
       <http://www.eastgate.com/StoryspaceOV.html> (10 Dec. 1996).

[14]   Eisenstadt, Marc. "About KMi Stadium." 1995.
       <http://kmi.open.ac.uk/stadium/aboutstadium.html> (10 Dec. 1996).

[15] Eisenstadt, Marc. "Virtual Summer School Project." 1994. <http://www.me.titech.ac.jp/=@=:kmi.open.ac.uk/kmi-misc/virtualsummer.html> (10 Dec. 1996).

[16] The Exploratorium. "Project LINK@The Exploratorium." 1995. <http://www.exploratorium.edu/learning_studio/link/> (10 Dec. 1996).

[17] Frahmann, Dennis. "Xerox Consultant Update, March 1995." 1995. <http://www.xerox.com/ConsultantUpdate/Mar95/Jupiter.html> (10 Dec. 1996).

[18] Fujihata, Masaki. "Global Clock Project." 1996. <http://www.flab.mag.keio.ac.jp/GClock/> (10 Dec. 1996).

[19] Georgia Institute of Technology. "GVU's Fifth WWW User Survey." 1996. <http://www.cc.gatech.edu/gvu/user_surveys/survey-04-1996/graphs/general/access.html> (10 Dec. 1996).

[20] Goldberg, Ken and Joseph Santarromana. "The Telegarden." 1996. <http://cwis.usc.edu/dept/garden/> (10 Dec. 1996).

[21] Goldberg, Ken and Michael Mascha. "USC's Mercury Project." 1995. <http://www.usc.edu/dept/raiders/> (10 Dec. 1996).

[22] Hamilton, Jacqueline D. "Harper's Tale Home Pages." 1996. <http://www.astroarch.com/HT/> (10 Dec. 1996).

[23] Hamilton, Jacqueline D. "Welcome to the Frontier." 1996. <http://lightsphere.com/frontier/> (10 Dec. 1996).

[24] Hillenbrand, Bob. "Night of the Comet: Big Fun with Hyakutake." 1996. <http://ccf.arc.nasa.gov/comet/index.html> (10 Dec. 1996).

[25] Infoseek Corp. "Infoseek." 1996. <http://www.infoseek.com/> (10 Dec. 1996).

[26] The Internet Movie Database Ltd. "Welcome to the IMDb." 1996. <http://us.imdb.com/> (10 Dec. 1996).

[27] Kaplan, Simon M. "wOrlds: An Open Environment for Support of Collaborative Activities." 1995. <http://acsl.cs.uiuc.edu/kaplan/worlds.html> (10 Dec. 1996).

[28] Lam, Mike and Alfred Hubler. "NetworkTA: Main Menu." 1995. <http://corwin.physics.uiuc.edu/cyberprof-bin/physics/101/nta05> (username: guest; password: guest) (10 Dec. 1996).

[29] Levine, Rick. "JavaSoft FORUM 1.0." 1996. <http://www.javasoft.com/forum/1.0.0.html> (10 Dec. 1996).

[30] Livingood, Jeb. "Revenge of the Introverts." 1995.
      <http://sunsite.unc.edu/cmc/mag/1995/apr/livingood.html> (10 Dec. 1996).

[31] Lotus Development Corp. "Lotus Development Corporation." 1996.
      <http://www.lotus.com/> (10 Dec. 1996).

[32] Lotus Development Corp. "Lotus Notes." 1996.
      <http://www.lotus.com/notes/> (10 Dec. 1996).

[33] Microsoft Corp. "Learn About NetMeeting." 1996.
      <http://www.microsoft.com/netmeeting/learn/#appshare> (10 Dec. 1996).

[34] Microsoft Corp. "Microsoft Project Home Page." 1996.
      <http://www.microsoft.com/msproject/> (10 Dec. 1996).

[35] Moore, Cindy T. "The Internet Vet Column." 1996.
      <http://www.zmall.com/pet_talk/tittle/pets/ivc/internet-vet.3.15.html>
      (10 Dec. 1996).

[36] Myers, James D. "Collaboratory for the Environmental Molecular Sci-
      ences." 1995.
      <http://www.emsl.pnl.gov:2080/docs/collab/CollabHome.html>   (10   Dec.
      1996).

[37] ——. "EMSL Collaborative Research Environment (CORE) Home Page."
      1996. <http://www.emsl.pnl.gov:2080/docs/tour/index.html> (10 Dec. 1996).

[38] National Center for Supercomputing Applications. "HyperNews Home
      Server." 1996.
      <http://union.ncsa.uiuc.edu/HyperNews/get/hypernews.html>   (10   Dec.
      1996).

[39] National Science Foundation. "REC NIE Program." 1996.
      <http://www.ehr.nsf.gov/EHR/RED/NIE/index.html> (10 Dec. 1996).

[40] Netscape Communications Corp. "Netscape Communicator." 1996.
      <http://home.netscape.com/comprod/products/communicator/
      datasheet.html#conference> (10 Dec. 1996).

[41] ——. "Netscape Navigator 3.0 | CoolTalk." 1996.
      <http://home.netscape.com/comprod/products/navigator/version_3.0/
      communication/cooltalk/index.html> (10 Dec. 1996).

[42] ——. "Netscape Suitespot." 1996.
      <http://home.netscape.com/comprod/announce/dss_suit.html>   (10   Dec.
      1996).

[43] ——. "Press Release." 1996.
      <http://home.netscape.com/newsref/pr/newsrelease81.html> (10 Dec. 1996).

[44] ——. "Welcome to Netscape." 1996. <http://home.netscape.com/> (10 Dec. 1996).

[45] NineCo, Inc. "The Bingo Zone." 1996. <http://www.bingozone.com/> (10 Dec. 1996).

[46] Northwestern University. "Learning Through Collaborative Visualization." 1996. <http://www.covis.nwu.edu/CoVis_Welcome.html> (10 Dec. 1996).

[47] NTT Data Corp. "World Fiction." 1996. <http://www0.nexsite.nttdata.jp/world-fiction/> (10 Dec. 1996).

[48] ——. "3D Entry Port." 1996. <http://www.construct.net/projects/ntt/3d/index.html> (10 Dec. 1996).

[49] Oracle Corp. "Welcome to Oracle." 1996. <http://www.oracle.com/> (10 Dec. 1996).

[50] Preece, Jenny. *Human-Computer Interaction*. Wokingham, England: Addison-Wesley, 1994.

[51] Putnam, Jeffrey. "Genetically Programmed Music." 1996. <http://www.nmt.edu/~jefu/bin/get-notes> (10 Dec. 1996).

[52] Roberts, Bill. "Groupwar Strategies." *Byte*. July 1996. pp. 68–78.

[53] Rensselaer Polytechnic Institute. "RPInfo at Rensselaer Polytechnic Institute (RPI)." 1996. <http://dcr.rpi.edu/> (25 Aug. 1997).

[54] Sabre Interactive. "Travelocity Home Page." 1996. <http://www.travelocity.com/> (10 Dec. 1996).

[55] The SenseMedia Network. "The Sprawl @ SenseMedia." 1996. <http://sensemedia.net/sprawl> (10 Dec. 1996).

[56] Sixth Floor Media. "CommonSpace." 1996. <http://www.sixthfloor.com/Products/CS/CS.html> (10 Dec. 1996).

[57] SoftKey Multimedia Inc. "Oregon Trail Online Demo." 1996. <http://www.mooc.com/internet/oto/otodemo/daily.html> (10 Dec. 1996).

[58] Starwave Corp. "ESPNET SportsZone." 1996. <http://espnet.sportszone.com/> (10 Dec. 1996).

[59] Stevens, Rick, et al. "LabSpace." 1995. <http://www.ccs.neu.edu/research/labspace/> (10 Dec. 1996).

[60] Sun Microsystems Inc. "Sun Microsystems." 1996. <http://www.sun.com/> (10 Dec. 1996).

[61]   ——. "VTS Home Page." 1996. <http://www.suned.com/> (10 Dec. 1996).

[62]   SunSITE. "Usenet Info Center Launch Pad." 1996.
       <http://sunsite.unc.edu/usenet-i/> (10 Dec. 1996).

[63]   Tennison, Jennifer. "Home Page." 1996. <http://spsyc.nott.ac.uk:8888/
       home> (10 Dec. 1996).

[64]   University of Wisconsin. "NetForum Home." 1996.
       <http://www.biostat.wisc.edu/infolink/nf_docs/> (10 Dec. 1996).

[65]   USA Today. "USA Today." 1996. <http://www.usatoday.com/> (10 Dec. 1996).

[66]   Virginia Tech Computer Science Department. "Virginia Tech." 1996.
       <http://linc.cs.vt.edu/nie-public/shared.html> (25 Aug. 1997).

[67]   Washington State University. "Welcome to the Virtual Gym." 1996.
       <http://134.121.112.29/fair_95/gym/index.html> (10 Dec. 1996).

[68]   Witbrock, Michael. "International Interactive Genetic Art." 1996.
       <http://robocop.modmath.cs.cmu.edu:8001/htbin/mjwgenformI>   (10   Dec.
       1996).

[69]   Yates, Kenneth R. "EMSL TeleViewer." 1996.
       <http://www.emsl.pnl.gov:2080/docs/collab/tv/> (10 Dec. 1996).

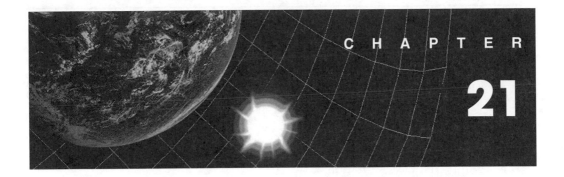

C H A P T E R

21

Education

by Paul Mather

*E*ducational uses of the Web in a kindergarten to twelfth grade (K–12) setting tend to focus, thus far, more on technology than pedagogy. This leads to systems that are technologically at odds with the typical K–12 classroom and educator, compounding the long-standing problem of refusal to adopt technology in K–12 education. Furthermore, existing Web applications typically follow the entrenched didactic model of instruction, serving mainly to alleviate the pragmatic problems of wide-area dissemination of lecture, testing, and course materials.

This chapter describes the typical milieu of the K–12 educator, and it shows how the Web can serve as an excellent enabling technology for a significant student-centered active-learning paradigm known as constructivism. With modest technology, the Web can be appropriately integrated into a constructivist classroom, providing access to a rich source of up-to-date raw information and all-important real-world audiences. The Web also serves as an excellent vehicle for educators to confront the pressing problem of critical literacy.

This chapter gives a general framework for the effective use of the Web in the classroom. It is biased toward curriculum and instruction issues rather than toward technology.

Chapter Content

1. Introduction

2. Foundations

- Technology vs. Pedagogy
- Environments
- Teaching Methodologies

3. Typical Current Applications and Approaches

- Wide-Area Dissemination
- Administration and Public Relations
- Online Resources and Projects

4. Realistic and Effective Applications

- Characteristic Features
- Guidelines and Examples

5. Critical Literacy: the Web's Great Potential
6. Conclusions
7. References

21.1 Introduction

In this chapter we look at the task of using the Web as an effective educational tool, primarily in a K–12 classroom setting. The intended audience is a reader who is moderately computer literate and interested in applying educational technology in a real-world classroom situation. It is assumed that such a reader has a good technological background but is unfamiliar with education, pedagogy, and the classroom environment. The aim of this chapter is to bridge this gap and to enable computer scientists to better understand the needs of educators. Without such an understanding and context, we cannot hope to create effective and usable educational technology for the classroom.

In essence, this chapter is a computer scientist's primer for the world of education and educational technology. However, educators will also benefit greatly from reading it, because it contains useful ideas for effectively integrating the Web into the classroom and curriculum. It also discusses appropriate and inappropriate teaching methodologies for use with educational technology, showing how one in particular is a natural "fit."

It may not be apparent, but computer scientists see the world through very different eyes from educators. Without understanding the world of educators, it is difficult for computer scientists to create effective tools for them. The the section on "Technology vs. Pedagogy" on page 394 looks at what problems this poses and highlights some common misconceptions.

In the the section on "Environments" on page 395 we look at the typical environments of the computer scientist and the K–12 educator so that the former can better understand and appreciate the milieu of the latter. Typically these two environments are strikingly different. If educational use of the Web is to be effective, it must be targeted to the level of available technology. This section points out some special concerns that anyone wanting to bring educational technology to the classroom should bear in mind.

At that point, the computer science reader should hopefully have a much better understanding and appreciation of the problems of the educator. Next, on page 398, we examine appropriate teaching methodologies. In particular, we focus upon two approaches: didactic and constructivist. Didacticism is the approach most commonly used in the classroom and taught to new educators. It is also, undoubtedly, the educational system with which most readers are familiar. However, it is not the most appropriate for use with educational technology, especially with the Internet and Web. Instead, we shall see that the other approach, constructivism, is a more natural "fit" in this respect, in that it meshes nicely with the strengths that educational technology has to offer. Educators may wish to dive into the chapter in earnest at this point.

Armed with the required educational context, the reader should now be equipped to look more critically at what has been currently achieved in the use of the Web for educational purposes. We look briefly, in Section 21.3, at how the Web is typically used today in education, noting how muchfalls under the shadow of the didactic umbrella. We argue that much more can be achieved, and that simply mimicking the didactic model is a severe impediment to the effective use of the Web in the classroom.

At this point we are well placed to determine what factors contribute to effective use of the Web in the K–12 classroom. An effective application is one that takes a realistic view of its intended environment and that contributes to learning (rather than simply to knowledge). We present in the section on "Characteristic Features" on page 404 several guidelines and an underlying rationale as to what we consider effective application of the Web. Computer scientists considering introducing educational technology into the classroom would do well to give these guidelines careful consideration.

Next, in the the section on "Guidelines and Examples" on page 406, we look at some effective applications of the Web in the classroom and describe why we consider them to be effective. Although superficially simple, these applications yield rich educational rewards and provide a fertile learning experience for their participating students and teachers.

A common thread running through the applications covered in this chapter is the goal of fostering critical literacy and information literacy on the student, discussed in Section 21.5. We examine this goal and determine why, in today's information age, it is a paramount one to pursue. Furthermore, we describe how the Web provides an accessible way of attacking the problem of critical literacy head on, showing that, in fact, this may be its greatest contribution to the classroom.

Finally, we end in Section 21.6 with a look toward future trends and some thoughts about where educational technology may be heading. We also offer some conclusions about the use of the Web in the classroom. By this point, the computer science reader in particular should have a much better appreciation of the lot of the average K–12 educator, and of the opportunities, problems, and pitfalls surrounding the use of educational technology in the classroom.

21.2 Foundations

This section gives the reader a necessary understanding of the world-view of the classroom educator. We cannot develop effective educational technology without knowing the realities of that world. Also included is a description of two important teaching methodologies that have great bearing on educational technology.

Technology vs. Pedagogy

Educational technology for the classroom combines, by definition, elements of education and technology. The question we need to address is that of balance and understanding. It is an inalienable fact that everyone sees the world in a different way. This can present problems when individuals with differing world-views come together to collaborate. Educational technology is a collaboration between computer scientists (the creators) and educators (the users), and so it is incumbent upon the former to understand the latter in order to create usable tools. The quote below captures the quintessential problem posed by individual world-views:

> "We do not describe the world we see; we see the world we can describe."
> [20]

The implication for computer scientists is that they are more likely to create educational technology skewed toward technology rather than education simply because this is the world they know and inhabit. It is very difficult for computer scientists to step outside their world and place themselves in the mind-set of educators; it is difficult to "unlearn" deeply ingrained, almost unconscious technological knowledge acquired over many years in order to see the world through neophyte eyes. Yet this is the challenge they face, and the barrier they must cross in order to produce usable, effective educational technology.

Our interests drive what we do and color our world-view. Computer scientists are interested in computer science; educators, in education. So, it is often the case that computer scientists seek to address computer science problems (e.g. distributed collaboration, real-time conferencing) wrapped in a blanket of education and call the often unsatisfactory result "educational technology." We deem the results unsatisfactory because they are often too complex or unwieldy for classroom use, or they make unreasonable demands upon resources: they cater to the wrong end-users. Education should be the focus, not technology. Because educators are the end-users, we should cater to their interests.

Our world-views can prejudice our perception of others. A common problem is to confuse a lack of knowledge with a lack of intelligence. However, the fact that someone does not know something does not make him or her stupid: the person just lacks knowledge of that particular thing. A lack of knowledge does not mean a person is *incapable* of knowing or understanding something. Computer science is infested with jargon, and this is acquired over a period of time. In effect, computer science is a dialect of the computer scientist's native language. We cannot expect educators to be fluent in, or even familiar with, what is essentially a *foreign language* to them. By the same token, computer scientists should endeavor to learn the language of educators and try to bridge the gulf between the two groups. Learning the language means learning not only the terms but also the concepts and theories behind them.

Finally, it is incumbent upon computer scientists to create *effective* tools for educators. Here, we deem a tool truly *effective* if it *goes beyond* what is already possible. Effective educational technology is, ideally, a synergy arising from joining the best educational practice with the *support* (not dominance) of technology. Technology should add something to the educational experience. Remember: an electronic worksheet is still just a worksheet. If (as many educators feel) worksheets have limited educational potential, then to use computers to create electronic versions only allows us to use something inadequate faster, more often, or with greater ease [1]. However, the fact remains, we are simply perpetuating poor pedagogy. Worse still, we may be attaching false importance to it by dressing it up in new, high-tech clothes. We must strive to improve on what the educator has, not create electronic facsimiles.

Environments

We have seen that experience separates individuals through differing resultant world-views. We now go on to examine how different milieus, or environments, also affect what can be achieved within those world-views. Table 21–1 shows the typical milieus of the computer scientist and the K–12 educator.

Before we discuss Table 21–1, let us first acknowledge that there is likely no such thing as a "typical" educator or classroom. Educators and their available facilities cover the entire spectrum from poor (nonexistent, even) to state of the art [11]. Even within the same school, facilities may vary wildly. One classroom may have several state-of-the-art PCs connected, via Ethernet, to a T1 Internet connection, while the classroom next door may have only a single, old, text-only Apple IIe with only a 2400-baud modem Internet connection through a shared telephone line. It is fairly safe to say that we are not yet at the stage where every

Table 21–1 Typical Milieus of Computer Scientists and K–12 Educators

Computer Science	K–12 Education
Familiar with technology; good infrastructure	Unfamiliar with technology; poor infrastructure
Excellent Internet connectivity	Variable, intermittent connectivity
High-performance equipment	Modest or poor equipment
Unrestricted access	Restricted access

classroom enjoys the luxury of its own computer (never mind one connected to the Internet). The situation is improving, however, as the government realizes the importance of the information age in which we now find ourselves.

Although more schools are going "online," the numbers are still tiny compared to the total number of schools. The Web66 registry of schools [23] attempts to track the numbers, but such demographics are hard to collect. For example, one could say that *every* K–12 educator in the state of Virginia in the U.S. is online because every one has, or at least is entitled to, an account on the Virginia Public Education Network [24]. This account gives them access to e-mail, Usenet, gopher, interactive talk, telnet, ftp, and the Web (via lynx) through a simple menu-driven text-based interface (though SLIP connections are also supported via *The Internet Adapter* software[1]). However, the fact that everybody is signed up does not mean that all can use the system on a daily basis in the classroom, or even choose to do so.

Let us look at the differences between the worlds of *typical* computer scientists and educators, as summarized in Table 21–1. Computer scientists are familiar and comfortable with technology, whereas educators typically have little or no formal technology training, especially that pertaining to curriculum and instruction. A typical response, therefore, is for educators to adopt avoidance strategies to deal with the introduction of computer technology into their environment [4]. Even colleges of education place little emphasis in their teacher training on the seamless integration of technology into the classroom and curriculum, and typically they turn out student teachers that are more like their predecessors who graduated decades earlier and less like today's children [21].

Allied to this, computer scientists usually enjoy a much better technological infrastructure than educators. Not only is their physical support stronger, but also it is more likely that they can obtain help for technological problems from their immediate colleagues. Educators do not enjoy such luxuries, and may feel isolated, technologically speaking, from their peers. We should bear in mind that

[1] http://marketplace.com

educators who integrate technology into their curriculum are more like lone pioneers; it is not part of their everyday lives.

Another difference is in the level of Internet connectivity. Computer scientists typically enjoy fast, permanent connections, usually at Ethernet speed or above. Although more schools are being hooked up with T1 or ISDN connections, Internet connections are usually much slower than that. Obsolete hardware is part of the problem. If an old computer does not have an Ethernet card, but instead has only a 2400-baud modem, it matters little if the school has a T1 line to the Internet.

Modem lines may present a problem due to a limited number of school telephone lines. For this reason, even if a computer is available, it may only be able to connect to the Internet for short bursts to avoid "tying up" the phone line. In overcrowded schools that use mobile units to provide extra classroom space, these satellite classes may not even have telephone connections at all. (This may also be a problem in older schools. In fact, rewiring for the information age is a problem afflicting many schools.)

Connectivity also applies to physical access. Often, computers are concentrated together in labs, for example in the library under the supervision of the school's media specialist. Such labs may be massively oversubscribed, with many classes vying for class time in them. These labs may be inconvenient to use because of intermittent access or physical separation from the regular classroom. We should be aware, therefore, that educators may only enjoy limited or sporadic access to both computer hardware and the Internet, and thus our educational technology should be designed to reflect this.

Like textbooks, computer equipment in our schools usually lags behind the state of the art. With limited budgets, longevity is a must in the school setting. This goes against the prevailing ethos of the rapidly evolving computer industry, which exhorts its users to upgrade continually in terms of hardware and software. This creates a disparity between the educational environment and that of the computer scientist. Many schools still have old or obsolete computers, often with limited graphical capabilities. Computers are often donated because they are being replaced by their donors with newer models capable of keeping up with current applications. Much of the hardware in public schools may be unable to support the heavy demands made by resource-hungry Web browsers such as Netscape and Internet Explorer. Many computers may be unable even to support graphical Web browsers because they are text-only systems. It is incumbent upon computer scientists, therefore, to design educational technology not with the leading-edge, but with more modest technology in mind, so as to create systems that are usable in the classroom setting. (Commercial computer game designers are well aware of this truism and design their game software comfortably behind the leading-edge, so as not to limit their potential market. Educational technology should be no different.)

Finally, an educator's access to the Internet may be restricted compared to that of a computer scientist. It may be restricted on several levels. Apart from the speed and availability restrictions mentioned above, other limitations may be imposed by various political and *in loco parentis* considerations. These may manifest themselves in terms of being only able to access, e.g., a subset of the Usenet newsgroups; certain sites or domains; or content filtered according to PICS ratings (see Section 19.9) [29, 19]. Restricted access may also extend to the fact that educators may not be able to install custom software and may only be able to use a predetermined set of programs and applications with which to access the Internet (e.g. via the VAPEN menu system). If an educator's Internet Service Provider (ISP) does not allow shell access, then development of applications that require this is not realistic. Once again, computer scientists need to be familiar with the educator's milieu in order to develop effective educational technology. In the next section, we shall also see that familiarity with effective teaching methodologies is the final key to understanding the educator's world. As well as being appropriate to the educator's environment, effective educational technology should adhere to an appropriate pedagogical model. We shall look at two such models next.

Teaching Methodologies

Education is a difficult application area to step into because, it seems, everybody thinks he or she is an expert, having "been there, done that." However, it is fair to say that most have seen the process from only one side of the desk, so to speak, and are largely ignorant of the view from the teacher's point of view. Worse still, it is likely that most have been exposed only to a very limited range of pedagogical styles and are unaware of other, perhaps much more appropriate, approaches.

Most people are familiar with the *didactic* style of teaching, even if they don't know it by this name. This approach, described below, is the dominant instructional technique in use in schools today. It has a considerable heritage. However, it is in many ways incongruous to the computer and information technology now available. In fact, reliance on the didactic approach may be a major contributing factor to the phenomenon of *technology refusal* affecting contemporary education [10].

An alternative approach, posited by many authors as being a more natural partner for integrating educational technology, is the *constructivist* paradigm [6, 27]. This approach is not as widely used as didacticism, but it dates back at least to the turn of the century when it was advocated by John Dewey [3], among others, and is once again coming to the fore.

Constructivism is primarily a locus-of-control issue. It addresses the question of who is in control of the learning process. It advocates that students become self-directed information managers, not information regurgitators. Constructivism focuses on knowledge construction, not knowledge reproduction. It also holds as an axiom that one constructs knowledge from one's experiences, mental structures, and beliefs that are used to interpret objects and events.

Table 21–2 A Comparison of Two Teaching Methodologies

Didactic	Constructivist
Passive	Active
Linear	Non-linear
Teacher as sage	Teacher as guide
Little or no student choice	Significant student choice
Part-to-whole	Whole-to-part
Skills taught in isolation	Skills taught in a relevant context

Accordingly, learning environments should support multiple perspectives or interpretations of reality, and allow knowledge construction using context-rich and experience-based activities [12]. An immediate consequence is the notion that there is no "right" way or sequence to learn anything; the "right" way depends on the student.

Table 21–2 highlights some of the salient features of the didactic and constructivist teaching methodologies.

In the didactic approach, learning is passive, with students receiving an incremental, ostensibly authoritative, predetermined linear sequence of facts from a teacher acting in the role of sage. Passive learning often involves memorization, rote, or delivery of material via lecture, slide show, handouts, etc. Active learning, on the other hand, is learning by doing.

The notion of teacher as a guide does not imply that the teacher has no control or is not in an active role. Actually, the teacher must be able to exercise great finesse in creating and controlling the learning environment. In the constructivist approach, the teacher often acts in the role of facilitator, as opposed to an ultimate authoritative dispenser of knowledge. The didactic and constructivist approaches can be summed up in this respect by the analogy "the sage on the stage versus the guide on the side."

Similarly, student choice does not imply a free-for-all. A definite learning objective is held in mind; the choice refers to exactly how this is to be achieved in terms of form and precise content. Student choice may be from a predetermined list or "menu": it may relate to how the information is presented (presentation, oral discussion, written article, hypercard stack, etc.), or it may be student-devised to fit into an overall theme or topic.

Learning in the didactic approach is linear and part-to-whole. Skills are taught in a sequence decided upon by the teacher, and not necessarily in the order in which they may be needed. Skills are often taught in isolation, without a relevant context for the student to ground them in and thereby retain them.

Although we may not realize it, almost everyone applies a constructivist approach to certain kinds of learning, such as learning how to use a word processing or an editor application on a computer. We typically do not learn all the commands such as how to underline, center, make bold, cut and paste, and so on, before starting up the word processor; we do not read the manual cover to cover before using the application. Instead, we learn functions in a demand-driven fashion. We get an overview of the capabilities of the package, and then, when we need to know how to achieve some needed task, such as underlining, we learn the keystrokes or menu navigations required to do this. Thus, we proceed in a whole-to-part, contextual manner. We learn things as we need them, when they are relevant and meaningful to us, making the learning process less abstract.

In the whole-to-part approach we start by looking at the "big picture" and then "zoom in" on specific parts or aspects as they become interesting or relevant to us. In part-to-whole we learn about each of the specific parts (usually in some arbitrary sequence), and then, at the end, we auto-magically integrate these disparate parts into a coherent whole. Thus, if we were learning how to play the guitar in a didactic fashion, we might proceed by first learning about musical notation and how to read sheet music. We might then learn which musical notes correspond to which fret positions on the neck of the guitar. From there, we might learn about scales and harmonics and how to form chords and progressions. When we have learned that, we might then be handed a classical acoustic guitar with the musical score to some classical piece like "Greensleeves" and told to play it in a certain scale. We are expected to integrate all the abstract theory we have been fed up to now and apply it by playing a rendition on the guitar. Never mind that we may be far more interested in playing high-volume blues/rock on an electric guitar instead; all the disparate theory is now supposed to make sense.

Of course, in practice, people are more likely to adopt a constructivist approach to learning the guitar. They start by learning the chords to a few songs of interest to them, then maybe a solo or two, progressively adding more finesse and theory to their repertoire as their skill improves. All the time, learning is non-linear, self-directed, and in a relevant context.

The great advantage of the didactic approach, and the likely reason for its entrenched success, is its ability to scale. It can work for relatively large numbers of students. Because all students have to conform to one set pattern of learning dictated by the teacher, all students are treated essentially alike. Their individualism is largely ignored, as all must fit into the "round hole" devised by the teacher. It matters little if the didactic approach is applied to five or five hundred students at a time, since the same delivery and assessment mechanism will be used for all.

Because constructivism is child-centered, scalability is much more of a problem. Smaller class sizes and higher teacher/student ratios are preferred for effective deployment of this technique. (Coincidentally, these attributes are also advocated by educators for improved achievement even in the didactic arena.)

This is not to say that constructivism cannot be applied in the average classroom. It can, but it is more demanding of a teacher. The rewards, however, are much greater, both for students and teachers. In addition, constructivism incorporates the notion of *multiple intelligences* [7, 8] naturally into its paradigm, resulting in more students' achieving their potential. The didactic approach typically caters mainly to visual and auditory learners. Although constructivism may be harder for the teacher to deploy than didacticism, we must judge the two approaches based upon their results. In those terms, constructivism becomes much more favorable, being more in tune with the real world outside the classroom.

Constructivism is also a very natural partner for the computer technology that exists in the information age we find ourselves in. In particular, the anarchy of the Internet, with its non-linear hypermedia, is a natural proving ground for constructivism. Hyperlinked documents within a Web page defeat almost instantly the notion of the linear, evenly paced approach of didacticism. Getting a lab full of eager students all to follow the same sequence of links, instead of exploring according to their own interests, is not only highly unnatural but functionally almost impossible. This extends also to the very open-ended nature of computer applications, which provide a fertile vehicle for expressing individual intentions and interests. Like constructivism, the computer can be seen as an excellent processor and manager of information, not simply a tool for storing and regurgitating it. It is likely, therefore, that constructivism will come more to the fore as educational technology is deployed centrally within the curriculum. The current position of educational technology at the periphery of the curriculum owes more to the poor supporting framework offered by didacticism than to lack of resources or desire on the part of teachers. Constructivism offers a way of integrating educational technology into the heart of the curriculum, as a natural tool in the learning process [2, 1].

21.3 Typical Current Applications and Approaches

The Web has made relatively little penetration into education. A large part of the problem, apart from the training and infrastructure problems mentioned previously, is the fact that most educators are adherents to the didactic method of teaching, and so they seek to employ the tenets of this philosophy in their use of the Web. This tends to constrain applications to become electronic extensions of lecture and assessment material—material provided by the teacher for consumption by the student.

Wide-Area Dissemination

By far, the greatest deployment of the Web in education as a whole is in solving the pragmatic problems of information dissemination, particularly wide-area information dissemination. Higher-education institutions such as universities appear to have embraced this as a means of delivering course content to a largely nomadic student population. An exemplar is the Educational Infrastructure project Web server at Virginia Tech [25], which hosts online course materials. The bulk of the material comprises static class lecture materials, online tests and assignments, news and course changes, and software and demos.

This mode of Web usage seems to follow the well-established videotext model which became more popular in Europe, with TeleText and Minitel, than in the USA. Videotext offers a carousel of information pages that may be called up via its page number using a TV remote control or similar device. TeleText uses spare lines of each frame in broadcast TV channels to deliver its content. A suitably equipped TV can decode and display this information on the TV screen, even overlaying it on the broadcast picture, allowing for subtitling of programs, for example.

A common use of the Web is the delivery of lecture material and handouts in electronic form, thereby creating "paperless classes" where everything is available for reading online. In practice, however, these "paperless classes" appear to generate more paper than their regular counterparts, as students tend to print out all the online materials to take to class. The poor presentational capabilities of HTML usually mean less effective use of the printed page when material is delivered through the Web, creating a higher page count when the material is printed.

Another major reason for students' printing out material from "paperless classes" is the poor annotation capabilities of the Web as currently implemented via HTML and HTTP. A much better system is one in which hyperlinks and documents are stored separately from one another. This enables users to create their own links between documents; to create their own "webs" instead of only being able to navigate those created by others. Such an approach is used in the *Iris Hypermedia System*[9] pioneered at Brown University, which was used successfully as a resource by students in an English literature course taught there. *Hyper-G* [14] also follows this general model of keeping links and documents separate, greatly improving both annotation capabilities and document maintenance.

Although wide-area dissemination addresses pragmatic concerns, it often ignores the educational dimension of the problem. For example, there is little educational difference between software (demos and applications) distributed on disc or on the Web. The problem being solved is not an educational but a pragmatic one. For example, running a simulation implemented using Java on a remote server is little different than running the same simulation as native code on a PC. In fact, the latter is less prone to problems of access caused by network and server failures. The main conveniences provided by the Java simulation are not having to distribute the software physically via disc or CD-ROM and also being able to rapidly obtain updated software. This increases availability and decreases costs. However, this solves an economic and pragmatic problem, not an educational one.

Similarly, Web-based applications providing distributed collaboration or test-taking are often artificial and cumbersome attempts at providing high-tech solutions to problems more easily solved face-to-face in the classroom. Collaboration between students within the same class is best performed in real life, rather than by artificial online means. By the same token, online testing is a high-tech facsimile of what many educators consider to be a poor assessment technique anyway. When proctoring problems are factored in, it is probably easier to administer a multiple-choice exam in class using a paper form graded by optical mark recognition, where time constraints and proctoring can be properly monitored, than by offering it online via the Web. Largely, such online applications are solving artificial problems and are not meeting the needs of educators. In many cases they create more work than they solve. For example, authoring computer-based testing is often far more laborious for the K–12 educator than simply delivering the same thing on paper, especially when taking into account the learning curve.

A central theme of this wide-area dissemination approach is that it seeks to emulate, electronically, current practice in the real world. However, such practice is usually derived from the didactic approach, and so the electronic counterpart inherits the inappropriate baggage of that approach, limiting its ultimate success [1].

Administration and Public Relations

Many of the K–12 schools that are on the Web use the medium for essentially administrative and public relations functions. Most online K–12 schools have pages that describe where the school is; delineate its policies, vision statement, and activities; list its staff; and, usually, include some school history. In many cases, links are provided to various grades or departments within the school, with those pages usually providing more detailed information about staff and facilities.

Here in Montgomery County, home of Virginia Tech, a concerted effort was made to bring all the county's public schools online on the Web. However, within each school, the school's Web presence is not integrated into the classroom. It usually falls to one or two lone volunteers in each school to maintain the pages. As a result, student-produced class material is usually sparse on the class pages. The school pages, out of necessity, restrict themselves mainly to relatively static information, such as that arising out of administrative or public relations material. A random sampling of other schools on the Web tells a similar story. It is only the pioneers of the medium who are beginning to see the relevance of the

Web to their classroom activities, and these people are both consuming and producing more Web material as part of their regular class work.

Another use of the Web is as a bridge between the school and the community. Web pages are an excellent vehicle for Parent-Teacher Association (PTA) and volunteer groups to promote their activities and solicit help. Again, though, this is just another manifestation of the administrative and public relations function related above.

Online Resources and Projects

More people are becoming aware of the collaborative knowledge possibilities of the Internet and the Web. Not only is it a fertile storehouse of information on almost every conceivable topic, but it is also a rich publishing outlet for locally produced information and resources. Increasingly, people are beginning to organize these disparate strands of useful information into topically organized pages.

As well as sharing "bookmarked" sites of interest, educators can find links to useful classroom resources and information. Yahoo [30] has a large education section [31], well organized with a good user interface, and even has an entire service targeted towards youngsters: its Yahooligans service [32]. These are good starting points for educators wishing to get in contact with other educators and materials on the Web. Web66 [23] also contains much practical advice on the mechanics of getting a school online on the Web.

Although this is very much a step in the right direction, such online resources are essentially passive repositories of classroom information, albeit useful. *Effective* use of the Web in the classroom needs to go beyond that, integrating the Web into the curriculum, both as a source of up-to-date information (both recorded and cultural) and of real-world audiences for student-produced material. The information potential of the Internet needs to be harnessed in the classroom.

21.4 Realistic and Effective Applications

Now that we know more about the milieu of the educator (Section 21.2), and have seen the course charted by typical current Web applications for education (Section 21.3), it is time to examine what realistic and effective applications are possible. We will present some basic guidelines, then a few examples.

Characteristic Features

Given the typical environments and teaching methodologies discussed in Section 21.2, what can we infer as being the characteristic features of *realistic* applications, i.e., those which can be implemented in the educational milieu previously described?

First and foremost, they should have relatively modest technology requirements. Not only does sophisticated and extensive technology typically not exist in many classrooms, but, also, the infrastructure and skills base is not yet there to support complex technology and applications. If a teacher has only text-based access to the Web through the character-only Web browser, then there is little point designing highly graphical Java applets. Similarly, if the educator has only a 14400-baud modem connection to the Internet, it is not feasible to deliver digital video and audio over such a low-bandwidth link, ruling out such applications as video teleconferencing. The available technology and bandwidth should be ascertained prior to designing applications, so that they are feasible within the environment they will be used in. Although the situation is improving, available bandwidth and technology are often relatively poor.

Second, any application or planned activity should require a negligible learning curve and preparation. Classroom teachers have notoriously little spare time. Typically, they have only a single 45-minute period per day for planning lessons. This time is also taken up with teacher and parent conferences, along with sundry other administrative tasks. There is precious little time left over for anything else, let alone the daunting task of learning an unfamiliar and arcane area like technology [4].

While most teachers can offset lack of time by doing much of their planning and preparation at home, this is often not feasible in the case of educational technology, which frequently requires hands-on use of equipment. This is especially true when browsing the Web and bookmarking sites of interest. If a proposed application requires special hardware, software, or connectivity, and the teacher does not possess these requirements at home, or cannot easily borrow what is needed, he or she will have no option but to find the time at school. Finding the time in an already busy schedule may be very difficult, at best.

It is important that teachers can see a ready return on their investment, especially its relevance to their classroom endeavors; a steep learning curve can deter many from seeing things through. Applications which build upon existing skills, such as using e-mail, Usenet, or browsing the Web, are ideal candidates.

Realistic applications must be reliable. Teachers soon lose faith in technology that lets them down [2]. If a lesson has to grind to a halt because the hardware or software crashes and someone has to be found to fix it, or the connection to a remote site goes down, then the teacher is going to be much more wary in future about using it. Reliability is an issue of trust. If the teacher cannot trust the technology, it will not find favor in the classroom. Complex hardware and software systems (especially software in alpha and beta release), tenuous remote links, and ephemeral online documents are to be avoided, if possible, at least in the early stages.

Designers of realistic applications must address the pragmatic concerns arising from the limited availability of computers and time versus many students. The low computer-to-student ratio found in many classrooms will usually necessitate a more hands-off than hands-on approach to educational technology applications. Also, students typically have fairly poor keyboarding skills, and so it is often inefficient for them to key in information themselves. Similarly, when lesson time or available connect time is limited (as with short-persistence modem connections), applications will have to be more offline than online; data gathering should be planned so that it takes place more outside class time (e.g., via e-mail requests for information), with the class period being reserved for the important task of *evaluating* the information gleaned.

As well as being a huge source of information, the Internet is an invaluable outlet for *publishing* information. Constructivism places emphasis on engaging in real-world tasks, and a basic requirement in the real world is to be able to convey information to others in an understandable fashion. Effective Web applications will therefore include a component in which students are both *producers* and *consumers* of information. Not only does this improve communication skills, but it also makes the activity more engaging and adds a greater focus. Alas, the teacher is not viewed as a real-world audience by students. However, knowing that their work may be read and judged by hundreds, thousands, or more readers all across the world leads to greater care being taken over presentation of material. Writing also becomes a more relevant task when the student knows he or she may obtain feedback from a vast potential audience from a huge variety of backgrounds.

Finally, we must remember that the computer is a *tool* and not the focus of educational technology or the classroom. It is a teacher's skill in interpretation and explanation that makes teachers invaluable. If people were able to learn solely by reading books, one could simply distribute a reading list, or put the material up on the Web, and people would become masters of the subject simply by reading it; there would be no need ever to attend classes or hire teachers and professors. Of course, we know that notion is nonsense, and it is the interpretative skill that teachers bring to a subject that makes them a necessary adornment to any classroom; it is their ability to restate concepts to fit the student's world-view, thereby making the material accessible and understandable to that student. Thus, educational technology should be seen as supporting this endeavor, and not replacing it. Computers lack the sophistication and flexibility to manipulate and convey concepts in the way educators can.

Guidelines and Examples

What are good guidelines for projects featuring the characteristics outlined above? One theme arising from our discussion so far is that flashy, advanced technology misses the point when it comes to effective classroom use. As far as the Internet is concerned, its great value in the classroom is as a very rich and copious supply of up-to-date information. This information exists in many forms. It may be as archived "knowledge" in Web pages, Usenet newsgroups, gopher sites, and Internet databases, or it may take a less tangible form such as cultural contact.

The Internet has vastly shrunk the world. It is now possible for individuals to contact and discourse easily and directly with individuals and organizations across the globe. Previously, such contact was usually unidirectional, in the form of films and videos, passively observed, which deliver only a very high-level impression (usually lacking in context) of what the culture is really like. They miss the richness of detail that direct contact can bring. After all, if one could know what another country was like just from reading a travel brochure or watching a video, there would be no need for people to go on holiday there. But of course we do, so we can gain the benefits that accrue from direct experience.

One way to use the Web effectively in the classroom, therefore, is to involve it directly in every lesson as a source of information. Textbooks are usually inadequate in terms of being up to date and in their depth and breadth of coverage. When local information resources are inadequate, one can turn to the Internet by posting a query to an appropriate Usenet newsgroup, or searching the Web using a search engine. The Internet is also an ideal outlet for timely and ephemeral information that likely would never appear in textbooks, or would take years to do so. One example of this is the impact of the Shoemaker-Levy comet on Jupiter in 1995. The Internet had contemporaneous digital video of this event, available over the Web, along with supporting information. Many sites also carried images of the Hyakatuke comet when it made its close pass of the Earth in 1996.

Another rich source of information, especially for the social studies curriculum, is the large amount of international news and statistics available on the Internet. Many newspapers across the world are now finding their way onto the Internet, and these can be usefully employed by teachers to highlight the different coverage of current events across the world, as well as obtaining a better insight into the daily existence of other cultures.

Another popular source of such cultural information is in the establishing of "keypal" networks, in which students discourse with students in other countries via the Internet. This is usually via e-mail, but, if technology and bandwidth allow, it can be via interactive talk or Internet video-teleconferencing. One thing to remember with synchronous forms of communication is that it may not be feasible to use due to time-zone differences. For example, there is at least a five-hour time zone difference between the eastern US and western Europe. However, video-teleconferencing and Internet telephony are useful adjuncts in the study of foreign languages, for example, as they allow discourse to take place directly with native speakers [18].

The Internet is a great source of real-world data, and many interesting projects can be planned around data collected and presented on the Internet. A global perspective can be introduced into the curriculum. For example, on the Internet we can undertake comparisons of social problems, consumerism, language usage, history, and so on, around the world. Once we devise a project, human contacts can be sought from online sources such as Usenet. Such projects are often gold mines of tangential discoveries and spin-off lessons that result. For example, a project run by a local educator [17] comparing social problems asked people around the world what they considered to be the greatest social problem in their country, and the students outlined what they considered to be theirs.

A reply from Hong Kong cited housing costs as the biggest problem there, with even small apartments costing huge sums of money. When asked the possible causes and solutions by the teacher, the students assumed that a shortage of land was the root of the problem. In fact, the Hong Kong respondent said land hoarding is the cause. Property developers buy up tracts of land and leave them undeveloped so their more favorably placed areas will accrue in value through artificial scarcity. The students suggested the government should step in and outlaw this practice, requiring developers to build on their land within a certain time period after acquisition, which, coincidentally, was the solution suggested by the Hong Kong contact. This led to an impromptu discussion of the role of government and society versus private enterprise and capitalism, within a highly relevant framework, none of which was envisaged when the project was devised.

Another important aspect of Internet projects in the classroom is to include the production as well as the consumption of information. In this way, students will have to exercise their communication skills before diverse real-world audiences. It is important to contribute as well as consume. Students should organize and present their findings. This can either be as a posting to Usenet or to a mailing list, or, better still, on a Web page for a more persistent outlet. However, publication is not limited to the Internet: presentations are another fertile outlet for student research. For example, one class project on violence in society eventually culminated in a student presentation by ten- and eleven-year-olds at a Virginia regional library conference.

A language arts project investigating the restricted speech pattern known as Cockney rhyming slang gathered examples from around the world and compiled a dictionary of Cockney rhyming slang. The dictionary was then made available to other educators around the world. Students became aware of how far their work had permeated when, months later, a postal letter arrived from Australia. It was from a teacher there who had no Internet access, but who had obtained a printout of the dictionary from another Australian educator. The dictionary reminded the teacher of the rhyming slang used by his grandfather, and, since he had found the students' rhyming slang dictionary useful, he sought to return the favor by sending them an Aussie rhyming slang dictionary. Although this collaboration was unsolicited and unplanned, it was very natural, with both parties acting as both producers and consumers of information for the other.

Publication of information need not be limited to the written word. The Web offers the possibility of full hypermedia. One proposed project involves students effecting the virtual preservation of a community. Riner, Virginia, is a community in flux. Its cultural makeup is changing rapidly, and its old identity is becoming lost forever. The student project seeks to preserve this on the Web by creating a "virtual historical Riner" online. Students would be assigned the task of gathering information on Riner, e.g., by consulting courthouse records, interviewing residents and obtaining oral histories, taking photographs of important buildings and landmarks, and so on.

This information would then be placed online on the Web in the form of a hyperbase. As well as documenting the results of their investigations, students would also digitize photographs, snippets of audio (to provide examples of regional accents, for example), and video. This would require students to become familiar with many aspects of information technology within a very directly relevant context. It is also a project that caould be inherently ongoing, with successive classes of students augmenting the online history. To do this, previous students would need to make their work accessible enough that it could be understood and extended, thereby further exercising their communication skills.

Finally, one may wonder whether anyone is actually using these techniques. The answer is yes. In fact, more and more people are realizing that using the Internet in the classroom does not require a lot of hardware or complexity, and that it can reap rich rewards. But can the Internet be *integrated* successfully into the classroom and the curriculum? To attempt to answer this question, a federally funded study began recently in a fifth-grade class in rural Riner elementary school in Montgomery County [26]. The project seeks to determine, via a three-year longitudinal study, whether a technology-rich environment and integrated curriculum have a positive impact on the learning of students. Although it is taken as an axiom by computer scientists that technology can improve education, the phenomenon of technology refusal reminds us that this assertion is far from proven. This study will be of great importance to the ongoing status of educational technology and its eventual deployment on a large scale in the future. Many interested parties will be keeping a close eye on its progress.

21.5 Critical Literacy: the Web's Great Potential

What we seek to achieve with educational technology requires us to step back and determine what it is we wish to achieve within our educational system. A common goal is to create self-directed lifelong learners who are well equipped to take up a productive role in society. Our society is rapidly becoming an information driven one, and so it is incumbent upon us to equip students of the future to be effective information managers.

Knowledge continues to double at an increasingly fast rate. Requiring students to learn facts, as is common under the didactic system, is no longer a viable proposition. We need to equip our students with all the necessary skills to be able to locate and evaluate any information they need. They must become information managers, not information regurgitators [16].

As part of this process, two key questions face students searching out information:

1. Is this information relevant to my needs?

2. How do I determine the credibility of the source?

In essence, the problem is to develop critical literacy [13]. In a society where we are bombarded with often contradictory information, we must cultivate the ability to evaluate it critically. We must become critically literate [15].

Students often have had neither the need nor the opportunity to develop critical literacy in the class thus far. The authoritative nature of the didactic approach, combined with the use of textbooks as the primary delivery mechanism for information, favors the largely uncritical acceptance of information.

Textbooks are static and usually out of date by the time they are printed. Worse still, because of budgetary concerns, textbooks usually must be adopted for a minimum of several years, and so students must face a built-in obsolescence in the information they receive. In addition, textbooks need to please a broad and diverse audience, leading to a dilution and compromising of their contents. (For example, one may not find a frank treatment of the Viet Nam war in a US K–12 classroom text.) Political concerns aside, textbooks also come to the student pre-filtered. Somebody else, either the author or the librarian that chose the book, decided whether the material was relevant or appropriate to the student's needs. For these reasons, students have little opportunity to gain access to raw, unfiltered, even contradictory information with which to challenge their critical literacy. Yet in the real world this is precisely the kind of information they must deal with [28].

The Web offers immediate access to up-to-date raw information on every conceivable topic from a huge variety of sources. While teachers use the Web as an important source of information in their classes, they can also use it to cultivate critical literacy in their students.

As an example, part of the social studies curriculum used in one county in the U.S. (Montgomery County, in Virginia) includes a unit entitled "Facing History" which centers around human rights, including a focus on the Holocaust. Teachers incorporating material from the Web might discover Holocaust memorial sites along with Holocaust revisionist (Holocaust denial) sites such as that run by the "Institute for Holocaust Research." Immediately, students are confronted by two diametrically opposing views of the same subject. They must determine which is the more credible. In doing so, they must call upon skills that cut across the entire curriculum to sniff out misinformation, disinformation, and bias. A knowledge of statistics, physics, chemistry, mathematics, and so on might be needed to uncover the flaws in a specious argument. It may be necessary to examine what is not said in order to reveal something telling. For example, the fact that Holocaust memorial sites contain links to Holocaust denial sites but not vice versa could indicate to the reader that the former are not afraid of presenting all the information and letting the reader decide, whereas the latter wish to confine the reader's available information to the skewed presentation they offer.

Critical literacy is a prerequisite skill that must be fostered when using information from the Internet. This invaluable skill will carry over into a real world that contains ever more sources and quantities of information. On the Internet, where anyone may publish anything relatively easily, the huge quantity of extant information makes the use of search engines commonplace. However, search engines cannot rank the returned documents for credibility. This is left to the student, with a potential mountain of chaff mixed in with tasty morsels of wheat. In such a diluted ocean of information, the source is not always easy to evaluate, especially according to reputation, because of the vast number of (often anonymous) authors involved. In the end, it is usually left to the document to speak for itself in terms of its content validity, and ultimate credibility lies in the critical literacy of the reader [5].

Although this may seem like a burden, it is also a great liberation. Critical literacy is needed for a true democracy to function. Also, the critically literate reader will be armed with the skills necessary to avoid the pitfalls of specious advertising, pseudoscience, narrowed reality (e.g. Holocaust revisionism, Scientific Creationism, cults), get-rich-quick schemes (time-share scams, pyramid schemes, innumerable mail frauds), political rhetoric, indoctrination, media bias, double-speak, twisted statistics, and other ills that prey on the gullible in this information society we live in.

21.6 Conclusions

Having pursued several themes throughout this chapter, we now reflect on the content. First, educational technology has been an uneasy fit in the classroom, giving rise to the phenomenon of technology refusal. A large part of the problem lies in the fact that the creators of educational technology are far more familiar with and interested in the technology part of the pairing, and this leads to a product that ill-meets the needs of its users, the educators. Computer scientists need greater awareness of the milieu of educators, and, more importantly, a much deeper insight into pedagogical approaches more in tune with technology. Knowledge of the former will lead to adequate educational technology; understanding of the latter will result in exceptional classroom applications.

We have seen that the shadow of didacticism permeates many of the educational technology applications in typical use today. The main reason is its entrenched status in the classroom, in colleges of education, and in the extant experience of the educational technology developer (the computer scientist). Didacticism does not fit well with the open-ended, flexible nature of the computer, and so, as the computer moves towards a central point within the curriculum, didacticism will likely have to move aside to accommodate it. Thus, it may be that technology will force the issue in the ongoing issue of constructivism versus didacticism, giving the upper hand to the former, which, for a multitude of reasons already examined, is a more natural partner for technology. Such a move toward constructivism will not come about without a radical reassessment of what we want our educational system to achieve, and what its ultimate goals and requirements are: it requires real reform.

We have seen that only modest technological resources are required to use the Internet effectively in the curriculum, and that such use is not highly intrusive in that it can be a natural and dynamic extension of the traditional available information resources. The thing to note is that the computer is merely one more *tool*, and not a replacement for the educator (which educational technology often mistakenly tries to be). Educators are necessary and, in fact, are the classroom's most valuable resource. The computer should support the educator, not the other way around.

To be truly effective, our schools should reflect the society around them. The Internet and technology increasingly permeate society, and so it is likely that they will make their way further into the classroom and, importantly, the curriculum as time goes on. Along with this will come an inevitable increased awareness and training. Although the telephone and the automobile are taken for granted today by people who have grown up in a world surrounded by them, we must recall that these technologies were once foreign and novel just two or three generations ago. Just as those technologies were assimilated into the everyday lives of successive generations through ubiquity, so, too, will the computer. (Already it is commonplace to see Web URLs in television and print advertisements, indicating the penetration of the Internet into the everyday world.) This will doubtless be reflected in the classroom, with an inevitable ubiquitous use of technology across the curriculum. Indeed, the drive towards increased K–12 networking is already afoot, a testament to the importance of the Internet in our present and future—a recognition of the information age upon us.

Finally, the dawn of an information age requires students to be equipped to exist in an information-driven world. A key skill is the ability to forage successfully for information and then, most importantly, to evaluate it critically. Critical literacy, then, must become a big goal in our curricula, and, as already seen, the Internet and the Web provide an excellent medium in which to cultivate and hone this skill.

Acknowledgments

I am indebted to Melissa N. Matusevich, Instructional Coordinator, Montgomery County Public Schools, Virginia, U.S.A., for many invaluable discussions about education and technology. Ms. Matusevich has for many years now pioneered the ideas expressed in this chapter, often with only primitive available technology, proving time and again that one can "do more with less." Her patient and illuminating explanations of the issues involved allowed me to glimpse the world of educational technology through the eyes of the educator, and to see the subject in a much wider context.

21.7 References

[1]   Campoy, Renee. "The role of technology in the school reform movement." *Educational Technology*, Aug. 1992, 17–22.

[2]   Collins, Allan. "The role of computer technology in restructuring schools." *Phi Delta Kappan*, Sept. 1991, 28–36.

[3]   Dewey, John. *Experience and Education*. Kappa Delta Pi Lecture Series, New York, NY: Collier Books, 1938.

[4]   Evans-Andris, Melissa. "An examination of computing styles among teachers in elementary schools." *Educational Technology Research and Development*, 43 (2), 1995, 15-31.

[5]   Farah, Barbara D. "Information literacy: retooling evaluation skills in the electronic information environment." *Journal of Educational Technology Systems*, 24 (2), 1995, 127–133.

[6]   Fosnot, Catherine Twomey (ed). *Constructivism: Theory, Perspectives, and Practice*. New York: Teachers College Press, 1996.

[7]   Gardner, Howard. *Frames of Mind: The Theory of Multiple Intelligences*. New York: Basic Books, 1983.

[8]   ——. *Multiple Intelligences: the Theory in Practice*. New York: Basic Books, 1993.

[9]   Haan, Bernard J., Paul Kahn, Victor A. Riley, James H. Coombs, and Norman K. Meyrowitz. "IRIS hypermedia services." *Communications of the ACM*, 35 (1), Jan. 1992, 36–51.

[10] Hodas, Steven. "Technology refusal and the organizational culture of schools." *Educational Policy Analysis Archives*, 1 (10), Sept. 1993. <http://olam.ed.asu.edu/epaa/v1n10.html> (8 Nov. 1996).

[11] Holland, Holly. "Needles in a haystack: the real have-nots in technology are rural schools." *Electronic Learning*, April 1995, 26–28.

[12] Jonassen, David H. "Evaluating constructivistic learning." *Educational Technology*, 31, 1991, 28–33.

[13] Jongsma, Kathleen Stumpf. "Critical literacy." *The Reading Teacher*, 44 (7), 1991, 518–519.

[14] Kappe, F., H. Maurer, and N. Scherbakov. "Hyper-G: a universal hypermedia system." *Journal of Educational Multimedia and Hypermedia*, 2 (1), 1993, 39–66.

[15] Macedo, Donaldo P. "Literacy for stupidification: the pedagogy of big lies."
     Harvard Educational Review, 63 (2), Summer 1993, 183–206.

[16] Mann, Christine. "New technologies and gifted education." *Roeper Review*,
     16 (3), Feb. 1994, 172–176.

[17] Matusevich, Melissa Nabbe. "Educational Projects." 1994.
     <http://pixel.cs.vt.edu/melissa/projects.html> (20 Nov. 1996).

[18] Mohn, Robert C. "Problems with integrating computer technology into the
     K–12 educational curriculum: a study of the use of the Internet and video-
     conferencing in a fifth grade classroom." MS thesis, Department of Com-
     puter Science, Virginia Polytechnic and State University, 1995.

[19] Resnick, Paul and James Miller. "PICS: Internet access controls without
     censorship." *Communications of the ACM*, 39 (10), Oct. 1996, 87–93.

[20] Senge, Peter (presenter). "Applying Principles of the Learning Organiza-
     tion, Part II." Teleconference, 1995. (Available from InNov.ation Associates,
     Inc., 3 Speen Street, Suite 140, Framingham, MA 01701, U.S.A.)

[21] Strommen, Erik F. and Bruce Lincoln. "Constructivism, technology, and the
     future of classroom learning." *Education and Urban Society*, 24 Aug. 1992,
     466–476.

[22] University of Minnesota. "Web66 Home Page." 1996.
     <http://web66.umn.edu> (25 Nov. 1996).

[23] ———. "Web66: International WWW School Registry." 1996.
     <http://web66.umn.edu/schools.html> (25 Nov. 1996).

[24] Virginia Department of Education. "Virginia Public Education Network."
     <telnet pen.k12.va.us> (5 Dec. 1996).

[25] Virginia Tech. "CS Dept. NSF-Supported Education Infrastructure Project /
     ei.cs.vt.edu." 1994. <http://ei.cs.vt.edu> (5 Dec. 1996).

[26] Virginia Tech and Montgomery County Public Schools. "PCs for Families."
     1996. <http://pixel.cs.vt.edu/edu/fis/> (5 Dec. 1996).

[27] Vygotskii, Lev Semenovich. *The Vygotsky Reader*. van der Veer, Rene and
     Jaan Valsiner (eds.), Oxford, UK; Cambridge, MA: Blackwell, 1994.

[28] Wilson, Marilyn. "Critical thinking: repackaging or revolution?" *Language
     Arts*, 65 (6), Oct. 1988, 543–551.

[29] World Wide Web Consortium. "Platform for Internet Content Selection."
     1995. <http://www.w3.org/pub/WWW/PICS/> (20 Nov. 1996).

[30] Yahoo! Inc. "Yahoo!" 1995. <http://www.yahoo.com> (25 Nov. 1996).

[31] Yahoo! Inc. "Yahoo!—Education." 1995. <http://www.yahoo.com/Education/> (25 Nov. 1996).

[32] Yahoo! Inc. "Yahooligans!" 1996. <http://www.yahooligans.com> (25 Nov. 1996).

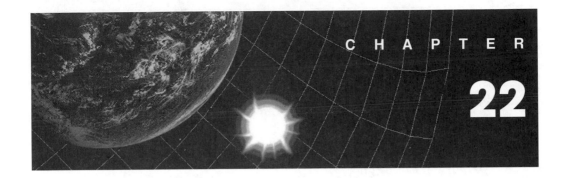

C H A P T E R

22

Web-Related Careers

by Felicia Doswell

*E*mployment in Web-related fields has been a growing trend for several years. We know the skills necessary, but what are the job titles to match these skills? Is there a one-to-one correspondence of "Skills X = Job Title Y"? A review of many of the jobs currently involving Web-related careers presents a confusing view. Web-related employment in these areas spans many different disciplines. Web usage, development and maintenance are just a few of the opportunities offered. The possibilities are abundant if you have skills in Communications, Marketing, Advertising, Art/Graphics Design, Network Maintenance, System Administration, HTML, Java, CGI Programming, and many others. What are the going salaries if you have "Web Experience"? The answer differs based on the number of skills possessed. The more of the above-listed skills one may have, the higher the salary one can demand. How will education to acquire "Web Experience" prevail in the future? The present trend is quick, learn-as-you-go techniques. With the growth of the Internet and the Web there will be a need for more structured educational programs designed to produce truly efficient "Webmasters." The employment outlook is vague but optimistic. Future employment in Web-related careers will require a person to be a "Jack" or "Jill" of many trades; however, those persons will be able to demand top salaries.

This chapter will first address the problems of distinguishing titles for "experts" that work with the Internet and the Web. It will then provide an overview of some of the more notable professionals that use the Web to perform job functions. This includes their job title, job description as it relates to the Web, salaries range, and education requirements. Finally, there will be a discussion on the potential future of the job market in relation to the Web, and the future of education for these professions.

Chapter Content

22.1 Introduction

The Internet and the Web have introduced an abundant amount of information to the world. The Internet is a large collection of computer networks connected via cables and telephone lines. The Web is just a communication tool giving access to all the information available on the Internet. People everywhere are becoming involved with Internet technology, either as a user or to profit financially. Internet and Web users include individuals that use it for personal work, students and teachers that use it for courses, and government and businesses that use it to perform job functions. In order to access the information, a person only needs a computer, a modem, a telephone line or Ethernet cable, access through an online service, and a Web browser. The types of information that are available electronically via the Web include magazines, newspapers, books, advertisements, games, and courses. The ease of accessing all of this information has made a major impact on academia and industry.

The usage capacity of the Internet is now more than 30 million users. How will we begin to control the type and amount of information available via the

Web? An even broader issue to be explored is who will create, manage, support, and present this wide array of information. To help manage the situation, college campuses and technical schools have produced many professionals geared to handle the creation, maintenance, and transmission of information on the Web. The professions that have emerged range from artists to "Webmasters." There has also been a rise of self-employed individuals who train and consult on a freelance basis to help bring more individuals, government organizations, and companies onto the Internet. This leads to the task of attempting to compile a list of Web-related careers and the necessary requirements for performing the jobs. The education requirements for many of the Web-related careers include backgrounds in Computer Science, Information Science, and Electrical Engineering. However, there are a larger number of Internet professionals being produced from other degree areas such as Art and Marketing. In all cases, the salary range of Internet professionals is based on the skills a person possesses and his or her job title and educational status.

22.2 The Job Title Confusion

Well-defined job titles in computer-related professions appear to be a thing of the past. What has happened to the times when job titles clearly defined the responsibilities of computer professionals? In the past, job titles specified what qualifications the employee had or the employer expected. There were the system analysts who did the planning and design of computer systems. The programmers implemented the design of the system by writing and testing code. If one was responsible for planning, design and implementation, then he or she was referred to as a programmer/analyst. Now we have the push toward client/server technology and a plethora of titles that come with it. Among the most prevalent is the title of "Webmaster." Therefore, with the new emphasis on the Internet and the Web, there has been a large addition to the confusion of job titles for computer professionals.

There are many titles applied to persons who are considered Web experts. Webmaster, HTML/CGI/Java Programmer, Web Site Administrator, Web Architect, and Web Page Designer are just a few. Notice that several of these names have Internet or Web attached to them. The reason is that the Internet and the Web are hot topics now. However, with each of these titles, there are some conflicting and overlapping job descriptions. One view is that anyone with experience in HTML can be characterized as a Webmaster (page 426). This is a narrow view. Although many persons carry one of the above mentioned titles, some of these persons may fit into other Web/Internet related fields. These other fields may require less or more specific responsibilities than a Webmaster. However, all of these professionals should be considered in the move toward the distributed information storage and access given by the Internet and the Web.

In the ten subsections under "Popular Career Titles" we will cover some of the more popular Web-related careers. Each career subsection will include a description, education requirement, and average salary demand.

22.3 Popular Career Titles

Artist/Graphics Designer

Description: Internet Artwork is now a popular component of personal Web pages, commercial Web sites, online magazines and online galleries [11]. Due to the increase in Web usage for commercial advertising and publishing, there has been a large increase in the need for people with art/graphics skills to aid in producing eye-catching art for advertising. The objective is to add enough graphics to attract a reader's attention.

The artist/graphics designer is generally responsible for Web page layout and design of magazines, newspapers, journals, and other publications. Since multimedia on the Web has become more prevalent, artist/graphics designers also create graphics for computer-generated media [7]. These persons either create HTML pages or communicate with the Web Page Designer (page 427) to produce quality artwork that properly represents the textual information. The skills necessary to do this are graphics design and creativity. The artist should have a working knowledge of the popular paint and scan programs such as Adobe Photoshop [11] and experience with some desktop publishing package. Another name for the occupation is visual arts.

Education Requirement: A degree in Graphics Design or Art would be a plus. However, if other Web-related skills are available, then a few classes in Graphics Design and Art are sufficient.

Salary: The demand for art/graphics designers is frequently for a freelance or consultant position. Magazines and commercial businesses will hire persons to perform graphics design on a regular basis if they have other skills to complement their design ability. The amount paid for this skill can range from $25–$50K annually [7]. The salary could be higher based on additional skills.

Author/Journalist

Description: Journalists and book writers are well known for the information they provide to the world in written form. These persons gather data, form it into meaningful information, and present it to their readers. With the move to provide material via the Internet, authors of books and journal articles have to keep up by providing their information as well. Therefore, in addition to having excellent writing skills, these writers will have to learn additional skills. They need to know how to set up a Web site, be familiar with HTML in order to present the information they desire, have graphics design experience, or hire someone to do these tasks. They must do all of these things and still meet deadlines [11].

Education Requirement: An author is usually someone who has a creative mind for putting thoughts and ideas on paper. The person may or may not have a formal education, but if so he or she usually has a degree in English, Literature, or some other liberal arts field. A journalist usually has a formal education with a major in History, Journalism, English, or Communication. Both types of writers may work freelance. Otherwise, journalists usually answer to a magazine or newspaper, and authors to an editor. To provide their material on the Web, authors also have to be trained in graphics design, HTML, and a navigation tool.

Salary: The pay can range from $35–$100 per article for a freelance journalist [11]. This pay scale also depends on the type of article written. For a freelance book author, the pay depends on the interest of the audience. Authors and journalists that work for a company or magazine could expect a salary range of $20K–$60. This depends on the firm for which they work and the number of years of experience they have in the field. The lower range is for beginning writers and the upper range is for editors [7].

Educator/Trainer

Many educators and trainers have jumped on the Internet/Web bandwagon. These persons are either training in corporations or teaching in secondary and post-secondary education. There are many titles for Internet educators and trainers. A few are named and described below.

Instructional Designer

Description: Businesses are finding it essential to provide training to their employees in order to remain productive and globally competitive. To provide this training, instructional technologists/designers are usually employed as corporate trainers. Due to the higher availability of information on the Web, these educators are using the Internet and the Web to teach job-related topics. They are also responsible for developing the training material and course format. In all of their tasks, they use the Internet for creating, editing, and presenting material. The necessary Internet skills include knowledge of how to create a Web site, HTML, basic Internet services such as e-mail and newsgroups, and experience with a Web browser. Other skills would be dependent on the topic being presented [11].

Education Requirement: Persons in this field usually have a degree in Instructional Technology, especially for developing training material and course format. Companies also employ workers who may have on-the-job expertise and can help in training new hires. These trainers have a degree in the technical field for which they generally work.

Salary: A person can receive a salary in the range of $30K–$80K depending on how technical their degree is [7]. Salary would also depend upon the experience in training and the topic being taught. For trainers with technical degrees, the higher end of the scale would apply. All others fall in the lower two thirds of the range.

Internet/WWW Instructor

Description: Internet instructors usually range from technical school instructors to college professors. They are the persons who have some expertise in the Internet and Web. They teach all aspects of the Internet and Web, from HTML/JAVA/CGI programming to internetworking technology. They usually teach as a part of a curriculum that leads to the students getting a degree or certificate stating they have completed Internet/Web training. The Internet instructor designs, implements, presents, and evaluates course material used for the course.

Education Requirement: The expected education level covers a wide range of educators and backgrounds. There are the professors who teach undergraduate and graduate courses, and they have M.S. or PhD degrees. There are the pregraduate degree and technical school instructors who have B.S. degrees with extensive experience in Internet/Web concepts and usage.

Salary: The salary range for Internet Instructors is $30K–$80K depending on education level. The technical school and pregraduate degree instructors are on the lower end of the pay scale. University professors are on the upper end, and their pay is based on rank [7].

K–12 Educators

Description: K–12 educators all over the world are starting to use the Internet to teach in primary and secondary education classrooms. They use the Internet to communicate with parents, other teachers, and administrators. They show students how to use the Internet for research purposes and for collaboration with students and teachers at remote locations. The necessary skills include knowledge of how to create a Web site, HTML, and basic Internet services such as e-mail and newsgroups. Teachers should have experience with some kind of Web browser.

Education Requirement: To teach in primary and secondary education, teachers should have a B.S. or B.A. in Education and have passed the state exams necessary to be certified. In addition they should have some training to acquire the above-mentioned skills (informally or formally). Consultants (page 423) are usually employed to train teachers for Web usage.

Salary: Salary may range from $20K–$40K depending on education level, state requirements, and experience.

Internetwork Engineer

Description: Internetwork engineers, network installers, and network architects design local area networks and then install the cabling, switches, routers, and firewalls. They also program routers and set up ftp sites. They have skills in a wide assortment of router products, know how to set and recover passwords, have experience with downloading operating systems images and configuration files via ftp servers, and have knowledge of file architecture of routers. These persons also provide troubleshooting capabilities for companies. In other words, they provide the installation and customer support for a company.

Education Requirement: Basic knowledge of networking and protocols is necessary. Therefore, having courses that cover this would be a plus. Many persons have a degree in Computer Science or Electrical Engineering, or a combination of the two, with advanced degrees typically commanding higher pay. At least a background in computer hardware and software would be sufficient. There are some companies that offer certification for Internetworking. Employers may reward employees for taking short courses that lead to certifications to encourage employees to stay abreast of new technologies.

Salary: The 1997 *Network World*/Deloitte & Touche Consulting Group Salary Survey found that companies expect to pay an average of $44,106 for a new hire. The survey was based on companies whose annual gross revenue is $1 billion or more. Companies surveyed currently pay $48,859 for an entry-level position (averaging 3.3 years of experience) and $78,596 for a senior position (averaging 8.8 years of experience) [6]. Respondents expected raises ranging from about 5% to 6% in the next 12 months, compared to an average increase of 3.2% for the average U.S. worker, reported by the U.S. Bureau of Labor Statistics.

Internet/WWW Consultant

Description: An Internet consultant is a person that provides training and support to individuals, companies, and schools. They are considered experts in Internetworking, Web browsers, Web creations, installation, and maintenance. They have extensive knowledge of HTML, Java, CGI, VRML and some scripting languages such as PERL or JavaScript. They must also be familiar with applications run on the Internet. In other words, they do it all! They are usually hired based on a reputation for getting the job done efficiently.

Education Requirement: A degree in a technical field such as Engineering or Computer Science is usually the education level for a consultant. However, since the Internet is such a new phenomenon, the majority of employees acquire their education from hands-on experience, either from working with companies that use the Internet, or by self-taught methods. Since they are usually hired based on reputation, they would have to market themselves in order to establish a working relationship with a company.

Salary: Consultants can be paid $25–$100 per hour [11]. This would be based on how they market themselves and whether they work for small or large firms on a consulting basis.

Marketing/Advertising Professional

Description: Due to the growth of the Internet and the number of people accessing information on the Internet, a large part of the commercial online services will be used to deliver advertisements. This is a positive step for job-seekers because it increases the number of jobs for Marketing/Advertising professionals. Employers want individuals with Marketing and Management skills and an understanding of the Web environment. They do not want programmers for their tasks, but they want individuals with creativity and a knack for product design and presentation [1]. These individuals use the Web as a platform for their products. They are sometimes hired as consultants (page 423), Web designers (page 427), advertisers, and/or marketing personnel.

Education Requirement: Persons working in Marketing and Advertising should have degrees in Marketing, Advertising, or Management. They generally acquire Internet knowledge via experience working with the Internet and Web. A background in graphics design (page 420) would be a plus.

Salary: Marketing and advertising professionals with Web skills can expect a salary in the range of $25K–$150K depending on education level and experience [7]. The higher end is for managerial positions and depends on the number of employees that the manager supervises.

Protocol Designer

Description: Persons that define Internet services are called protocol designers. They write protocols for Electronic Mail (e-mail), File Transfer Protocol (FTP), TELNET, USENET News, Gopher, and Hypertext Transfer Protocol (HTTP). These persons should have knowledge of existing protocols, creativity to design/modify protocols, ability to test the protocols, and experience with networking. Many of them have performed or do perform Internetwork Engineering (page 423) tasks as well.

Education Requirement: Most protocol designers have an education background in Electrical Engineering and/or Computer Science. There are some technical schools that offer one to two year programs of courses to be certified in writing protocols.

Salary: The salary can range from $40K–$80K depending on experience and education.

Software Engineer/Programmer

Description: The software engineer (or client/server programmer, development manager, programming manager, programmer, systems analyst, Web/Internet application developer, software developer, or database administrator) designs and develops a variety of software that runs interacts with networks. One type of software is server software (e.g., router, firewall, Web server software); another type is applications programming, especially client/server applications. A software engineer may design and/or implement the software. The individual may also set up Internet accounts for a company, and insure that everything runs smoothly.

Their skills include basic knowledge of operating systems, programming languages, internetworking, and software development methodologies. They should know several languages and utilities such as Java, HTML, C++, and CGI. They should have experience with UNIX systems, have some knowledge of database systems, and be familiar with several Web browsers. Communication skills are necessary to provide support to users of the Web sites, servers, or applications.

Education Requirement: Software engineers usually have degrees in technical fields such as Electrical Engineering, Computer Engineering, or Computer Science. They acquire their basic training from their formal education and get some Internet coverage via these degrees. However, with the rate at which new Web and Internet technology is introduced, these persons acquire the majority of their Internet knowledge on their own and from experience working with the Internet and the Web. Reading many books and articles is a big part of acquiring knowledge about the Web. The Internet itself can provide a large volume of helpful information.

Salary: Software engineers/programmers can demand a salary in the range of $30K–$70K depending on education level and experience [7].

Webmaster

Description: Webmaster is the title of a person who manages a Web site. It includes persons that develop, install, and maintain Web sites. These persons interact with Web Page Designers and Graphics Designers or perform these duties in order to create quality Web sites. Their responsibilities include design of textual and graphical layouts, maintenance of sites via verification of links and contents, and creation and installation of applications to be used within the site. Necessary skills include knowledge of HTML/CGI/Java, understanding of internetworking, knowledge of many applications available on the Web, and excellent communication skills.

According to Paul Kozeniowski, a Webmaster is expected to understand server operating system and languages such as Java, as well as to create HTML pages [8]. One "Webmaster" for Telegroup International Inc. describes the tasks performed under this job title as follows:

- Designing and maintaining the company's intranet. This includes gathering content to be presented on the Web.

- Composing company documents in HTML.

- Training colleagues about proper construction of Web pages, and how to use Web specific applications.

- Critiquing and editing HTML pages before making public on a Web site.

- Maintaining Web servers by staying current in new technologies and Web developments [2].

Other job descriptions taken from various job postings include responsibilities such as requirements analysis, interface design, application implementation, Web page design, graphics design, C++ and Unix knowledge, technical support, database management, and writing, presentation and management skills. Notice that the description above gives a long list of skills required by many companies and that the list encompasses many fields other than computer-related fields. Therefore, Webmaster is a tag attached to almost anyone in any profession that can perform the listed skills.

Education Requirement: The usual education background of a Webmaster is a minimum of a B.S. degree in Computer Science, Information Science, Electrical Engineering, or other computer-related fields. Experience with the above-mentioned skills is normally required of a Webmaster. Finally, a Webmaster might be a member of a professional organization, such as the International Webmasters Association [10].

Salary: The salary given for a Webmaster can range from $45K–$80K, depending on experience and the breadth of knowledge acquired [11]. This salary range is based on the requirements stated in the job description and the education background.

Web Page Designer

Description: Web page designers are persons that convert text or printed documents to HTML format. These are usually not the only skills they have, and they sometimes refer to themselves as Webmasters (page 426). The latter should only apply if the person does the graphics design (page 420), text conversion, Web site setup, and maintenance. Otherwise, their only tasks involve designing the layout of the textual information and presenting it via HTML. However, they are required to work with the graphics designer and persons providing the content in order to provide quality Web pages. Web page designers also need to have expert knowledge of HTML, a browser, and good communication skills to accomplish their job.

Education Requirement: Knowledge of HTML is the largest educational requirement for Web page designers. HTML is a language that one can learn by reading a book. To be an efficient and productive Web page designer, one should also have skills in graphics design, some programming ability in scripting languages (e.g., Javascript), and knowledge of CGI and Java.

Salary: These persons can demand $20K–$50K depending on experience, skills beyond basic HTML knowledge, and education level [11].

22.4 Future Opportunities

The Internet and Web are changing the way people perform information searches and presentations, sell and buy products, and communicate with others. Although there are many new Web-related careers that may result from the growth of the Internet, the professions that may benefit most in the future are education, law and Internet security, and Internet commerce.

Education

The Internet and Web have had a major impact on academia. College students are performing many academic endeavors using the Internet, including correspondence and collaboration. Faculty are using the Internet to develop courses, exchange information, and examine students' progress. This leaves ample room for the Internet to expand in the academic environment, from producing Internet programmers to designing quality applications to be used in education. The Internet technology will have an even larger impact on K–12 education (see Chapter 21). It is presently changing the way students collaborate, and will continue to allow communication that was otherwise limited by distance in the past.

Law and Internet Security

Although the Internet has provided society with many new capabilities, this grand new communication medium comes with problems such as legal and security issues. However, these changes and problems have produced the potential for new jobs and the expansion of existing jobs. Legal issues come about from misbehavior such as e-mail fraud and breach of confidentiality. International export laws produce restrictions on taxes, licenses, and transport of goods across boundaries. Managing proprietary information, programs, and technology is a prominent concern and will continue to be in the future. Limits to freedom of speech will be challenged (see Chapter 19). All of this creates a whole new arena for the legal profession. Security issues can abound on the Internet due to unauthorized access, denial of service, malicious altering of information, and theft of information. This opens a host of career opportunities for programmers/analysts who design and code encryption algorithms and use other techniques to ensure privacy and information security on the Web (see Chapter 12).

Internet Commerce

With the growth of the Internet, there has been a major increase in conducting business using this technological medium (see Chapter 13). Some of the advantages of Internet commerce include 24-hour access for customers and rapid customer-service response. Among the organizations that offer online services are financial institutions, home shopping networks, and magazine publishers. The future for these businesses encompasses bringing more interactive services and publications to a larger spectrum of the population. There will also be many more entrepreneurships, new opportunities for distribution, and more businesses interacting among each other [9]. Internet commerce is an umbrella for a variety of existing career opportunities and therefore will be an exciting creator of jobs for many highly motivated individuals.

All of the above results in a promising future market in Web-related careers. Presently, many of the Web related skills are acquired via self-taught methods. A training trend has begun in which Internet schools are being started to teach the necessary skills to work in Internet/Web related jobs. The success of the Internet/Web will determine if these schools are a good investment idea. For now, colleges, universities, and technical schools will have to accommodate the students attempting to acquire these Web-related skills.

22.5 Conclusion

Look through the classified advertisements, and you will see a company requesting computer professionals with Internet/Web skills. How will the potential employees and employers find a match with the inconsistent list of job titles that conflict and overlap? Webmaster is a title everyone wants to have, but what are the skills necessary to truly be called a "master" of the Web? The Web is too new for anyone to claim to be a "master." Some approach mastery by having many of the skills that are presently known for Internet/Intranet/Extranet set-up, development, maintenance, and analysis. To imply you do everything necessary to have a Web Site, you would have to be able to do at least the following:

- Deliver T-1 and T-3 connections

- Install routers and firewalls

- Set up FTP sites

- Help customers set up and develop a Web site

- Register URLs and Domain names for customers

- Set up accounts

- Apply and teach HTML, Java, VRML, CGI

- Integrate various database, and other applications into the site

- Work with all multimedia applications available

- Have experience in graphics design, and marketing [4].

So, what should people call themselves if "Web designer" is too restrictive, and "Webmaster" is too broad? The present chaos will probably continue for another couple of years, until the topic phases out or the jobs are absorbed by some existing titles, or standardization of titles occurs. The upside to all of this is that anyone with any of the above skills can demand top dollar for their knowledge and need not have extensive education to get it. Therefore, the career outlook for future employment in Web-related fields is positive.

22.6 References

[1] Bennahum, David S. "Our Brilliant Careers." *NetGuide* (April 1, 1995).

[2] Buchanan, Leigh. "What IS a Webmaster?" *Webmaster Magazine*. <http://www.cio.com/Webmaster/wm_job.html/> (1996, accessed 23 Oct. 1996).

[3] Corcoran, Elizabeth. "On the Internet, a Worldwide Information Explosion Beyond Words." *The Washington Post* (June 30, 1996).

[4] Doyle, T. C. "Where the Dollars Are." *VARBusiness*. (February 1, 1996).

[5]   Dreyer, Steven M. and Isabelle Fymat. "He Who Staffs Last." *Webmaster Magazine*.   <http://www.cio.com/Webmaster/0596_tracks.html>   (1996, accessed 23 Oct. 1996).

[6]   Duffy, Tom. "Write Your Ticket," *Network World* 14, No. 5, Sept. 1, 1997, pp. 1 and 44–48.

[7]   Fullerton, Howard N. "The Occupational Handbook, 1996–1997." <http://stats.bls.gov/ocohome.htm> (accessed 23 Oct. 1996).

[8]   Korzeniowski, Paul. "Mastering the Webmaster." *InfoWorld,* 18.32. (5 Aug. 1996). pp. 53–54.

[9]   Netscape Communications Corp. "Internet Commerce Overview." *Netscape White Paper Series*. <http://home.jp.netscape.com/comprod/business_solutions/commerce/overview/white_paper.html> (accessed 23 Oct. 1996).

[10]   International Webmasters Association. "About the International Webmasters Association." <http://www.irwa.org/about/>. (3 Sept. 1997).

[11]   Thompson, Lianne. "CyberSpace Jobs." <http://www.best.com:80/~lianne/index2.html/> (accessed 23 Oct. 1996).

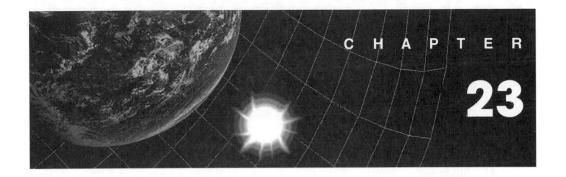

HTTP: Present and Future

by Mir Farooq Ali

The Web has grown dramatically in the last five years. The primary protocol for the Web, HTTP now accounts for the majority of Internet traffic. With this change has come a need to revise the existing HTTP (1.0) protocol. HTTP-NG was a proposed extension to the HTTP protocol, increasing the basic functionality and extending it. HTTP/1.1 followed, as a new standard. The growth of the Internet has fueled a lot of interest in Web commerce too. This forces the issue of security on the net. This resulted in S-HTTP, a proposed extension to HTTP to make it more suitable for "secure" transactions on the Web. When we have many proposed extensions to HTTP, then there is a need for coordination between the different versions. Protocol Extension Protocol, or PEP, allows HTTP clients, servers and proxies to use custom extensions to HTTP. In this chapter we present a brief introduction to the basic HTTP protocol and its design issues, before talking about HTTP/1.1, HTTP-NG, S-HTTP and PEP.

Chapter Content

23.1 Introduction

The main protocol behind the Web is the Hypertext Transfer Protocol (HTTP). It forms the basis for the transfer of documents between Web servers and clients. It runs on top of the TCP/IP protocol suite. In this section a brief history of HTTP, the need for it, and the design issues behind the original HTTP are presented.

History of HTTP

Around the time when the Web started gaining popularity, there were a host of specialized data-transfer protocols related to file transfers, news broadcasts, mail transfers, search and retrieval facilities. But the Web brought along its own specific needs. The protocol needed mainly a subset of file-transfer functionality, the ability to request and index search, automatic format negotiation, and the ability to refer a client request to another server. This initiated the development of HTTP.

The original HTTP developed in 1991 was a very simple-minded protocol [1]. Its main purpose was to do raw data transfer. This protocol is HTTP/0.9. It has facilities for making connections, initiating requests, and getting back responses. All the responses are simply streams of ASCII characters.

This protocol was replaced by HTTP/1.0, described in RFC 1945, which added MIME-like messages, header lines containing information about the data being transferred, and modifiers for the request/response messages. This protocol also has disadvantages that are overcome by the next proposed enhancement, HTTP/1.1. HTTP/1.0 and HTTP/1.1 are described in more detail in the next two sections.

HTTP/1.1 considers hierarchical proxy servers, caching, adding persistent connections, and virtual hosts. HTTP/1.1 became an Internet Engineering Task Force (IETF) proposed standard, RFC 2068, in September 1996.

HTTP-NG (Next Generation) is another proposed modification to HTTP/1.0. It preceded development of HTTP/1.1 (draft 7). It was supposed to be an enhanced replacement for HTTP/1.0. HTTP-NG is discussed in detail in Section 23.4. Since it was first proposed, many changes have been suggested for HTTP-NG. The World Wide Web Consortium (W3C) has an HTTP-NG activity. The HTTP-NG discussed here is now referred to as classic HTTP-NG. Some of the key ideas behind HTTP-NG include persistent connections, the ability to make multiplex multiple requests/responses over a single transport connection, and the ability to pass URLs to a protocol in a response message.

S-HTTP (Secure HTTP) was developed to provide secure communication mechanisms between an HTTP client-server pair to simplify commerce transactions that are increasingly important to the Web.

Design Issues of Original HTTP

The design of HTTP presented some new problems because it dealt with information retrieval for hypertext [2]. Decisions had to be made related to the underlying protocol and other issues related to the data transfer. There were various distinct possible bases for the protocol. Choices could be made between something based on an Internet protocol, something based on an RPC standard, or something based on the OSI stack. Current HTTP as well as the original version decided to follow the first option and run over the existing TCP/IP protocol, since it had the advantage of being well understood, and existing implementations were readily available.

Another issue arising was whether the protocol would be idempotent or not, which determines whether the server needs to keep any state information about the client. The current protocol is idempotent.

Decisions also had to be made regarding the two main commands under HTTP, requests and responses, as well as status codes depending on the result of command execution.

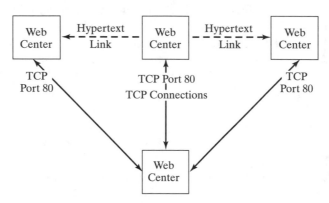

Figure 23–1   Interaction between Client and Server

23.2 HTTP/1.0

Background

The Web client (commonly called a browser) communicates with a Web server using one or more TCP connections (see Fig. 23–1). The well-known port for the Web server is TCP port 80. HTTP is the protocol used by the client and server to communicate over the TCP connection. Typically, the browser invokes some hypertext document. This document may itself contain other hypertext links to other documents. They may even be links to FTP, TELNET, or other protocols.

Description

Some of the main features of HTTP/1.0 are summarized below.

1. *Message types:* There are two kinds of messages: requests, and responses. Requests are made to get information and responses are the replies to requests. There are three kinds of requests:

    a.   The GET request returns whatever information is requested.
    b.   The HEAD request returns only the server's header information.
    c.   The POST request is used for posting electronic mail or news or for sending forms that can be filled in by and interactive user. This is the only request that sends a body with the request.

2. *Header fields:* With HTTP/1.0 both the request and the response can contain a variable number of header fields. A blank line separates the

header fields from the body. A header field consists of a field name, followed by a colon, a single space, and the field value. Field names are case sensitive. Headers can be classified into three categories: those that apply to requests, those that apply to responses, and those that describe the body. Unknown header fields should be ignored by a recipient.

3. *Response codes:* The first line of the server's response is called the status line. It begins with the HTTP version, followed by a 3-digit response code, followed by an English response phrase.

Performance Problems

Given the increasing use of HTTP, its impact on the Web is considerable. As mentioned earlier, HTTP/1.0 and earlier versions suffered from some serious performance problems. Some of the problems were due to the design mismatch between HTTP and its underlying TCP layer. A fundamental problem has to do with the mismatch between the byte-oriented TCP stream and the message-oriented HTTP service. An ideal solution is a session-layer protocol on top of TCP that provides a message-oriented interface between an HTTP client and server over a single TCP connection. This approach is used in HTTP-NG and is described in Section 23.4.

The biggest problem, however, is due to the use of one TCP connection per file. This causes connection setup and slow-start costs, leading to high latency costs. This is further increased by the protocols returning only one object per request. In general, HTTP/1.0 spends more time waiting than transferring data.

These factors seriously affect the performance of HTTP. The latest versions of the protocol, HTTP/1.1 and HTTP-NG, address these problems.

23.3 HTTP/1.1

HTTP/1.1 seeks to enhance the scope of HTTP/1.0, remove many of the inconsistencies surrounding different implementations, and improve the performance. It seeks to add to HTTP/1.0 features such as hierarchical proxies, persistent connections, virtual hosts, and caching, as well as to act like a generic protocol for communication between user agents and proxies/gateways to other Internet systems, including those supported by the SMTP, NNTP, FTP, Gopher, and WAIS protocols. HTTP/1.1, which as of draft 08 is a draft standard of the IETF, RFC 2068 [4], is still in an evolving state. As of this draft, there are still several implementation issues that must be resolved. In this section we discuss the main features of HTTP/1.1.

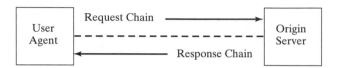

Figure 23–2 Interaction between User and Server in HTTP/1.0

Main Features

The HTTP/1.1 draft standard [4] uses certain terminology. First, the *user agent* is the client that sends requests to a Web server. The most familiar user agent is a Web browser. Second, the standard refers to *Uniform Resource Identifier* (URI). A URI is either a URL or a *Uniform Resource Name* (URN). To understand a URN, note that a URL names a specific Web server, thereby encoding the physical location of a document into the name that people use for the document. If the document is moved to another Web server, a URL becomes invalid. A URN allows a yet-to-be-adopted mechanism to be introduced into the Web, in which the name that people use for a document does not contain a physical location, but rather some logical name. Third, the server that contains the original copy of a document, as opposed to a cached copy, is called the *origin server*. In the URL http://ei.cs.vt.edu/, Internet host ei.cs.vt.edu is the origin server. The term origin server is used because an HTTP request, such as a GET for a document, might be satisfied by some server other than the origin server, such as a caching proxy server.

The main features of HTTP/1.1 are summarized below.

1. *Intermediaries*: HTTP/1.0 uses a simple model for data transfer between the user agent and the origin server over a single connection, as illustrated in Fig. 23–2.

   HTTP/1.1 recognizes that one or more intermediaries may exist. The most common forms of intermediaries are proxies, gateways, and tunnels. According to [4], "A proxy is a forwarding agent, receiving requests for a URI in its absolute form, rewriting all or part of the message, and forwarding the reformatted request toward the server identified by the URI. A gateway is a receiving agent, acting as a layer above some other server(s) and, if necessary, translating the requests to the underlying server's protocol. A tunnel acts as a relay point between two connections without changing the messages; tunnels are used when the communication needs to pass through an intermediary (such as a firewall) even when the intermediary cannot understand the contents of the messages." An example of multiple intermediaries is illustrated in Fig. 23–3, where A, B, and C are intermediaries

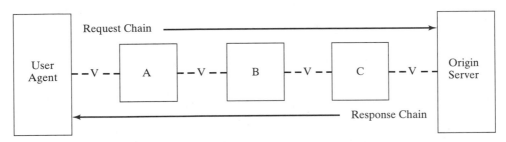

Figure 23–3 Interaction between User Agent and Server in HTTP/1.1

between the User Agent and the Origin Server. Each network link is denoted by V in the figure.

One of the goals of HTTP/1.1 with respect to caches and proxies is "to support the wide diversity of configurations already deployed while introducing protocol constructs that meet the needs of those who build Web applications that require high reliability and, failing that, at least reliable indications of failure" [4].

2. *Messages*: HTTP messages consist of a request sent from user agent to server and a response returned server to user agent. Most types of messages consist of a start-line, one or more headers, an empty line indicating the end of the headers, and an optional message body.

   a. *Requests*: The HTTP/1.0 requests are GET, HEAD and POST. HTTP/1.1 adds four more request types, listed below. The HTTP/1.1 PUT and DELETE types, together with the HTTP/1.0 GET, changes a Web server function from that of just returning documents into that of a conventional network file server, by allowing documents to be stored on, deleted on, and read from the Web server.

   • DELETE: Client can delete a document on the Web server by using DELETE and naming a URI to be deleted.

   • PUT: Client can write a document to a Web server. The document is stored on the server in a location named by the URI in the PUT.

   • OPTIONS: A request for information about the communication options available on the request/response chain identified by the Request-URI.

   • TRACE: Used to involve a remote, application-layer loop-back of the request message.

b. *Responses:* After receiving and interpreting a request message, a server responds with an HTTP response message, which consists of a status line, headers, blank line, and the message body. The status line consists of the protocol version followed by a numeric status code and its associated textual phrase.

3. *Persistent Connections*: In the earlier versions of HTTP, a separate TCP connection was established to fetch each URI, as described in the section on "Performance Problems" on page 435. These corrections led to a decline in the performance of HTTP by increasing the load on HTTP servers and causing congestion. HTTP/1.1 uses persistent HTTP connections, which have a number of advantages. Persistent connections are the default in HTTP/1.1.

   a. TCP connections work most efficiently for transfers of a large number of bytes (e.g., megabytes), whereas many Web documents are fairly short (e.g., thousands of bytes). (TCP uses an algorithm to identify the effective network bandwidth between the two connection endpoints, called *slow start*, which often introduces a stall in data transmission after the first few packets of data are sent. If the data transfer requires many packets, the delay for this stall is negligible compared to the total transfer time.) Pipelining HTTP requests and responses, or using the same TCP connection for multiple short requests and Web document responses, takes advantage of TCP's design.

   b. Establishing a TCP connection requires at least three packets to be sent between the user agent and the server *before* the HTTP protocol can use the connection. This delay can be avoided by reusing the same connection for multiple requests and responses. In addition, by opening and closing fewer TCP connections, CPU time is saved, and memory used for TCP protocol control blocks on the user agent and origin server computers is also saved. Finally, fewer connections means less overhead for the Internet, in terms of TCP connection establishment and release packets.

   c. HTTP can evolve more gracefully, since errors can be reported without the penalty of closing the TCP connection.

4. *Caching:* The goal of caching in HTTP/1.1 is to use intermediaries to minimize the need to send requests, and, if a request must be sent, to minimize the need to send full responses. Not sending a request reduces the number of network round-trips required for many operations, while not sending a response reduces network bandwidth

requirements. Caching is implemented in HTTP/1.1 through a number of mechanisms such as expiration models, document freshness, and validators. HTTP/1.1 also allows the use of caching and non-caching proxies. Caching in HTTP/1.1 is complex and is described in the draft specification in detail.

5. *Access Authentication:* In some cases, the user may need to authenticate their identity with the server. HTTP provides a simple challenge-response authentication mechanism by which a server may challenge a user agent request and the user agent many need to provide authentication information (e.g., the user agent then prompts the user for a password, which the user agent sends to the server). This scheme guarantees that only authenticated user agents are allowed to access the document(s) at the server.

6. *Content Negotiation:* Content negotiation is the process of selecting the best representation for a given response when there are multiple representations available. Most HTTP responses include an entity which contains information that may be interpreted by a human user. It is desirable to provide the user with the "best available" entity corresponding to the request. Unfortunately for servers and caches, the definition of "best" may vary from person to person. For that reason, HTTP provides several mechanisms for content negotiation. Two kinds of content negotiations are possible in HTTP: server-driven and agent-driven negotiation. In the former, the selection of the best of representation for a response is made by an algorithm located at the server, while in the latter, the selection is made by the user agent after receiving an initial response from the origin server.

Many more features in HTTP/1.1 are elaborated upon in [4].

23.4 HTTP-NG

This section deals only with the classic HTTP-NG as proposed by Simon Spero. HTTP-NG is an enhanced replacement for HTTP/1.0. It is designed to correct the known performance problems in previous versions of HTTP and to provide extra support for commercial transactions, including enhanced security and support for online payments. In this section, we present the architectural overview of HTTP-NG, implementation exercises, and the current status.

Architecture

According to Spero, "the protocol is designed to make it easy to implement the basic functionality needed for a simple browser whilst making the addition of more powerful features such as security and authentication much simpler than it is for HTTP" [7].

Instead of using a single connection per request as in HTTP/1.0, HTTP-NG allows multiple requests to be sent over a single connection. These requests are asynchronous. This means that there is no need for the client to wait for a response before sending out a different request. The server can also respond to requests in any order it sees fit. In order to make these multiple data streams easy to work with, HTTP-NG sends all its messages and data using a session layer. This divides the connection into a lot of different channels, making it easier to provide the ability to pass a URL to a protocol in a response message and to use a media-specific protocol for things like audio and video over media-aware networking technologies, such as Asynchronous Transfer Mode (ATM).

HTTP-NG provides a general security framework into which various security components can be fitted. This provides the facility to incorporate different security schemes and policies. The HTTP-NG message wrapper has fields which can carry arbitrary authentication and security information. This allows each message to be individually authenticated. HTTP-NG also allows an intermediate server to perform security related operations on behalf of its clients.

Implementation

There are several ways to implement HTTP-NG. Three of these are outlined below.

1. The first approach is to use a synchronous Remote Procedure Call (RPC) mode. The client establishes a connection to the server and then sends out a request. This is the most common implementation practice among older HTTP versions.
2. This approach uses an event-based model, in which a simple dispatcher can be wrapped around the connection.
3. The final approach is to use a multithreaded implementation, in which each request and channel gets allocated its own thread, allowing multiple requests to be processed in parallel.

Current Status

After the recent completion of the HTTP/1.1 proposed standard by IETF, steps are being taken to re-engineer the basic protocol structure of HTTP. There is an ongoing HTTP-NG activity within the W3C which intends "to design, implement, and test a new architecture for the HTTP protocol based on a simple, extensible distributed object-oriented model" [10]. This HTTP-NG will build on the classic HTTP-NG.

23.5 S-HTTP

Background

Secure-HTTP or S-HTTP describes a syntax for securing messages sent using the HTTP protocol. It tries to enable spontaneous commercial transactions by negotiation of different algorithms, modes and parameters needed for security. It also provides independently applicable security services for transaction confidentiality and authenticity/integrity. S-HTTP allows different parties to negotiate a variety of key-management mechanisms, security policies and cryptographic algorithms for each transaction. Cryptography is discussed in Chapter 12.

Main Features

Some of the main features of S-HTTP are summarized below.

1. S-HTTP is a secure message-oriented communications protocol designed for use in conjunction with HTTP. It is designed to coexist with HTTP's message model and to be easily integrated with HTTP applications.

2. S-HTTP deliberately mimics the format and style of HTTP to ease integration. However, certain headers are promoted to be Secure HTTP headers. In such messages, the request line will look like the following:

```
Secure * Secure-HTTP/1.2
```

3. The response line will look like the following:

```
Secure-HTTP/1.2 200 OK
```

4. S-HTTP provides a variety of security mechanisms to HTTP clients and servers, providing the security service options appropriate to the wide range of potential uses for the Web. It is particularly useful for commercial applications, which may involve transfer of confidential information across the Web.

5. S-HTTP supports interoperation among a variety of implementations, and is compatible with HTTP. This means that S-HTTP-aware agents

can communicate with S-HTTP-oblivious agents, and vice versa, although obviously such transactions would not utilize S-HTTP's security features. One way this is done is through the use of a new kind of URL. This starts with "shttp://" rather than "http://". The new prefix indicates that the target server is S-HTTP capable.

6. Several cryptographic message format standards may be incorporated into S-HTTP clients and servers. S-HTTP provides full flexibility of cryptographic algorithms, modes and parameters. Clients and servers can openly negotiate to agree on transaction modes, cryptographic algorithms, and certificate selection.

7. Message protection can be done in three ways: signature, authentication, and encryption. Any message may be signed, authenticated, encrypted, or any combination of these. S-HTTP has features to allow all these facilities.

8. Special header lines are provided in S-HTTP to accommodate HTTP facilities that may interact with security, such as caching and proxies.

9. S-HTTP also permits persistent connections between client/proxy and proxy/server pairs through the use of special headers.

Basically S-HTTP attempts to make the existing HTTP more secure by providing many features. Some of the main features have been presented here. These and other features are presented in greater detail in the SHTTP draft proposed to the IETF [6].

23.6 Protocol Extension Protocol (PEP)

HTTP is increasingly being used for applications like distributed authoring, collaboration, printing, and remote procedure calls. Modifying HTTP is a long and complex process. There are times when specialized changes to HTTP are designed (e.g., for electronic commerce) that would be used by a subset of the world's Web servers and user agents. Also, private parties in the Internet may wish to run a specialized version of HTTP between their user agents and Web servers to accommodate a new function. These specialized changes are inappropriate for worldwide standardization by a change to HTTP, yet must be accommodated for the Web to grow in functionality.

"The Protocol Extension Protocol (PEP) is an extension mechanism designed to address the tension between private agreement and public specification and to accommodate extension of applications such as HTTP clients, servers, and proxies" [3]. HTTP has the facility to provide extended facilities using additional message headers. These are referred to as *custom extensions*. PEP has features to allow the negotiation of these extensions between clients and servers. It also has features for expressing the scope, strength and ordering of such extensions.

Background

HTTP is increasingly being used in applications that require more facilities than the standard version of the protocol provides. HTTP messages can be extended with additional header fields and content formats. PEP introduces the concept of protocol extensions to systematically address these issues at a higher level of abstraction. With PEP, HTTP agents can interoperate correctly with known and unknown protocol extensions, select protocol extensions available to both sides, and query partners for specific capabilities. This eliminates the confusion between the clients and servers and allows dynamic operation.

PEP has been developed over the last few years by the collaboration of many parties, including W3C/CommerceNet Joint Electronic Payment Initiative (JEPI).

Extensions

PEP uses the HTTP header space to describe extensions. Extension declaration bags are used to indicate that PEP extensions have been applied to an HTTP message. Two attributes that are used are map and strength. The map attribute contains a URI identifying the extension and a list of any header field names. The strength attribute indicates whether the extension is to be followed or not.

Extension policy bags are used to indicate the extensions that may be applied to a message. These are different from extension declarations because they indicate the extensions that *have been* applied to a message.

Interaction between PEP and HTTP/1.1

HTTP requests are "bound" if they include at least one PEP extension declaration of strength "must." "PEP uses the HTTP request method name to extend existing HTTP/1.1 methods and to introduce new methods" [3]. PEP can be used by either extending existing HTTP methods or adding new HTTP methods.

A new status code with number 420 is introduced to indicate bad extensions that may indicate refusal to meet the appropriate extensions.

PEP also provides facilities to interact with caching and non-caching proxies. Practical considerations for PEP-extended HTTP applications involve dealing with existing HTTP/1.1 methods and headers.

In conclusion, PEP provides facilities to extend the features of applications like HTTP clients, servers, and proxies.

23.7 Summary

This chapter has examined some old, existing, and emerging Web protocols. In particular, it has summarized the main features of HTTP/1.0, HTTP/1.1, HTTP-NG, S-HTTP, and PEP.

With the explosion of the Web there has emerged a need to revamp the existing underlying HTTP protocol, to make it more powerful by adding new features, and also to remove many of its known performance problems. HTTP/1.1 and HTTP-NG focus on trying to enhance the performance of HTTP using concepts like caching, proxies, and persistent connections. S-HTTP makes HTTP more suitable for commercial transactions by making HTTP more secure. S-HTTP permits cryptographic features to be incorporated into HTTP. PEP is a system for HTTP clients, servers and proxies to reliably negotiate to use custom extensions to HTTP.

Currently HTTP/1.1, S-HTTP and PEP exist as Internet drafts. The latest information about these standards can be obtained from W3C [11]. The current use of HTTP as the leading protocol for the Web suggests that it will be the protocol of the future, too. But there are also alternative protocols, such as the Handheld Device Transport Protocol [9], designed for the Handheld Device Markup Language (HDML) discussed in Section 3.2 for cellular phones. Therefore protocols for the Web will continue to be an active area of change in the future.

23.8 References

[1]   Berners-Lee, Tim, "The HTTP Protocol as Defined in 1991." 1991.
      <http://www.w3.org/pub/WWW/Protocols/HTTP/AsImplemented.html>
      (5 Oct. 1997).

[2]   Berners-Lee, Tim. "Design Issues for HTTP." 1991.
      <http://www.w3.org/pub/WWW/Protocols/DesignIssues.html> (5 Oct. 1997).

[3]   Connoly, Dan, Rohit Khare, and Henrik F. Nielsen. "PEP—an Extension Mechanism for HTTP." WD-pep-970714. 14 July 1997.
      <http://www.w3.org/TR/WD-http-pep-970714> (5 Oct. 1997).

[4]   Fielding, R., J. Gettys, J. Mogul, H. Frystk, and T. Berners-Lee. "Hyper Text Transfer Protocol—1.1," January 1997.
      <http://www.w3.org/Protocols/rfc2068/rfc2068> (5 Oct. 1997).

[5]   Nielsen, Henrik F. "Classic HTTP Documents."
      <http://www.w3.org/pub/WWW/Protocols/Classic.html> (5 Oct. 1997).

[6]   Rescorla, E. and A. Schiffman. "The Secure Hypertext Transfer Protocol." Draft 04. March 1997.

<ftp://ds.internic.net/internet-drafts/draft-ietf-wts-shttp-04.txt>   (5   Oct.
1997).

[7]   Spero, Simon E. "Analysis of HTTP Performance Problems." 1995.
       <http://sunsite.unc.edu/mdma-release/http-prob.html > (5 Oct. 1997).

[8]   Spero, Simon E. "HTTP-NG Architectural Overview." 1995.
       <http://www.w3.org/pub/WWW/Protocols/HTTP-NG/http-ng-arch.html>
       (5 Oct. 1997).

[9]   Unwired Planet, Inc. "HTTP Specification, Version 1.1." July 1997.
       <http://www.uplanet.com/pub/hdtp11.pdf> (6 Oct. 1997).

[10]   W3C. "Overview of HTTP-NG."
       <http://www.w3.org/pub/WWW/Protocols/HTTP-NG/> (5 Oct. 1997).

[11]   W3C. "Protocols." <http://www.w3.org/Protocols/> (30 Sept. 1996).

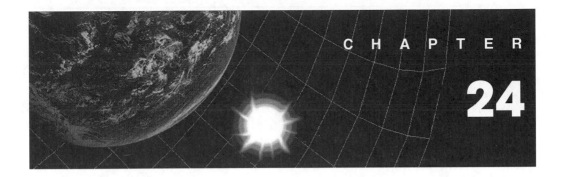

Caching and New Ways to Improve Response Time

by David C. Lee

To some people, the acronym WWW means the World Wide Wait. This is caused by a lack of bandwidth and poor response time. Bandwidth and response-time problems will most likely increase as more people use the Internet. Thus, improving bandwidth and response time for the primary Internet traffic source, the Web, is a major research area. This chapter provides an overview of potential solutions to the bandwidth and response-time problems, including protocol modifications (such as binary protocols, transaction-based protocols, and document compression), document caching (caching hierarchies and document pre-fetching), and new distribution mechanisms (multicast and remote distribution sites).

Chapter Content

3. Document Caching Strategies

- Caching Schemes/Hierarchy
- Metrics
- User Caching
- Proxy Caching
- Server Caching
- Prefetch Caching

4. Alternative Distribution

- Multicast
- Replication

5. Conclusion

6. References

24.1 Introduction

As of April 1995 the Web was the largest single component of traffic on the NSF-NET backbone in both packets (21.4 percent) and bytes (26.5 percent) [18]. The emergence of the Web has stretched network technology to the point that "brown-outs" frequently occur on the Internet (a collection of networks). High network traffic typically causes these failures.

This high-traffic problem will continue to plague the Internet for the fore-seeable feature, especially considering the emergence of new multimedia traffic (video and audio). Thus, one important consideration to the Web's current architecture is how to reduce network traffic. Approaches to reducing traffic include removing it entirely from the network and moving it from congested backbone networks to higher-speed local networks.

The other common complaint is poor user response time. Response time is generally measured as the time between when a request is issued and the response is received. It is closely related to the time it takes to transfer a document. This metric is very important to the user, since it provides a measure on how long it takes for a document to be received.

The most obvious way to improve Web performance is to obtain higher-bandwidth connections and faster routers. To get the improvement, the upgrades must occur. These are the connection end-points and all the intermediate networks. This is prohibitively expensive to do on a worldwide scale. Another way to obtain better Web performance is to reduce bandwidth consumption by intelligently sending data only when absolutely necessary. This is the primary solution that is discussed in this chapter.

There are three general intelligent bandwidth-consumption methods to improve Web performance. These are protocol modifications, document caching, and alternative distribution methods. Protocol modifications have an immediate impact on performance but may result in significant infrastructure changes that users may not accept. Document caching is generally transparent to the users and Web document designers and is under active research. Alternative distribution schemes may help alleviate the problem but do not hold the same potential as the other methods.

24.2 Improving HTTP

The Hypertext Transport Protocol (HTTP), version 1.0 [5], is the primary mechanism used to transport Web documents. It is designed so that it can theoretically run on any underlying communications network. Most, if not all, Web implementations use Internet's TCP/IP protocols. This section will discuss methods to improve HTTP performance by outlining general problems with the current protocol and detailing performance features of proposed protocols. It is assumed that the reader has basic knowledge of networks and HTTP. Stevens [22] and several others provide a detailed discussion of TCP/IP networks, and Chapter 23 of this book presents HTTP.

Problems Caused by HTTP 1.0

The performance of HTTP has been heavily analyzed [21, 16, 23]. Some of the common shortcomings include redundant information transfers, short single-document transactions, and unused negotiation features. These will be described below.

HTTP uses a stateless protocol that results in using a separate connection for every document retrieved. Use of a stateless protocol means that negotiation information must be transferred on every request, even if it is for items that are part of the same document. Spero [21] speculates that this redundant information factor is around 95 percent of the header information transferred. Lee's [12] analysis shows that a typical worst case is 86 percent. Regardless of the exact differences, a large amount of redundant information is transferred. This problem is reduced in HTTP 1.1 [9] by its use of persistent connections.

The single-request nature of HTTP means that some unnecessary transfer delay is added by TCP's round-trip time negotiation and slow start algorithm [20]. TCP essentially has features that deliberately slow down the first hundred milliseconds of a connection. The shorter the connection, the greater the slow-start effect. Since the problems caused by TCP are due to the short-document

Figure 24–1   HTTP 1.0 Communications Path

nature of Web documents, Stevens [23] suggests using T/TCP to help alleviate this problem. Padmanabhan and Mogul [16] describe and test some potential protocol modifications that improve response time. The short-document nature of the Web may change over the future as HTTP is used to replace FTP and other older transfer protocols to retrieve files. This replacement is evidenced by the fact that most large FTP sites have Web interfaces.

Web clients and servers can perform feature negotiation, such as preferred language to use and acceptable image types to view. A significant amount of the automatic client-server negotiation that occurs is worthless, since client implementations do not use the negotiation information. The most frequent negotiation scheme is performed by displaying the item to be sent and having the user manually select that item. This implies that this information does not need to be sent. Not using these fields will reduce both the transfer time and the amount of redundant information. However, correct future use of these features cannot be ruled out.

Solutions and Ideas in HTTP 1.1

HTTP version 1.1 [9] introduces the notion of *persistent connections*, which reduces the amount of redundant information that is transmitted and provides improved caching support. HTTP 1.1 also provides some more methods and other features. One of the most significant performance features is the Keep-Alive directive, which provides persistent connections. The NCSA team [14] shows that a time savings of approximately 33 percent occurs through the use of one long-lived connection. The connection is used to make multiple requests as opposed to single requests. This concurs with the approximately 30 percent connection-time to transfer-time ratio observed by Lee [12]. This ratio shows that 30 percent of an average document transfer is used by the TCP connection negotiation.

Other performance-related additions in HTTP 1.1 deal with caching support. HTTP 1.0 was essentially designed to support direct connections from user agents (clients) to origin servers, as illustrated in Fig. 24–1. In HTTP, the server that has the original copy of the document is referred to as an origin server.

HTTP 1.1 recognizes that there may be many intermediaries in the network, including proxy servers, firewalls, and gateways. This is illustrated in

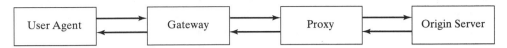

Figure 24–2   HTTP 1.1 Communications Path

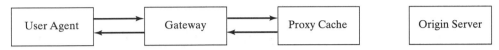

Figure 24–3   HTTP Cache Communication Path

Fig. 24–2. These intermediaries serve various network control functions, such as limiting access to and from a particular site.

If these intermediaries perform caching functions, the communications path looks like the one in Fig. 24–3. Assuming that the proxy cache has the requested document, there is no need to obtain the document from the origin server. Several new headers were added for caching support. These include allowing cache routes to be traced, allowing client and servers to issue instructions to a proxy cache, addressing issues such as cache coherency, expiration, when to store and when not to store, and other caching concerns. A general discussion of caching issues is included in this chapter; for a detailed discussion of caching features of HTTP 1.1 see Fielding [9].

HTTP 1.1 also allows for partial document retrieval through byte ranges and document compression techniques. These are discussed in the section on "Other Solutions and Ideas" on page 452.

Solutions and Ideas in HTTP-NG

The HyperText Transfer Protocol-Next Generation (HTTP-NG) [21] is a proposed replacement to HTTP. It is discussed in Chapter 23 of this book. HTTP-NG is a *binary protocol*, which essentially compresses the protocol information, and a *stateful multiplexing protocol*. The protocol introduces the concept of a session and a channel. State is maintained across different requests, whereas in HTTP 1.0, each request is a separate connection. HTTP-NG's multiplexing capabilities allow multiple outstanding requests to be issued at once. This is somewhat similar to the multiple-protocol-instance solution discussed in the next section.

HTTP-NG provides features comparable to HTTP 1.1 and provides a significant performance improvement. HTTP-NG attempts to solve the generic transport problem by allowing other media-specific protocols to be used. (Presently in the Web, media such as streaming video and audio bypass HTTP 1.0 and 1.1.)

However, HTTP-NG is unlikely to be used, since it would require substantial changes in the existing infrastructure and it requires highly complex software. HTTP 1.0 is fairly simple to implement, which may have contributed to the Web's quick growth. Large software houses should be able to develop HTTP-NG implementations relatively quickly, whereas freeware authors may not.

Other Solutions and Ideas

Several other ideas exist that may ease the response-time and bandwidth problem. Certain client-side techniques can help, such as displaying the document while it is being download over the network. Other ideas include partial document retrieval, document compression, and multiple protocol instances. These are discussed below.

- *Partial document retrieval:* Partial document retrieval allows for selective retrieval of portions of a document. This retrieval is performed through selecting a byte range of the source document to receive. The rationale for this partial retrieval is that users can retrieve sections of a large document as they need it. This reduces bandwidth usage by not retrieving unnecessary portions, and it helps performance since the user does not have to wait for the complete document to download. Adobe Acrobat Amber was one of the first applications to use this mechanism. This was originally proposed as an extension to HTTP 1.0. It has recently been incorporated into HTTP 1.1.

- *Document compression:* The Web primarily uses seven-bit ASCII text transmitted over an eight-bit data channel. Using the one extra bit for dictionary encoding could result in a sizable performance improvement with little or no extra overhead. See Bell [4] for an explanation of various text-compression schemes. From results presented by Lee [12], more than 64 percent of the documents transferred are text based. For typical text documents, compression can range from 40 percent to 70 percent of the original size [4]. Document compression could have a significant effect on bandwidth. Several browsers do support automatic decompression of *gzip* and UNIX *compress* documents. However, the document authors are usually required to manually compress the document before it is published.

- *Multiple protocol instances:* Multiple protocol instances are the equivalent of wanting to retrieve n separate files and using n simultaneous FTP sessions to retrieve them. This, in theory and in most practical cases, is faster than n sequential FTP sessions. Netscape Navigator uses multiple protocol instances to improve response-time performance. The penalty for using this method is that additional network load is created, since there are now n sessions active at once.

As the protocol is improved, security and other non-performance-related improvements will be implemented. These are not discussed here.

24.3 Document Caching Strategies

The general principle behind document caching is moving the document closer to the end user. This is achieved by transparently storing the document on servers closer to the user. These servers are typically called proxy cache servers, or proxy caches for short. Document caching in the Web is analogous to well-known methods to improve memory response times in computer design through hierarchical memories. The concept behind hierarchical memory is to move data from a slower memory to a faster memory: pages are moved from disk to main memory, and lines are moved from main memory to cache memory.

Caching Schemes/Hierarchy

Data caching is a common method to improve performance in computer systems. For example, CPU caches in static memory improve performance by avoiding the need to retrieve data from slower dynamic memory. Another example is disk caching: memory is used to cache data that is being read from or written to a disk drive, because disks are orders of magnitude slower than memory. The general goal is to move data closer to where it is used. Web document caching is an active research area with several projects underway or completed.

The user-access model is an important consideration when designing caching schemes. The model attempts to characterize how the user will access Web documents. By knowing the user-access pattern, better caching predictions can be made as to what documents will be requested. For a particular model, cache performance may be excellent. But, if the model does not accurately follow the user's actual access pattern, then performance can degrade substantially. User models for hypermedia include [1, 7, 24].

1. *Directed-search browsing:* The directed-search model implies that users spend time searching for information within a specific locality of the Web. The users have specific kinds of information in mind that they are deliberately seeking.

2. *General-purpose browsing:* Users behaving according to the general-purpose model spend some time within one Web locality and then go to another. This is repeated throughout the session. Users have some

vague idea as to what they want to find and the they are looking around for it.

3. *Random browsing:* The random model is the "window shopping" model. The user has no real objective in mind and is briefly looking at many documents.

The user model used by a specific scheme to increase performance must be suitable to the task. Designing for worst-case user behaviors may create a suboptimal design for 99 percent of user-access patterns. For example, assume that a server is expecting an average of 100 connections per minute. One hundred processes are started to handle the expected connections. However, if only a dozen requests are made, then substantial server resources are wasted. This implies that the way in which users are characterized and the performance criteria that result from the characterization are issues that need to be considered.

Other ways of providing the basis for caching include heuristics similar to the above, statistical methods, and graph theory. Statistical methods generally use user-access information as a probability estimate for future accesses. Concepts from graph theory can be used to convert the hypertext space into graphs that can be used to determine what documents to cache. A hypertext system typically can be mapped into a hierarchical graph [6]. Some researchers combine the various methods. A detailed discussion can be found in Lee [12].

The general caching hierarchy is as follows.

1. User caches, which are also called browser or client caches,
2. Proxy caches, which are also called cache or proxy cache servers,
3. Server caches, which are also called site caches.

Each of the caching systems above will be discussed below. All caching systems can either fetch the document before a request is made (prefetch) or fetch the document after a request has been made (postfetch). Post-fetch systems are distinguished by the fact that they already have, in cache, the document that is being requested. Prefetch systems attempt to request a document to cache before any user requests it.

Metrics

Several metrics are commonly used when evaluating caching systems. These include the following.

- *Hit rate:* The hit rate is generally a percentage ratio of documents obtained though using the caching mechanism versus the total documents requested. It expresses the percentage of time that the document can be retrieved from the cache without requesting the document from the origin server. A higher hit rate means that the cache is better.

- *Miss rate:* The miss rate is typically defined as unity minus the hit rate, or 100 percent minus the hit-rate percentage. The miss rate is the complement to the hit rate. The miss rate is the number of documents not found in the cache versus the total documents requested. It expresses how often the cache misses documents. A lower miss rate means that the cache is better.

- *Bandwidth utilization:* An efficiency metric, such as bandwidth utilization, may be calculated in several ways. The general use is to measure how effective a cache is at a particular task. A reduction in the amount of bandwidth consumed shows the cache is better.

- *Response time/access time:* The response time is the time it takes for a user to get a document. The amount of reduction in the response time can be used to determine the performance of a cache.

Individual caching algorithms may have various parameters (such as cache size and how long to cache a document) that can significantly affect the performance of the cache.

User Caching

User caches can be described as caches on the local system on which a particular user works. Almost every browser implements some form of user caching. User caches vary from storing every document retrieved for some specified criteria (typically time based) to just storing the documents retrieved in the current session.

Luotonen [13] recommends against user caches, primarily because there tends to be a significant amount of duplicated material in each individual user cache. He also notes that proxy caches may be able to obtain better performance than user caches.

Proxy Caching

Several experiments have been conducted using proxy-caching servers [2, 10, 13, 15, 18, 25]. These are generally based on the concept that a browser obtains documents through a proxy server, as opposed to directly retrieving the document. If the proxy server does not have the document in its cache, it can request it from the origin server. Thus, if a group of users with the same interests access the same proxy cache, they will most likely access a cached document.

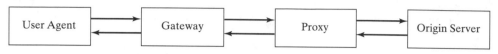

Figure 24–4   A Cache Hierarchy

Multiple proxy caches may exist in the access route. The recommended organization of these caches is to use them in a hierarchical system, as shown in Fig. 24–4. For example, cslab.vt.edu would have a proxy cache. If the document was not in the proxy cache, cslab.vt.edu would attempt to retrieve it from a proxy cache at the cs.vt.edu level. If the document was not found again, cs.vt.edu would attempt to retrieve if from a cache server at the vt.edu level. And if the vt.edu cache server could not find it, it would retrieve it from the origin server.

Most organizations are hierarchically organized, so this solution closely matches how people work. However, the proxy-cache arrangement may be performed in any method desired. Typical commercial sites have a security mechanism known as a firewall, and HTTP requests from machines inside the firewall are sent through a proxy located at that firewall.

Difficulty in maintaining consistent copies is one of the obstacles in development caching systems. HTTP 1.1 provides methods (expiration models and cache validation) to alleviate this problem. Another problem in using caches is that many browsers do not allow automatic alternative routes to be taken if a proxy cache fails. This can cause unnecessary service outages until the proxy is fixed or manual browser reconfiguration is used. Note that browsers may allow domain-based proxy access. This is useful, since obtaining local subnet document through a cache typically takes longer than directly accessing the origin server.

Caching research has indicated a wide variety of hit rates, typically within the range of 30–50% [2, 25, 10]. Due to the differing implementation methods and study limitations, it is hard to draw general conclusions. Many of the limitations come from the fact that the composition of Web documents and user populations vary significantly.

There are several open issues with regard to proxy-cache design today. First, when the cache's disk space is full, which document(s) should be replaced to make room for a new document? Comparative studies include [25]. Some recent work has examined estimating the time to refetch documents that are removed from the cache, which are kept in caches that are fetched over low-bandwidth links (e.g., documents from another continent) or highly utilized servers [26]. Second, can caches automatically configure themselves to discover who should be their parent in a hierarchy? Without automatic discovery, caches require the equivalent of routing tables, which makes maintenance of caches labor-intensive.

Server Caching

Server caching is best described as (origin) server site caching. A large site with large number of users, such as NCSA, requires multiple servers to properly serve all users. The NCSA design will be discussed in detail; however, other sites may vary.

The NCSA [11] system has several Andrew file servers on a high-speed fiber network (FDDI). These file servers are not accessible by the outside world, but a set of intermediate origin servers are available and accessible. The intermediate servers, all which have a set of unique IP addresses and host name, are assigned an alias to a generic host name. The system is set up so that over a period of time, the generic host name points to a different intermediate server. This round-robin access to load balancing on the intermediate servers is achieved by modifying the return value of a Domain Naming System (DNS) server. Servers may still become overloaded and they may forward requests to other servers.

Since the intermediate services do not have the actual documents, they typically are set up to cache documents to improve performance.

Prefetch Caching

Lee [12] and Padmanabhan and Mogul [17] explore the issue of document prefetching. Document prefetching consists of determining which documents will be accessed in the future, and pre-loading them into the cache. This cache can be at any level in the cache hierarchy. Lee's research shows that a typical user appears to spend about one minute reading each document. This time, in which no network activity generally occurs, can be used to preload documents. There are several methods to perform document prefetching, which generally fall into those that are based on Web graphs and those that are based on statistical methods.

Web graph based prefetching uses the graphical nature of hypertext links to determine the possible paths through a hypertext system. These links can be weighted on a statistical or heuristic scale. The links can be non-weighted as well, which is effectively a unity weight on all links. The prefetching is done based on the weights of the links: the higher the weight (or access probability), the more likely the user will read the document. For example, preloading the first link from the current document is a form of Web graph-based prefetching. All the links within the current document are preloaded so that the user response time is reduced when the user decides to view the document.

The other method to prefetch is based solely on statistical methods. The graph-based method may also use statistical methods. Cache and origin servers are typically configured to record access statistics. The statistics gathered on a cache server generally reflect the interests of a pool of users at a site. The statistics gathered on an origin server tend to reflect the interests of users on a more global scale. The performance of the prefetching based systems depends on the accuracy of the statistical model and the real-life access patterns.

Another form of statistical method prefetching is to use heuristics to categorize documents. For example, the root document of any Web server is generally an index of some type. One would assume that indices have an access probability associated with them. Instead of using server access statistics, the statistics are generated from the assumed document type. Problems with this method include significant administrative overhead and inaccuracies with the categorization method.

The downside to prefetching is that additional bandwidth is consumed by the act of preloading unviewed documents. Thus, research activity includes developing better algorithms to perform prefetch caching. Another problem with prefetching is the question of how to get information from the server to the client (or another proxy cache). This can be dealt with by adding HTTP or HTML extensions to send the information to the client.

24.4 Alternative Distribution

Another method to reduce bandwidth usage along the backbone is to use alternative distribution means. These include using multicast document delivery and remote-site distribution methods.

Multicast

Multicast delivery of Web documents is an experimental concept in which an alternative network delivery, or transport, mechanism is used. Typically Web document delivery is accomplished through the use of point-to-point (unicast) network connections, effectively creating a virtual wire from the source to the destination. Multicast Web services are on the point-to-multipoint model. That is, an origin server (document source) will send one copy to multiple recipients. Multicast allows one copy of the message to be sent to multiple destinations, whereas multiple copies are needed in a unicast service.

One idea behind multicast Web services is that documents will be broadcast on a round-robin schedule and that clients join the multicast group and listen for the document that they are interested in. The primarily benefit is that packet traffic is reduced, since multiple copies are not sent. However, the proposed scheme has an increased-latency problem due to the round-robin document broadcast. It also may result in wasted bandwidth if nobody wants the document. An alternative idea is that the document is multicast after a certain number of requests or elapsed time period. One general problem in any multicast scheme is that multicast services are not currently available to every user.

An experimental version of NCSA Mosaic that implements multicast document delivery is available at [8].

Replication

Distributing documents by replication is similar to mirroring FTP sites. Under this scheme, multiple server sites that contain copies of a set of document. These sites are generally closer to the user (e.g., one might replicate a Web site on each continent in the world). This reduces the load and bandwidth requirements for individual servers. Since the site is closer to the user, response time is improved.

The primary difference between this method and caching is that the user is aware of the fact that the Web server is replicated. In fact, the user often chooses the site closest to him or her in this model, where "closest" means in terms of geographic location, not necessarily in terms of number of network hops. In contrast, in a cache hierarchy, the user's request for a document will be filled by the cache that is closest to the user in the caching hierarchy.

24.5 Conclusion

Many methods exist to improve Web performance. These include protocol modifications, caching mechanisms, and innovative distribution methods. To date, most work has been in the areas of protocol modifications and document caching, as they have the highest promise to reduce bandwidth consumption. Each method is not necessarily independent of the other. Protocol changes can significantly help improve the performance of the cache, and caching may help improve the performance of alternative distribution mechanisms. On the other hand, since the composition of the Web is rapidly changing, assumptions made to improve performance today may not work in the future.

The quest for improved Internet performance is unlikely to vanish anytime soon. Usage is still increasing, and new competing Internet services will result in a continual search for inexpensive and more efficient ways to provide network services.

24.6 References

[1]   Abdulla, G., Edward A. Fox, and Marc Abrams. "Shared User Behavior on the World Wide Web." *Proc. WebNet97*. Toronto, Oct. 1997. <http://www.cs.vt.edu/~chitra/docs/97webnet/> (30 Sept. 1997).

[2]   Abrams, Marc, Charles R. Standridge, Ghaleb Abdulla, Stephen Williams, and Edward A. Fox. "Caching Proxies: Limitations and Potentials." *Proceedings: 4th Inter. World-Wide Web Conference*, Boston, MA, Dec. 1995, pp. 119–133.   <http://www.w3.org/Journal/1/abrams.155/paper/155.html> (30 Sept. 1997).

[3]   Abrams, Marc, Stephen Williams, Ghaleb Abdulla, Shashin Patel, Randy
      Ribler, and Edward A. Fox. "Multimedia Traffic Analysis Using Chitra95."
      Proceedings: ACM Multimedia '95. San Francisco, CA. November 1995.
      pp. 267–276.
      <http://www.cs.vt.edu/~chitra/docs/95multimediaAWAFPR/>
      (30 Sept. 1997).

[4]   Bell, T.C., J.G. Cleary, and I.H. Witten. *Text Compression*. Englewood Cliffs,
      NJ: Prentice Hall, 1990.

[5]   Berners-Lee, Tim, R. Fielding, and H. Frystyk. "Hypertext Transfer Proto-
      col—HTTP/1.0." RFC 1945. May 1996. Available at
      <ftp://ds.internic.net/rfc/rfc1945.txt> (30 Sept. 1997)

[6]   Botafogo, R.A., E. Rivlin, and B. Shneiderman. "Structural Analysis of
      Hypertexts: Identifying Hierarchies and Useful Metrics." *ACM Transac-
      tions on Information Systems*, 10:2. (April 1992: 142–180).

[7]   Catledge, L.D. "Characterizing Browsing Strategies in the World-Wide
      Web." *Computer Networks and ISDN Systems 27*, 1995, pp. 1065–1073.
      <http://www.gatech.edu/lcc/idt/Students/Catledge/browsing/
      UserPatterns.Paper4.formatted.html>. (30 Sept. 1997).

[8]   Ecole Nationale Supérieure des Télécommunications,
      <ftp://sig.enst.fr/pub/multicast/mMosaic/> (30 Sept. 1997).

[9]   Fielding, R., H. Frystyk, and T. Berners-Lee. "Hypertext Transport Proto-
      col—HTTP/1.1." RFC 2068. Jan. 1997. <ftp://ds.internic.net/rfc/rfc2068.txt>
      (30 Sept. 1997).

[10] Glassman, Steven, "A Caching Relay for the World-Wide Web," *Proc. of the
      First International World-Wide Web Conf.*, Amsterdam: Elsevier, 1994,
      pp. 69–76. <http://www1.cern.ch/PapersWWW94/steveg.ps>
      (30 Sept. 1997).

[11] Kwan, T.T., R. E. Mcgrath, and D. A. Reed, "UserAccess Patterns to NCSA's
      World Wide Web Server." 1995.
      <http://www-pablo.cs.uiuc.edu/Papers/WWW.ps.Z> (30 Sept. 1997).

[12] Lee, David C. "Pre-Fetch Document Caching to Improve World-Wide Web
      User Response Time." Master's Thesis. Virginia Polytechnic Institute and
      State University (March 1996).

[13] Luotonen, Ari and Kevin Altis. "World-Wide Web Proxies." *Proc. of the First
      International World-Wide Web Conf.* 1994.
      <http://www1.cern.ch/PapersWWW94/luotonen.ps> (30 Sept. 1997).

[14] NCSA *httpd* Server Development Team. "Features of NCSA HTTPD 1.5." 1995. <http://hoohoo.ncsa.uiuc.edu/docs/features-1.5.html#KeepAlive> (30 Sept. 1997).

[15] Network Research Group, "Virginia Tech's Network Research Group," <http://www.cs.vt.edu/nrg/> (30 Sept. 1997).

[16] Padmanabhan, Venkata N., and Jeffrey C. Mogul. "Improving HTTP Latency." *Proc. of the Second World-Wide Web Conference*. Oct. 1994. <http://www.ncsa.uiuc.edu/SDG/IT94/Proceedings/DDay/mogul/ HTTPLatency.html> (30 Sept. 1997).

[17] Padmanabhan, Venkata N., and Jeffrey C. Mogul. "Using Predictive Prefetching to Improve World Wide Web Latency." *Computer Communications Review* (July 1996).

[18] Pitkow, James E. and Margaret M. Recker. "A Simple Yet Robust Caching Algorithm Based on Dynamic Access Patterns." *Proc. of the 2nd World Wide Web Conference*. 1994. <http://www.ncsa.uiuc.edu/SDG/IT94/Proceedings/ DDay/pitkow/caching.html> (30 Sept. 1997).

[19] Pitkow, James E. "GVU Center NSFNET Statistics." Graphics, Visualization, and Usability Center, Georgia Institute of Technology. May 1995. <http://www.cc.gatech.edu/gvu/stats/NSF/merit.html> (30 Sept. 1997).

[20] Spero, Simon E. "Analysis of HTTP Performance Problems." July 1994. <http://sunsite.unc.edu/mdma-release/http-prob.html> (30 Sept. 1997).

[21] ———. "Progress on HTTP-NG." 1995. <http://www.w3.org/pub/WWW/Protocols/HTTP-NG/http-ng-status.html> (30 Sept. 1997).

[22] Stevens, Richard W. *TCP/IP Illustrated, Volume 1: The Protocols*. Reading, MA: Addison-Wesley, 1994.

[23] Stevens, Richard W. *TCP/IP Illustrated, Volume 3: TCP for Transactions, HTTP, NNTP, and the UNIX Domain Protocols*. Reading, MA: Addison-Wesley, 1996.

[24] Valdez, F., M. Chignell, and B. Glenn. "Browsing Models for Hypermedia Databases." *Proc. of the Human Factors Society—32nd Annual Meeting*, Anaheim, Cal., Human Factors Society (Oct. 24–28, 1988: 318–322).

[25] Williams, Stephen, Marc Abrams, Charles R. Standridge, Ghaleb Abdulla, and Edward A. Fox. "Removal Policies in Network Caches for World-Wide Web Documents." *Proc. ACM SIGCOMM*, Stanford, CA. Revised Aug. 1997 <http://www.acm.org/sigcomm/sigcomm96/papers/williams.html> (30 Sept. 1997).

[26] Roland P. Wooster and Marc Abrams. "Proxy Caching that Estimates Page
     Load Delays." Proc. WWW6. Santa Clara, CA. April 1997, pp. 325–334.
     <http://www.cs.vt.edu/~chitra/docs/www6r/> (30 Sept. 1997).

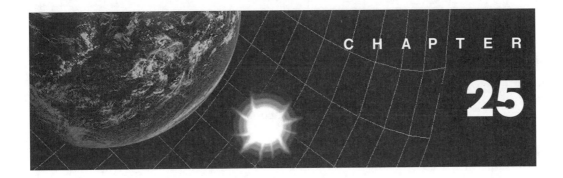

Ubiquitous Internet Computing

by Ingrid Burbey

The goal of ubiquitous computing is the production of devices that are so commonplace and natural to use that they become almost invisible. The term *ubiquitous* means that there will be hundreds of tiny computers in an office or home, each doing its own specialized task.

This chapter discusses the concepts of ubiquitous computing, as defined by Mark Weiser of Xerox PARC, the current state of ubiquitous computing, where it may lead, and the current areas of development. Some non-Web examples are shown, such as the Active Badge created by Olivetti Cambridge Labs and the PARC TAB from Xerox PARC. Other examples of computation-enhanced objects are mentioned.

The second portion of this chapter explores other devices accessing the Internet. We tend to think of Internet access through typical desktop computers or workstations, but that may not always be the case. In this section, Internet phone, video, and other uses of the Web are discussed, along with some of the technical and social challenges that lie ahead for widespread use of these devices.

Chapter Content

25.1 Introduction

"The Internet revolution has barely started. It won't be done until everything is on the Web. Light switches, pagers, copiers, printers, as well as PCs, benefit from Web connections." Mark Weiser [44]

Currently, when we think of accessing the Web, we think of parking ourselves in front of a PC, a workstation (Section 3.2), a network computer, or perhaps interactive TV-top boxes. What these devices all have in common is that they force the user to focus on a single device, actively access the Internet, and have the technical knowledge to perform that access.

Of course, there are all sorts of devices other than computers connected to the Web [49], including Coke machines, robot arms, cameras, pagers and even someone's plaster cast [23]. But most of these are interesting experiments and are not used in everyday work or home life.

Nevertheless, future access to the Web may not always be through desktop computers. Common equipment, such as telephones (page 53) or even toasters, will connect to the Web, and the user may not even be aware of which appliances in the home are actually connected. Instead of the user taking an active role in connecting to the Internet, the user's tools will automatically connect, without the user's participation.

This concept of ubiquitous computing began not as an exercise in using the Internet, but as a study of how people work, how they use tools, and where the future of computing might lie. The goal of ubiquitous computing is to move computers away from the central focus of the user's attention and into the invisible world, where they are used subconsciously, to enhance existing tools or communications. This article looks at the current state of ubiquitous computing, where it may lead, and how it will get there.

25.2 What Is Ubiquitous Computing?

Ubiquitous computing [36] puts computing in the periphery of our lives, as a tool, not a focus, out of the way so that we can get on with the true tasks we wish to accomplish. The term "ubiquitous" is used because computers and computation will be everywhere, embedded in the fabric of our lives. It envisions appliances that can dial in and download or schedule repairs, control panels that know the location of your co-workers, or even clothes that know when they need to be washed. The "Things That Think" [14] group at MIT phrases it succinctly:

In the past, shoes could stink.
In the present, shoes can blink.
In the future, shoes will think.

A future like this would help with the problem of "information overload." Instead of filling our minds with all sorts of things to remember, the things could remember for us. Your car could remind you that the oil needs changing; your kitchen cupboard could tell you that you are out of coffee. In fact, why not have the kitchen doing the shopping, by sending an order directly to the grocery store? The type of music coming out of your alarm clock in the morning could tell you what kind of day to prepare for [35].

An example of a ubiquitous technology present today is literacy [31]. Words are displayed on every surface and body part imaginable, and they convey information to us automatically, without invoking our conscious mind. We don't suffer from "literacy overload," or cases of stress, because we are being surrounded by too many words (unless it is that stack of journals every engineer feels compelled to read). We automatically read a street sign, and it guides us without undue effort on our part.

Ubiquitous computing will bring the Internet into our daily lives with less effort. Instead of keeping lists of pertinent URLS or "favorite places" on our browsers, the devices that need the information can find it themselves. Instead of "surfing" to find and sift through all of the information available to us, some other agent or device will do the searching for us.

25.3 The Visionary: Mark Weiser

Mark Weiser [37], Chief Technologist at Xerox Palo Alto Research Center [45], is the originator of ubiquitous computing, or "ubicomp." Xerox PARC studies the way people work and the tools they use. Weiser realized that the best uses of a tool occur when the tool requires less of the user's attention, and the user can devote attention to the work being done. He compares an amateur musician who needs to consciously think about every note and fingering, to an accomplished professional who knows the tool so well and so unconsciously that he can focus on the higher qualities of the music being played.

Weiser also studied trends in computing [38]. When computer mainframes were installed, many people used each mainframe. With the advent of the PC, one person uses one computer, and this relationship is common in offices today. A typical office worker spends the day in a cubicle staring at the monitor, with the workstation taking the bulk of his attention. In the future, we will have hundreds of computers per person, each quietly performing its specialized task without impinging on the user. This is already happening in the home, where embedded microprocessors are showing up in everything from ovens to thermostats and VCRs.

Weiser began this research in 1988. He realized that the current technology wasn't sufficient to create the vision. He focused first on different features of ubiquitous computing, such as devices that were portable and whose location was always known, or devices that would make it easier for people to work together. The first prototypes were TABs, Pads, and Boards [31]. TABs are similar to little electronic Post-it notes, and there could be hundreds in an office, each corresponding to some small surface with information. Pads are like yellow pads, or scrap computers, meant to be used temporarily and then left for someone else. Boards are electronic whiteboards, to allow group collaboration, and are in use today. TABs are discussed in more detail in Section 25.6.

25.4 The Vision: Calm Technology

The ultimate goal of ubiquitous computing is to implement calm technology, a world where computers do not cause stress, but enhance our lives and make many tasks easier. Eyeglasses are an example of calm technology. They help us to see the world more clearly, but they do not distract us from what we are doing, and we are barely aware of their existence. According to Weiser, the purpose of a computer is to help you do something else. The computer should extend your unconscious, and the more you can do by intuition, the smarter you are. Like Donald A. Norman [16], he believes that the best computer program is the one in which the computer "disappears" and the user seems to be working directly on the problem.

The way these devices control information overload is by making the machine conform to the user, not the other way around. Information is presented in the manner the user decides, and is easily accessible. Accessing the information doesn't require the user to work, it just appears. For example, a personalized newspaper could have the news that the user wishes to read displayed on it each morning, so the user doesn't have to search through the entire paper, or access the Internet to find it.

Research directly related to the Internet is looking at browsers that can present information more efficiently and provide real-time delivery of complex information. Xerox has invented a "hyperbolic" browser that can display hundreds of pages and their links simultaneously. It has also developed video conferencing tools and developed the Multicast Backbone (MBONE), which broadcasts audio and video over the Internet [33].

25.5 We Know Where You Are: the Active Badge

Active badges [17, 30] were developed by Olivetti Research Labs between 1989 and 1992. They are worn like employee badges, but their location within the building is always known. This simple piece of information creates the opportunity for a myriad of applications.

The badge is small and lightweight and includes a tone generator, a button, and two LEDs for simple communication with the wearer [18]. It operates like a beacon, sending a location signal out to a sensor every 15 seconds. The badge is sensitive to light, so that when light levels drop, the interval between signals is extended. This conserves power on the badge at night or when it is left in a drawer. There is no on/off switch, so the user will not have to remember to turn the badge on. Smaller badges are available for sticking onto objects.

One of the first applications of the Active Badge was telephone call routing. When employees wear active badges, the receptionist actually knows where someone is and can route phone calls to the handset nearest the employee. The LED on the employee's badge blinks to let the employee know the call is for her. There are many additional features to this system. The system can also notice that if the employee is in a location with many other people, maybe she is too busy to take the call, and it can be routed to voice mail. With a press of the button on the badge, the employee can notify the system that she is busy and doesn't want to be disturbed by phone calls. The tone generator on the badge can be used to notify a "busy" employee that a call has come in or that a visitor has arrived. The system can even make decisions like not forwarding calls if the employee is in the boss's office [30].

Another application of the active badge is to update an on-line diary. The diary notes which potential meeting attendees are currently in the building. If someone returns from an off-site meeting early or late, it is reflected in the on-line diary. If a badge wearer is walking to a meeting, the badge can warn him if he is heading in the wrong direction.

Newer models of the active badge include a badge authorization mechanism. The mechanism consists of an encrypted challenge request message sent to the badge. The badge must respond with the correct response. The responses change with time, so a "copy-cat" badge will be unable to just copy and send a correct response. This scheme was added to provide a level of security and deny rogue badges access into secure places.

The possible uses of the active badge can be extended to include access to secure areas of the building, automatic logon to a workstation when a badge wearer sits down in front of it, environmental control (heat, AC, lighting level, music, or not heating areas of the building where no one is present) [4]. Active badges could also be used to update the contents of an electronic bulletin board to reflect the interests of the badge wearer.

The active badge is not connected directly to the Internet, but it can be indirectly. Currently, Olivetti's Web site [19] provides for queries about the location of an employee wearing an active badge.

25.6 The World in the Palm of Your Hand: the PARC TAB

The PARC TAB [46] was Xerox PARC'S first ubiquitous computing device. Development started in early 1992, and the first TAB was released in March of 1993. The designers wanted to create a device that was extremely portable, yet connected to the office workstation and with a known location. They developed a palm-sized computer with a wireless interface to the workstation.

The TAB [47] is about the size of a pager and weighs 7 oz. It includes a display, three buttons, a touch panel and a piezoelectric speaker, in an ergonomic package that can be rotated for right- or left-handed use. It communicates at 19.2 Kbaud with a transceiver [48] located on the ceiling.

The TAB's function is similar to that of a Post-it note, and after looking around a typical office, one can imagine several applications for it. Instead of having multiple windows open on a workstation display, the contents of each window could be moved to a TAB. Like pieces of paper, the TABS could then be arranged on a desk and sorted. To take the project to another location, the user could just carry all the associated TABs. A project manager could have a TAB focused on an employee's project, keeping "tabs" on the progress of his work.

Other uses of the TAB include the "weather" button, which downloads the latest weather information from the Internet, and the "e-mail" button, which allows the user to scan, reply to, or save his e-mail. Other papers refer to the possible use of a palmtop computer as a porthole [7]. The TAB would serve as a window into another object or place. For example, the TAB could be held up to a city on a map, and details about the demographics of the city could be displayed on the TAB. In a library, a TAB could guide a user to a desired book, even if the book was sitting on a reshelving cart or incorrectly shelved. An active badge on the spine of the book could blink or beep to distinguish itself. The TAB could then be pointed at the spine of the book, and the table of contents would be displayed on the TAB.

A TAB, or any other device, could also be a window onto a remote location. The Ontario Telepresence project at the University of Toronto developed an application where snapshots are taken and sent regularly to subscribers [28]. This provides background awareness of other people, or remote offices.

25.7 Augmented Reality and Telepresence

Augmented Reality is another branch of computing making use of the Internet. Augmented Reality adds computation to a physical object or enhances human perception by adding information not normally conveyed by the human senses. One example is computer-assisted repair, where a headset is used to display part outlines and instructions to a technician while he is looking at an instrument [6]. A group at UNC uses Computer-augmented Vision Technology [27] to allow a doctor to see inside of a patient. It could even be used to try on "virtual" clothes to see if they fit before ordering them from an online catalog, or to rearrange "virtual" furniture [5] around your living room.

Telepresence is the label given to projects that focus on giving a "presence" in a remote location. The Ontario Telepresence project at the University of Toronto [28] has installed many prototype projects to study the way people work. These include the following:

- Active desks, which work as an electric drafting table.

- Portholes, for background awareness of remote locations.

- Hydra, for video conferencing, where remote participants are represented by a "video surrogate," an 11-inch-high monitor.

- Door Access Control, for environmental control and to divert phone calls.

- Reactive Room, which serves as an office for electronic visitors [29].

25.8 Internet Phone and Video

Several companies sell Internet telephone products [41] to save long-distance charges by placing phone calls over the Internet. Netscape and Internet Explorer both ship with telephony support, but currently there is no telephony standard, making widespread use impossible. When the standards battle [42] is finally settled, Internet phone use could skyrocket. International Data Corp. [8] predicts 16 million users of Internet phone by 1999, with a potential $560 million in sales. (For more information on Internet telephony, see Chapter 15 or [24, 1].)

Once standards are in place, video conferencing, shared whiteboards and shared programs will become common applications of the Internet.

25.9 Smart Homes

Computation is being added to homes, desks, clothing and other everyday items. Eventually, these items will also be communicating with each other through the

Internet, but current research focuses on enhancing the physical object with computation. MIT's Media Laboratory has built smart rooms [13], which use sensors to recognize people in the room. Offices can use the smart desk [12] to recognize workers and adapt to their preferences. A digital desk [40] has been built which can read the user's interactions (via pen or finger-pointing) with a paper document and copy items to an electronic document. Nissan is working on smart cars, which sense the driver's intentions before an action is taken in order to share control of the car with the driver [21]. Someday an intelligent car will read traffic reports [3] and optimize the traffic route.

The X-10 Corporation [43] markets "smart home" devices which allow telephone or PC control of appliances. It will just be a matter of time before these devices are connected to the Internet as well.

25.10 Getting There

Several research areas are studying the technology and capabilities needed to support true ubiquitous computing, such as the following:

Low Power: One of the first requirements of small, ubiquitous devices is that they are inexpensive, low-power devices. No one wants to have to change the batteries in hundreds of devices every year. Cheap computers will need a source of cheap, inexpensive power and will use low-power components.

Mobility: Mobility of computers is the focus of much current research. In the next decade, MIT expects its students to have portable, book-sized computers with wireless Internet access [2]. Internet connections need to be in place to support mobile applications and devices.

Mobile IP: Currently, the Internet Protocol (IP) assumes that the location and connection of a computer remain fixed. One aspect of current research in mobile computing is that of Mobile-IP, where IP is enhanced to allow a computer to roam and keep the same IP address [11]. The Internet Engineering Task Force (IETF) [9] maintains a Mobile-IP Web page [10] to develop the standard. Basically, Mobile-IP works by assigning a home agent on the permanent network for a computer. When the mobile computer (or the "mobile host") moves from one network to another, it notifies its home agent of its new location. The home agent then intercepts and forwards packets destined for the mobile host. (See Chapter 16 for more discussion of wireless connectivity.)

Mobile Applications: Research is also being done on movable applications. Applications will need to move off a workstation onto a TAB, or perhaps the application will move with the user. Olivetti Research Laboratory has created the ORL Teleporting System [20] to create mobile applications using the

X Window system. A proxy X server routes the input and output of an X application to any X display.

Low Cost: Research is also being done in the hardware necessary to create low-cost devices which can connect to the Internet. The trend will be toward small, disposable computers. The MIT Media Laboratory is proposing a design of an network interface chip that would be small and inexpensive. It's called the "Filament Chip" [22]. Weiser envisions buying a six-pack of computers [39].

Effective User Interfaces: These devices are meant to be practically invisible, and casually used. That means the user interfaces must be simple, apparent, and obvious. An awkward user interface could negate the whole purpose of the device.

25.11 Conclusion

Ubiquitous computing is the wave of the future. We have microprocessors in most of our appliances and office equipment. One day, these devices will be even "smarter" and also able to communicate with each other. The user interfaces will develop to the point to that the devices are calming, because they enhance our lives; make information easier to access, digest, and understand; and improve our quality of life. "Our computers should be like an invisible foundation that is quickly forgotten but always with us, and effortlessly used throughout our lives," says Mark Weiser [32].

For further reading on ubiquitous computing, see one of the following:

- [34]: Mark Weiser answers to the charge that Xerox PARC is the head of "big brother" technologies.

- [26]: Discusses some of the privacy and security concerns of mobile computing.

- [25]: "We moved into the smartest house in the neighborhood." A humorous look at the automated house of the future.

25.12 References

[1]   Abate, Tom. "Net Telephony: Talk is Cheap," *Upside*. (25 Sept. 1997: 74–85.) <http://www.upside.com/texis/archive/search/ article.html?UID=9611011004> (25 Sept. 1997).

[2]   Abelson, Harold, *et al.* "Ad Hoc Committee on Education via Advanced Technologies: Final Report." Ad Hoc Committee on Education via Advanced

Technologies, Massachusetts Institute of Technology. 31 July 1995.
<http://www-evat.mit.edu/report/> (25 Sept. 1997).

[3]   Caltrans. "Smart Traveler." <http://www.smart-traveler.com> (Nov. 1996).

[4]   Elrod, Scott, Gene Hall, *et al*. "Responsive Office Environments," *Communi-
      cations of the ACM*. (July 1993: 84–85.)

[5]   European Computer-Industry Research Centre, "ECRC GRASP Project."
      <http://www.ecrc.de/research/uiandv/gsp/Outlook/ARinfovis.html> (25 Sept.
      1997).

[6]   Feiner, Steven, Blair MacIntyre, and Doree Seligmann. "Knowledge-Based
      Augmented Reality," *Communications of the ACM* (July 1993:52–62.)

[7]   Fitzmaurice, George W. "Situated Information Spaces and Spatially Aware
      Palmtop Computers," *Communications of the ACM*. (July 1993: 38–49.)

[8]   International Data Corporation. "International Data Corporation."
      <http://www.idcresearch.com> (25 Sept. 1997).

[9]   Internet Engineering Task Force. "Home Page."
      <http://www.ietf.cnri.reston.va.us/home.html> (25 Sept. 1997).

[10] ——. "IETF Mobile IP Working Group."
      <ftp://software.watson.ibm.com/pub/mobile-ip/mobile-ip.html>
      (25 Sept. 1997).

[11] Lancki, Ben, Abhijit Dixit, and Vipul Gupta, "Mobile-IP: Supporting Trans-
      parent Host Migration on the Internet," *Linux Journal*. Aug. 1996. <http://
      anchor.cs.binghamton.edu/~mobileip/LJ/index.html>
      (25 Sept. 1997).

[12] Massachusetts Institute of Technology Media Laboratory. "SmartDesk."
      <http://www-white.media.mit.edu/vismod/demos/smartdesk/>
      (25 Sept. 1997).

[13] ——. "Smart Rooms."
      <http://www-white.media.mit.edu/vismod/demos/smartroom/>
      (25 Sept. 1997).

[14] ——. "The Things That Think Vision."
      <http://ttt.www.media.mit.edu/Vision.htm> (27 Sept. 1997).

[15] ——. "Wearable Computing Intro Page."
      <http://wearables.www.media.mit.edu/projects/wearables/> (25 Sept. 1997).

[16] Norman, Donald A. *The Design of Everyday Things*. Doubleday, 1988.

[17] Olivetti Research Laboratories. "The Olivetti Active Badge System." <http://www.cam-orl.co.uk/ab.html> (25 Sept. 1997).

[18] ——. "The Active Badge." <http://www.cam-orl.co.uk/thebadge.html> (25 Sept. 1997).

[19] ——. "ORL—The Olivetti and Oracle Research Lab." <http://www.cam-orl.co.uk> (25 Sept. 1997).

[20] ——. "The ORL Teleporting System." <http://www.cam-orl.co.uk/teleport/> (25 Sept. 1997).

[21] Pentland, Alex and Andy Liu. "The Driver's Intention Project (Smart Cars)" <http://pathfinder.cbr.com/people/andy/Projects/dr_intention.html> (25 Sept. 1997).

[22] Poor, Robert, *et al.* "The Filament Chip." Massachusetts Institute of Technology Media Laboratory. October 1996. <http://ttt.media.mit.edu/pia/Research/Filament/index.html> (25 Sept. 1997).

[23] Poor, R. Dunbar. "R. Dunbar Poor's Digital Cast Signing Page." <http://ttt.www.media.mit.edu/cgi-bin/r> (25 Sept. 1997).

[24] Pulver.Com. "Voice on the Net." <http://www.von.com> (25 Sept. 1997).

[25] Schrage, Michael. "Smart House," *LA Times*. <http://www.eclipse.net/~amw/silly/house.shtml>

[26] Spreitzer, Mike and Marvin Theimer. "Scalable, Secure, Mobile Computing with Location Information," *Communications of the ACM*, July 1993. p. 27.

[27] University of North Carolina at Chapel Hill. "Ultrasound Visualization Research." <http://www.cs.unc.edu/~us/> (25 Sept. 1997).

[28] University of Toronto. "Ontario Telepresence Project Home Page." <http://www.dgp.utoronto.ca/tp/tphp.html> (25 Sept. 1997).

[29] ——. "Welcome to the Reactive Room Media Space." <http://www.dgp.utoronto.ca:80/people/rroom> (25 Sept. 1997).

[30] Want, Row, and Andy Hopper. "Active Badges and Personal Interactive Computing Objects," *IEEE Transactions on Consumer Electronics*. (Feb. 1992: 10–20.) <ftp://ftp.cam-orl.co.uk/pub/docs/ORL/tr.92.2.ps.Z> (25 Sept. 1997).

[31] Weiser, Mark. "The Computer for the 21st Century," *Scientific American* (Sept. 1991: 94–104.)
     <http://www.ubiq.com/hypertext/weiser/SciAmDraft3.html>
     (25 Sept. 1997).

[32] ——. "The World Is Not a Desktop." *ACM Interactions.* (Nov. 1993).
     <http://www.ubiq.com/hypertext/weiser/ACMInteractions2 (25 Sept. 1997).

[33] Weiser, Mark and Andy Garman. "Bleeding Edge Technology—From Lab Coats to Market Caps," *The Red Herring Magazine* (August 1995).
     <http://www.herring.com/mag/issue22/edge.html> (25 Sept. 1997).

[34] Weiser, Mark. "The Technologist's Responsibilities and Social Change." *Computer-Mediated Communications Magazine,* 2 (4). April 1, 1995.
     <http://sunsite.unc.edu/cmc/mag/1995/apr/last.html>

[35] ——. "Open House," *Review.* March 1996. (25 Sept. 1997).

[36] ——. "Ubiquitous Computing."
     <http://www.ubiq.com/hypertext/weiser/UbiHome.html> (25 Sept. 1997).

[37] ——. "Mark Weiser." <http://www.ubiq.com/weiser.html> (25 Sept. 1997).

[38] ——. "The Major Trends in Computing."
     <http://sandbox.parc.xerox.com/weiser/10year/sld037.gif> (25 Sept. 1997).

[39] ——. "Computer Science Challenges for the Next Ten Years."
     <http://sandbox.parc.xerox.com/weiser/10year/> (25 Sept. 1997).

[40] Welher, Pierre. "Interacting with Paper on the Digital Desk," *Communications of the ACM.* (July 1993: 86–96.)

[41] Williams, Tish. "Competition Is Fierce for Your Net Phone Calls," *Upside Magazine.* Nov. 1996.
     <http://www.upside.com/print/nov96/telephony.oa1.html> (Nov. 1996).

[42] ——. "The Battle to Define Internet Telephony," *Upside Magazine.* Nov. 1996. <http://www.upside.com/print/nov96/telephony.oa2.html> (Nov. 1996).

[43] X-10 Corporation. "X-10 Home Page."
     <http://hometeam.com/x10/index.htm> (25 Sept. 1997).

[44] Xerox Corporation. "Xerox Names Computing Pioneer as Chief Technologist for Palo Alto Research Center." Press release. 14 August 1996.
     <http://www.ubiq.com/weiser/weiserannc.htm> (25 Sept. 1997).

[45] Xerox Palo Alto Research Center. "PARC Go Page."
     <http://www.parc.xerox.com/> (25 Sept. 1997).

[46] ——. "Xerox PARCTAB." <http://www.ubiq.com/parctab> (25 Sept. 1997).

[47] ——. "PARCTAB Mobile Hardware." <http://www.ubiq.com/parctab/tab-pic.html> (25 Sept. 1997).

[48] ——. "PARCTAB Basestation." <http://www.ubiq.com/parctab/tspic.html> (25 Sept. 1997).

[49] Yahoo! "Yahoo!—Computers and Internet:Internet:Entertainment:Interesting Devices Connected to the Net."
<http://www.yahoo.com/Computers_and_Internet/Internet/Entertainment/Interesting_Devices_Connected_to_the_Net/> (25 Sept. 1997).

25.13 Glossary

Augmented Reality: Enhancement of a user's perceptions or of a physical object using computation.

Calm Technology: Technology that leads to calm and comfort. Calm technology uses both the center and the periphery of a user's attention.

Mobile-IP: Extension to Internet Protocol (IP) which allows a computer to disconnect from the base network and move to another network.

Teleport: Extension to X-Windows system that allows an application to move from one X-terminal to another.

Telepresence: Use of technology to collaborate remotely.

Ubiquitous Computing: The research area in computers which seeks to put small, inexpensive computers throughout the user's environment, so that the computing tool becomes invisible and easy to use.

Weiser, Mark: The originator of ubiquitous computing. Mark Weiser is now Chief Technologist at Xerox Palo Alto Research Center.

INDEX